CHILLA BULBECK

Chilla Bulbeck is Emeritus Professor in the School of Social Sciences at The University of Adelaide and Honorary Professorial Research Associate, School of Social Sciences and Communication Studies, University of Western Australia. Her research interest in gender and difference has led to the publication of a number of books: *Shadow of the Hill* (1988), *Australian Women in Papua New Guinea: Colonial Passages 1920-1960* (1992), *Re-orienting Western Feminism: Women's Diversity in a Postcolonial World* (1998), *Living Feminism: The Impact of the Women's Movement on Three Generations of Australian Women* (1997) and *Sex, Love and Feminism in the Asia Pacific: A Cross-cultural Study of Young People's Attitudes* (2009). She has taught Australian studies and/or gender studies in three Australian States, Beijing Foreign Studies University and Tokyo University.

This book is available as a fully-searchable pdf from
www.adelaide.edu.au/press

IMAGINING THE FUTURE

Young Australians on sex, love and community

by

Chilla Bulbeck

School of Social Sciences,
The University of Adelaide

THE UNIVERSITY
of ADELAIDE

UNIVERSITY OF
ADELAIDE PRESS

Published in Adelaide by

University of Adelaide Press
The University of Adelaide
Level 1, 230 North Terrace
South Australia
5005
press@adelaide.edu.au
www.adelaide.edu.au/press

The University of Adelaide Press publishes externally refereed scholarly books by staff of the University of Adelaide. It aims to maximise the accessibility to its best research by publishing works through the internet as free downloads and as high quality printed volumes on demand.

Electronic Index: This book is available from the website as a down-loadable PDF with fully searchable text.

For the full Cataloguing-in-Publication data please contact the National Library of Australia: cip@nla.gov.au

1.   Youth — Australia — Attitudes
2.   Youth — Australia — Sexual behaviour

I.   Bulbeck, Chilla, 1951–

ISBN (paperback) 978-1-922064-34-9
ISBN (ebook) 978-1-922064-35-6

Project Editor: Patrick Allington
Cover design: Emma Spoehr
Cover image: Ayad Alqaragholli, '*highness*', *Sculpture by the Sea, Cottesloe* 2012
Book design: Zoë Stokes

'My most favourite thing in the world is books — after my family'
(Ella Churchill, 28 February 2011)

For Ella; and for my cousins, Anna, Bronwyn and Tessa; and for my 'old uncle' Newell.
With thanks for your love, grace and wit.

CONTENTS

ACKNOWLEDGEMENTS

When I googled 'If you can read this, thank a teacher', attempting to locate the origins of this bumper sticker, I discovered two common alternative phrasings: 'If you can't read this, thank the Teacher's Union' and 'If you can read this in English, thank a soldier'. Another kind of literacy is required to deconstruct these alternatives: civic, political or sociological literacy. I both thank and applaud the teachers who opened their classrooms to me. Teachers like these across Australia are working with their students in order that they may 'read this', read books like this one. Their work is underpinned by labours of love in the home: mothers giving the lion's share in most homes, but also fathers, siblings and others featuring in young people's stories. My thanks go especially to those young people and their parents who granted me interviews in which we explored attitudes and hopes concerning our place in family, work, and society.

The participating schools and youth services which so generously gave me access in South Australia are: Adelaide High School (especially Colleen Tomlian), Christian Brothers College (especially Bob Bowes and Brother Patrick Cronin), Croydon High School (especially Annie Hanson and Tammy Edwardson), Gepps Cross Girls High School (especially Michael Darley), Marden Open Access College (especially Sharon Morrison), Mitcham Girls High School (especially Susanne Owen), Pembroke School (especially Erica Baker), Prince Alfred College (especially Dr Adrian Brown), St Aloysius College (especially Elizabeth Fitzgerald, Liz Kelton and Neville Stapleton), Wilderness School (especially Carolyn Grantskalns), Windsor Gardens Vocational College (especially Angela Falkenberg), Murray Bridge High School (especially Chris Searle), St John's College (especially Charlie Allen and Sharon Rouse), Inner City Youth Service (especially Karen Walters), Christies Beach, City and Elizabeth Second Storey Youth Service localities (in particular Dorian Marsland, Jill Faulkner, Caroline Ninnes and Christine Shetliffe), Kumangka Youth

Service (especially Margaret Jackson). Thanks also to the students in my social sciences and women's studies classes.

Western Australian samples were secured largely through contacts provided by my colleagues in Perth (thanks to Helen Temby, Lenore Layman, Kathleen Pepall, Jane Long and Tanya Dalziell), Fremantle Christian Brothers College (Barry Tognolini and Kelly O'Mara), Eastern Goldfields Senior High School (Ingrid Klein and Dan McCormack), Newman College (Christine Roper and Anita Hobbs), Balga High School (Chris Parry), Guildford Grammar School (Barbara Wright), John Curtin College of Arts (Barrie Wells and Phil Allen), Applecross Senior High School (Veronica Lake), the University of Western Australia women's studies students (Jacqueline Van Gent), students participating in the S.M.A.R.T.S. Programme at the University of Western Australia (Tanya Dalziell) and other participating schools that have chosen to remain anonymous.

In New South Wales, my thanks go to Julia Ryan and Kate Cameron for assisting me with contacts, Holroyd High School (Dorothy Hoddinott and Jenny Wilkins), St George Girls High School (Linda Garrad), Dale Young Mother's Program (Jenny Baldwin), Caroline Chisholm College (Christine Howe, Matthew Barry), St Andrews College (Dr John De Courcy, David Bourne), Cerdon College (Paul Dolan, Fiona Forsyth) and Newington College (Neville Dawson).

In Victoria, my thanks to Dr Sylvie Shaw who made her sociology class at Monash University available, St Bede's College (Brother Kenneth Ormerod), Elwood College (Greg Prichard), Melbourne Aboriginal Youth Sport and Recreation (Donna Wright and Jasmine Wright), Same Sex Attracted Youth Project (Lee Fox), Country Awareness Network (Adam Wright), Quantum Support Services (Liz Jones), Hobsons Bay City Council Youth Services (Marina Popovic-Nunn). My thanks also to Carolyn Wallace, Paul Ellander and Bo Svoronos for putting me in touch with regional youth services, and to Ilse Mathews for attempting to secure regional school samples.

Daniela Bogeski and Simon Davey undertook interviews with young people in South Australia. Michael Willis and Robert Campain were effective local researchers in Victoria. I am particularly grateful to Lara Palombo for her tireless work in recruiting participating schools in New South Wales, and in completing insightful interviews. Jenni Rossi and Saul Steed devised the coding manual, coded all the questionnaires and created the ever-expanding SPSS and comments files to our mutual satisfaction. Peter Mayer alerted me to the life story essay research technique used by Anne Summers in her 1970 honours thesis, which underpinned the approach I took in my own research. My intellectual mentors over the last decade and more have generously assisted me to clarify my thinking and let my creative impulse breathe: Anita Harris, Raewyn Connell, Hester Eisenstein and Ros Prosser.

The Australian Research Council funded two large projects that supported data collection, coding and analysis between 2000 and 2007: 'Failing feminism? Generational, gender and socio-economic differences in the impact of feminism on the life course and values of Australians' and 'The limited promise of equality biographies: Young Australians negotiate modern gendered identities, family and citizenship engagements in a divided society'. Just as importantly, ARC support for teaching release provided relief from the wheel of university administration and teaching.

I would also like to thank Patrick Allington of the University of Adelaide Press for his faith in the project. My warm thanks to Ayad Alqaragholli, whose buoyant sculpture graces the cover of this book. His generosity and enthusiasm was the final pleasant punctuation mark on this book's journey, a passage that gave me hope for a future where all Australians can reach out to know and embrace each other.

INTRODUCTION

Background to the Research: The future is female (is it?)

> I don't think I've ever really seen any inequality. I mean, our lit teacher, Mrs Lake, she constantly says there is but honestly, personally I've never really experienced any of it. (Carina, middle class government high school student, Perth)[1]

> I have so many opportunities in life, and I don't feel that my gender or anything … is really holding me back in any way. (Verity, participant in high achieving high school student program, Perth)

Young interviewees in my 'equality biographies' research project, Carina and Verity, assert their belief in gender equality. They do this in the face of an older generation of feminists telling them otherwise: 'our lit teacher, Mrs Lake' and Verity's mother, Jane, an academic who has taught women's studies. As another young woman writes in her questionnaire:

> I think that we (women) have come a long way since the early 1900s and before. I am quite happy with where women stand now. (female, Catholic college, Adelaide)[2]

The research project that yielded these comments was framed in the mid-1990s. At the time, a 'generation debate' raged between so-called 'second wave' (women's liberationist or baby-boomer) feminists and their putative daughters, or 'third wave' 'Gen X' feminists. Young third wave feminists celebrated a diversity of glamorous, sexy, powerful women as opposed to the 'dowdy' 'politically correct' 'fully down-for-the-feminist-cause' second wavers (Walker 1995: xxxi). Echoed by Carina and Verity, young feminists advocated 'power feminism' to counter what they saw as second wave 'victim feminism'.[3] Women had the weight of voting numbers, they were outstripping males in university entrance, and choosing their own partners

1

because of their financial independence. Claiming that discrimination and gender stereotypes no longer held women back, some popular third wave feminists argued that women had become no different from men: no purer or more caring, and no less capable of violence, crime or killing in war (Denfeld 1995: 167–8; Wolf 1993: xvii; Benn 1998: 224; Walter 1998: 184), as can be seen, for instance, from female involvement in torturing prisoners in Abu Ghraib prison in Baghdad (c.f. Enloe 2004: 91, 99–100).

Second wave feminists agreed that women's status had been utterly transformed in many western countries, including Australia. Anne Summers (1994: 507–8) described these changes in her 'Letter to the next generation', addressed to women born after 1968 who she called 'daughters of the feminist revolution':

> The world began changing for women as you were being born. … By the time you came of age, the changes were so great that the world was almost unrecognizable to women like myself who had come of age as you were being born. … You may not be able to imagine a world where married women were not allowed to be permanently employed teachers (or any other profession on the government payroll), where pregnant women could be fired, where you could be refused a job or course of study because you were female, where abortion was illegal and dangerous, where it was the law of the land to pay women only 75 per cent of the male wage. … Then, women Members of Parliament were rare (and the handful who were there mostly occupied seats left vacant by the deaths of their husbands or fathers); the only women we saw on news and current affairs television were the 'weather girls'; it was virtually unheard of for women to be managers or bosses, except of other women; … women were starting to go to university in large numbers but more often to find a husband than to acquire career training, and the thought that a woman would retain her own last name after marriage was considered a dangerous and rebellious act.

Summers (1994: 506) lamented that the daughters appeared uninterested in seizing the torch of feminism. She wondered whether younger women would feel 'gratitude, a debt, a responsibility' to the older feminists and their movement. Summers' letter made 'hundreds' of young women 'angry' and 'insulted' (Genovese 1996: 149). They claimed that their 'ability to *do anything* comes from being a naughty girl', playing with the Sega Mega Drive instead of the 'dolls mummy gave her' (Rice and Swift 1995: 195).

By the turn into the new millennium the generation debate had faded and arguments about 'postfeminism' had replaced it. Feminist commentators, including Anne Summers (2003), were no longer confident of the forward impulse of changing gender relations. They blamed a neoliberal agenda instituted by conservative

2

governments,[4] which rolled back the welfare state and support for progressive movements such as feminism (see Segal 1999: 1 for Britain; Epstein 2001: 2, 5 for the USA; and Chunn et al. 2007: 15–16 for Canada). Summers (2003: 6–7) bemoaned *The End of Equality*, the end of 'the national conversation about women's entitlements and women's rights'. She lamented that the path to gender equality had stalled or gone into reverse, citing evidence from the realms of economics, power and intimate relations (Summers 2003: 3–5).

In 2008 there were still only four women CEOs in Australia's top ASX200 companies (Medd 2008). Although 2011 was the first year that a woman — mining magnate Gina Rinehart — headed the *Australian Business Review*'s 'Rich 200' list, women were no better represented than in previous years (Macintyre 2011). In September 2011, based on data released in a CommSec report (Sebastian 2011), women's average weekly earnings were the lowest vis-à-vis men's in 25 years — despite nearly four decades of court decisions granting equal pay, dating back to the Whitlam government's equal wage case in 1972. Indeed, a Fair Work Australia decision on 1 February 2012 ruled that 150,000 workers in the community sector, including lawyers, social workers and community development workers, were paid less because women dominated the industry. Pay rises of up to 45 per cent were awarded, indicating a very large gender gap. When part-time and casual work is taken into consideration, the average 25-year-old man is likely to earn a total of $2.4 million over the next 40 years, more than one-and-a-half times the prospective earnings of the average woman. Even among graduates, females may be pulling ahead in terms of the proportion with degrees,[5] but the gender wage gap for graduates widened from 6 per cent to 9.5 per cent in the three years to 2009.[6] Women are over-represented among those relying on government income support or experiencing sexual or partner violence. Women are more likely to experience unwanted sexual relations.[7] Although Australia had its first female Prime Minister in 2010 and first Governor-General in 2008, men, not women, still dominate the houses of parliament, as well as religious and judicial hierarchies and the trading floors that produced the global financial crisis.

Hester Eisenstein (2009: 133) argues that second wave feminism has been 'seduced' by capitalism: 'the central idea of mainstream feminism — paid work represents liberation for women — was deeply useful both to corporations and the governments backing them'. Paid work was the solution for women everywhere, forcing single mothers into the labour force in the west and women into wage exploitation in the export zones in the east. Women oppressed by Muslim regimes were to be liberated at gunpoint to participate in democracy and modernity — education and paid work. This was one meaning of 'postfeminism', the demise of feminism, and this was the meaning understood by second wave feminists like Anne Summers identifying the 'end of equality'.

Beyond the women's movement, 'postfeminism' is more often understood to mean that feminism is no longer necessary now that women have 'power'. Commentary on young women proclaims 'the future is female' (Budgeon 2011a: 10). Young women are represented as 'more confident, assertive, self-assured' than either their male peers or their foremothers (Harris 2004: 43; see Wilkinson 1994: 2, 21 for Britain). They are celebrated in the media and in social policy as 'the vanguard of a new subjectivity' (Harris 2004: 1), enthusiastically and flexibly embracing the challenges of expanding globalisation, labour market casualisation and the privatisation of education, health and social security. If education is the solution to so many social ills, female university graduates are 'trailblazers', the idealised subjects of educational reform and imagined labour market participation: *generation makers* in fact (Andres and Wyn 2010: 91, emphasis in original). In this frenetic age, ideal citizens complete their tertiary education and then effortlessly combine parenthood and career, retaining their youthful good looks and athletic figures throughout.

As former Prime Minister John Howard said more than once, 'we are in the post-feminist stage of the debate. Of course women are as good as men' (quoted in Summers 2003: 21). In proclaiming women's equality, Howard was justifying his government's actions: dismantling gender equality machinery; requiring women's services, such as rape crisis centres and domestic violence refuges, to renounce their feminist orientation as the price of continued funding, and; changing the social security and taxation system to favour a male breadwinner and dependent spouse family over a dual income/dual carer family (e.g. see Sawer 1999; Summers 2003: 130–1; Maddison and Partridge 2007).

As with Howard, other leaders of western nations proclaimed their commitment to gender equality as a sign of national modernity and economic efficiency by comparison with 'backward' 'third world countries' where women are oppressed by religion (Budgeon 2011: 13–14; Eisenstein 2009). President George W Bush, for example, invaded Afghanistan in part in the name of feminism.[8]

The Howard government introduced a citizenship test in 2007, which included gender equality as a defining national characteristic:

> Australians believe in the dignity and freedom of each person, the equality of men and women and the rule of law. (Department of Immigration and Citizenship 2007)

Feminists have been baffled and blind-sided by this new scenario in which 'we are all feminists now (except the feminists)' (Dux and Simic 2008: 151). It seems a positive sign that gender equality is a celebrated national characteristic. At the same time, conservative commentators and politicians use this 'fact' of gender equality to reprimand western feminists to stop navel-gazing and focus on the lot of their benighted Muslim and other oppressed sisters. Any evidence of ongoing inequality is explained away as the result of personal preference (women don't want to be CEOs) or something that time will fix (the pipeline theory: women are on their way up into the positions of power and influence).

One conceptualisation of this contradictory scenario posits a detraditionalisation of some aspects of gender relations along with a retraditionalisation of other aspects. Given the rapid improvement in women's public opportunities and lives, some theorists argue for a 'detraditionalisation' of gender. This signals both the weakening of tradition as the justification for action and 'the abandonment or reconfiguration of sociocultural traditions that had previously been in place' (Gross 2005: 287). Whereas women in the 1950s and 1960s expected to leave school early, work for a few years, marry and have children, this changed rapidly from the 1960s. More young women completed high school and entered university, mothers began to work, the contraceptive pill decoupled sex and parenthood, and women's liberation proposed that women become participants in the public realm. When Summers applauded the changes in women's lives in the mid-1990s she was articulating the advances of detraditionalisation.

However, some aspects of women's liberation could not easily be incorporated into the dominant ideologies, and they were excluded from mainstream acceptance, demonised as 'radical' feminism, as excessive and man-hating. As a result, some social 'fields', to use Pierre Bourdieu's formulation (e.g. see Threadgold and Nilan 2009: 50–2), have changed more rapidly than others. Individuals 'play' the 'game' in the fields, using their personal resources. Bourdieu and Passeron identify economic, cultural and social capital that flows from the habitus of each individual (Bourdieu and Passeron 1990: 74–6). The habitus of a given individual is the intersection of 'outside' elements of family, friends, education, geography, class, race and gender, and 'inside' elements such as taste, appearance and bodily dispositions: 'Habitus is a set of dispositions that form a matrix of realistic choices or actions in which one may engage in particular situations' (Threadgold and Nilan 2009: 52). When fields are aligned, individuals move from one to another more or less seamlessly, what Bourdieu calls 'knowledge without concepts' where 'the social order is progressively inscribed in people's minds' (Bourdieu in Threadgold and Nilan 2009: 50).

If there are disjunctions in gender relations between social fields, contradictions might lead to reflexive consideration of their lives by social actors. Women who completed university met resistance in workplaces that remained organised in gender hierarchies. Feminists campaigned to remove obvious discrimination in public environments and women can now move into paid work in most occupations, with little ongoing resistance, even though this challenges some of the taken-for-granted practices in the work sphere (McNay 2000: 53). However, Lesley Andres and Johanna Wyn (2010: 231) found that, while the generation born just after 1970 might belong to an 'education generation', an ever more precarious labour market has not delivered the rewards their education promised. Instead of the simple transition from education to work that was 'standard' for the baby boomer generation, *unsicherheit*, or 'uncertainty, unpredictability, and flexibility', characterises the individual struggle this generation has made to enter the workforce, most experiencing 'long hours in either a full-time job or several part-time jobs' (Andres and Wyn 2010: 18). Young women who were successful at education and who enter professional jobs are 'the least likely of any group to be employing their educational credentials in the workplace' by their mid-thirties (Furlong, Woodman and Wyn 2011: 365), indicating an inter-field contradiction between education and work. Many young people express regret that they have delayed marriage and parenting (Andres and Wyn 2010: 181) as they search for work-life balance. Mothers in particular experience this inter-field contradiction that is called 'work-life balance'. Workplaces have not changed to allow equal participation by workers with significant caring responsibilities and men remain unwilling to share housework. Women's entry into the workforce has not freed women from primary caring and emotional responsibilities at home, whether for husbands, children or ageing parents (McNay 2000: 41; Adkins 2003: 28–9).

Gøsta Esping-Andersen (2009: 54) agrees: 'one of the greatest tensions in modern society has to do with the reconciliation of careers and motherhood' — women's 'quest for motherhood remains strong'. In *The Incomplete Revolution*, he (Esping-Andersen 2009: 10–11) argues that society is in an unstable equilibrium between a past equilibrium (the patriarchal male breadwinner and female homemaker family) and a coming 'gender-equality equilibrium'. He also notes the impact of women's education and employment, particularly of mothers returning to work. Birth control and divorce laws allowed women to express new preferences, for example choosing partners on the basis of their commitment to childcare (Esping-Andersen 2009: 13–14, 20–1). The revolution is incomplete because women's values and behaviour have changed more than men's, and more in their public (educational and working) lives than in their home lives. Women with the most education have changed the most, in terms of both their engagement in the labour force and the tendency towards more equal housework and childcare, so that another — and widening — stalling of the revolution concerns the difference between middle class and working class households (Esping-Andersen 2009: 24). A third inequality is between the generations, the baby-boomers taking retirement benefits based on the post-war economic boom while young people struggle in an uncertain comparatively lower paid labour market (Esping-Andersen 2009: 4, 9). In this situation, neither the old nor the new social arrangements are normative, and people, women especially, cannot achieve their desires (Esping-Andersen 2009: 511).

Kathleen Gerson (2010) also argues for what she calls *The Unfinished Revolution*. As in Andres and Wyn's study, she suggests that the largely shared ideals for egalitarian mutually supportive relationships stumble against economic and social obstacles — in particular a vulnerable job market exacting long working hours — 'pressures to parent intensively, and rising standards for a fulfilling relationship' (Gerson 2010: 104). Gerson (2010: 12) calls the gender revolution 'unfinished' because young people's 'highest aspirations' cannot be met, and they 'fall back on less desirable options' (Gerson 2010: 12). Women resort to becoming 'self-reliant' women, who see personal autonomy as essential for their survival, choosing to make a family without a man if necessary. Men resort to becoming neotraditional men, who see work success as a key to self-respect and imagine wives who will be primary care-takers (Gerson 2010: 105). These are 'not just different but conflicting fallback strategies' (Gerson 2010: 123), as I explore in Chapter Three.

In summary, in response to 'detraditionalization' (McNay 2000: 1, 22), there has been a 'retraditionalization' of gender in new patterns (e.g. Adkins 2002; Arnot 2002). Many Australians, including those in my research, live with these contradictory notions of gender sameness, largely in the public sphere, and gender differences, particularly in our private lives, where we tend to treat the sexes as preformed categories (see Connell 2000: 18; Flood 2005). Separate studies by Esping-Andersen, by Gerson and by Andres and Wyn highlight that 'educated women either forgo marriage or childbearing to pursue their careers or forgo their careers to take up the role of motherhood' (Furlong et al. 2011: 366). This unstable and contradictory situation may encourage some elements of reflexivity, women's consideration of why they face obstacles to mobilising their career capital, realising higher career aspirations and changing partners' contribution to heterosexual relationships.

The discourse of gender equality combines with an anti-discrimination discourse to produce the contemporary understanding in many people's minds that to *notice* differences based on gender (or class, race or culture) is discrimination. This serves to increase gender inequality due to failure to attend to the gender aspects of public policy and other decisions. Australia has become 'a culture in which women are bullied into invisibility', a climate actively cultivated by Australia's leaders, as well as against them (Cunningham 2011). In March 2010, *The Monthly* commissioned

Louis Nowra to write the cover story celebrating 40 years since the publication of *The Female Eunuch*. Nowra's descriptions of Greer's 'uninspired', 'meaningless', 'dreary', 'repetitive' and 'dull and graceless prose' (Nowra 2010) leave readers wondering why *The Female Eunuch* had such a huge impact on so many Australian women. In 2009 and 2011 not a single female author was short-listed for the Miles Franklin Literary Award (Cunningham 2011). The response to the global financial crisis did not consider increasing women's employment, for example in childcare and teaching, but focused on blue collar building trades.[9] Australia's first female prime minister failed to identify the portfolio of women's affairs (and Indigenous health).[10] Later, her government initially refused to support the Fair Work Australia pay case for community workers, mostly women.[11]

This book is an exploration of the changing grounds of sameness and difference, with a focus on gender relations. According to Esping-Andersen (2009: 1–3), most of the research on changes from one generation to another focuses on what sociologists call 'institutions', in particular of work, family and education. These changes are generally explained in terms of the growth in the services sector, globalisation, technological change, and new social movements such as the new left, the women's movement, and environmentalism. Esping-Andersen suggests that the over-arching story is in fact 'the quiet revolution in women's roles'. Similarly, my study focuses on the values and attitudes young people express when talking about their 'roles', how they express gender, class and culture in their own lives, and how they imagine these relations in the future and in wider society.

This book applies the analytical frame of difference to discuss gender, but also class and cultural/race relations in several ways. First, and particularly in relation to class and gender, I argue for sameness or equality at the level of rhetoric and difference and inequality at the level of 'practices'. Young people accept, even embrace, categorical gender differences. They imagine lives marked by persistent gendered preferences, such as romance versus sex or cars versus friends. Those from other than English-speaking background ethnicities are often proud of their ethnic identity, their difference, as are Aboriginal respondents. They incorporate these expressions of identity into individual uniqueness. By contrast, aspects of cultural or class difference that express inequality, that suggest 'victim' or 'loser', are eschewed. Their rhetoric expresses equality but their practices are of gender, class and ethnic difference, expressed in often profound inequalities. They can deploy individualism to good advantage in promoting the rights of individuals but are stumped to identify or discuss collective or structural bases for inequality and difference.

I contrast the differences in the way young people understand their present lives and imagine their futures with their insistent refusal to entertain such inequalities.

They claim gender equality, are unwilling to acknowledge class relations and have enormous difficulty discussing Indigenous disadvantage, concerned about sounding racist. They are almost sociologically autistic, unable to discuss structural impacts and patterns in any but the crudest terms — like Laurel Richardson's (1997: 164) single mother interviewee Louisa May, who 'resists categorization into and through … sociology'. The rare glimpses of structural constraints that appeared in young people's responses were often nebulous and phrased in universal literary tropes rather than the cultural specificity that comes from the lens of history, anthropology or sociology.

My research explores how young people, in contrast with their parents, negotiate a contradictory gender and class scenario and the limitations of the discourses available to them to confront the complexities of their current lives. Young women are sanguine that gender equality has been achieved yet readily report instances of ongoing discrimination, particularly in the workplace. Young women, and to a lesser extent young men, endorse sharing housework and childcare, yet almost no young men write of being stay-at-home fathers or otherwise challenging traditional gender roles in the home. Young people are insistent advocates of the equal worth of every individual and many advocate the right to free expression of sexual preference and opinions — and yet they cleave just as insistently to an imaginary of gender differences. They are so concerned about expressing gender equality that they are unwilling to notice gender-differentiated treatment, fearing this to be an expression of sex discrimination.

Methods

> all (YOU) or who ever is reading it wants to hear is that we will get married and become barefoot & pregnant. (female, Sri Lankan background, Catholic college student, Sydney, bracketed text in original)

Anne Summers wrote her honours thesis in 1970, amidst the excitement of the newly arrived women's liberation movement.[12] She addressed 'Women's *consciousness* of their role-structure' (added emphasis),[13] or 'what women think their role-structure is' (Summers 1970: 4), in three domains: in Australian women's magazines, in Australian novels written by women and in 'schoolgirls' perceptions of adult roles'. In relation to the last domain, Summers asked 117 schoolgirls in their last year of high school to write an essay imagining their future lives. Summers presumed this would reveal 'what these girls see, at this point in their lives, as the future possibilities available to them' (Summers 1970: 8).

Instantly attracted to this research tool, I decided to replicate Summers' study a generation later, thus allowing for a 'social generation approach' (see Furlong et al. 2011: 366–7, discussing Mannheim 1959). I make intergenerational comparison in the context of structural changes shaping each generation's opportunities and experiences. As Andy Furlong, Dan Woodman and Johanna Wyn (2011: 366) claim, the social generational approach 'enables us to understand the significance of subjectivities and the unevenness of capacity across groups (gender, class, race) and across time and place to enact these subjectivities'. Both Summers in 1970 and myself between 2000 and 2006 surveyed young women in the last year of high school, thus allowing comparison of the 'future possibilities' envisaged by young women before and after the impact of women's liberation. Like Summers, I was interested in the difference in hopes expressed by young people from different class backgrounds, and so sought to include a wide range of school types in my sample. Unlike Summers, I chose also to survey young men, thus allowing a gender comparison in my sample. Furthermore, given the larger reach of my ARC-funded project, I was interested in extending my sample beyond high school students to capture voices often excluded from representative samples,[14] such as Indigenous youth, same-sex attracted youth and early school leavers.

Most of the data for my sample was collected between 2000 and 2005, largely in South Australia and Western Australia. Some additional data was collected in 2006 and 2007, largely in New South Wales and Victoria. I secured ethics approval from The University of Adelaide, from each State department of education (for government schools) and the state Catholic Education Office (for Catholic schools). I personally administered the surveys in classrooms in South Australia (apart from one school in Adelaide and one in Whyalla) and Western Australia. Otherwise, a local researcher administered the questionnaires and conducted interviews, doing all the survey work in New South Wales and Victoria.

At the centre of my sample are 743 year 11 or 12 high school students from a wide range of schools, including regional centres (see Warner-Smith and Lee 2001 for the effect of schools on opportunities, attitudes and outcomes; see also Table A2.1 in Appendix 2). Julie McLeod and Lyn Yates (2005: 65, 55–6) claim that research in the school setting elicits the 'good student' persona. While many in my sample expressed such a persona — diligently completing the task with the answers that a teacher-like adult would favour — others chose to be 'bad students', taking the mickey out of my presumed values, or just enjoying their own fantasies.[15] Questions about feminism partly provoked negative responses such as 'lesbian communists (feminists) do not deserve to be a part of society' or 'I couldn't give two shits about feminism'. It was also clear that students collaborated and conferred in producing their answers.[16] Scourfield et al. (2006: 34) also found such collaboration.

Almost no school granted me access unless I had a contact to smooth the way, the exception being the Catholic schools, which were the most willing to participate in my research. Therefore, my sample, while large, is not random, although I hope it is largely representative. Once the principal approved my project, a class teacher was usually willing to take it on. These teachers were committed to an ongoing conversation with their students about how Australian society operated and their students' roles in that society. Elaborating on the teachers' union bumper sticker, 'If you can read this, thank a teacher', the teachers with whom I worked demonstrated that 'If you can think critically and optimistically about your personal life, your employment options, your civic engagements, thank your teachers' (see McLeod and Yates's (2006: 16, 10–11, 143–58) study of 'biographies in interaction with schooling', which addresses the impact of the social justice curriculum on students' attitudes). Given teachers were self-selected, their students might well have a higher than average knowledge of social affairs, while it was clear that many teachers were committed to educating their students in gender issues.

I sought participant classes from four school categories: elite Protestant colleges, parochial Catholic colleges, middle class government schools and working class government schools. I also sought to sample schools in capital cities and regional towns (see Table A2.2). I entered middle class academically-oriented government classrooms where young women and men worked hard to do well and go to university. For example, one mother I interviewed, Jenny, who was forced to leave a violent husband, moved into the catchment area of such a school, even though she struggled to find the rent. She wanted her daughters to have the best educational opportunity she could provide. This school takes its public service seriously, proudly displaying the sticker 'Public education — our future' in the reception area at the time of my visit. In working class government classrooms, teachers battled to impart basic skills that would improve students' success in their interactions with the Australian justice system or in employment. At one such school, students had taken a 'dole abstinence pledge', a promise not to go on the dole when they leave school. These students were featured in a local newspaper article pinned to the noticeboard alongside pictures of students working in neighbourhood stores and workshops.

To further extend the socio-economic range of my sample, I surveyed clients of youth services, in particular those supporting Aboriginal youth, early school leavers or young people with sexuality issues.[17] The youth service clients were mostly aged 15 and 16 (36 per cent), although there was a sample of younger respondents from an Aboriginal youth service (20 per cent of the sub-sample were 14 years old or younger) as well as a number of older respondents (including 26 per cent of the sub-sample who were aged 17 to 22). A sample of 144 first year university students, largely aged 18 and 19 and enrolled in social sciences or women's studies, were young 'cosmopolitans', that is, those whose education in the social sciences is positively correlated with left-liberal attitudes on gender and other social issues (e.g. see Simons 2004).

The high school students took a questionnaire home to their parents of the same sex (if available) to complete and post to me. This yielded a sample of 226 parents, to supplement my intergenerational comparison with Summers' 1970 essayists. These results are introduced in Chapter One and discussed largely in Chapter Two. Most parents were aged between 40 and 50 (the average age was 45). Born between 1950 and 1960, parents are either defined as baby boomers or, less often, 'Gen X' (depending both on when they were born and how these two generations are distinguished) while the 'young' respondents[18] are early Generation Y (Andres and Wyn 2010: 33).[19]

The intergenerational comparison with Summers' essayists and the comparison of young people with their parents in my sample allows exploration of intergenerational transmission. This change and continuity has been little addressed in explorations of changing gender and class relations, by contrast with the more common longitudinal studies that follow the same cohort through time (Woodman 2009: 254). Chapters Two and Three explore the complexities confronting youth in their family relations and the contribution of parents in assisting young people to forge alternative gender identities.

The questionnaire

> [in relation to gender equality]: I didn't really know much about this topic, but then the person that was doing the … survey next to me, gave me an idea. And so, that's how I came to that. ('Sam' (female), middle class government high school student, Adelaide)

I explored the attitudes of young people and their parents via three research instruments: a questionnaire, a life story essay and a follow-up interview. Karen Walters, a youth services worker, suggested I change the questionnaire to make it more accessible to her clients who were early school leavers. Appendix 1 shows the two versions of the questionnaire. The questionnaire commenced with a task in which respondents were asked to complete ten 'I am …' statements (see Emmison and Western 1990: 247). Their answers focused not on 'structural' attributes such as gender and class but personal attributes (such as personality, sporting interests, intellectual capacities). Once coded, the 'I am' responses assisted me in analysing differences in subjectivity according to generation, gender, class and ethnicity.[20]

These self-descriptors were particularly pertinent for my exploration of the relationship between understanding oneself in terms of independence from others and interdependence with others (see Chapter Three).

The questionnaire also contained questions on attitudes to gender issues like sharing housework, abortion or homosexuality (adapted from Pilcher's (1998) interview schedule), attitudes to feminism and the women's movement (taken from a CNN poll: see Bellafante 1998), and attitudes to the social issues of reconciliation, multiculturalism, the environment, the welfare state and unions. My interest was in young people's attitudes towards social issues that dealt with the distribution of resources and recognition to social groups (see Fraser 1995). Each item asked for respondents' degree of agreement, followed by space to make comments. Attitudes to social issues, including citizen engagement, inform Chapter Five. The responses to the gender questions are discussed largely in Chapter Three, where I explore the differences between young women's and men's imagined family relations. An intergenerational comparison of attitudes towards the women's movement and feminism is in Chapter Two.

The questionnaire contained a section for personal details if the respondent was willing to be interviewed. Around 150 follow-up interviews, discussing the questionnaire answers (see Lupton 1999: 299 for a similar research design), were completed with willing respondents (in which parents, particularly mothers, were over-represented and school students under-represented; see Table A2.4 in Appendix 2).[21] The interviews canvassed the respondents' questionnaire answers, seeking elaborations and explanations. In addition, I asked the parents to reflect on intergenerational changes in gender relations (see Chapter Two) and the young people to reflect on class through discussions of consumption and on politics (see Chapter Four). Interviews with mothers of around my age flowed easily in a 'natural discourse', yielding incisive insights concerning my theoretical framework and presumptions (Bourdieu in Bourdieu et al. 1999: 613–4). My interviews with young people only rarely achieved this fluency, for example when they shared my feminism or interest in other social issues. I turned to young interviewers to bridge the cultural gap. I was surprised to find that they often had almost as much difficulty in securing thick narratives from their interviewees, suggesting that the research topics that interested me rarely fired the enthusiasm of the young participants, although it was clear from their comments that some gender and social issues engaged their interest — in particular abortion rights (see Chapter Three), an apology to Indigenous Australians, and the environment (see Chapter Five).[22]

Writing the future: Imagined life stories

> It's the sort of story that you would actually hear somebody say. (Kelly, working class government high school student, South Australia)

> That's what most people want, partial of what everyone gets. (Naomi, working class government high school student, Adelaide, commenting on her life story, which covered university education, a 'highly satisfying career', 'true love', children)

To my mind, the most intriguing element of the data, but also the most difficult to analyse, were the life story essays. The last section of the questionnaire for high school students and youth services clients consisted of four lined pages in which they were asked to write an essay imagining their future (see Appendix 1 for the two questionnaires). Seven hundred and sixty-six respondents completed life stories (90 per cent of the females and 85 per cent of the males), ranging from a sentence to three closely typed pages (see Table A2.3 in Appendix 2). While this research method is rare,[23] a number of interview-based studies ask young people to imagine their futures (e.g. see Wierenga 2009 for a Tasmanian study; McLeod and Yates 2006 for a Victorian study; Henderson et al. 2007 for a longitudinal British study called 'Inventing Adulthoods'; and Dwyer and Wyn 2001 for a longitudinal Victorian 'Life Patterns' study).

The authors of *Inventing Adulthoods* explain that

> we adopted a longitudinal, qualitative, biographical approach in order to examine the micro-processes that contribute to the diverse biographical projects in which young people engage. We use the term 'biographical' here to distinguish an approach in which a life story is privileged and which is based on the collection and analysis of biographical and autobiographical accounts. (Thomson et al. 2004: 222)

Interviewers in this study constructed a 'narrative analysis' of each interviewee based on two interviews and 'life lines' in which the young people predicted their futures. The authors are aware that this approach 'of "walking alongside" young people' and its interpretation 'give[s] rise to distinct challenges in terms of validity and reliability' (Thomson et al. 2004: 220).[24] As Andres and Wyn (2010: 29) note of the longitudinal Victorian study, 'reading the aspirations of school-aged youth onto their future lives is itself risky'. However, the 'biographical' method produces rich and unexpected results, revealing the constantly changing relationship between 'the variability and contingency of young people's individual biographical trajectories, and socially structured factors such as class, locality, gender, "race", and religion, which were related to the inequalities that they were experiencing' (Thomson et al. 2004: 220–2).

As my study was not longitudinal, I have been unable to assess the extent to which imagined life stories were realised. Nor did I ask biographers to write a 'realistic' prediction of their future as in 'Inventing Adulthoods'. The young people in my study were allowed to invent adulthoods much more freely than is usually done in interview-based studies. This very freedom, we will see, encouraged young people to express the gender differences that they often repressed when more aware that they should conform with the hegemonic discourse of gender equality, for example in commentary on sharing housework. The life stories are more unguarded expressions of the enduring impact of gender and class on shaping the subjectivities of young people.

One essayist — despairingly — concludes of her essay 'Honestly how could I write anything else?', suggesting the weight of the cultural in channelling the psychodynamic in the production of a life biography:

> 'At the age of 26 I had my first child and while I am happy in my job I take maternity leave followed by reduced hours at work. … My husband has an extremely well paying job as well as being a lawyer. … Of course our relationship was a happy one and my husband is supportive.' Honestly how could I write anything else? I believe that no one plans to have an unhappy life and frankly at the age of 16 or 17 no one wants to believe they may die alone, having failed at everything and achieved nothing they believed they were possible of. The future is completely unpredictable … and I think this honestly is a waste of time. (female, middle class government high school student, Perth)

This essayist realises, but deplores, that the self is '"found" in cultural forms', especially dominant discourses, as much as '"created" through personal feelings' (Luttrell 2003: 167; see also Quinn 2005: 23; Henderson et al. 2007).

For those essayists I interviewed, I handed them the essay they wrote and asked them the extent to which stories were desired, predicted or total fantasies. Most responded that their tales were written between hope and expectation, what Audre Lorde calls 'bio-mythography' (in hooks 1989: 158), an interplay of embellished desires, utopian dreams and realistic plans. In interviews, respondents sometimes expressed surprise at what they had written a scant two to three months previously. Consider this, for example, from a young woman in a group interview:

> Florence: Ooohh!!! When I wrote this, my story that I wrote, this is the story of the days when I was going out with B-B Kim but that's all changed now, all changed. Jeez Louise. … I have many

boyfriends but I kind of, what's that, I'm kind of explaining how I don't believe in marriage and all that kind of stuff. ... Kim and I, it's kind of like we have a de facto relationship and we had a couple of kids and went around the world. And [with ironic self-parody in voice] we were able to educate the kids by ourselves because we were, you know, so good. And I had two boys, I forgot about them, yeah. ... Umm, yeah, but [said with some surprise] I end up retiring in Ireland, I lived in Ireland, yeah. ...

Chilla: So now that story, did you write it like, to what extent do you think it was what you wanted and to what extent did you think it might happen?

Florence: ... I still don't believe a lot of this marriage stuff. But, Kim's not in the picture [all laugh]. ... But I still, I want to move to Ireland and I want to run a, I think it would be great to have a pub — that's just like hope. But otherwise, yeah. ('Florence', girls' middle class government high school student, Adelaide)

Florence compares her enduring beliefs about marriage and her hopes to travel with the obsolescence of the boyfriend. In the same interview, Patricia writes more dramatically of starring in 'a biographical film about the life of Marilyn Monroe', shortly before her actor husband dies in a car crash. In the same group interview, Patricia actually fears that her life won't contain 'something good' and describes her story as 'just made up' ('Patricia', girls' middle class government high school student, Adelaide). Even when 'just made up', the reiterated themes in the life stories demonstrate the persisting relevance of gender, class and ethnicity in young people's lives.

The patterns found in these 700 life stories are of sociological significance, not because they predict what will happen to this generation in adulthood, but in terms of 'consciousness', as Summers put it, or identification as it might be put today — how young people express their gendered, classed and raced imaginaries. Almost invariably they understand themselves to be unique individuals. The patterns in their stories reveal the limited remit of individuality, still hemmed in by the social expectations of gender and the structural limitations of class and race.

Outline of the book

Fate or destiny played an important part in my life. So did society, but times were forever changing and I'm sure the cycle of society's pattern has begun again, always telling us how to live etc. (female, Catholic college student, Adelaide)

16

Through the life stories, this book explores the persistence of gendered and classed imagined life trajectories and subjectivities, an analysis that commences in Chapter One with a summary of differences on the basis of gender, class and ethnicity. My use of the term 'equality biographies' signals that young people yearn for and believe in equal opportunities, but the very marrow of their life stories indicates massive inequalities in the personal resources that will allow them to achieve their goals. The horizon of their desires is bracketed by socio-economic location. I am not claiming that the life stories tell us what these young people will actually do. But they do tell us that their dreams and desires are still strongly gender-coded, class-marked and ethnically differentiated.

Sameness and difference across the generations is the subject of Chapter Two, exploring how respondents believe men's and women's lives have changed across the generations. While women of the parents' generation told a progressive tale of women's increasing freedom across the generations, such a narrative was totally obscured to men, apart from two who read these generational changes through the lens of feminism. Like their mothers, daughters also enthusiastically embraced a teleological tale. Having inherited the gains identified by Anne Summers in her 'Letter to the next generation', young women generally have a very monochrome view of women's history, a terrible 'dark ages' of women's oppression compared with the equality of now. The chapter then compares the gender identities of the fathers, who are dumb to a story of changing gender relations, with their sons. Some young men found the question concerning changes in men's lives across the generations as baffling as their fathers did. Others deflected the messages of feminism in an ironic parody of patriarchal attributes. The chapter concludes with an analysis of attitudes to feminism and the women's movement, noting the greater concern with men's presumed disadvantage than women's continuing inequality.

Chapter Three explores the shape of heterosexual partnerships when gendered life stories meet under one roof. On top of young women's and men's differently imagined futures, discussed in Chapter One, are different subjectivities and expectations concerning their partnerships, discussed in Chapter Three. Young women envisage equal relationships in which partners will share their dreams, activities and desires. Some of them explicitly talk of what this means in terms of 'working' on and in a relationship. They imagine independent lives, for both themselves and their partners, but which are expressed in interdependence, thus envisaging interdependent independence as a work in progress. This will require considerable 'psychological capital', and the young women demonstrated more of this than did the young men in my research.

Chapter Four addresses how young people understand economic inequality in a world of 'capitalism without class' (Beck 2002: 205), a world where access to economic and cultural resources is ever more crucial in determining life chances but where class identity and explanations have almost completely vanished from mainstream discussion. Young people are aware of socio-economic differences, readily visible in the lives of many, and can finely parse ownership of cultural capital in expressions of taste. However, they are unwilling to identify themselves in the category of 'working class' or 'struggling class', seeing this as the abject identity of a loser, the one whose biography has failed. Privileged respondents were also uncomfortable in discussing their 'good fortune'. As with sex discrimination, there is a sense that to notice social inequality is some kind of breach of the widely endorsed commitment to equality. However, unwillingness or inability to explain class differences in structural terms meant that ultimately people were individually blamed for living in poverty.

If young people are more individualistic than previous generations, as is suggested by the pervasive neoliberal discourse, how do they imagine citizenship or social action? While some researchers have rejected Generations X and Y as apathetic and alienated from politics, other researchers question the definitions of politics and citizenship. Chapter Five suggests that the old forms of parties and parliament do not capture the forms of local or intimate citizenship that characterise the civic involvement of many young people, responding to the lure of celebrity or the processes of social media rather than politicians and the mass media. This chapter also extends the analysis in Chapter Four, exploring young people's attitudes to those beyond the intimate circle, to those marked as 'other' in terms of ethnicity or race, in particular how personal experiences influence attitudes to Indigenous Australians and detention of refugees. Insistence on equality and tolerance creates great discomfort, even inarticulateness, when addressing differences produced by dispossession, culture and religion. Refusing notions of superiority and lacking an understanding of structural literacy, some young people resort to what I call 'intimate citizenship', hopeful forms of engagement, particularly around psychological issues, individual rights and the environment.

This book also gives space for the young Australians' own words, their energetic conviction that each person's story is unique and precious, while also linking these individual biographies to the structural constraints and discursive contradictions within which they are expressed. This plaiting commences in Chapter One, which introduces the respondents by comparing their life stories on the basis of generation, gender, class and race/ethnicity.

Notes

[1] In the body of the text, interviewed participants are referred to in terms of their name (either their real name or a pseudonym, the latter in quotation marks). Indented quotations are sourced by gender, Aboriginality or ethnic background if identified in their 'I ams' (but English-speaking country background is not noted), respondent source (school, university, or youth service category), whether they are a young person or a parent, and their geographical location (either capital city or State in the case of regional respondents).

[2] As most of the government high schools were co-educational, I have only indicated girls' government high schools. Conversely, as most of the private schools were single sex, I have only indicated co-educational private schools, which I have called 'colleges'.

[3] There are several and sometimes contradictory strands to this debate, made more complicated by the different positions taken up by academically located third wavers, who focus more on what they see as the lack of diversity in second wavers' identification of 'women', and popular authors, such as Naomi Wolf (1993), Rebecca Walker (1995) and Rene Denfeld (1995) in the US, Natasha Walter (1998) in the UK and Kathy Bail (1996) in Australia. For an analysis of the debate see the contributions to *Outskirts* volume 8 (2001), http://www.outskirts.arts.uwa.edu.au/volumes/volume-8) and, more recently, Henry (2004).

[4] Although James Walter (2010: 307–9, 288) argues that the Hawke Labor government from 1983 was a 'direct precursor of what would become Howard's mantra after 1996', adopting economic rationalism and commencing financial and labour market deregulation.

[5] According to the Australian Bureau of Statistics (2012), 29.8 per cent of males and 41.0 per cent of females aged 25–29 had bachelors degrees or higher in 2011, the gap widening from 7 per cent in favour of females in 2001 to 11 per cent.

[6] A Graduate Careers Australia report found that women earn $7200 less than men three years after leaving university, that males are more likely to be in full time employment (91 per cent compared with 84 per cent), and that the wage gap is still seven per cent when discipline differences are taken into account. 'It definitely shows that there remains some form of labour market discrimination in terms of earnings on average for women', GCA senior research associate David Carroll concluded (Healy 2010).

[7] Some studies have found up to 63 per cent of women experiencing sex 'not because they wanted to, but because [they] felt it would be inappropriate to refuse' (Powell 2008: 169). One in seven young males agreed with the statements that 'It's okay for a boy to make a girl have sex with him if she has flirted with him or led him on' and 'It is okay to put pressure on a girl to have sex but not to physically force her' (Flood 2005: 4). For a summary of statistics on violence against women, see Michael Flood, XY, <http://www.xyonline.net/content/violence-against-women-australia-facts-and-figures-3-pp>, accessed 23 July 2010.

[8] While the war might have been justified in part in terms of women's rights, the provision of aid is no longer directed towards this goal. The US Agency for International Development (USAID) no longer requires contractors to identify how they promote women's rights, such being described as 'pet projects': 'All those pet rocks in our rucksack were taking us down' and 'Gender issues are going to have to take a back seat to other priorities' according to the director of USAID's Office of Afghanistan and Pakistan affairs. This was promptly denied by Secretary of State Hillary Clinton (Parker 2011).

[9] The Rudd government's response to the global financial crisis in 2008 was a stimulus package plucked straight from John Maynard Keynes. School building programs increase unskilled blue

collar and trade employment: jobs for unemployed men rather than for women. To guard against a fall in female employment, the Australian Human Rights Commission suggested that some stimulus package funds should have been directed at training more early childhood educators, teachers and care workers to staff the new buildings (Australian Human Rights Commission 2009). Paid parental leave would have been another successful strategy, but was only grudgingly introduced by the Gillard government in January 2011.

[10] Albeit her cabinet had a higher percentage of women than any cabinet before, rising from 5 per cent in 2001 to 20 per cent in 2011. The Opposition leader, Tony Abbott, also 'forgot' women, although prompted, both remedied the oversight (Australian Bureau of Statistics 2011a).

[11] In November 2010, the federal government, claiming it would threaten their hoped-for balanced budget, refused to support a pay equity case before Fair Work Australia for 153,000 community-sector workers, mostly women who were paid 30 per cent less than comparable workers in government jobs. Only an outcry from unions and the Australian Council of Social Services changed the government's strategy. The outcome in May 2011 was heralded as 'equal pay' based on work of 'comparable value' (Cox 2011).

[12] In the summer of 1969–70 women returning from the United States announced the inaugural meeting of the Women's Liberation Group in Sydney. By 1971, there were women's liberation groups in every major town in Australia, clustering in the inner-city suburbs and around the universities (Burgmann 1993: 77; Curthoys 1992: 430; Kaplan 1996: 32). In her honours thesis, Summers thanked 'Miss Anna Yeatmann [sic]' — now an internationally renowned professor — for a willing ear, and 'the members of the Adelaide Women's Liberation Movement who allowed me to argue several of my theories at their meetings'.

[13] The term 'role-structure' expresses a negotiation of social expectations and structures with individual agency (Summers 1970: 1–2).

[14] For example, Andres and Wyn (2010: 14) report that, in their longitudinal study of Victorian youth, cell sizes were too small in relation to same-sex attracted and Indigenous samples to explore the experiences of these groups.

[15] My local researcher, Simon Davey, was woven into the life story of a young woman at a co-educational school who wrote, 'I found a man, Simon Davey, I loved and we got married. We have a hot sex life.'

[16] For example, in the school class that Simon Davey surveyed, two students wrote life stories in which they both won Olympic gold medals, saved the world's wildlife, and lived in exotic places such as Antarctica and the Amazon.

[17] The sexuality youth service clients represent four per cent of my sample of young people (38 of the 1000 young people). Depending on the source, between three and 11 per cent of the population are not exclusively heterosexual. As self-declared in the 2001 ABS census, 99.53 per cent of couples are heterosexual, 0.26 per cent are male homosexuals and 0.21 per cent are lesbian (de Vaus 2004: 83). There are more gay couples among those aged 20–24, where 0.55 per cent are male gays and 0.54 per cent are lesbian (de Vaus 2004: 83). A survey of 19,000 Australians in 2001/02 found that 97.4 per cent of men identified as heterosexual, 1.6 per cent as gay and 0.9 per cent as bisexual; 97.7 per cent of women identified as heterosexual, 0.8 per cent as gay and 1.4 per cent as bisexual. However, 8.6 per cent of men and 15.1 per cent of women reported feelings of attraction or some sexual experience with the same sex (Australian Research Centre in Sex, Health and Society circa 2003: 2). A repeat survey in 2004 of the first national study in Australia of same-sex attracted young people (by Hillier et al. in 1998) found many more support groups

and community programs and more young people feeling positive about being lesbian, gay or bisexual, which produced a greater tendency to come out to fathers as well as mothers (Lindsay and Dempsey 2009: 80–2).

18 In their study of young people, McLeod and Yates (2006: 76–7) ponder the use of 'adolescence' as too psychologised, 'youth' as being normatively male and associated with studies of deviance, 'teenager' as signalling market research and 'young women' and 'young men' as potentially clichéd and patronizing. I generally refer to my sample as 'young people', 'young men' or 'young women'.

19 The appellation of 'Generation X' was first applied by Coupland (1991) to describe those born in the 1950s and the 1960s (Walsh and Bahnisch 1999: 60), although some commentators extend the definition of baby-boomers to those born in the 1950s and even early 1960s (e.g. Everingham et al. 2007: 421). Generation Y, born in the 1970s and 1980s, are 'echo boomers', children of the baby boomers (Huntley 2006: 10). Andres and Wyn (2010: 33) provide a 'summary of current thinking' in which they identify early baby boomers (born 1946–1954), late baby boomers (1955–1965), Generation X (1966–1976), early Generation Y (born 1977–1990) and late Generation Y (born after 1991). By this definition, my sample is early Generation Y (Andres and Wyn 2010: 33). The 'generation — born just after 1970 — … initiated the flurry of so-called generational naming in the mass media' (Andres and Wyn 2010: 242). As they remained living with and financially dependent on their parents for longer, they have been called a 'yo-yo generation' or 'boomerang generation' (Andres and Wyn 2010: 160). Their hopes for the future and belief in a multitude of choices have earned them the appellations 'options generation' (McKay 1997) or 'generation blue sky' (Huntley 2006).

20 Subjectivity and identity have slightly different meanings in the social sciences. Identity refers to common positionings, such as gender, ethnicity, race, sexual preference by which individuals inscribe themselves into the social world (Clammer 2000: 211; Cranny-Francis et al. 2003: 33). Subjectivity is the outcome of 'subjectification (the production of "the subject" in discursive practices) and subjectivity (the lived experience of being a subject)' (Walkerdine et al. 2001: 176). Subjectivity refers to unconscious and conscious emotions and thoughts which are historically and socially produced and contextualized as an individual places herself in the social and material world (Hobson 2000: 240; Weedon 1987: 32). Subjectivity and identity are 'precarious, contradictory' (Weedon 1987: 33) works in progress, individuals torn between desires and drives on the one hand and cultural and social demands on the other (Cranny-Francis et el 2003:11).

21 Although around half of my high school sample was male, 80 per cent of those interviewed were female, probably a combination of my gender, the research topic and mothers' engagement with their children.

22 Of the gender issues, abortion, pornography and role reversal provoked the most comments. There were few comments on the industrial relations items and the feminism items (although attitudes towards feminism constituted the last section of the questionnaire, which might have contributed to the lack of comments; see Table A3.6 in Appendix 3).

23 Besides Summers' (1970) research, on which I modelled mine, I have since discovered three other studies that use this 'imaginative life story' approach, all of them with younger writers than in my study. An English study in 1969 asked 11-year-old children to write 'on the topic of how they imagined their life at age 25' (Elliott 2010: 1073); Ani Weirenga's (2009) study 'commenced' with the individuals writing 'essays about their futures', after which she interviewed them every two years until early adulthood, along with families, teachers and significant others (Wierenga 2011: 374); Maureen Baker undertook an unpublished Canadian study (pers. comm.).

24 The authors interviewed and re-interviewed 100 young people aged 15–21, also asking their interviewees to complete 'memory books' and 'life lines'. In their life lines, interviewees were asked to predict their lives in home/housing, education, work, relationships, travel and values in three years, 25 and 35 years time (Henderson et al. 2007: 170). Based on this material, the interviewer constructed a 'narrative analysis' of each young participant's imagined and actual lives, which paid attention 'to narrative structure, the identity of the teller, and the presumed audience' (Thomson et al. 2004: 220).

1

ESSAYING DIFFERENCE: COMPARING ESSAYS ACROSS THE SUB-SAMPLES

Introduction: 'Choice' or 'risk' biography?

> When I was younger I thought that I would be very good at school and complete year 12 then I would travel and do everything I wanted. I thought I would get my licence straight away and have a car already and I would have my freedom and do whatever I wanted to do. I dreamt that I would live my life the way I wanted to and enjoy it and then around the age of twenty-five I would have the man I love — be married to him and start a family. I would have a good job that pays well and I would be paying off my house and I would have a nice new car and would be living comfortably, but when I started high school that all changed. At the age of fifteen I found out about drugs and got involved with them and started going down in my schoolwork because it didn't interest me any more, my mind wasn't on it. I started getting more and more involved with drugs and at the end of year 10 I quit school and just did nothing any more. ... I became involved with [friend's cousin] and then I ran away with him. And then my parents moved away so I moved into a flat with him, and now I'm pregnant with his baby. And I'm confused about my future now but I hope that everything works out and I marry him and have a happy life with him. (female, working class government high school student, Adelaide)

Many essayists in my sample write assertively about being independent authors of their world and words, prizing the 'authentic self' (Weedon 1987: 32; see also

Budgeon 2003: 67–8). The young woman quoted above once believed she would do 'everything I wanted', but drugs lead to truancy, pregnancy and confusion, out of which she still hopes for the 'happy life'. In an imaginative cautionary tale, Zarya writes two essays, 'how I hope my life will unfold, and how I hope it will not unfold'. The difference between becoming 'a bit of a celebrity' journalist leading a fulfilling useful life and the dark alternative of nights in 'cheap hotels, drinking cheap whiskey, wallowing in loneliness and despair' is ascribed to the protagonist's willingness to pursue one's dreams: 'if you stick to your guns, against all odds, anything is possible' (Zarya, youth services client, Adelaide).

Anthony Giddens (1991: 14) argues that 'Modernity is a post-traditional order, in which the question, "How should I live?" has to be answered in day-to-day decisions.' With the weakening of ties of family, kinship, work, class and locality, people are exhorted to craft their own lives in a self-reliant fashion. The 'choice biography' is based on the 'pure relationship' entered into 'until further notice' (Giddens 1991). The social philosophy of neoliberalism chimes with a do-it-yourself biography in which we are self-disciplined authors responsible for our own lives, for crafting an 'entrepreneurial self' (Kelly 2006).

By contrast, Ulrich Beck is careful to eschew the 'choice' biography. Beck agrees with Giddens that collective and group identity, ethnic identity, class consciousness and faith in progress are breaking up to be replaced with 'hybrid identities and cultures', emerging in 'intersection and combination through conflict with other identities' (Beck and Beck-Gernsheim 2002: 26). In place of the former collective identities, individuals must now coordinate contradictory 'multiple differentiated aspects as students, consumers, voters, patients', integrating themselves across these identities because society fails to do this for them (Beck and Beck-Gernsheim 2002: 23, 2, 163). State institutions force responsibility for the risks that arise from the 'global risk society', such as the challenges of global warming, environmental devastation, global financial crises, back onto individuals (Beck and Beck-Gernsheim 2002: 164). Dan Woodman (2010: 739–40) gives the example of individualising time demands as service providers offer extended hours that require young people to manage often contradictory work timetables, study timetables, and also find space for interaction with significant others to build and maintain relationships.

Thus, Beck is not identifying an opportunity for freedom ('do whatever I want to do', as the essayist cited above writes) but a compulsion to manage increasingly difficult life circumstances:

> The normal biography thus becomes the 'elective biography', the 'reflexive biography', the 'do-it-yourself biography'. This does not necessarily happen by choice, nor does it necessarily succeed. The do-it-yourself biography is always

a 'risk biography', indeed a 'tightrope biography', a state of permanent (partly overt, partly concealed) endangerment. (Beck and Beck-Gernsheim 1996: 25 in Woodman 2009: 243)

Beck describes the institutional response to these unintended consequences and insecurities as 'institutional individualization':

> You may and you must lead your own independent life, outside the old bonds of family, tribe, religion, origin and class; and you must do this within the new guidelines and rules which the state, the job market, the bureaucracy etc. lay down. (Beck in Beck and Beck-Gernsheim 2002: 11)

'Outside the old bonds' suggests that people now craft 'choice biographies'. In fact individuals have no choice: 'you may and you must'. Beck is interested in how people are *forced to* craft their 'own life', 'personalized costumes of independence' in the contemporary 'epidemic of egoism' (Beck in Beck and Beck-Gernsheim 2002: 22). Individualization is 'a compulsion … to create, to stage manage, not only one's own biography, but the bonds and networks surrounding it' (Beck in Beck and Beck-Gernsheim 2002: 4). As Zygmunt Bauman (2001: 144) argues, 'individualization' consists in transforming human 'identity' from a 'given' into a 'task' and charging the actors with the responsibility for performing that task and for the consequences (also the side-effects) of their performance.

The next section introduces intergenerational change and continuity in women's lives by comparing life story essays written in 1970 with the millennium sample. I then compare my sample of young women and men, revealing the persistence of gendered aspirations and preoccupations. Some of the hot spots of future gender contention are revealed in the comparison of young people's essays: short-term sex versus long-term love and romance; interest in things like cars versus interest in relationships like friends; growing together through constant negotiation versus accumulating possessions and accolades. The heterosexual imaginary of these stories is highlighted with a brief analysis of the life stories of gay youth. I then address the limited horizons imposed by socio-economic disadvantage, revealing that essayists across the socio-economic groups asserted the need for individual self-reliance. However, life story essays reveal the painfully limited horizons of disadvantaged respondents compared with middle class students who imagined worlds spun away from the perceived restrictions of their parents' lives into a future that embraces the playground of the globe and the highest reaches of career success. There follows a brief analysis of the different themes — family, country and sport — that interest Aboriginal writers. The chapter concludes with the stories from another group identifying strongly in cultural terms, those from non-English speaking countries.

This comparative survey of life stories demonstrates the persistence of classed, gendered and raced subjectivities, as structures continue to shape young people's world views, despite being expressed in *choice* biographies, in imaginative essays young people write about their future.

Young women and their mothers: From caring for family to caring professions

> I have various ideas — perhaps environment law. I do care about the environment and I'm quite interested by the legal system but then again I'd maybe like to help people like psychology, exploring like deep things — not particularly like health. Perhaps teaching or like university lecturing because so many teachers I've had have helped me to become the person I am and I believe that it's very important that children have a good role model to teach them, to inform them about the world, and teachers basically make or break a person's education and how they respond to it, so perhaps something like that I'd like to do, but I'm not sure what. (Stephanie, Catholic college student, Sydney)

Summers (1970: 95) reports an 'alarming tendency on the part of a few [of her essayists: she cites four] to posit their existences solely on their children': 'children are seen as effortlessly acquired and inevitable accompaniments to marriage' (Summers 1970: 94). One-third of Summers' young essay writers completed their lives with the comment that they got married and had x children (Summers 1970: 103): 'Most seem to think that they should be content to experience a few years of freedom', 'exciting and interesting work' before 'settling down' to domesticity. Only one essayist explicitly rejected marriage, although half the private school sample did not discuss it. Another essayist wrote that she 'had no right to have [children]' (Summers 1970: 94, Tables 1 to 4, between pages 75 and 76). Children figured more prominently than husbands, who in several cases were divorced for handsome alimony or killed off (Summers 1970: 102).

If their life story essays are any indication, young women today appear no less committed to marriage and motherhood. Chart 1.1 suggests that the life stories written by the baby boomer generation at the end of high school and young women today are remarkably similar, the major difference being today's much greater expectation of university education and greater commitment to paid work, particularly returning to work after having children. The generation born just after 1970 have been called an 'education generation' (Andres and Wyn 2010: 64) because they pioneered 'mass post-secondary education', subsequent cohorts (like the one in my sample) following in their footsteps. The major difference between the two

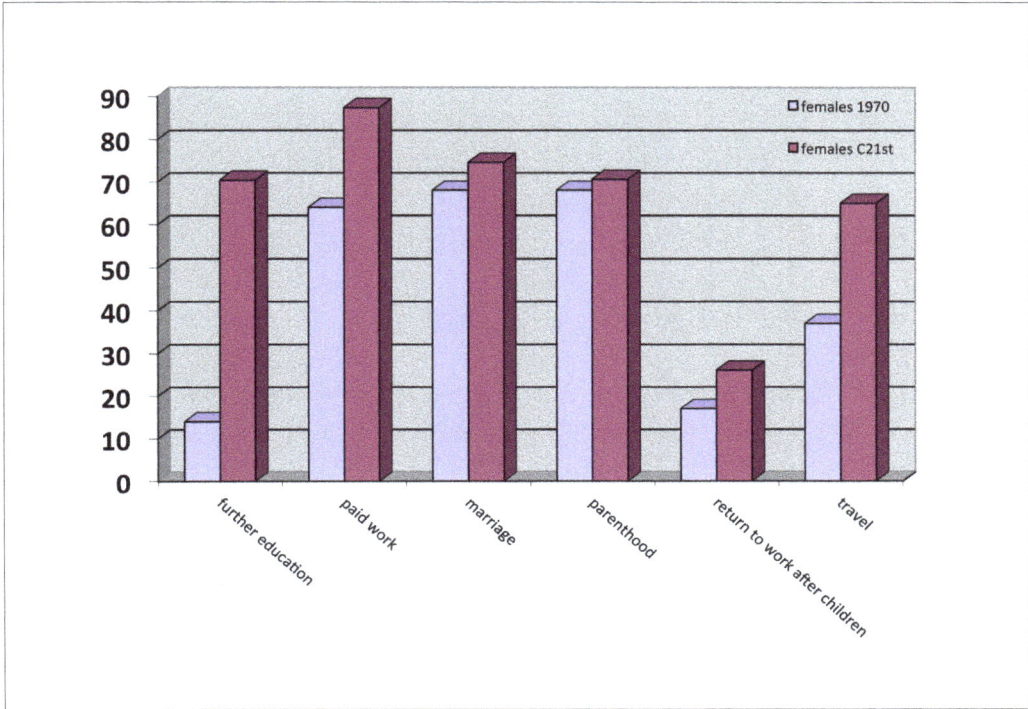

Chart 1.1: Generational life story differences: Female high school students in 1970 and twenty-first century compared

Notes:
1) The 1970 sample was collected by Summers (1970: tables 1-4, between pages 75 and 76). However, there is not complete comparability between her results and the millennium sample, as the essay topics are different and there may be differences in coding.
2) 'Further education' includes attended university: 4 per cent for Summers' cohort (c.f. 9.5 per cent who describe post-school education) and 59.1 per cent for millennium females.
3) 'Marriage' includes long-term relationships not formalized with marriage: 3.4 per cent of females and 2.1 per cent of males in millennium cohort.
For full data on the life stories content see Table A3.1 in Appendix 3.

generations in my study, then, is the issue of combining work/career with a family, although, as Chapter Three explores in more detail, young women seemed little concerned about this in their imagined life stories.

In Summers' 1970 sample, only five (of 117) students wrote of going to university. Three of them completed law, medicine, and a B.A. respectively, while two did not specify their fields of study (and one of these did not complete her degree). Nine essayists attended teacher's college and two the 'institute of technology'. By contrast, 60 per cent of the young women in my sample wrote of going on to tertiary education. Many 'middle class' respondents imagine cashing in their educational capital with professional careers. Whereas 12 per cent of Summers' essayists trained for a profession (the majority going to teachers' college), 30 per cent of my female sample describe work in the caring professions or sub-professions while a further 10 per cent choose legal or managerial careers (see Table A3.3 in Appendix 3). A full 16 per cent of female Protestant college respondents imagined becoming doctors, many of them specialists (see Table A3.4 in Appendix 3).

One-third of Summers' essayists do not mention any job at all, this being most common among the commercial stream and technical school girls and least common in the private school and government high school academic stream (Summers 1970: 78). The jobs chosen were almost all within a traditional band of professions (teacher, nurse, chiropodist, social worker) or clerical occupations (travel consultant, 'office work', bank work, typist, receptionist, secretary). The more adventurous chose glamorous occupations (air hostess, model, pop singer, interpreter for the UN, diplomatic post in Malaysia). One was a 'waitress' and 'maid on a ship' and two became 'governesses' (both private school respondents). Unusual occupations were 'working with scientists creating a dream world' (high school academic stream), policewoman (technical school), building and plans tracer (high school academic stream), oceanographer (high school academic stream), laboratory assistant (high school academic stream) and commercial artist (private school). One writer's husband 'prevented her' from working (Summers 1970: Tables 1 to 4, between pages 75 and 76). Summers (1970: 78–81) notes that many jobs were chosen because of travel, with the focus being on 'meeting people' and occasionally to 'help people' — for example, missionary work in 'New Guinea'.

The traditional choices of modelling, 'air hostess', clerical work and hairdresser, to which most of Summers' essayists who did not become teachers confined themselves, are only favoured today by the female students at disadvantaged government schools (see Table A3.4 in Appendix 3). They sometimes transformed even these traditionally feminine jobs into something more like careers: a crew attendant in the air force, the dream of her 'whole teenage life', joins her husband (a pilot) in running a successful flying school; a hairdresser hones her skills in Paris and 'By the time I was 26 I was doing hair for TV stars.'

However, the *reasons* for choosing careers still tend to be framed in socially sanctioned female terms: 'love' of children or the desire to 'really help' people. Thus, Stephanie, quoted at the head of this section, imagines every prospective career choice — from environmental law to psychology and teaching — in terms of 'caring', either about the environment or about people. One essayist chose midwifery 'because I love babies and the experience of birth is amazing, and to help women along with that would be great'. Anna ruminates about occupational therapy or counselling, as this would involve 'helping' and 'reaching out' to people (Anna, working class government school, Sydney).

The desire to 'really help' people meant two young women even enthused about retail and nannying:

> I loved my job, working in a variety store. I loved the customers, I loved having authority, I loved the people that rang up and asked me questions, but most of all I loved the people that I worked with. (female, middle class government high school student, Adelaide)

> a nanny exchange for a year overseas … was an experience that I would never forget. Having to look after somebodies[1] children while they worked at the busy career, having the responsibility and looking after their children was excellent, making life long friends that I still talk to now occasionally. (female, working class government high school student, South Australia)

By contrast with Summers' essayists, some young women today, particularly in the Protestant college sample, imagine managerial responsibility rather than a professional career. They write of becoming a magazine editor, CEO of a corporate law firm or senior manager in the corner office. But uneasiness sometimes accompanies these choices. A self-proclaimed female 'high-flyer' is 'a little ashamed to admit it but I can be a little uncaring sometimes'. Interestingly, her father is her role model, and she reclaims her imagined career with: 'I have a businesswoman's mind. Can't you just see me behind the big desk in the spacious office wearing a power suit? I can.'

Whereas two-thirds of Summers' sample wrote of paid work, only 17 per cent returned to work after having their children (Summers 1970: 82–3). Six teachers, three nurses and one social worker in Summers' sample returned to their professions. Two essayists returned to part-time work, one as a chiropodist and another until her fifth child was born. Some switched jobs, for example to breed dogs, manage a fashion boutique, manage top models, write for a magazine or sell a painting 'now and again' (Summers 1970: Tables 1 to 4, between pages 75 and 76). Only one essayist had any notion of financial exigency as a reason for working (Summers 1970: 84). The background against which these young women wrote was that one quarter of all married women were in the workforce in 1966. Indeed, many of the technical school essayists mentioned that their mothers worked (Summers 1970: 83, 91). Yet they did not generally imagine this in their own lives.

A quarter of the female essayists in my millennium sample explicitly wrote about returning to work after having their children, and only six per cent explicitly wrote of choosing not to return to paid work once they became mothers, a shift found in the population at large.[2] For some, combining partnering and parenting was a carefully choreographed aspect of the choice biography. This is revealed in the different foci of attention between the generations. The millennium sample worry about when they will marry (26.4 per cent compared with 18.8 per cent of Summers' sample) whereas Summers' sample identify the name (28.2 per cent compared with 14.5 per cent) and occupation of husbands (18.8 per cent compared with 14.5 per cent), who functioned as 'meal tickets' without which motherhood was impossible to imagine. In Summers' sample divorce (two essayists, by contrast with the twelve per cent of marriages then ending in divorce), or more commonly death followed by remarriage (five essayists, two as serial widows), were the only conceivable escapes from marriage, chosen by six per cent in Summers' sample (compared with 3.9 per cent of females in the millennium sample).

As Tables A3.3 and A3.4 in Appendix 3 indicate, even in the potentially wide compass of dreams rather than predictions, while desire for education has exploded, the gendered nature of occupational desires has shifted but not shattered. Other studies report similar findings (McLeod and Yates 2006: 8; Probert and Macdonald 1999: 144; Dwyer and Wyn 2001: 104–5). Whereas much popular commentary — and many young people in my research — claim that the gender gap has narrowed to near extinction, the texture and substance of the imagined life stories are still remarkably gendered. The enduring gender differences in young people's life stories are explored next.

Young men's and women's life stories compared

> I left university with a master's degree in accounting and business and went on to be a merchant banker and at the age of 27 bought the Playboy mansion from Hugh Hefner. ... I bought myself a factory in Thailand where I get a car made for free each week. I bought a 50% share in a Lamborghini factory and I got married at the age of 30 to an 18 year old, blonde Playboy playmate. Then at the age of 32, when she was 20 I dropped her and married a 19 year old brunette and then a few years after that I retired and bought my own island in the Caribbean and named it What Island, where I moved to and now live there and shoot anyone that comes on it. (male, co-educational Catholic college student, Perth)

> When I was 20 I played professional basketball in the NBA with the Magic, and then for the NRL for the Warriors. I had sex for the first time when I was 13 and World War 3 changed us forever. ... I got married to a mail order bride from Asia and we had 1 child ... then I worked on the mines up north and made millions of dollars. (male, Protestant college student, Perth)

> Then there was George. Oh how can I forget him. My first real love. It was love at first sight and I couldn't forget the day he asked me out. I was ecstatic. But

of course I can't forget him, as he has now been my husband for forty years. We did a lot together. We saw the world. … We saw the sights, spent romantic nights under the moonlight travelling in Venice in the gondolas and in Paris under the Eiffel Tower. …How can I forget when Liam was born, our first son. He looked so much like his father, lucky boy. His first steps, his first words, his first love — Just memorable moments. (female, Catholic college student, Adelaide)

When my initial findings were published in the *Sydney Morning Herald* in 2004, by-lined 'still cavemen and cave-women at heart', they provoked a flurry of coast to coast media interest, arising from the widespread presumption of gender equality in today's society. By contrast, feminist researchers are not surprised that young men and women give 'meaning' to their lives via commonly available 'gender scripts' (Thiel 2005: 187; McLeod and Yates 2006: 4–5, 10–11, 151, 184–5, 213–4; Wierenga 2009: 61; Coates 2003: 44, 117–8, 130; Wyn 2009: 97; Flood 2008; Nicolopoulou et al. 1994; Gilbert 1994: 126–7, 135).[3] The timeworn opposition between pink for people and blue for things seems little altered, as the extracts quoted above suggest. The young male writers focus on 'actions' (like sex, drinking and sports) and mastery over 'things' (like cars and technology). Young men write about wars and technological change while young women write about their grief when loved ones suffer or die. Young men are more likely to see themselves as famous or well known, young women as engaging in philanthropy. The young women discuss how they 'feel' (friendships, romance, family) even when they are talking about 'actions' (such as travel); they seek mastery over their bodies and their emotions.

In relation to marriage, the only item on which men write more than women is in a flight from commitment: young men are more likely to divorce or kill off their wives. Young men are more likely than young women to conclude that they were discontented with their lives, although more young men were contented than were discontented. This may reflect young female writers expressing an acceptable femininity in which love, marriage and children are rewarding (see Chart 1.2, which shows the items favoured by female essayists, and Chart 1.3, which shows the items of more importance to male essayists, and Table A3.1 in Appendix 3). Given that female stories were on average longer, statistically they are likely to canvass more issues, rendering the items which young men mention more frequently particularly noteworthy.

Young people reach for gender scripts that, in many respects, appear little changed despite forty years of feminism. Not only do young men write more often about cars, sports and sex, they also code them in gendered messages and, in many cases, write in a gendered style. By contrast with young women's emotion-laden stories,

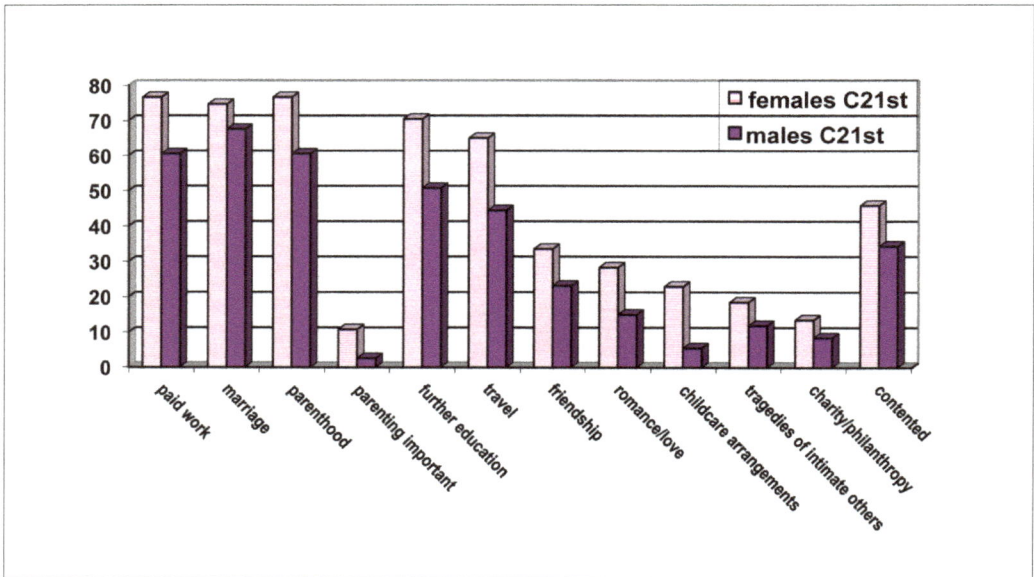

Chart 1.2: A selection of events mentioned more frequently in life stories written by female than male high school students

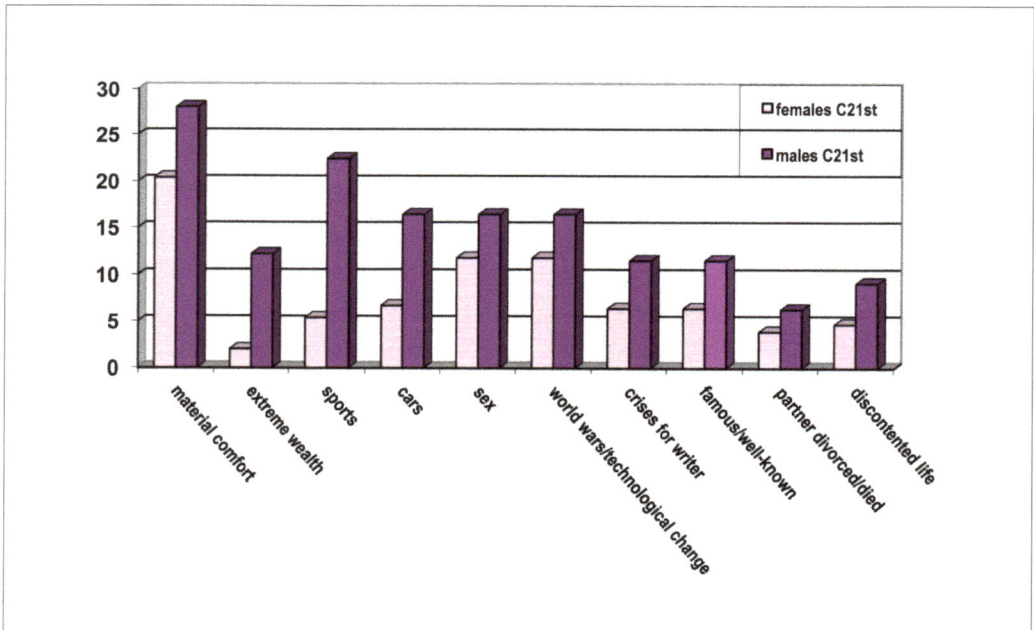

Chart 1.3: Events mentioned more frequently in life stories written by male than female high school students

many young males write truncated sentences lacking emotional colour or reflection on their internal states. Milestones such as 'multiple sexual partners', 'marriage' or 'children' are ticked off, enumerated, rather than described or embellished:

> Happily married for 45 years. 3 children, 2 boys and 1 girl. Retired at age 67. Got an ENTER score 78. Studied at Melbourne Uni for 4 years to become a secondary school P.E. teacher. At age 33 worked at St. Bede's and worked there for 34 years. Travelled overseas with wife and kids 4 times and with wife 3 times. Travelled Europe with family twice for 1 month at a time. Went to Hawaii once to Asia once. Both for 3 weeks. Travelled Europe 2 times, 6 weeks each, went to Brazil for 3 weeks. First house was medium 4 bedroom house in Mordialloc, paid $500,000 when 27 years old. At age 55 bought a big 5 bedroom house in Parkdale, $1.5 million.
> Cars — 4 cars.
> age 19 — Holden commodore 2001 model
> age 27 — new 'SS' commodore 2016 model
> age 40 — Holden land cruiser 2025 model
> age 60 — Holden larina 2040 model Kids left home all aged 23. (male, Catholic college student, Melbourne)

One male essayist 'wished' that he would become '4 times Brownlow Medallist, 7 times Club Champion, 5 times All Australian, and 3 times AFLPA MVP, but to be brutally honest I have no skill or talent'.

Young men: Cars and sports

> Married and 3 kids — two boys, 1 girl. Be a mechanic, Travel to America. Own Valiant Charger (six pack R/T). House in Balga, Play Colts football and AFL. Must own the Valiant Charger R/T. (male, working class government high school student, Perth)

Young men across the socio-economic range wrote about cars, from Fords to Ferraris, from 'protest' masculinity (for example, hot-wiring cars or 'burn-outs'; Kenway et al. 2006: 179–80; Walker 1998; Wyn 2009: 97) to owning a car race, the Bathurst 1000. The car is the ultimate goal in the disadvantaged male's story quoted above. Furthermore, three young men expressed gender coding through cars: 'a Mercedes for me and a Ford Territory for my wife'; 'two cars 1 for the wife and kids and 1 for me'; 'We both bought our dream cars. Nicole bought a pink Porsche and I bought a dodge viper (red)' (this gender coding was also expressed by 11-year-old male essayists in 1969: Elliott 2010: 1084).

Even more so than cars, young men wrote about sports, both because sport is a 'site where males learn to perform culturally revered masculinities' — through physical aggression and competitiveness, drinking with mates, and father-son bonding (Kenway et al. 2006: 181) — and because it is a site where boys can perform their masculinity from an early age (Bartholomaeus 2012: 68–75). Young men's loving embellishment of sporting careers sometimes contrasted sharply with their casual mention of love and marriage. A rower, describing a career that culminates in the 2012 Olympics, offers a single line on 'the girl of my dreams that I met somewhere along the way'. Another Olympic winner meets a 'very beautiful Russian gymnast' 'and before I knew it we were making love'. He is 'sad' that 'Maria Sharapovia' never rang him, only to later find out that 'she had lost all her facial skin due to a car accident. … She never called because she was scared I wouldn't love her anymore, which is true' (male, Protestant college student, Perth). These casual or hard-hearted approaches to 'true love' compare starkly with young women's lovingly crafted stories of romance, discussed below.

Only six per cent of the young women's life stories mention sport (media coverage and unequal payment to male and female sports players probably influencing this result, e.g. see Connell 2005: 1816). At Leila's Protestant college, P.E. is compulsory only to year 11 and takes place once a week, whereas at the 'sister' boys' college, 'compulsory sport' involves nights and weekends. Young women are still policed in terms of their sporting preferences. For example, Cheryl's daughter has 'been called a bloke sometimes at school' because she is a BMX rider (Cheryl, working class government high school mother, Adelaide). Despite all this, several female essayists dream of Olympic gold. One young woman, Verity, in reality represents Australia in baseball:

> when I was Verity's age, it was considered just not the done thing to be interested in sport or really to get stuck into it and to excel. That was considered unusual and pretty daggy. (Jane, middle class government school mother, Perth, speaking of her daughter)

Jane compares Verity's situation with her school days, when a line of embarrassed, menstruating teenagers excused themselves from each physical education class.

Sex and love

> In particular I missed a man. His name was Danny and I knew from the moment I met him that I was going to love him forever. And I did. We got married when I was 19, he was 23. We themed the wedding of a midsummer nights dream and held in the evening of May 17th with fairy lights sparkling everywhere. He wore a black suit with the coat long, and a black shirt with 2 buttons undone at the top. My flower girl was his sister's daughter and I had

the twins as jnr bridesmaids, Corey was pageboy. It was great. Everyone got drunk. … The only times we ever fought was when I spent too much money, or when he let the kids do something that pissed me off. The main purpose of my life is 2 love Danny & be happy with him, because he is my life. (female, Protestant college student, Perth)

The above excerpt echoes Summers' findings that young women's main goal in life was marriage and motherhood: 'The main purpose of my life is 2 love Danny & be happy with him'. This was an unusually single-minded focus on love and marriage, but young women are almost three times as likely to write about romance than sex, whereas young men are more likely than young women to write about sex (although only slightly more likely to write about sex than love and romance, albeit more often in the clipped terms described above). For young women, the 'love conquers all discourse' 'suggests that relationships with men are the key to women's overall life satisfaction' (Phillips 2000: 69). A discourse found most commonly in women's teen magazines, it covers the 'fairy tale wedding and the fairy tale life' (Phillips 2000: 75). The protagonist meets 'the man of my dreams', 'the love of my life', 'the one', a 'soul mate'. 'True love' is expressed in the white wedding, described in loving detail by the female essayist quoted at the head of this sub-section: 'the most beautiful memory of my life', 'exactly how I had planned it since I was six', 'what I had always dreamed of', a ceremony 'where I connected myself to my chosen one'. Like the young woman who marries George, essayists remain 'unconditionally', 'everlastingly' and 'forever' loving and faithful, 'happily ever after': 'I loved my husband with all my life and I still do.'

Young women are also more likely than young men to write about friends (see McLeod 2002 for similar findings). 'Friendship' is a sentiment that stretches across and stitches together connection with family, lovers and the environment ('environmentally-friendly'). Feminism gave women back to each other as friends, beyond a crutch when heterosexual relationships go bad, a real alternative to the marriage and motherhood package: 'My lifetime of friends are the ones that got me this far'; 'friends … enriched my life so much':

When I am 80 my best memories will be travel and the little things in life like bbq's at friend's houses and calling a friend when they are down. (female, co-educational Catholic college student, Perth)

In high school, friendships are 'priceless', their loss mourned by daughters of fathers (usually) who had peripatetic jobs. Female essayists party with friends, share households with friends, travel to Europe with friends, holiday with friends, set up businesses with friends and don't forget their friends even when they become famous (see Coates 1996: 42–3 and Aapola et al. 2005: 117 on the significance of female friendships).

Male essayists' friends are usually called 'mates' with whom essayists play sport, drink and party: 'On weekends I'd hit the pubs and clubs with my mates, ingesting copious amounts of alcohol and generally having a great time.' The sexual passages in many young men's stories are akin to 'warries', as the ADFA interviewees call their 'stories about military training, war, funny situations or incidents, drinking, and sex, where *warry* is a portmanteau word created out of *war* and *story*' (Flood 2008: 353, emphasis in original). Warries cement male bonding, so that a common negative epithet at ADFA is WOM, or 'Woman over Mates' (Flood 2008: 344). One male essayist in my sample makes the function of male bonding clear:

> I started going to parties and got a bit of play, the girls look bloody good when your gone. I started going to lots of parties and chilled with my friends, me and Nick would see who could score the most girls in one night. He usually won, but eventually I beat him. We went on lots of trips to Venus Bay and Corny Point, we had fun and talked about chicks. (male, co-educational Protestant college student, Adelaide)

While young women do everything with their friends, in male stories sex is the constant companion: 'a lot of women', 'heaps of girls ha', 'lots of sex', 'enormous amount of sex':

> Play senior football — (mentone tigers). Girlfriends — sex. Successful job — (own business). Wife/golf/lots of sex. Holidays/honeymoon — enormous amount of sex. Kids. Golf — with lots of sex. Travelling — with lots of sex. Retirement — with lots of sex. Nice house — car (good back seat). Golf/scuba diving/travelling. Die peacefully — with lots of sex. (male, Catholic college student, Melbourne)

> My life is all about sex with girls and 10–15 at the same time, what I am saying is that I like sex. (male, Catholic college student, Melbourne)

One writer becomes 'Time Magazine's Sexiest Man of the Year. Time Magazine's Bachelor of the Year. Magery [sic] medallist' (for Australian Rules Football). Multiple sexual encounters with 'beautiful' 'hot' supermodels and playmates or compliant wives and girlfriends lace every stage of young men's progression through life. A self-described 'Italian stallion' describes his 'first true love' as 'stunning, brilliant and easy to manipulate'. After marriage and fatherhood, he notes that 'I own a strippers chain of clubs and spend my time there' (male, Catholic college student, Adelaide).

Summers' (1970) female essayists mentioned sex, if at all, in heavily laden metaphors, for example the high school academic stream student who experienced 'the full meaning of love' on her wedding night. Apart from this writer, only the working class students described sex, and usually confined themselves to their first kiss, although one lost her virginity (Summers 1970: 101, 98). Indeed, survey research indicates that first intercourse for most of Summers' young women was still to come, the average age then being 19. By the millennium, however, the average age of first intercourse was sixteen (Australian Research Centre in Sex, Health and Society, circa 2003: 1–2). A handful of young women in my sample enjoy sex without love, for example 'Sexual experiences. I hope they are plentiful!!!' or 'casual sex every day'.

To be clear that these young men's views are not safely corralled private male fantasies, Jane describes her boyfriend's university football club where 'they get fined for say sleeping with an ugly girl' or for sitting next to their girlfriends during the football match. Jane's boyfriend defends this childish behaviour in a 'testosterone-fuelled arena: "it's not me personally, it's just a cult sort of thing which yes, I'm really against"' (Jane, women's studies university student, Perth).

Obsession with sexual identity, sold and marketed as it is (Hawkes 2005: 21), crowds out other identities. As Tamara puts it, 'women are their sex' and so, increasingly, are men (Tamara, social sciences university student, Adelaide), so that 'other things or skills such as raising children in a good environment … are not considered as important' (female, social sciences university student, Adelaide). A minority of young women resisted the sexualisation of self discourse with an 'abstinence' discourse, usually grounded in religion (see Magill 2004: 3; McRobbie 2004: 4; Burns and Torre 2004) and often discursively linked with the 'special' nature of 'the wedding night' and the marriage partner (e.g. a female, Turkish background, Catholic college student, Sydney). More commonly, young women yoked premarital sex to love: 'I don't plan on being a virgin until I'm married, but I want to sleep with people when I'm in love with them.' The regular marital sex imagined by some male essayists ('a sexual experience at least once each day'; 'I was quite the ladies man now I have a beautiful wife, who I make love to every night') is greater than the frequency with which most actual wives desire sex (see Arndt 2009; Dempsey 2001: 62).

Gendered career aspirations

> I'm 78 retired from a fulltime macanic with 1 daughter Ellie a lovely home by the beach with my VL Walkinshaw + Nissan Skyline R33 parked under my house in my garage my daughter will have her cars and she can do what she wants, like she does not have to be like me a fulltime macanic … I have been in car magazine modelling my cars not pornografic but in swimmers and small clothes I enjoyed my life living alone with my daughter. (female, young mothers' Christian school student, New South Wales)

The continuing gendered nature of career aspirations, discussed above when comparing Summers' sample with the millennium sample, is even clearer when the millennium sample of young men and women are compared (see Tables A3.3 and A3.4 in Appendix 3). Professional careers in the caring professions are imagined much more enthusiastically by the females than by the males. Young middle class men are more likely to write of becoming senior managers or CEOs, or enter the traditionally male careers of engineer, information technology, scientist or soldier. Thus, 6.6 per cent of male essayists compared with 1.1 per cent of the females enter the armed forces: 'around Australia and the world serving my country', as one young man writes. Only nine female essayists become engineers and only one female, the essayist quoted above, writes of entering a skilled trade, mediating it by assuring us that she has the feminine body to model her cars in motor magazines.

Young men in every sub-sample are three times more likely than young women to imagine becoming CEOs or owners of large businesses. Young men from privileged backgrounds or middle class government schools write of building financial empires based on their inventions, such as 'revolutionary new computer operating systems', thus becoming 'the next Bill Gates, only not ugly like he is'. Another Bill Gates owns 'a multi billionaire company', becomes a 'merchant banker' and owner of Playboy mansion. Instead of becoming Bill Gates, a young woman marries 'Will [sic] Gates'. Males are more likely to be filmmakers, musicians, casino or night club owners and females the actors, sex workers or strippers (because 'that would be fun') who work in them. Young men do not yet have access to the full range of activities that make up adult masculinity, in particular those associated with breadwinning and fatherhood. How the young men envisage these performances in the future is further discussed in Chapter Three.

Where enumeration substituted for emotional storying in many young men's essays, I often grappled to discern the meaning of the essays. The focus on incidents rather than narrative, on facts rather than feelings, suggests narrative subjects with little history and thus, perhaps, less ability to imagine their future. By contrast, the young middle class women have a future that unfolds towards 'goals', built on a presence in the present and a known past, sometimes forged in reflection on the bildungsroman of their mothers. This is further addressed in Chapter Two, exploring intergenerational transmission of gender stories and role models, to reveal that young women are exploring their changing options more fully with their mothers than young men are with their fathers. In their life stories as in the interviews and 'I am' statements, the young women express a fund of psychological capital, of knowing themselves and what they desire from others. This psychological capital appeared to be deficient in most of the young men in the sample, as further explored in Chapter Three. Young women embrace their 'choice biography' usually in imagined partnership with a companion. The evidence for a matching emotional literacy and commitment to equality from young men is addressed in Chapter Three.

The homosexual imaginary

> I've been with my partner since I was 21. The high lights of our relationship would be first and formost the legalisation of same-sex marriage and our subsequent wedding. It was the most beautiful day I have ever had. Jess looked so stunning in her wedding dress. Our next highlight was the birth of our first child, Josh. … Experiencing Jess get pregnant with technology that uses embryos from both of us was fantastic. A child that was truly of our own making. (female, sexuality youth service client, Victoria)

Only two life stories written by male high school students mentioned male-to-male sexual attraction. One male writer 'began to question my own sexuality, once even actively' after his 'best [female] friend left me for another man, then for a woman'. Ultimately he marries his 'best friend'. A young man at a Catholic college divorced his wife after cheating on her 'with my personal fitness male instructor'. He stayed with his male lover until the latter died and then 'found a younger partner, no doubt enticed by my wealth, but as long as he was good in bed, I did not mind'. This was the first in a succession of younger male partners. Among several female high school students who write of gay feelings, a Protestant college female student 'got with a girl' at university, went out a couple of times, 'but then I thought it was too weird … and just broke the relationship. My other relationships were normal (with a guy)'. She felt 'at times' that these relationships were 'quite boring' but later married and does martial arts with her husband (in her 'I ams' she identifies herself as a black belt).

Homosexual love might be rare in the mainstream sample's stories; in the gay sample's stories it often looked a lot like heterosexual love. As the quotation above reveals, young gay women also imagine 'true love' and 'white weddings', many of their stories differentiated from the heterosexual imaginary (Ingraham 1994: 203) only by needful overcoming of legal obstacles or homophobia in their path to marriage equality and 'normal' happiness more generally. Indeed, Netta says of her life story: 'it looks like other people would see it as being very nuclear, traditional and I'm a lesbian' (Netta, sociology university student, Melbourne). Almost all the sexuality youth services clients identify as gay, homosexual or queer ('as queer as queer can be'). Some eschew the 'nuclear family' to bring up children 'in a community of close

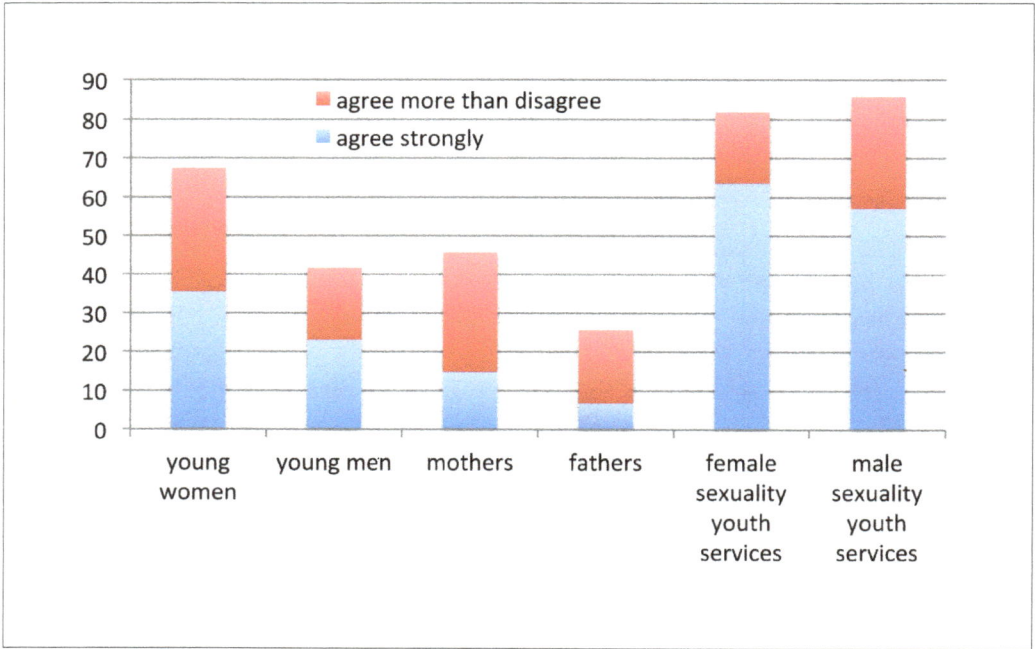

Chart 1.4: Support for gay sexual relations between people over the age of 16: Sex by respondent type

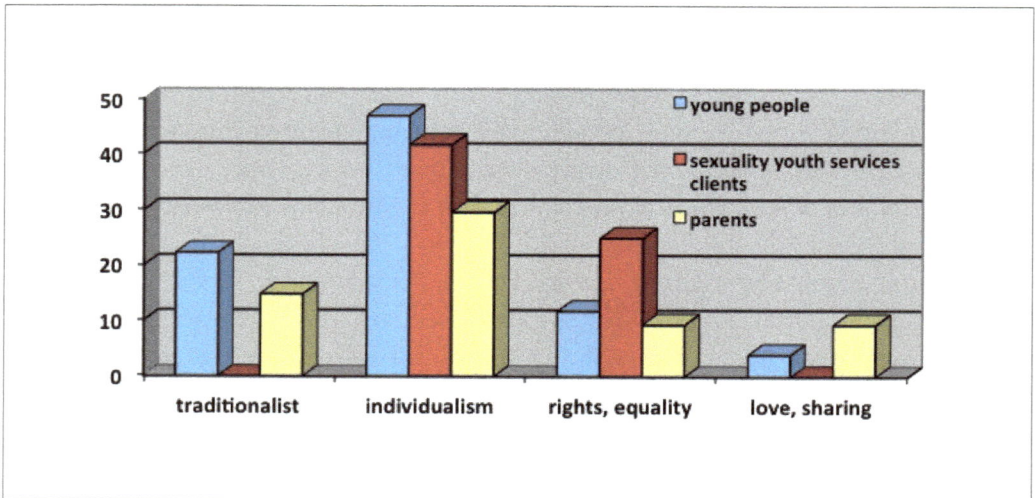

Chart 1.5: Vocabularies* used to oppose or support homosexual relations between those over the age of 16 (percentage of responses)

* For a discussion of vocabularies, see the explanation at the end of Appendix 3.

friends' or to remain childless and still 'have a delicious life'. But the majority 'find my one true love', marry and have or adopt a family in the vein of the essayist quoted above.

The major distinction from heterosexual stories relates to overcoming barriers to happiness, such as a cure for AIDS, legalisation of marriage, or technological changes that facilitate parenting. A further hurdle to the fulfilment of their 'normal' family lives includes homophobia and discrimination: 'My children … were questioned by peers about having two mums but they dealt with it respectfully and were well informed — they were happy' (female, health service client, Victoria). In expressing their attitudes to gay relations, young women were much more tolerant than young men. This item also recorded the greatest intergenerational difference, although some of the parental disagreement was expressed in the opinion that the age of 16 is too young for *any* kind of sexual relations (see Chart 1.4). Mothers sometimes lacked a comfortable language with which to discuss gay relations and expressed anxiety that gay children would experience ostracism. As one young gay woman wrote:

> I have an amazing fear of being oppressed for my sexuality by parents who have old-school values. All I want is to fit in. I know they'll find out one day I want to postpone it as long as I can. (female, sexuality youth service client, Adelaide)

Although the small size of the sub-sample is a caveat, gay respondents were more likely to support same sex sexual relationships on the basis of rights and equality whereas other young respondents argued for individualism ('their choice'; 'It's better than living the rest of your life a lie or in doubt about who you are') or 'true love' (mainly the female respondents: 'They love each other and they are happy, that's good enough! isn't it?'; see Chart 1.5). Chart 1.5 also shows that heterosexual respondents who oppose gay relations do so largely based on 'traditional claims' (against God or nature).

A substantial minority of young men, but none of the young women, responded to the questions concerning female nudity in magazines and homosexuality from the perspective of a heterosexual male viewer, approving 'the ladies choice to please men'. They welcomed 'good looking' lesbians but not 'fat chicks' or 'old ladies'. Others drew a sharp distinction between 'poofters', 'faggots' and 'male homosexuals' as compared with 'lesbians', 'girls' or 'chicks': 'we hate fagits! Don't mind lesos'; 'gay people are disgusting, especially guys. Lesbians are OK though'; 'NO WAY unless it's 2 women!'. These strident comments dismiss the possibility that women might enjoy each other's sexuality, and confirm the role of 'pornography-inspired fetishisation of lesbians as objects of heterosexual male desire' (Flood and Hamilton

2008: 27), while also conflating femininity and homosexuality and denigrating both (Flood 2005: 2).

Rejection of homosexuality by men is not surprising, given that the hegemonic definition of being male excludes being gay (Flood 2005: 3): 'everyone will answer the same as it is "cool" to be homo-phobic'. I witnessed this policing at a working class government school in Perth, where students noisily compared answers as they completed the questionnaire. One young man, looking at the answer of the student next to him, queried, 'You're not a poofter, are you?' and called my attention to this answer. The other young man quickly changed his answer to 'disagree strongly [with gay sexual relations]', muttering that he had not understood the question. This encounter suggests that some of the hostility expressed in the questionnaire was a public performance of masculinity. This factor might also be expressed in the young men's life stories, which (apart from those written by sexuality youth services clients) contained the merest smattering of homosexual incidents.

The fragility of sexual identity is expressed in both constant performance (Sedgwick 1990: 34, 75–89) and constant reference, or 'lexical density' in conversation (see Coates 2003: 70–1 on the 'hyper-heterosexuality' of young English men's conversations). In completing their 'I am ...' statements, 10 per cent of young men noted that they were sexually desirable, and this was more significant than family group membership or friendship (see Table 3.5 in Appendix 3). The young Italian-Australian males, in particular, liked to describe themselves as 'hot', 'built like a tank' or 'Unbelievable (ask the ladies)'. None of the male sample outside the sexuality youth services clients identified as gay. Furthermore, five defined themselves as 'not gay' and eight as 'heterosexual'. By contrast, several female respondents outside the sexuality youth sample were relaxed enough to describe themselves as 'a lesbian'; 'a lesbian ... I think' but 'confused'; 'right now, I'm not too sure if I am one'.

The most imaginative challenge to the heterosexual imaginary was written by a young woman in a class of peers enthusing about their white wedding to the love of their life. Describing herself as 'capable of comprehending complex issues, eager to talk over my thoughts and feelings', she presents the reader with three alternatives to the 'normal' family: adoption without marriage, single fatherhood and a lesbian family:

> I fell in love a few times but usually nothing happened. ... [O]ne day I realised that the guy I was with would make a perfect father. ... We decided to adopt rather than have a child ourselves. I'm so glad we did. Su-sim provided something we always wanted. We adopted three children, all from different backgrounds, before having a child that was ours biologically as well as emotionally. We had never seen it as important to marry. ... [Their son] James

has children of his own now — he's a single father. [A daughter] Skye adopted too and her partner, Lily already had a child from her last relationship. So now they have two. Su-sim found she loved painting and Claire is studying engineering. We couldn't be prouder of them all. (female, Catholic college student, Adelaide)

As suggested in the Introduction, the media celebrates limitless opportunities for young women. Every girl is expected to be a 'can-do' girl, encouraged in one recent children's book to start learning her entrepreneurial skills at the age of nine (Sade and Neuborne 2011). As Anita Harris (2004: 8–10 and passim) argues persuasively in *Future Girl*, the 'can-do girl' or 'professional career women with glamorous consumer lifestyles' is the reality for only 'a small number'. Indeed, the media also represents her doppelgänger, her abject double, the 'at risk' girl who expresses excessive sexuality in early unmarried pregnancy and deviant consumption in drugs, alcohol or shoplifting. Those who rely on the public sector — for their health, education and money — are blamed as 'losers' and 'bludgers'. Implicitly, media images also represent the raced as well as classed nature of the 'can-do' girl. She is usually 'white' and almost never Indigenous or a Muslim clad in a headscarf. Thus, the choice and self-determination paradigm obscures 'the classed and raced constitution of the "successful" feminine subject', causing 'a fundamental misrecognition of the causes of social disadvantage as explanations for inequality' (Budgeon 2011b: 285). The next section turns to expressions of class in life stories.

Disadvantaged stories: No bridges from now to the future

— Play football.
— Make trouble with Beau.
— I [go] to the teals this weekend with Beau.
Work part time, but I am quitting to play AFL.
I had bottle smashed over my head.
I had a b.b bat in the head,
which gave me a broken nose. I have a broken thumb.
I go clubbing and get paro [paralytic]. (male, working class government high school student, Adelaide)

Got into a fight and got a fractured rib — The other girl had a broken nose and her front tooth fell out. I dance at a nightclub (under age) I am not a striptease … [I want to] study journalism and become an English teacher. I would not mind owning my own business, eg: restaurant. Eventually I plan on having a family one day, but not yet. I will travel the world. (female, working class government high school student, Adelaide)

Just as I could normally tell the gender of the writer within a sentence or two of reading a life story, class background declared itself almost as immediately. Even in the proportions who wrote a life story, class is clearly evident: students in the private schools were more likely to write a life story than those in the public schools; students in middle class government schools were more likely than those in working class government schools (see Table A2.3 in Appendix 2). Most of the essayists from disadvantaged schools and youth services, in particular the young men, wrote short life stories, sometimes only a sentence or two. Some, like the essayist quoted above, listed a handful of dot points, following my suggestion when young men baulked at the idea of writing an essay.

Discursive capacities are not only correlated with class and gender; so are the more material resources of quality of education, parental finances, family networks providing information, mentoring and so on. As a result, the remit of life stories told by disadvantaged youth differed significantly from the dreams of the more privileged. Chart 1.6 expresses the classed nature of past experiences and its effects on future horizons. More students at working class schools and clients of disadvantaged youth services know that they will not go to university than dream that they will. They are less confident even in achieving paid work. They are less likely to write about travel

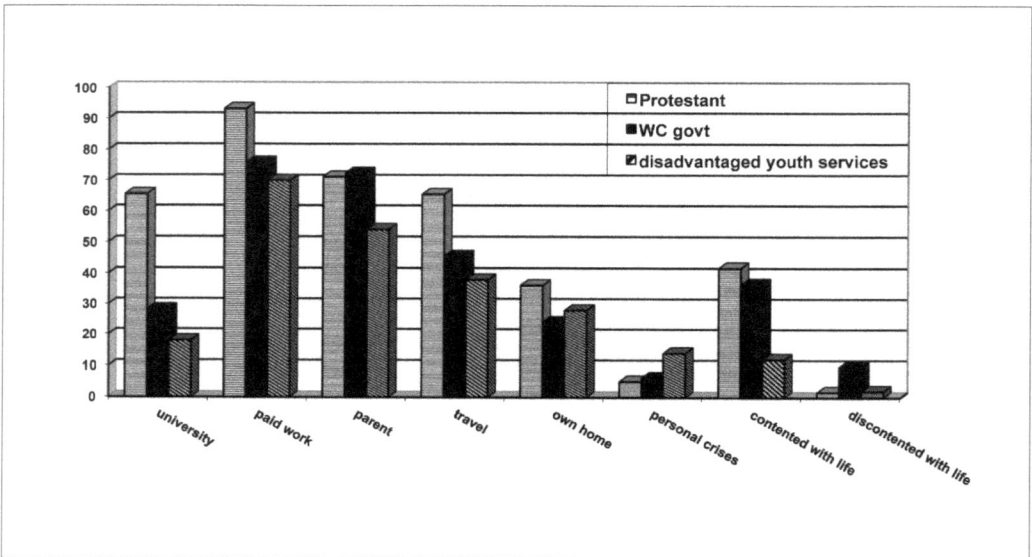

Chart 1.6: Class effect on selected aspects of life stories: Protestant college, working class government schools and disadvantaged youth services clients compared

Note: Some of the differences for the youth services clients are due to a slightly differently worded essay task (see Appendix 1) but the working class school students completed the same essay as the other students.

or owning their own home. Their lack of belief in economic security is also expressed in the percentage who write of extreme wealth: 3.2 per cent in the working class government schools, 4.2 per cent in the middle class government schools, 6.3 per cent in the Catholic colleges and 10.7 per cent in the Protestant colleges (see Chart 1.7). Ultimately they are more likely than middle class students to be discontented — while remaining positive enough to write of contentment more often than discontentment.

In Summers' sample, too, the technical school students were much less likely to write of travel and much more likely to write of personal disasters. Fifty-three per cent of the technical schoolgirls wrote of road accidents and injuries and a further 16 per cent of hospitalisation (Summers 1970: 106), while none wrote of wider social events (apart from one who doubts her place in the world) (Summers 1970: Tables 1 to 4, between pages 75 and 76).[4] Similarly, in my study the youth services clients and working class students are more preoccupied with personal crises, although they are also more likely to mention technological change (see Table A3.1 in Appendix 3). The former reflects their lower socio-economic status (see Henderson et al. 2007: 98 for similar findings) while the latter appears to be influenced by the guidance offered by one of the youth workers.

Summers (1970: 103) found a correlation between class and the essayist's capacity to project herself into the future, noting that one third of the working class essayists recounted their school history and then sometimes added a sentence or two on a post-schooling job, concluding 'almost perfunctorily' with marriage and x children (see also Luttrell 2003: 49 for similar findings among underprivileged single mothers). Similarly, in her study of regional Tasmanian youth, Ani Wierenga (2009) identifies four types of imagined futures, deriving from the intersection of the class and gender of her respondents. Young working class males, and some working class females, imagined 'settling' or 'wandering' futures. Settling futures often meant following in their father's footsteps in the small Tasmanian town where Wierenga conducted her research. An example from my sample is the following:

> I want to finish schooling and TAFE courses. Try different jobs. Reach retiring age. (total life story, female, working class high school student, Adelaide)

Because the town in Wierenga's study offered young women only casual work and motherhood, many dreamed of 'wandering', leaving home for a glamorous career. However, their stories were based on unrealistic dreams, often prompted by the mass media, with no lines of connection to the interviewees' present situation. Such 'wandering' stories emerge from lives of chaos, social isolation and low trust.[5] Even sadder were the disadvantaged interviewees who could see no hope in the future and told 'retreating' stories. Such essayists are unconsciously 'refusing what is anyway refused' as Bourdieu put it (in Mackinnon 2006: 283): the media-celebrated 'can-do' girl future. In a study of Adelaide youth in two alternative education schools, Alison Mackinnon et al. also found quotidian 'settling' dreams, such as becoming a bricklayer so he doesn't have 'to go out and steal' (Mackinnon et al. 2010: 2) as well as helplessness and retreating stories: 'In twenty years time I'd like to be dead. But that might change in the future' (Mackinnon et al. 2010: 24).

Wierenga's middle class interviewees, and some of the working class females, draw clear lines connecting what they are doing now — 'the right choices' — to their future dreams. They offer 'thick' descriptions about themselves and the world around them, with a variety of exit and entry points, and the resilience to learn from mistakes: full of 'plans, contingencies, past experiences, hopes, anecdotes, beliefs and impossible dreams' (Wierenga 2009: 55):

> Assumptions about futures and being able to plan them belong to the privileged: ... those who come from stable worlds, those who have a measure of control over their own lives, and those who know that they have. (Wierenga 2009: 113; see also Smart 2007: 106)

Wierenga calls these 'exploring' stories, noting that her interviewees construct their available options by reference to 'people like me', this pool being 'diverse' and including 'thinkers who inspire them' and such like for those with 'access to different crowds and places' by contrast with the 'local' role models chosen by the male working class respondents (Wierenga 2011: 180). The 'highly honed reflexivity' of middle class girls reveal that they are aware how their actions in the present position them for their desired futures (McLeod and Yates 2006: 7), constructing biographies that align with an 'entrepreneurial self' (Kelly 2006; see studies by Threadgold and Nilan 2009; see also Nollmann and Strasser 2007). Wierenga (2011: 379) 'found that there was a strong correlation between individuals' storying and their capacity to act, and between voicelessness and stuck-ness'. Another indication of the fuller lives bequeathed by cultural and financial capital is expressed in the percentage of essayists who wrote about hobbies or other leisure pursuits, both sports and other activities such as playing a musical instrument, writing or going to the movies (see Chart 1.7).

Not only are chosen jobs/careers class and gender-inflected, so are the motivations for them — financial or social versus philanthropic or self-fulfilling, for example (Threadgold and Nilan 2009: 57, 59). Where the middle class respondents in my sample were more likely to imagine extreme wealth or philanthropic pursuits (see Chart 1.7), the working class respondents were more likely to focus on the

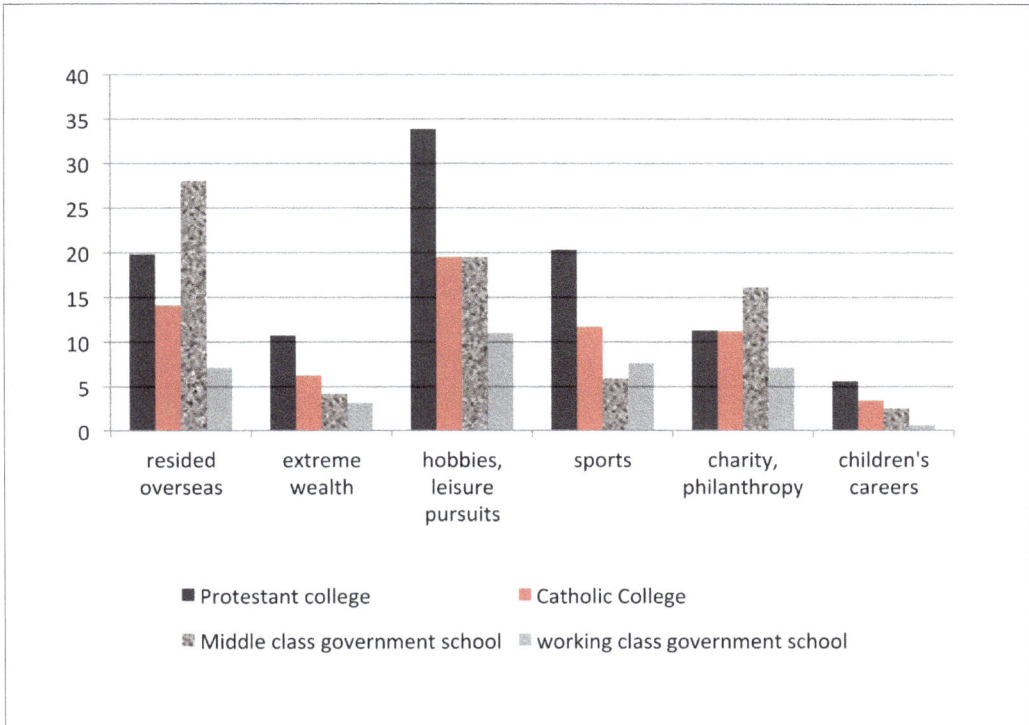

Chart 1.7: Class effect on selected aspects of life stories: High school students' essays

extrinsic social aspects of their work. Three friends at the Perth working class high school in my study 'take it as it comes' and enjoy themselves along the way: 'endless weekend on end going out to parties, getting totally wasted' and 'hooking up' with successive boyfriends. In the interview, I asked Kiri what she plans to do when the party is over:

> I still have no idea what I'm going to do, I have no idea. … Like I'm working at the courts now, Family Courts, and that is cool, I love it, I love the people. I don't see myself working there like in another ten years time but I have no idea still so I'll just stay there for the time being until, you know, maybe I might find something. … I've been over in the records section just filing and I've been in the call centre, but my favourite was when I was doing subpoenas with one of my friends, that was really good, I liked being there. (Kiri, working class government high school student, Perth)

It would appear that the social aspects of Kiri's job experience of 'doing subpoenas' are more important than its intrinsic merits, a point also made by Alex, a youth service client, who favours a particular course of study because she can socialise with a friend who works nearby.

Julie McLeod and Lyn Yates (2006: 101,184) found that interviewees' time horizons correlated with class background, the working class respondents being more likely to 'take it as it comes' (McLeod and Yates 2006: 184; see also Mackinnon et al. 2010:1 01).[6] As one young woman in my study writes, 'I take each day as it comes; I only plan ahead for long term things like holidays' (female, working class government high school student, South Australia). This future-time orientation is expressed in the percentage of students who wrote about their children's careers, highest in the Protestant college essays and lowest in the working class essays (see Chart 1.7).

There is perhaps a good reason for turning away from present limitations to dream of an unlikely future, given the different nature of obstacles or challenges faced by the middle class and working class respondents. Middle class youth engage fulsomely with the DIY biography, representing hurdles as *positive* learning opportunities. Two write: 'Although it sounds corny, my mistakes were good learning experiences' and 'I will be happy and still learning … from my mistakes … and growing at 80'. A similar conviction is expressed in this essay:

> I want to love my whole life, the good and the bad cause the bad always comes but I want to accept that. I want opportunities to open and me to take them. I want to do something different in my life, and I am going to actually do those things not just wish. I know I have to make my own opportunities. (female, Protestant college student, Adelaide)

Middle class youth's imagined obstacles are internal, such as a failure of resolve, whereas disadvantaged youth confront external challenges, such as financial problems or the interference of other people. Disadvantaged writers are more likely to express the need to *overcome* obstacles through struggle (see Kacen 2002: 19 and Watson 2008 for studies that classify disadvantaged young people's essays according to the 'constant struggle between weakness and strength'). The 'risk biography'[7] is an enforced response to institutional individualisation, risk and the 'liquid society', something engaged in because there is little choice:

> We find the sociological notion of 'risk' … provides the most useful way of understanding the link between reflexivity and habitus, where the reflexive negotiation of risk highlights the habitus in action through the operation of cultural capital. (Threadgold and Nilan 2009: 48)

The fragile dreams of disadvantaged essayists flutter against large, even insurmountable, impediments: inadequate literacy and lack of education, poor health, poverty, indifferent treatment by Centrelink, fights, single motherhood, childhood rape, violence at home, pregnancy, entering a series of bad relationships 'cos I needed a guy to support me'. 'Before I fell pregnant', a young Aboriginal mother dreamt of playing netball — 'league or even play state' — and becoming a hairdresser. She hopes that 'After I have my kid I'll go back to TAFE and continue on with my hairdressing', but is not sure (female, Aboriginal youth service client, Adelaide). Alex, a young mother at sixteen as a result of rape, was, when I spoke with her, reporting monthly to a youth worker for break and enter, struggling to keep off drugs and cigarettes and in a custody battle with her uncle and aunt to regain custody of her infant son. She was also considering, with little enthusiasm, a limited range of training and work options (Alex, disadvantaged youth service client, Adelaide). Another youth service client cannot 'follow her dreams' because she left home at thirteen due to 'the conflict, violence and emotional abuse'. On the streets, 'I was always getting locked up' and now 'a really violent boyfriend is still wanting to find me and hurt me' (female, disadvantaged youth service client, Adelaide).

At the same youth service centre, Tim starts his story with a plan but then reflects unhappily on his lack of options, before recovering himself for the appropriate DIY approach:

> I want to get a loan from my grandmother so that I can buy a bobcat and a tipper truck so that I can sub-contract for the Housing Trust or something. But to do that I need to go and do a small business traineeship and a horticultural course so that I can get there. But at the moment I am in shit so I can't do fuck all. Sorry about the language but I know that I will sort myself out and eventually do what I want to do and what I am capable of doing to my full potential. (Tim, disadvantaged youth service client, Adelaide)

While many disadvantaged essayists adopt the discursive ploy of the DIY biography, it is often a rhetorical gesture revealing the lack of alternative discourses, rather than a detailed program for achievement, a real DIY biography in which present accomplishments provide the solid grounding for future possibilities. Many young essayists are forced into the self-help discourse because they lack any other alternatives, the sociological literacy by which to understand social structures dealing life changes. The self-help discourse is the dominant 'meaning constitutive tradition' or 'pattern of sense making', which influences 'the thinkability of particular acts and projects' (Gross 2005: 296). This influences the following assertions:

> if you want some thing bad enough you can achieve any thing you want.
> (female, young mothers' Christian school student, New South Wales)

I believe life hold for me in store are the think which I built throughout my life. I belive I control my life, therefore I get out what I want in store. I strongly belive that I control my life. (male, working class government high school student, Sydney)

Steven Threadgold and Pam Nilan (2009: 47, 54) suggest that the working class respondents in their sample were expressing reflexivity, responding with awareness to the challenges in one's life — doing their best to improve their chances, for example, by finishing high school. However, their reflexivity was met with greater external obstacles, which reduced their capacity to express successful reflexivity (Threadgold and Nilan 2009: 47, 54).

In the English 'Inventing adulthoods' study, disadvantaged youth who failed to achieve 'competence' and 'recognition' via investment in education turned to other avenues (Thomson et al. 2004: 237) such as recreational drug and alcohol use, club culture or violence, this being the response of the second respondent quoted at the head of this section (Henderson et al. 2007: 78–9). Instead of being 'suckers' for the do-it-yourself biography, a study of Adelaide youth in two alternative education schools also found some young people 'resist' the inequities of structural risk by embracing escapist risk (Mackinnon in Mackinnon et al. 2010: 95) or giving free reign to disturbing 'illegitimate' beliefs such as violent racism or sexism (Mackinnon et al. 2010: ix, 34, 46),[8] although others expressed elements of the self-help discourse ('You can't help anybody else … if you don't want to help yourself first': Mackinnon et al. 2010: 13).

An innovative rejection of the self-help biography in my sample was what might be called 'parodic disadvantage', an unseating of inequality in fantasy. Both the essayists quoted below refer to class differences, living in dustbins 'next to a flash hotel' and being 'homeless because the Liberal government don't want people from Western Sydney in their world'. They escape their circumstances by becoming a 'whore' or winning the lottery:

I had 10 kids — 5 boys & 5 girls when they were old enough I kicked them out on the streets. They then became homeless & lived in dustbins next to a flash hotel. My husband left me when I had my last kid. I was a single mother. I got paid from Centrelink, I was very poor bum. I then had to become a whore to earn more money. It was very pleasuring nearly every day. It was a good experience. I caught STD's, had crabs & had to retire from my whore job. Then I became a tranny. I had grey hairs, wrinkly. (female, working class government high school student, Perth)

I'm going to be homeless because the Liberal government don't want people from Western Sydney in their world so I'll eat out of rubbish bins then find a winning lottery ticket and claim it then I will be a multi millionaire and live in a mansion and do what I feel. (male, working class government high school student, Sydney)

Sheila Henderson et al. (2007: 100) suggest of the British 'Inventing Adulthoods' project that mobility is a central idea in all the biographies they collected: 'getting around', 'getting on' or 'getting out'. My results suggest that disadvantaged youth focus more on 'getting around' and perhaps dream of 'getting out' while middle class youth have elaborate plans about 'getting on'. In summary, the differences between disadvantaged and middle class life stories revolve around wide or narrow time horizons, crafted as realistic 'exploring' stories or realistic 'settling'/'retreating' stories, so that disadvantaged youth only escape narrow horizons with unrealistic 'wandering' stories. Disadvantaged youth, I argue, are forced to deploy the DIY biography due to few available alternatives (such as structural understanding of disadvantage). But it is largely an empty rhetorical gesture, with little detail giving it backbone. Where the middle class respondents almost enthuse about obstacles as learning experiences, the working class writers are more likely to confront impediments as insurmountable, and certainly as undesirable. The kinds of jobs imagined, as well as the likelihood of writing about further education, travel or material comforts are also clearly classed (see Tables A3.1, A3.2 and A3.3 in Appendix 3). Disadvantaged youth are more likely to write about personal accidents and ultimately to be discontented (see also Andres and Wyn 2010: 78).[9]

The disadvantaged youth in my study imagine lives with limited horizons and few goals, unless they write of elaborate unlikely scenarios. While Indigenous Australians are the most disadvantaged group of Australians, other issues are revealed in young Aboriginal people's life stories, in particular constant upheaval and disruption, against which writers cleave to family and country.

Aboriginal youth: Family and politics

When I was 4 my mother died and I don't see much of my dad. I use to live with my grandma until I was about 7 and then moved in with my aunty. We moved over to Kalgoolie W.A. for about a year or so. We come back cose my aunty and unck broke up. My aunty was pregnant with twins at the time which made it hard. I have 3 brothers and 3 sisters including me. The oldest 23, Raymond, then Tasha 18 then Edward 17 then Johnny 14 then me 12 then Christopher 11. The 3 older same dad him and my mum were married he was very abusive to my mother so I hear and then they got divorced then my sisters dad that was just a over night stand. My mum gave Johnny to my aunty because she thought she couldn't have kids and then she had me my dad's half

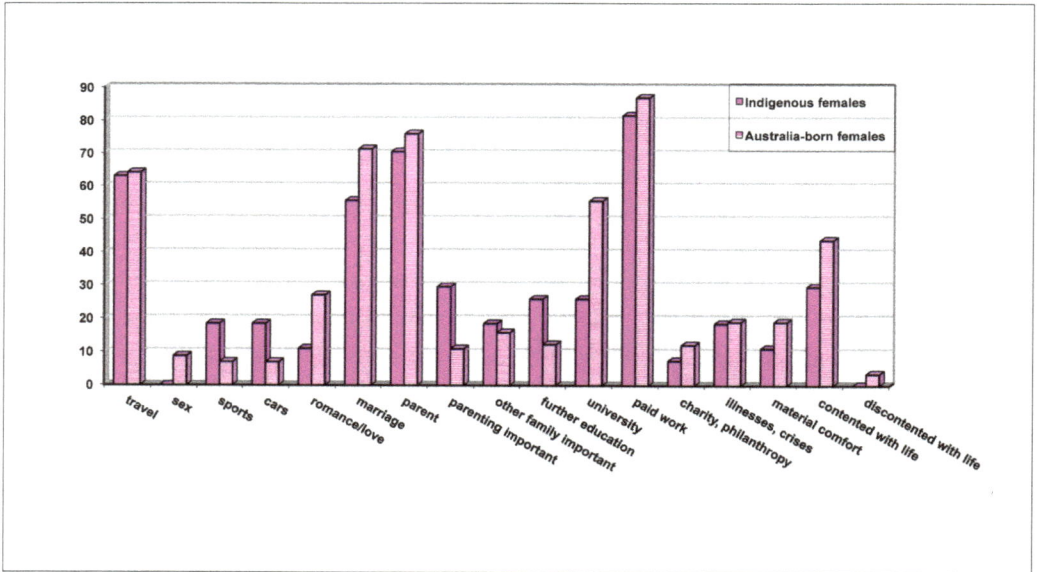

Chart 1.8: Events mentioned in life stories: Gender by Indigeneity: Females

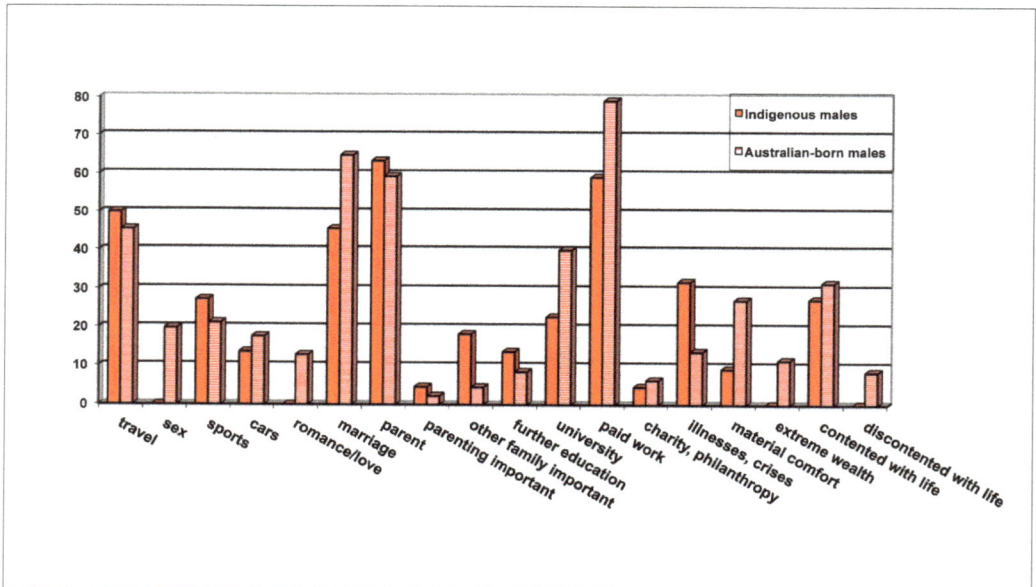

Chart 1.9: Events mentioned in life stories: Gender by Indigeneity: Males

Scottish. I see him once and a while then my mum met this great man since my dad was never around he was kind of my dad figure for a while. I was kinda brought up a greek as well. I never really understood where my mum went until I got older we still go down to her grave now and then but it's hard to get the whole family 2gether now theres been so much arguments. But I still go on. THE END. (female, Aboriginal youth service client, Adelaide)

Only in identifying sports, cars, the importance of parenting and family beyond the nuclear family, do the Aboriginal female essayists focus on any aspect of their imagined lives more often than the other Australian-born writers. The Australian born non-Indigenous females write more often of love and marriage, and of outcomes based on privilege (travel, material comfort and, most particularly, attending university), leaving them more likely to be contented with their lives. Some of the same differences are recorded for the male essayists, with Aboriginal male writers more likely to write of illnesses and other family tragedies, less likely to imagine material comfort and less likely to be contented. They are also less likely to write of paid work or a career, a difference that is greater for the Aboriginal males than the Aboriginal females by contrast with the other Australian-born essayists (see Charts 1.8 and 1.9):

I lived a long, healthy life, playing a lot of sport. I don't want to be troubled by the law. I want to stay free of drugs. I want to be rich and handsome. (male, Aboriginal youth service client, Melbourne)

There is a caveat, however. After removing those youth services clients who were under the age of fifteen, for example the essayist quoted at the head of this sub-section who writes of constant changes in her family situation, the Aboriginal sample consisted of only 27 females and 22 males. Only these are included in Charts 1.8 and 1.9, meaning that only the large and patterned differences are likely to have any significance. Commitment to family — particularly relationships beyond the nuclear family — is also expressed in Aboriginal 'I ams': for example 'A proud Big sister, a proud aunty and godmother'; '18 years old, An Aboriginal, Going to be a mother, A sister, Granddaughter, A daughter'. In a total life story, caring for relatives is a goal along with wealth and fame:

Living with my wife, Got one leged chopped off by a car, Live in a manchen, Give all cuzies money and my family. Famous around world for something. (total life story, male, aged 12, Aboriginal youth service client, Adelaide)

Aboriginal respondents are 'proud' of their culture and therefore 'special'. They are engaged in their communities: 'I am Kaurna/Ngarringjeri descent and fight for land rights and support my elders.' They write of becoming an elder or a 'respected woman' whose work 'gives me a sense of drive and understandment of my people'. In her interview, Caitlin says:

> in the wider world, I want to do something incredible, kind of thing. Do something that can be recognised. … The thing is … I'm not too bright (chuckles). So it's kind of hard. Like even if it's making a stand for a certain group, … I just want to do something that can help others. … I do want to make a difference. I don't want to just be someone else that kind of wastes their time. (Caitlin, Aboriginal service client, Victoria)

In discussing her identity, Caitlin notes family, pride in her culture and community closeness, although she says this sounds 'dopey'. She is troubled that she learned about her Aboriginality 'through school' rather than from her family.

Sporting involvement is important to young Aboriginal people. One essayist, who would like to become an elder, writes 'I like boxing — I like knocking people out, I hate school — school is shit.' His disaffection from school suggests why few young Aboriginal males imagine further education. Instead, sports, in particular football, offer a path of upward mobility. Sports-related friendships can bridge cultural difference, as suggested by a young male Melbourne Aboriginal youth service client:

> I didn't know many people but after a while I got used of it and by the end of year 9 I knew alot of people I am playing sport I love my footy I am playing for prestan RSL I enjoy playing there all me mates.

Some Aboriginal writers combine sporting success with a middle class career, for example rising to 'Commissioner of the Fire Department' after a stellar AFL career.

Two young women imagine themselves as proud mothers and successful professionals. Caitlin writes of becoming a health worker, affording the 'luxuries of a nice car and to take the kids away to see the family' (Caitlin, Aboriginal services client, Victoria). The other young woman becomes a lawyer, something she had wanted from the age of 15; both career success and motherhood are important to her:

> When I was 25, I graduated my law degree, my greatest accomplishment. I also married that year, to my long time boyfriend and best friend since attending High School. After working 1 year at Aboriginal Legal Rights I left and landed myself a job at a well known Law firm in Adelaide, which then enabled myself to practice Criminal Law, my long time dream. … Being a mother to a beautiful boy and a wife to a loving husband, and being a lawyer at a law firm meant the world to me. More than anyone could ever imagine.

… When my first child was 5 years old, myself being 31, I broke down in tears after watching my son toddle off into the schoolyard with his spider-man back pack and matching lunch box. (female, Aboriginal university student)

Young migrants' dreams

My life is normal and on my track, but it is boring too compared to other teenagers. I do not have as much freedom as they do. My parents are these traditional type of Chinese (well not the very typical ones, a little better than that) but they are still the same as most of the Chinese, expect me to be well behaved, be respectful and work hard for my work. Sometimes I feel really tired of being like this and the most important is I am not allowed to date guys before finishing University. (female, Chinese background, middle class government high school, Adelaide)

When I became more mature, my parents and I have come to an agreement that I would be allowed to have a boyfriend and would be able to go out with him each month. But I have to study (which I wanted to do) and think about my own actions. (female, Asian background, middle class government high school, Adelaide)

The thing I have to mention here is that my dad was so strict about me studying medicine at Adelaide Uni, and he would remind me every single day that I have to make it otherwise the whole family and friends back in Iran would laugh at me. As you can imagine I was really stressed those two years of my life when I was studying year 11 and 12. (female, 'Persian' background, middle class government high school, Adelaide)

The children of overseas-born Australians are often portrayed in the sociological literature and the media as straddling cultures, sometimes with rich consequences, at other times with less success (e.g. see Butcher and Thomas 2006 for Australia; Smart and Shipman 2004 for England). A successful hybridity or 'place polygamy' (Beck and Beck-Gernsheim 2002: 23) is expressed by the essayist who mobilises her identity strategically in different situations (see also Noble et al. 1999: 136; Smart 2007: 82–93). A Jew, she felt that living in Israel was 'like finally being home', a place where she could pursue her classical music. Back in Perth with her 'childhood friends' and 'familiar surroundings':

I felt as though I was home there as well. At first I couldn't understand this, but then I realised that there are so many different parts to who I am; Perth satisfies some — my sense of fun, my need for genuine lifetime friendships, while Israel satisfies those aspects somewhat closer to my core. (female, Protestant college student, Perth)

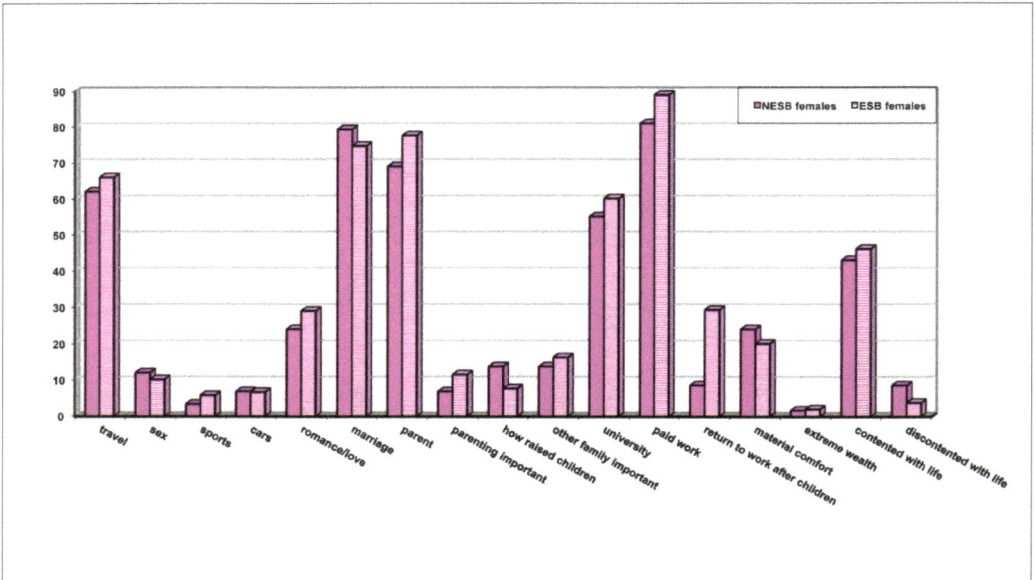

Chart 1.10: Events mentioned in life stories: Gender by ethnicity: Female high school students

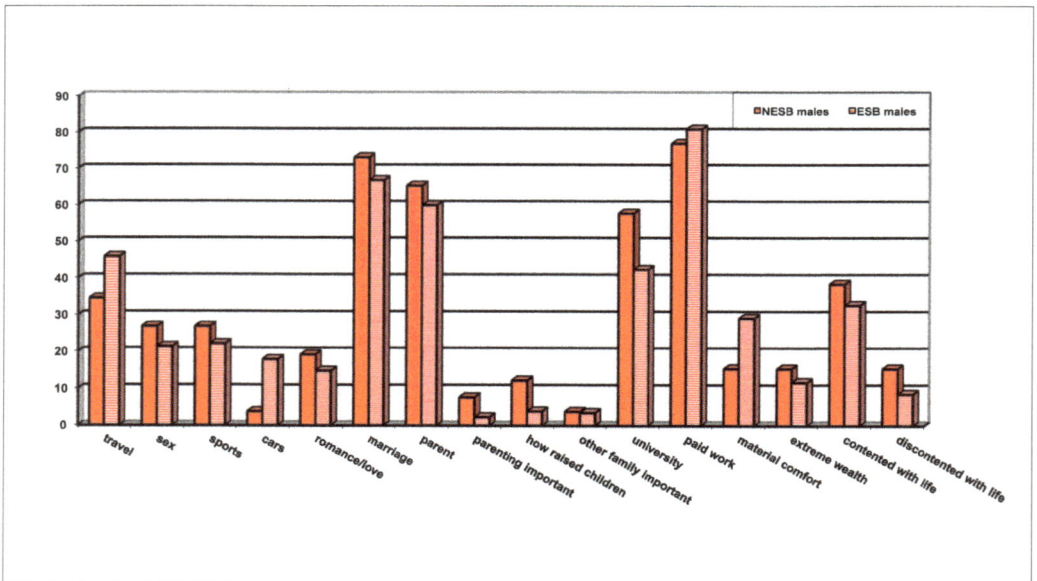

Chart 1.11: Events mentioned in life stories: Gender by ethnicity: Male high school students

Note: The samples born in non-English speaking countries are small, 60 females (compared with 374 ESB females) and 26 males (compared with 276 ESB males), so little should be made of the low incidence items in Chart 1.11 such as sex, sports and cars.

Another essayist writes more ruefully: 'kind of in between … I don't know what I am'. Thirty-one per cent of overseas-born CALD (Cultural and Linguistic Diversity) high school respondents noted their ethnic identity compared with only 10 per cent of the rest of the high school students (see Table A3.9 in Appendix 3). A male Filipino youth writes 'I wanna represent mah race. — PINOY PRYDE!!'. Another young man defines himself as 'AZN', a term associated with 'Asian pride'. A female Muslim essayist travels to Mecca: 'the wonderful feeling it gives surrounded with such beauty is the best experience in life for me'. Other essayists travel to better understand their ancestry and culture.

As in the essay extracts at the head of this section, daughters note the parental pressure to stay home, study hard and marry well. Sons must study even harder to become doctors or lawyers. Thus, a self-defined female 'Chinese' 'youth' writes despondently:

> Your health deteriorate when you study — you get fat, unfit — you are eat unhealthy foods and your eyes deteriorate. My life is a misery. So boring. My high school year is a rat race to get to the end. … This pursuit is fuelled by parental expectations, but also to help with the pressure from parents. My last romance was in year 6. Sad. (female, girls' middle class government school, Sydney)

By contrast, a young man matures to appreciate his parents' wisdom. He notes that 'the emphasis has always been on working hard … in school to get a good job like Doctor, Dentist or some Engineering course, and then work hard at that occupation and become respected'. He becomes a 'successful' doctor and parent: 'I educated them on the virtues of Buddhism, my religion, and they too grew up to have "respectable" occupations, which ironically, is based on the same principles as my parents.' Like the story at the head of this section, parental expectations are felt acutely, but they are also understood and not usually rejected, although the first essayist quoted above notes of her parents' injunction against dating, 'I do not really listen to them in this. I think that is the only thing that I hide from them.'

As Charts 1.10 and 1.11 reveal, there are few significant differences in the concerns of essayists from non-English and English-speaking (largely Australian-born) backgrounds. The young women from English speaking countries write more of romance and those from non-English speaking backgrounds of (not having) sex; the former are slightly more latter to marry but the former write more often of motherhood. English-speaking background essayists evince more workforce attachment, ranging from a greater likelihood of attending university, entering paid work and returning to their careers after having children. By contrast, the non-English speaking background female essayists write about material comfort. They are slightly less likely to be contented and more likely to be discontented. Young ESB men focus on their cars (although interestingly not their sports) vis-à-vis NESB males, writing less often of attending university but more often of paid work; more of material comfort and slightly less of extreme wealth. Non-English speaking background males are more likely to be either contented or discontented with their lives. The greater likelihood of discontentment among the CALD-background essayists may reflect the tensions of cultural bridging (see Butcher and Thomas 2006).

There is no clear evidence that the non-English speaking background female students are more committed to family, being less likely to write of the importance of parenting or family beyond the nuclear family, although they are more likely to write about how they raised their children. Concerning the male students, family is more significant for those from non-English speaking backgrounds, the greatest difference being a discussion of how children are raised. Family is also important to many Anglo-background young people, this fact occluded by a 'cultural predilection' that emphasises young people's early independence and freestanding individualism in work, education and leisure (Aapola et al. 2005: 92).

One reason that the expected commitment to education is not found in Chart 1.10 and is less significant for the males from NESB backgrounds than one might imagine (Chart 1.11) is that my sample does not only include east Asian students, who do write of this struggle to meet (or resist) parental expectations. Students from other countries, such as Syria, the Philippines and Fiji, express more modest goals. A young 'Syrian' hopes to become a teacher before marrying and having '4 kids'. Another university graduate married 'Ali', a 'Muslim and we now have 3 children — 2 boys and one girl'.

Among the CALD essayists, assertive self-identification based on ethnicity suggests that this particular group-based identity is not rejected in the way that class identity is (further explored in Chapter Four). However, the similarity in life story essays supports Ulrich Beck and Elisabeth Beck-Gernsheim's suggestion that 'detraditionalization' leads to 'hybrid identities and cultures' emerging in 'intersection and combination through conflict with other identities' (Beck and Beck-Gernsheim 2002: 26). Chapter Five returns to a discussion of how those marked as 'other' in mainstream society — Indigenous, Asian, 'Third World-looking' (Hage 1998: 116) — are treated by the English-speaking background respondents.

Conclusion

Dan Woodman (2009: 247) suggests that the 'individualization thesis' is often deployed as a 'straw theory' against which the researcher's own evidence is posited to propose that constraints still limit choices and that class, gender and ethnicity continue to shape people's lives. In support of this, some researchers have found little empirical support for Giddens' claims concerning a flight from the certainties of family (e.g. see Jamieson's 1998 review of the literature), kinship (Smart 2007) or the desire for employment security (Andres and Wyn 2010). Carol Smart discovered among her interviewees that 'secure roots and a known heritage are vital for ontological security'. The families in her study spoke neither of a wide buffet of choices nor of only one true origin story: 'They also tried to ensure that their children had the foundations for "choice" drawn from their own biographies and identities' (Smart 2007: 106). These foundations melded individual personality traits with 'the cultural, the biographical, the historical and the spatial', so that the interviewees' narratives expressed class, gender and ethnicity (Smart 2007: 107).

The review of life stories in my sample also reveals the 'persistence of inequality' (Andres and Wyn 2010: 243) and difference based on gender, class and Indigeneity. The majority of young people have fairly traditional hopes and expectations, although social scientists argue that these are less likely to be met in precarious labour markets (Andres and Wyn 2010), combined with a lack of institutional support for women's desires for both rewarding work and rewarding motherhood (Esping-Andersen 2009). In response, some young people prize mobility as the antidote to the loss of a 'lifelong profession' (Beck and Beck-Gernsheim 2002: 162). But this imposed freedom becomes a cage and some people may desire escape back into the comforts enjoyed by the previous generation. This condemnation to shift for oneself cracks through the stories written by disadvantaged youth, as further discussed in Chapter Four. Andres and Wyn's findings reveal the 'reality of [social] generation' (Andres and Wyn 2010: 243), of young people sharing social conditions and responding to them differently from the way their parents engaged with the central projects of work and family (Andres and Wyn 2010: 33). This is the subject of the next chapter, exploring intergenerational change and continuity.

Notes

1 I have retained the essayists' own English usage and not signalled incorrect grammar or spelling with sic, unless indicating incorrect spelling of proper names.

2 Only four per cent of young Australian women aspire to be full time at home with family in midlife; 75 per cent of young women aspire to more educational qualifications, 90 per cent want paid work and children by the time they are 35 (Harris 2004: 42). As a result of women's focus on career, the median age for first confinement had risen from 27 in 1982 to 30.2 in 2002 for mothers; for fathers it was 32.5 (Office of the Status of Women 2004: 4).

3   Gender saturates the texture of stories, subject matter and identity markers, as revealed in a study of single-sex conversations in England. Men tell tales of 'conquest', women relate stories of 'community', with further sex differences concerning the heroic and the everyday, action and people (Coates 2003: 35, 50, citing Barbara Johnstone). Nicolopoulou et al. (1994) discovered that these distinctions start early. Four-year-old girls write of family groups and relationships and boys of powerful or frightening warriors or monsters engaging in violent action or dramatic events. As Pam Gilbert (1994: 126–7, 135) puts it, girls — drawing on stories around them in magazines, romance fiction, television soaps and so on — take up a narrow range of stereotypical narrative positions in which they 'learn to construct femininity and masculinity within a hierarchical dualism'; teenage female writers find it hard to resist a storyline with a romantic heterosexual closure. Indeed, in my sample, more male writers disrupted the realist autobiography with a fantasy, and there were more monsters in the young men's fantasy tales than in the young women's. My results bear similarities with essays written by British 11-year-old children in 1969 (Elliott 2010: 1080).

4   Summers (1970: 103) found that only seven per cent of the technical schoolgirls mentioned travel, compared with half of the private school girls. Half the private school girls wrote of world disasters (Summers 1970: 104–5) but only one (out of 26) of personal disasters (suicide). Those who wrote of 'war, peace, world hunger, pollution and the increased mechanization of our existence' 'were not interested in anything else', barely discussing their own personal lives.

5   Ani Wierenga (2009: 160, 64) captures this in a poignant vignette: Laura used to ride a lot until, as she tells Wierenga, 'Dad sold my horse when I was at school one day'.

6   McLeod and Yates (2006: 184) summarised the class differences in their three Victorian sub-samples as becoming a 'somebody', seeking a 'good life', or aiming only for 'a comfortable life' and being ready to 'take it as it comes'. Similarly Mackinnon et al. (2010: 101) identify disadvantaged youth respondents who are present-time oriented, focusing on helping each other and having fun with friends rather than expressing the 'hallmarks of the individualizing biographical project': 'you deal with the cards you get … Yeah, whatever happens, happens, just deal with it as it comes' (Mackinnon et al. 2010: 101).

7   The notion of 'risk' biography has overlapping meanings: character failure, for example lacking 'persistence and foresight' (Elias (1991 [1940s–1950s]: 129); 'ontological insecurity' and 'existential anxiety', as Giddens (1991: 8, 47–55) renders Norbert Elias' (1991) formulation. Another meaning indicates the effects of persisting inequalities of class, gender and culture in our society (Lemert and Elliott 2006; Mills 2007: 70).

8   Their comments were confronting in their racism ('In the future there wouldn't be any Asians. They'd all be shot by skinheads'; Mackinnon et al. 2010: 34) and sexism ('In 20 years I can see myself with a nice job, a fuckin' pimped-out fuckin' car, a hot little bitch, maybe kids'; Mackinnon et al 2010: 46 in their a study of Adelaide youth in two alternative education schools).

9   Australian males with non-university credentials were the least content in reporting satisfaction levels and university educated females the most positive about achieving fulfilment (Andres and Wyn 2010: 78).

2

LEARNING FROM THEIR PARENTS: INTERGENERATIONAL CHANGE AND CONTINUITY

Introduction

> The women's rights campaign of 2020 turned out to be a war against men. Masculinity prevailed and we fought females back and out of Earth. They now reside on the moon (except my wife). We have learnt that by doing stupid feminism surveys that it seeds the idea that feminism has a right to live. (male, Catholic college student, South Australia, who describes himself as 'A man, Aussie, bored already, not female, a mad mad man, young and immature')

In my first interviews with women of the baby-boomer generation for my book *Living Feminism* (1997), I asked 'How have the lives of women changed as a result of the women's movement?' Several interviewees began to sketch their answers and then added, 'You must talk to my daughter.' These mothers were proud of, and a little awed by, daughters who were apprenticed jewellers, in the police force, who believed they could do anything. Because they reached for their daughters' stories to highlight the changes in their own lives, I began asking each interviewee to compare her mother's, her own and her daughter's life and opportunities (see Bulbeck 1997: 9). I also decided to interview some of the daughters, asking them to reflect on the differences between their mother's generation and their own. And I decided to write another book, based on the experiences of these young women who believed they had inherited the whole wide world.

This was the genesis of the research undertaken for this book, in which women told me the same progressive narratives that I had heard in the 1990s. The story of a revolution in female education, work and politics has become commonplace. The mothers in my research predicted their daughters would not put up with the gender-differentiated relationships that many of them had lived through, and automatically presumed equality between the genders. With a less readily available public language, but offering something not so often explored intergenerationally, several mothers in my sample identified a confidence, independence and worldliness in their daughters, a knowing psychic freedom, which they contrasted with their youthful misplaced idealism or lack of self-esteem. In general their daughters agreed with this story.

In *Living Feminism* I had not researched the experiences of men, a task I set myself in the current research. I blithely sat down to my first interview with Gordon, a blue-collar public servant in a working class suburb on the fringes of Adelaide, and asked him to compare his father's life, his own and what he imagined for his son. He was utterly stumped by my question. Only three fathers in my sample spoke readily about changes in male roles: all had been exposed to feminist ideas. Whereas daughters embrace an assertive confidence and belief that they are as good as any man, as John Howard put it (in Summers 2003: 21), the young men are more ambivalent in their response to feminism's message. Some are struck as dumb as their fathers by my questions concerning intergenerational gender changes. Some express an angry response to feminism, like the young man cited at the head of this section. Some perform a parodic 'postfeminist' masculinity: postfeminist both in the sense that these men's responses acknowledge the impact of feminism on gender relations and in the sense that they reject the most revolutionary aspects of women's liberation (see Budgeon 2011a: 10–14; McRobbie 2004: 4; Thomas 1995: 4–5 for further discussion of postfeminism's limits).

Based largely on the 100 interviews undertaken with young people and 45 of the high school students' parents, this chapter explores the 'consciousness' of change across the generations, to use Summers' (1970: 4) formulation, that is, the changes young people and their parents sketch in institutions and psychological frameworks. The chapter concludes with an analysis of intergenerational attitudes towards feminism and the women's movement. Young women, by comparison with their mothers, locate feminism firmly in the past, as no longer necessary in an age of gender equality. Interviewees are more concerned about men's presumed disadvantage than women's continuing inequality.

Narratives of becoming: Women change their lives (and minds)

> We lived at Somerton Park in a very small home. It was spotless. Absolutely spotless. … A woman was judged by how she could do the pickles or do the cucumbers. … [B]ut certainly Dad was the dominating one. Very much so. … We had a stick by the fridge and all that kind of stuff. … Dad was the ultimate disciplinarian. … And often Mum would say, if she wanted to get something or needed to get something a bit different, 'We'll have to wait for your father'. … Women today are quite — . See, we've got more freedom to have our own money. Dad died eighteen months ago and I think now she's realising, umm, that her total life was to care for him, look after him and bring up her children. (Susan, Protestant college mother, Adelaide)

> My mother … always felt stuck. I don't think she knew what to do about it. She knew there was more in life and I think she's still frustrated now at the life she led. … I don't think my parents paid a lot of attention to my career. It was about marry a man with a good trade, you know, and you won't starve, that kind of thing. … I think as a result of that I always felt kind of caught between, I never had it in me to think about what are you going to do for the rest of your life in terms of, you know, supporting yourself. … I wanted to work, but I didn't quite know what to do, so feminism was attractive. I used to take a bit of ridicule in my family because they saw feminism as a side-issue [Lynette's parents were active Marxists]. … I started off in office work when I first left school so there was this sea of women and a man in charge. … I worked in a bank, sea of women … the same at school, you know, the role models weren't there. (Lynette, middle class government high school mother, Melbourne)

> From when I was about seven, I've always played the aunty [in childhood games] no matter what and have always been, 'No, no, I'm not a mother, I'm not a mother'. ('Daria', women's studies university student, Perth)

According to Hugh Mackay's (1997) three generation comparative study, the 'Lucky' Generation were born in the 1920s, the 'Stress' Generation were born in 1946–1955 and the 'Options' Generation were born in the 1970s. The fulcrum of his naming, as in many studies, is based on the weight of the 'baby-boomer' generation born following the Second World War. In my sample, most parents were born between 1950 and 1960 (the average age was 45 at the time of the interview) and most of the young people were born between 1985 and 1990 (81 per cent were aged between 16 and 18 when surveyed, an average of 17.52 years old). On this basis, I have labelled the three generations discussed in this chapter as follows. I have called the parents of my sample of parents the 'wartime' generation, as a gesture to one of the differences that some fathers identified when comparing themselves with their fathers. The parents are (late) 'baby-boomers' and their children are 'Gen Y' or 'young people' (see Andres and Wyn 2010: 33 for a discussion of generational classification).

Women's lives transformed by access to paid work

The first question I asked the mothers I interviewed was 'What is the difference between your mother's life, your own life and what you imagine for your daughter?' Almost every interviewee responded with a variation on the story told by Susan and Lynette above (although Henderson 2006: 45 suggests my framing of the question encourages a progressive narrative). The wartime generation of women understood their central life task to be that of wife and mother, albeit sometimes feeling 'stuck' and 'frustrated' by this, but lacking the confidence and the legal and social support to re-enter the workforce. The baby-boomers are 'caught between', as Lynette suggests, raised in the expectation of motherhood but seizing opportunities for education and work that were not available to the wartime generation. As one working-class background baby-boomer put it, 'Finishing year 10 was the goal' with '[h]igh expectations of working at Woolworths, Coles' prior to marriage. Their re-entry into education and work was often somewhat haphazard, coming after their children were in primary or secondary school. They were lured by growing labour force demand for white collar workers, pushed by the 'empty nest' once their child-rearing years were behind them and encouraged by feminist ideas advocating new ways for women to imagine their lives and worth (Curthoys 1994: 16; Everingham et al. 2007: 425–6).

These women entered a gendered workforce, with its 'sea of women' in clerical and retail jobs. Lynette started in clerical work but returned to university to study social work. After this, Lynette secured a supervisory position. Unlike a previous generation of women workers, Lynette 'had a young man working for me', going on to note 'and he had absolutely no respect for me at all'. Lynette noticed this prejudice (and declared she would never employ another male). Discrimination at work fired feminist understandings among the baby-boomers when they, for example, discovered they were denied equal pay, forced to resign because of the marriage bar or required to 'ask permission' to continue working as a casual employee, which excluded them from superannuation. Jane remembers the requirement to perform femininity at work: 'women couldn't be seen in their uniform outside of work — in case they went to a hotel, that would be bad' (Jane, Catholic college mother, Adelaide). The male Leonie worked alongside before she 'first left to have children, is now the Head of the Department', while Leonie's preference for part-time work has restricted her to a succession of casual contracts (Leonie, middle class government high school mother, Perth). By contrast, 'Gen Y' carefully plan careers while still in high school, and imagine working lives in which 'the world is her backyard', as Lynette says of her daughter working in Dublin and likely to 'end up living with a Swiss boy that she's met'.

For Daria, the young interviewee cited above, marriage and motherhood are a choice. In the generation of women who married following the war, only four per cent (and eight per cent of men) never married. This was also the most fertile generation in Australian history in terms of having at least one child (McCalman 1993: 210). As Penelope, a young woman who, like Daria, asserts her right to 'be by myself', ponders: 'I don't really know anyone in their seventies who has never been married or doesn't have children' (Penelope, middle class government high school student, Adelaide).

Compared with the wartime and baby-boomer generation who lived in benighted times, the young women in my research imagine themselves free to choose the shape of their lives, paid work generally understood as the pivot on which other freedoms hinge. In the past — 'ye old English colonial times' — women were 'forced to cook and clean', 'stay indoors and look after the children' and 'weren't allowed to work … whereas now they can do what they want'. Suffrage, owning property, and dress choices were also part of 'doing what they want': 'we're all wearing bathing suits and that sort of stuff, and not long ago they weren't allowed to do that'. Young women generally have a skimpy — albeit positive — notion of the changes in women's lives across the generations. Because of 'something about burning bras' or 'then they got a female president and she changed everything around', women are no longer 'submissive' and 'just like a prize for a man'. Boyfriends no longer believe that women are 'there for their benefit and nothing else'. Tash elaborates that the 'something' to do with bra-burning was 'equal respect', whereas in the past women were told 'respect your men':

> Like my auntie found this old book which said, oh, 'Before your husband gets home, make sure all the dinner's cooked and your hair's all nice and washed, and make sure you have a cup of tea for him', and stuff like that. And I think a lot of feminism is about just having equal respect. (Tash, working class government high school student, Adelaide)

The improving story of women's journey was comfortable and familiar for the baby-boomer mothers and Gen Y daughters, only two interviewees describing a 'declension narrative' (Shoemaker 1991: 39) in which the changes brought about by feminism are rejected or deemed irrelevant to the interviewee's life. In one case,

Nancy Margaret's wartime generation mother wanted to become a doctor but her family's resistance meant she had to settle for teacher training. Nancy Margaret places herself in this story as a lonely latch-key four year old, 'left with neighbours and crying on the swing'. She rejects the widespread current social expectation that women enter paid work and reveres motherhood as women's sacred duty ('Nancy Margaret', Catholic college mother, South Australia). In the other case, Rita's achievement of the 'small' position of teacher's aide, which she attributes to being an Italian migrant, disappoints her profoundly. However, Rita believes she will 'be able to assist' her daughter to achieve her 'very high expectations' (Rita, Catholic college mother, Sydney).

Psychic transformation

> before that [exposure to feminism] I always thought if you didn't agree with something, you were like, a troublemaker or something. ... Now I have a much greater feeling of what is right and what is fair, and so I'll voice it. (Jane, Catholic college mother, Adelaide)

For most baby-boomers, then, their lives were a leap outward into extra education and paid work, away from the 'small' goals of yesteryear and the 'small' social circle of home and, for some, involvement with similar women in charity work. Gen Y daughters are making another quantum leap in terms of geography (the locations in which they might study and work), in terms of the forethought they are putting into planning education and career, and in the less concrete terms of psychic freedom. Compared with the expansion in women's social roles, changes in expectations concerning social relations are far less frequently researched: the psychic freedom to express oneself, to respect oneself, and to expect to secure what one wants. This change in imaginative space is articulated by Lyn, a member of parliament in the baby-boomer generation, when she compares her daily experiences with the circumscribed routine of her wartime generation mother.

As with Susan's mother quoted above, Lyn feels widowhood meant her mother's 'life really stopped'. At the age of 81, 'she's become very dependent on me [Lyn]', Lyn feeling the need to ring her mother 'about three times a day'. Lyn's mother barely understands Lyn's life as a member of parliament, graphically described in one of these phone calls, on a significant day for Lyn. Lyn had received a 'really good reception' at a conference on refugee children (a speaker describing Lyn as 'a politician who's had the guts to speak out about our detention system') and won a coveted place on a committee. Lyn knew her mother would not understand the joy or success she felt. Instead her mother itemised her own preoccupations:

what she was going to have for lunch. She was going to cook a wiener schnitzel and she thought she might make some potato and a bit of carrot. She likes a bit of pumpkin so she's going to have a bit of pumpkin. Then, then the big decision was, Kate, my daughter, is coming there for a meal tonight because I'm away, so she didn't know what she'd cook for Kate, but she thought she might give her some chips, but then she doesn't think she likes chips. So this was the nature of the conversation and my head was spinning thinking, you know, I've got this to do and this to do and this to do and this to do. 'Um, yes Mum, right Mum'. And that's the difference between our lives. (Lyn, Catholic college mother, South Australia)

However, Lyn is in parliament, she says, for the sake of her children:

I'm here because of my children, because I wanted a better life for them and I knew what I was doing I couldn't create that better life for them. … Mum judges success as a mother in whether your daughter's got a clean uniform and whether she's had her lunch packed for the day. Whereas Kate, I judge it that she's been and seen things and she's met women — you know, famous people and had her eyes really opened by my life with her.

While many baby-boomers sketched wartime parents' marriages based on equal respect or mutual devotion, others had fathers who were 'a bit of a bully' or 'controlling'. As Jane (mother of Verity, participant in high achieving high school student program, Perth), a baby-boomer, put it, her wartime mother was more 'prepared to tolerate bad behaviour from men in her life' than she did herself. Her mother stayed whereas Jane left an unsatisfactory husband. Susan's mother, confronted with unusual requests for expenditure or outings, said to her children 'We'll have to wait for your father'. Once women returned to work, as (another) Jane, a baby-boomer in my sample, puts it, women who previously 'had no power basically because they had no money' raised their voices in the household (Jane, Catholic college mother, Adelaide).

Paid work was not always sufficient to confer psychic autonomy on baby-boomer women. Jenny, when aged nineteen and 'about the idea of getting married and the wedding dress and … changing my name', married a man from 'a very traditional Christian family where, as bizarre as it sounds, women didn't actually have an opinion, let alone have a job'. In her mid-thirties, Jenny finally fled her 'very violent' marriage: 'I took my three children, put them in a thousand dollar car and ran away, literally.' Given Jenny believes she will never own her own home, it has taken some time to relinquish her anger and bitterness:

It was hugely unfair. It was abusive. He tried to hurt me. He tried to hurt my children. I lost everything and I had to leave my job. I had to leave my friends. It was hugely unfair. But I can actually remember the day when I made a choice. And I said, 'I will stop being bitter. All my children are seeing is me being angry and bitter and yelling and horrible and if that's what they see then that's what they are going to become, so if they see me being happy and moving on, then that's hopefully what they will do.' I mean, I know that sounds very simple and it doesn't always work that way, but I just saw it as, make that choice and move on and hopefully they can as well. (Jenny, middle class government high school mother, Perth)

Reflecting back on her marriage, Jenny now realises that she was not the 'empowered woman' she had believed her employment had made her: 'Now I look back on it, now I'm starting to feel like I'm empowered and I have an opinion and I will express it and how I feel.' Jenny sloughed off her smiling façade, her femininity of agreeability (see McCalman 1993: 128) in her journey away from her violent husband:

know that your opinions are worthwhile and to not have that constant fear of offending or upsetting someone. Be able to put forward your point of view, however distasteful it may be to another person and be able to put it forward in a very non-aggressive way and be able to say, well this is how I feel and if it makes you feel bad, well, that's not a good thing, but it's still my point of view. ... I always grew up thinking, don't say that, it might upset someone. ... [B]rush your hair, put your mascara on and keep your mouth shut. (Jenny, middle class government high school mother, Perth)

Other baby-boomers also remember being concerned about 'upsetting someone', trying to live up to 'expectations of me or society', or being branded a 'troublemaker', as Jane cited at the head of this sub-section put it — until feminism opened her eyes and her mouth.

In her life story essay, a middle class teenager articulates her desire for these intergenerational psychic changes, rather than the outward signs of 'occupation, husband or kids':

It is too complicated to explain, but basically when I am 80 I want to be able to look back on my life and be confident that all my choices are my own, and not have a stuffed up life at 50 because I've tried to keep up an outer respectability and been so caught up with other people's opinions that I've convinced myself I'm something I'm not. That's all I know. I have no vision of my future occupation, husband or kids. (female, Protestant college student, Perth)

The essayist both understands and rejects her mother's life choices. Her mother has low self-esteem because her own wartime generation mother had 'told her she was ugly and would never get married'. So 'at 21 she got married to my father, believing herself lucky not to be "left on the shelf"'. The essayist's father had 'millions of affairs' and 'sexually harassed' his patients. Even so his wife 'stayed with him "for the kids" etc'. This young writer understands, but rejects for herself, that her mother's low-self esteem explains why she cleaved to the prized social role of doctor's wife and mother of private school children, despite its hollow 'outer respectability'.

As Jo, a baby-boomer mother, says of her daughter, Tash, she has more 'freedom to live the life that you could possibly live'. Tash's freedom requires additional emotional skills: 'deeper understanding' of herself, her feelings and how she relates to others. Thus armed, Tash's self-knowledge and interactive skills 'just blows' Jo away:

> we have all got, you know, a way of all talking about our feelings now that my mother didn't have. … [Of Tash:] I'm amazed at … the decisions she's making about her life and the way she is considering all these different things and the openness of it. It just blows me away. (Jo, Protestant college mother, Perth, interviewed with her daughter Tash)

Tash sees herself as a member of the 'options' generation (Mackay 1997), with bountiful information and choices:

> I've probably, yeah, like Mum was saying, learnt about a lot of, you know, life's lessons a lot earlier and kind of what the broadest spectrum of life is about, whereas maybe, you know, that we do have a lot more options just because of the different generations. (Tash, Protestant college daughter, Perth)

Kathleen, a baby-boomer, suggests that she and her wartime mother were both 'sheltered from the horrors of the world'. Gen Y have been exposed from childhood to the 'cruelty and ferocity in the world'. This tempers their passion, idealism and belief in social justice with a 'reality check', with objectivity, critique and analysis. Kathleen's daughter is both 'very good at empathising with people', including men, and

> doesn't accept anything really without questioning it. She questions authority. She questions everything — which you would expect, coming from our family [laughs]. (Kathleen, middle class government high school mother, Adelaide)

Baby-boomer Lynette 'let things happen to her', even though she was brought up by 'free thinking' socialist parents. Her daughter 'makes decisions' and blends her 'social conscience' with 'a smart mouth, she can stand up for herself, but she's a lovely person too' (Lynette, middle class government high school mother, Victoria). Baby-boomer Lyn, the member of parliament, laughingly compares her confidence with that of the young female staffers who work around her: with their sense of self-worth, 'my God, I'd be John Howard'. She cites a recent parliamentary committee meeting in which 'here I am at fifty-two years of age realising I'm still waiting for them [men]. Letting them speak before me'. By contrast, her daughter Kate knows:

> that she can do anything she wants to do. She's not held back by — I mean, when I was young I'd sort of dream about politics, for example, but women couldn't do it. You know, that was a man's job. (Lyn, Catholic College mother, South Australia)

As young women's emotional and physical boundaries expand, so does their worldliness, knowledge, and aplomb. Some baby-boomer mothers claim they are passing similar skills in emotional literacy to their sons: 'he just thinks of girls as being equal. ... He expects that when he gets married, he'll be sharing all the things equally' (Jane, Catholic College mother, Adelaide). Linda is less sanguine, suggesting her son is 'more tolerant and accepting of people's differences' but still emotionally challenged. Linda believes most young men have not 'seen the range of emotions expressed by, you know, a role model', a father who has moved beyond traditional gender boundaries (Linda, middle class government high school mother, Perth). This seems a fair assessment of most of the baby-boomer fathers I interviewed, although two fathers have grappled with changing their masculinity.

Men's disadvantage or opportunity?

> [men] have less control over aspects of the life/world, less opportunities, are increasingly compared to the achievements of women (particularly boys and girls in school) and are often criticised for being insensitive as they do not understand or support women's plight. (male, Catholic college student, Perth)

I asked a class of restive male students, who had completed their truncated life stories, to write a response to the question 'Are men and women better off now than they were twenty or thirty years ago?'. The questionnaire, which they had just completed (see Appendix 1), no doubt primed these nine young men to respond in terms of women's greater equality. They informed me that women are no longer confined to the 'stereotypical "housewife" trait', 'earning respect', 'have more rights' or 'don't have to do the cooking'. While all who expressed an opinion agreed that women are better off, there was much more uncertainty about the changes in men's lives. One young man suggested both sexes have greater 'freedom' than in the past. Another suggested that men are now 'more understanding'. Others reported that men are better off because they are 'more sensitive', have the option to be a stay-at-home father, because living standards are higher, or the amount of required physical work has declined. Two respondents believed little has changed in men's lives. As one put it:

Men remain very much the same in today's society as they have through countless generations. They are still the figure head of society and will continue to be well into the foreseen future. (male, Catholic college student, Perth)

The young man quoted at the head of this section also resisted the feminist narrative, complaining that, as women's lives have improved, men have suffered.

These results suggest that the progressive tale in relation to women's lives is known to young men as well as to women, both of whom can articulate grounds for improvement. The young men are more divided and uncertain concerning if and how men's lives have changed (see Gerson 2010: 189 for similar findings).[1] Perceptions of intergenerational changes in masculinities are the subject of this section.

Fathers grope for stories of moving masculinities

Chilla:	So the question I want to ask is this: how do you think your life is different from your father's (and what's the same as well), and how do you think your son's life will be different from yours?
Gordon:	Ermm, in what way?
Chilla:	Well, I suppose, anything really. I mean, yeah, just when you, do you sort of, when you think about your father's life and your own life, are there particular differences that you think about, or not?
Gordon:	I think there's more freedom down through the, down through the ages. (Gordon, girls' working class high school father, Adelaide)
Ray:	[of his son] Umm, as to what sort of life he'll lead, I don't really know. I can only hope that he leads the best life he can.
Chilla:	I suppose I was thinking of things like, you know, there's a lot of talk about men and women sharing housework now that women are working, and that kind of stuff.
Ray:	Okay, we're on the equality thing. (Ray, Catholic college father, Adelaide)

While mothers effortlessly retold the progressive narrative of women's escape from the domestic domain to financial independence and reproductive freedom, the fathers lacked access to a ready-made intergenerational imaginative landscape. The small number of fathers interviewed is a caveat here (but see similar findings concerning men's difficulty in discussing changing gender relations in Coates 2003: 76–7; Henderson 2006: 224–35; Townsend 1994: 34–9, 56).[2] I was struck by the absence of any kind of story by which to discuss generational change, Ray implying such narratives are the stuff of feminism: 'Okay, we're on the equality thing.' With further prompting from me, Gordon offers different job opportunities (fewer for his generation who lack the 'paperwork' as well as experience, and even fewer for those among the next generation who lack computer skills), two other fathers also noting this shift from manual to white collar jobs. Gordon finally suggests that gender relations are 'more equal now' because more women are in paid work.

Other fathers grasped for external factors, such as war, or migration from class-bound England to the 'best part of the whole world'. Such global changes may well overwhelm subtle generational differences. For example, Paul compares his father's time in the Polish resistance and consequent discrimination by the Soviet regime with his own life as an émigré in Australia. Ray pointed to the language barrier distinguishing him from his Italian father, while his communication with his son is more open ('we talk about things that I certainly wouldn't have been able to discuss with my parents'). When I pushed Ray on changes in the 'relationship' between father and son or husband and wife, Ray answered

> Well I'm sure my parents did the best they could and umm this is what I'm trying to do. But of course what you're trying to do also is trying not to repeat any mistakes that, err, you think they may have made, which, but they may not think so. Err, I'd say, I don't know. Well, I'd hope the relationships were okay between, err, between me and all the family members, but err, I guess, err, that depends on what day you ask the particular person [laughs, and so does Chilla]. (Ray, Catholic college father, Adelaide)

The fathers' bafflement was echoed by the few sons to whom I put the question. Nick's father is different in being 'English for one', but Nick is 'sort of like my dad' in terms of 'similar features', attitudes to 'America, the war in Iraq' (Nick, Protestant college student, Perth). Matthew refers to shared interests while Edward notes the implication of his father being born in England in terms of class-based opportunities:

> growing up in a sort of a middle-class would have helped him a lot in his studies, and things like that. Umm whereas here, it doesn't really matter what sort of a class you grow up in — if you've, umm, for my age group, wherever you grow up, there's equal opportunity for everyone, I would say. (Edward, Protestant college student, Perth)

Among the seven fathers interviewed, only three, Tony, Keith and Paul, could talk like a woman about the changes in gender relations across generations. Paul's story is a 'declension' narrative drawn from his Catholicism, which he has tested in the fire of a women's studies major at Murdoch University. Paul's enduring belief in the sanctity of life and 'natural law' rather than 'positivist law' (human-made law), 'relativism' and 'liberalism' means he opposes abortion, homosexuality, euthanasia and fathers (rather than mothers) staying home with very small children. Now that sex is freely available outside marriage and divorce a ready weapon in a wife's hands ('She will take everything, my children' and the house), Paul believes that men no longer feel committed or responsible towards women who 'have lost a lot on this'. Although Paul worries that blurring gender roles is destroying the family, he also says everyone should be able to reach their fullest potential. He reconciles these positions by admitting that distinct gender roles may not be a perfect solution, but maintaining they are preferable to today's confusion. Paul bewails loss of respect, for example by the young for the old, and loss of certainty in the 'moral framework' conferred by religion (Paul, Catholic college father, Perth).

Tony and Keith have also been exposed to feminist ideas, taking a positive message from this exposure. In the mid to late 1980s, Tony acquired his emotional literacy through counselling and a men's group. He was propelled there by a second wife who would not accept his alcoholism: 'a person that was prepared to be there with me and I was wanting to be there with her but it wasn't going to be on my terms'. Before this, Tony was 'a rubber stamp of my father and my father was a rubber stamp of his', public bonhomie disguising dysfunctional family relations. Tony discovered that men 'were able to really relate and discuss and talk and be there for one another', instead of talking 'about nothing but women, boats, racing cars'. Through 'going into myself', Tony has moved beyond blaming his father, can 'quite openly cry', and is getting 'on with what I have got and what I'm going to do with it'. Despite all this work, Tony regrets that he still raises his voice when he gets angry, revealing the obstinacy of habitual gender performances (Tony, Catholic college father, Perth).

Keith has also struggled to avoid repeating the 'traditional' male role and attitudes. Keith's father was a toolmaker, although the 'focus' of his life was captainship of the New Zealand soccer team: 'he liked to stay out drinking and partying ... my father would come home late, and there would be a lot of arguments'. Over time, the marital relationship became more equal, as Keith's mother entered paid work and handled 'the money and all of that'. At the age of nineteen Keith left New Zealand for England where he trained as a railway engineer. Keith chooses his words carefully to describe his early attitudes towards women:

> There was a feeling that the male was dominant and the woman was subservient. ... I mean, not dominant in the aggressive or nasty sense. Just a feeling —. [Chilla inserts 'A presumption?'] A presumption that that is the way in which life ... that's obviously definitely not politically correct at the moment. But you can't change the past. You can't change the way in which you were brought up. (Keith, co-educational Protestant college father, Adelaide)

73

Keith believes that men of his generation (those who are self-reflective like Keith) 'can see the intellectual necessity for the change. We can see the logic of it' but this runs aground on the role models they grew up with:

> that ability to intellectualise doesn't necessarily transpose into your ability to actually make day-to-day sense, you know, to conduct your life in accordance with what you intellectually believe is, should happen. And, as I said, there's little doubt that that's had a significant impact. Probably to a point a negative impact, because, umm, it means that I guess relationships are not as full as they should be.

From Keith's perspective, both partners at times operate with 'a measure of hypocrisy', saying one thing (the right thing that our minds agree with) but feeling another (the 'wrong' thing that our parents did, for example women wanting their husbands to investigate the suspicious 'bump in the night'):

> so there are these two levels; there is the intellectual level and the emotional/ internal level. And in people of my generation I don't think that's going to be resolved. Hopefully it'll be better resolved through our children.

Keith predicts 'it will be much easier for my son because the more traditional role is not evident to him'. Keith plays squash with his son, 'coached his soccer' and they share intellectual activities ('through helping him with schooling and that sort of thing'). In terms of traditional gender role disruption:

> My wife has always worked. … My son sees me ironing, he sees me cooking. … My son is seeing a *completely* different person. Umm, so that is going to be a *completely* different role model for him than I had with my father. Equally, my wife does the gardening. She's very good with restoring furniture. … I think he's much more comfortable with women than probably I would have been at his age.

Whereas Paul believes gender relations have changed far too rapidly, other interviewees — like Tony and Keith — experience entrenched 'often unconscious investments in conventional images of masculinity and femininity which cannot easily be reshaped' (McNay in Adkins 2003: 28), unconscious blockages that hinder transparency of the self to itself and others (McNay 2000: 13). As Valerie Walkerdine suggests, the sexual pleasure and desires we have as subjects are only half-consciously articulated and do not yield readily to children's literature in which young girls do 'men's' work (Walkerdine 1984: 183). Despite the apparent challenges to the institution of the heterosexual gendered family from divorce and fertility decline, narratives of romantic love, marriage, reproduction and fidelity remain resilient and cherished (McNay 2000: 93).

Not only Keith, but also some of the women I interviewed, are baffled by a discourse of 'choice' and 'freedom' in the face of institutional barriers as well as the resistance of their own psyches, moulded to a more traditional femininity. Several wondered to me if their actions mean they are yielding inappropriately to a man's wishes or doing something because they genuinely wish to please their partner — for example, dressing in a certain way. Like Keith, Myles, a social studies university student in Melbourne, notes female connivance in traditional gender relations:

> I think women … take on a lot of the stereotypes that are taught to them, without often not even having a problem with it. So I've come to this point where I'm really confused … because if the woman isn't saying it's a problem, is it? And weighing that up against things that are obviously not equal.

Men like Myles experience 'gender vertigo' (Connell 1990: 470-1), or 'total confusion', as Nicola (Protestant college mother, Adelaide) puts it, with no guidance concerning how to respond to women's changed roles. Gabrielle agrees, but suggests:

> it may be that the original women involved in the feminist movement have maybe concentrated on their daughters and forgotten their sons a bit. They've assumed that their sons are like their husbands and fathers, and therefore are perfectly well off. But it will be just that group. I think my son's generation have a fair idea of where they fit and don't have any of those false expectations, I hope. ('Gabrielle', Protestant college mother, Adelaide)

Nettie's son 'jokes about [how] he's going to marry a rich woman and he's going to be the househusband'. Nettie suggests this is both 'a joke' and 'a possibility', given that they have two good friends who 'have sort of had role reversals' ('Nettie', Catholic college mother, Perth). While a number of young men in my sample stridently rejected feminism or women's equality, a handful 'joked' about this, embracing a traditional masculinity but doing so tongue-in-cheek, with a knowingness that is 'postfeminist', only possible for those who are acquainted with feminist ideals, but also, I suggest, less than fully comfortable with them.

Sons deflect feminism in parodic masculinity

> I am 70 years old, I am a retired janitor. I lived my life like a candle in the wind. Never knowing who to cling onto when the rain came in. I am still looking for some emotional stability in my life i.e., someone besides Mrs Palmer (my last name is Palmer). Damm, that woman annoys me. I caught her in watching the TV the other day, I had to shorten her lead. Married life was fun, but impotency is a bitch. (male, co-educational Catholic college student, South Australia)

Keith's and Tony's life changes and young women's claims that they have never experienced any inequality suggest that gender has been detraditionalised (e.g. see Gross 2005: 292), its impact less significant in our lives than it was forty years ago. But some researchers argue that the picture is more complex, and there are ways in which gender has also been 'retraditionalised' in new patterns (e.g. see Adkins 2002; Arnot 2002), revealing that 'masculinity and femininity are dynamic *gender projects*' (Connell 2000: 28, emphasis in original). Where almost all the essays could immediately be identified in terms of the gender of the author, there were also challenges to normative gender scripts. Not only from young women becoming engineers, or proposing to the men they marry, or refusing the mundanity of motherhood — but also from young men who become models, read Jane Austen or drink champagne, but who almost never (apart from the sexuality youth services sub-sample) express homosexual orientation.

Terms like 'mosaic' (Coles 2008) and 'hybrid' masculinities (Messner 2007 for US political leaders; other writers coining 'hybrid' femininities: Paechter and Clark 2007) suggest men now have a wider range of masculine performance available to them. The 'mosaic' performer chooses those aspects of dominant masculinity that suit his capacities, while rejecting others (Coles 2008: 241). In one study of male school students, such reflexivity only arose in one-on-one interviews and only with prompting by the interviewer, after which a number of boys were able to encompass their more egalitarian notions of gender and sexual performance within definitions of masculinity (Imms 2008: 42): 'Let me get what you are saying straight. My ideas are my masculinity and by sticking to them I'm asking others to be more tolerant of a different masculinity? Jeez, I'd dig that!' (Ishmael, in Imms 2008: 34).

As kudos accumulates around jobs that require personal style and performance (e.g. see Sullivan 2004: 209; Barber 2008: 469–70), the fashion industry attracts elite boys' school graduates, such as Nick and Edward. Edward writes of becoming a part-time model as well as joining the army reserves and becoming a forensic scientist. Other young men write of becoming dancers, fashion designers or a butler. However, even if some 'feminine' attributes such as reflexivity and attention to 'appearance, image and style at work' have become 'key resources', particularly in the new service occupations (Adkins 2002; Adkins 2003: 32–4; Adams 2006: 519), gender marking has certainly not disappeared from the work place, and these 'non-traditional' choices are made far less often by young men and women than traditional careers and jobs (see Chapter One).

Less challenging to hegemonic or dominant ideas of masculinity is reflexivity expressed in an ironic parody of pre-feminist masculinities, which 'spring[s]from not being able to inhabit old forms of behaviour without some distance' (Coward

1999: 93; see also Adkins 2003: 36–9). Bourdieu's 'unthought categories of habit … are themselves *corporealized* preconditions of our more self-conscious practices' (Lash 1994 in Adkins 2003: 25, emphasis in original). Lisa Adkins (2003: 36–7) suggests that ambivalence allows a gap between habitus and field, so that it is not mere mimicry but possible ironic parody that occurs when the body expresses a distance from the field: 'Such procedures, moreover, would allow a move away from problematic notions of liberal freedom of the sort found in recent sociological accounts of reflexivity and social change, indeed from the very dilemma of determinism versus freedom' (Adkins 2003: 38–9). Andrea Taylor (2003) argues that young women's postfeminism is this kind of parodic or ironic performance of femininity. The 'postfeminist girlie' *knows* about feminism's critique of femininity and so can be feminine at the same time as she distances herself from the performance. We now live in a world where feminism has made patriarchy visible, thus allowing performances of apparently 'subordinate' femininity as an expression of 'choice', a choice that was not available when subordinate femininity was obligatory. Some academics make a similar claim for the 'new bloke'.

Margaret Henderson (2008: 38) notes that the self-deprecating humour in 'etiquette guides' for men questions the codes of masculinity in a 'postfeminist male under reconstruction' narrative. The 'new bloke' 'gets a laugh' out of 'mock chauvinism', for example by telling 'outrageously sexist jokes' that are 'designed to "take the piss" out of his mates, not out of women' (Mackay 2007: 56). He acknowledges the 'legitimacy of masculine urges, masculine images and masculine culture', while also understanding 'the real point about the gender revolution: men and women, for all their obvious differences, are equal' (Mackay 2007: 60). Rebecca Huntley's (2006: 53) 'New Bloke' is less assured, aware that the 'line between cool, hetero guy and being gay still has to be negotiated carefully by [heterosexual] Y men'.

In attempting to apply the 'male under reconstruction' perspective, it was not always clear to me where the values of my essayists lie, and maybe they were not always sure themselves. In one class with a feminist teacher, three Perth co-educational Catholic school students conclude their essays with a reality check, a statement that their sexual fantasies did not 'really' happen: 'WARNING — this essay <u>does not</u> reflect me in any way'; 'Only joking, I didn't marry any 18 year olds'. The third essayist dreams his politically incorrect fantasy of marrying 20-year-old Playmates in his sixties and seventies, but woke up and 'realised I was still married happily to Jessica with my children old. LIFE WAS GOOD THOUGH!' Two male writers in the co-educational Protestant college school Keith's son attended reverse gender roles, one eschewing firefighting as 'hard work' to become 'a check out chick', the other marrying an 'old millionaire' and inheriting her money (males, co-educational Protestant college students, Adelaide).

Two year 12 literature students in another class with a feminist teacher contributed to each other's questionnaires. Josh, who describes himself as 'sexually frustrated', draws a penis in Nick's essay, which Nick annotates as 'Please note — the above picture is a self portrait of my friend Josh. Anyway, back to me.' In retort, Nick adds a comment to Josh's answer concerning domestic democracy:

> [in black ink:] it must be remembered that women belong in the kitchen. [in different handwriting and blue ink:] Also, changing nappies is not the role of the man — he must be worshipped as a sex god [in black ink and original handwriting:] (my 'friend' Nic wrote that last comment). (Josh and Nick, middle class government high school students, Perth)

Nick, who also describes himself as 'sexually frustrated' even though he is 'better looking than most models', avers he will be 'dead before I am 70' as the 'old are a hassle to others. ... But here is my life story up until I rid this world of the great evil that is myself.' He then describes a life of:

> wild drunken orgies where I am worshipped as a God — after all, who needs a job when you are worshipped as a God. Also, every week there must be a sacrifice made to me in the form of another shipload of sex slaves. ... By the age of 37: I will have been appointed Prime Minister by the people of Australia. ... The most important things I will do in my life are the laws I will pass as PM, as well as replacing America with Australia as the almighty nation. Acts as PM:
> 1. Clone Hitler from DNA strands and people the island of Australia with little Hitlers (n.b. All cabinet members will be sex slaves)
> 2. Sterilisation will be made compulsory
> 3. women will be banished from the workplace and all areas of society that require a minimum intelligence of a monkey's half-brain
> 4. it will be illegal for men to cook, clean or do any housework what so ever
> 5. bigamy will be made compulsory
> 6. naked women's mud wrestling will become Australia's national sport
> 7. our flag of Australia will be replaced with a picture of our mud wrestling champion Olympic team
> 8. I will do to gay men what Hitler did to the Jews
> NAH JUST KIDDING — I'M NOT THAT EVIL (WELL, JUST WAIT AND SEE....)
> HOPE I'VE BEEN A RAY OF SUNSHINE ON YOUR DAY. (Nick, middle class government high school student, Perth)

Apparently responding to the feminist ideas they have learned from their literature teacher, these young men challenge political correctness in what they see as humorous, and occasionally self-deprecating, parodies of traditional male conquest stories in a world where women wait on men 'hand and foot'. This masculinity may be parodic, but I do not think it is self-assured; it appears to require constant cultivation.

Keith's son, who describes himself in his 'I ams' as 'content … goofy, aching, moody', casts himself in his life story as a three times loser in love. The women to whom he proposes 'knocked me back' until his expanding wealth, accumulated through gambling, make him a 'multi-millionaire'. Alas, however, he and his wife divorce after two years. Keith related his son's capacity to mock po-faced feminism with a chauvinism that 'winds up' other family members. Accordingly, I have some confidence in reading this essay, at least, as a knowing parody of traditional masculinity:

> He's also mischievous in that he will trot out some of the traditional male [attitudes]. … And it works *every* time. He reels my daughter in *every* time. So I think it will develop later in her life than with my son. My son seems to have come to some kind, some kind of knowing that my daughter doesn't seem to have stumbled on yet. … She has less of an ability to, to intellectualise about what she's doing, where she's going, what she's trying to do. My son has much more ability to do that and to reflect. … [H]er extreme views — her views about her grandmother [wasting her life as a stay-at-home mother] really did disappoint me. …She has much more difficulty in relating to me than my son does, umm, and he winds me up, too! (Keith, co-educational Protestant college father, Adelaide)

Keith's son can only wind up other family members because he 'knows' them, has an emotional virtuosity that is more often attributed to women, and he 'knows' feminism. The next sub-section identifies the capacity for quite sophisticated analyses of 'mosaic' gender performances among several interviewees.

Girly girls and blokes: Young people's consciousness of gender performance choices

> Ryan does drama and Jacob is extremely cultured, he's the most cultured person I've ever met. He knows wine, coffee, cooking, books, music. He's amazing actually. Any wife he has will be set up for life. He's financial, entrepreneurial, whatever. … Like in my group we don't have any blokes, at all. We have Tanya who does sport, but she also does drama and like we focus on the academics of it. So that's sort of what I'd say with our friendship group. We do have guys but they're not blokes at all. (Zoe, middle class government high school student, Perth)

Zoe, a very bright year 12 student in the same class as Nick and Josh, says her mixed sex friendship group contains neither 'blokes' (sporty muscle-heads) nor 'girlies' (who lack academic ambition). Zoe's understanding that sex-marked bodies (guys) can be distinguished from gender performances (blokes) offers a coherent challenge to traditional gender boundaries (see Paechter and Clark 2007: 342; Heywood 2008: 72). Dominic, a university sociology student, describes the four females in his high school friendship group as 'very, very strong female characters' who challenge gender boundaries by acting 'like a guy' in the case of the 'skater punk girl' or conquering 'the males in terms of academic achievement' in the case of the academic girls, although one of them is also a 'princess' who combines a belief in her ability to 'be anything that she wanted' with the desire to marry a 'bread-winner of the family' (Dominic, sociology university student, Melbourne).

At another school, Edward drinks champagne and loves Jane Austen, believing this could be classified either as the performance of class ('wealthy') or sexuality ('homosexual'), but feels his friends lack the intellectual capital to thus interpret his interest in Jane Austen. Edward asserts that feminism has assisted males and females to 'come more into their own, rather than being ostracised', claiming that women can wear trousers and men 'dress how they want to', although he qualifies, 'probably not skirts' (Edward, Protestant college student, Perth). Elise, a student in the young mothers' Christian school in New South Wales, is less coherent, but grasping for the same point. Army Corps is not for her, as she is a 'real fussy girl', but it is a boys' thing that she believes should be totally available to girls: 'If they want to get involved in it, it's up to them. ... If they want to act more like a girl or if they want to learn about ... boys' stuff.' Kelly dresses and acts comfortably as 'one of the guys', rather than as someone 'girly' who 'doll[s] themselves up' to 'let people know that they are girls'. As a result, when she was attending an agricultural college, Kelly's male co-students never 'really saw me as being a girl, so to speak ... they'd get me to help them [e.g. move furniture] and I did' (Kelly, working class government high school student, South Australia).

These stories of gender diffusion are countered by other tales, experiences of continued gender boundary policing. Leila would, like Kelly, prefer to dress comfortably but her friends

> say things that, you know, show that they have succumbed to conventions like, 'But you can't do that, it's just not girly. It's too butch you know. You're such as tomboy.' ('Leila', Protestant college student, Perth)

Karen's grandson 'never worried about telling everyone' that he learned ballet. But this did not mean his friends accepted his choice without criticism. Karen explained to a taunting boy that ballet improves her grandson's balance and strength for football: 'this kid just said "Oh yeah, sure; it's still a girl thing"' (Karen, middle class government school mature age student, Adelaide).

While required to be 'a bit feminine', as Leila's friends recommend, young women must also avoid being a 'victim', 'the pathetic female' who, for example, complains about abuse by men or cannot stand up for herself. The 'girly-girl' has only herself to blame for not seizing opportunities, or is 'the one to look bad' if she complains about sexual harassment at work (Rich 2005: 501, 502, 504 for an English study; see similar findings for sexual assault complainants in Gotell 2007: 142, 151–2; Easteal and Judd 2008: 336, 341–2).[3] Jasmine feels uncomfortable when her boyfriend makes fun of his mother who is a part-time secretary, but Jasmine admits she is 'quite ditsy' and 'girly' (Jasmine, women's studies university student, Perth). Alannah disparages a female teacher who was 'a complete mess, crying all the time' because she was unable to control her male pupils in a mixed-sex class (Alannah, middle class government high school student, Perth). Furthermore, gender performances are 'accountable' (West and Zimmerman 1987: 136) in the sense that others subject our performances to 'gender assessment' (West and Fenstermaker 2002: 54), usually against widely practised standards.[4]

The boundaries of acceptable femininity have shifted a little but hardly dissolved: being clever or athletic is feminine as long as a girl is not big or ugly or a lesbian. Being in paid work is acceptable as long as a mother puts her husband and children first and does not yearn for the heights of corporate power. Likewise, young men's masculinity tales run the gamut from anxiety concerning blurred gender relations and re-assertion of traditional stereotypes (wives in the kitchen and sex with 18-year-olds), judgment that contemporary gender relations are unfair (particularly concerning divorce settlements), a more benign 'mosaic' playfulness or self-mocking mournfulness for their 'loss of power' (Walter 1998: 161), through to forging 'new men' who are crafting more egalitarian and complex masculinities informed by the feminism of their mothers, fathers and others. Only in this last category are there young men who would heartily agree with many of feminism's ideals for women.

Little wonder, then, that social scientists have discovered the contradiction between females asserting their equality despite evidence of inequality in sharing housework and childcare (Bittman and Pixley 1997: 145–71), in intimate relationships (Chung 2005: 450 and Phillips 2000: 7, 18 on 'date rape'; see also Wilkins 2004 for a Goth scene), or the contortions of managers and equity officers trying to explain the under-representation of women in engineering or IT. According to a European study, managers find this under-representation inexplicable because they eschew the 'victim' and structural inequality discourses (Kelan 2007: 507).

Similarly, an Australian study suggests 'a politics of ignorance and a refusal to know and challenge the role of sexual politics in workplace cultures' (Franzway et al. 2009: 102). The next section explores contradictory attitudes towards gender equality and feminism: awareness when directly asked that gender equality has not been achieved, support for the women's movement's accomplishments, but scant identification with feminism.

Feminism: Too far, too soon, too same

Chilla: Okay, so tell me what you think feminism is, what sort of idea of feminism you've got from these places, sort of thing. …

Hannah: Is it just, I don't know, like male friends talk about girls and they're, they're just for sex, and how girlfriends complain about it, and then you see it in the newspapers, so [unclear as Hannah and Claire talk over each other]. … Okay that chiko roll ad … There's some woman on a motor bike and she's spreading her legs with a chiko between her legs and it had a big write-up about it saying it was a sex symbol and they had to change it. So —

Chilla: So those things shouldn't be, women shouldn't be used that way in advertising?

Hannah: I'm not really fussed to tell you the truth, but it doesn't do anything for me like.

Claire: It annoys me though because every advert I've seen, every bit of music I've seen has got —

Hannah: Has got —

Claire: Half-naked women on it wearing bikinis and they're all pretty and they're all fairly slim.

Chilla: And what, you think that's bad or it's limited or?

Claire: It's bad for young girls because they —

Hannah: And they get a bad rep. [she kindly translates this as 'reputation'] as well and it makes girls heaps self-conscious about themselves because not all girls are slim and they're not all pretty and they've not all got money and stuff. (Claire and Hannah, working class government high school students, Adelaide)

I suggested above that the 'postfeminist girlie' and 'parodic masculinity' are examples of postfeminist gender subjectivity. The common element in the various definitions of postfeminism concerns the purported 'pastness' of feminism. But pastness may be a critical rejection of the women's movement due to obsolescence now that gender equality has been achieved; it may be a mourning for the demise of an activism that is still necessary; it may be a 'backlash' or 'retrosexism' attempting to reverse the gains of feminism. In this move, it is sometimes claimed that men are now suffering disadvantage vis-à-vis women. For example, former Prime Minister John Howard established enquiries into the education of young men in response to claims concerning 'boys' disadvantage' at school (Standing Committee on Education and Training 2002). He proposed amending the sex discrimination legislation to allow Catholic Education to offer scholarships open only to males, to 'correct' the gender balance of teachers in schools (Bacchi and Eveline 2010: 165). In response to men's groups, his government passed the *Family Law Amendment (Shared Parental Responsibility) Act 2006*, which introduced a presumption of equal shared parental responsibility and a new definition of family violence, some feminist commentators arguing that this exposed mothers and children to a greater likelihood of sexual and physical assault. For the first time, in 2010 sexual harassment claims by Western Australian men outnumbered those made by women.[5]

Finally, postfeminism identifies a limited and particular entanglement of feminism and neoliberalism, a co-option of feminist goals to fit 'individualized conservatism and neoliberal depoliticization' (Budgeon 2011a: 10). Conservative commentators have appropriated claims concerning gender equality and contained them within a neoliberal framework, at the same time rejecting feminism's more radical tenets. As Angela McRobbie puts it, feminism has been 'transformed into a form of Gramscian commonsense, while also fiercely repudiated — indeed almost hated' (McRobbie 2004: 4; see also Thomas 1995: 4–5). In the hands of apologists for neoliberal capitalism, the transformative revolutionary movement imagined by women's liberationists — 'smash the patriarchy' — has become little more than individualist entitlement to consumption. Feminism in practice is no longer critical of and opposed to institutional power but has been incorporated as a pale version of liberal feminism, focusing on technocratic and managerial outcomes, on evaluation and best practice. Where these initiatives have been assessed, there is evidence of some rhetorical shifts but little evidence of substantive changes in the status of women (Budgeon 2011: 14). This section explores the contradictions in respondents' attitudes towards feminism and gender equality.

Given that baby boomers lived through and made women's liberation while their daughters only read about and inherited it, there are generational differences in the sources of feminism, younger women being much more reliant on second-hand stories, relayed in classrooms or the mainstream media (see Campo 2005: 67–8; Bulbeck 2011). Naomi suggests that young people find feminism as

> just little bits and pieces. ... Because, you know, I don't go out and do big rallies or anything like that, so I'm not there myself. So the next best thing

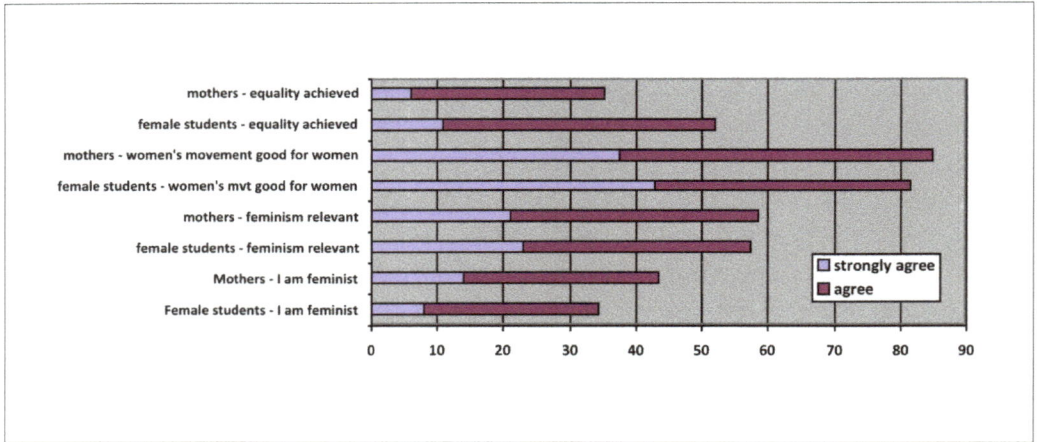

Chart 2.1: School students and their parents compared on attitudes to feminism and the women's movement: Gender by generation: Females

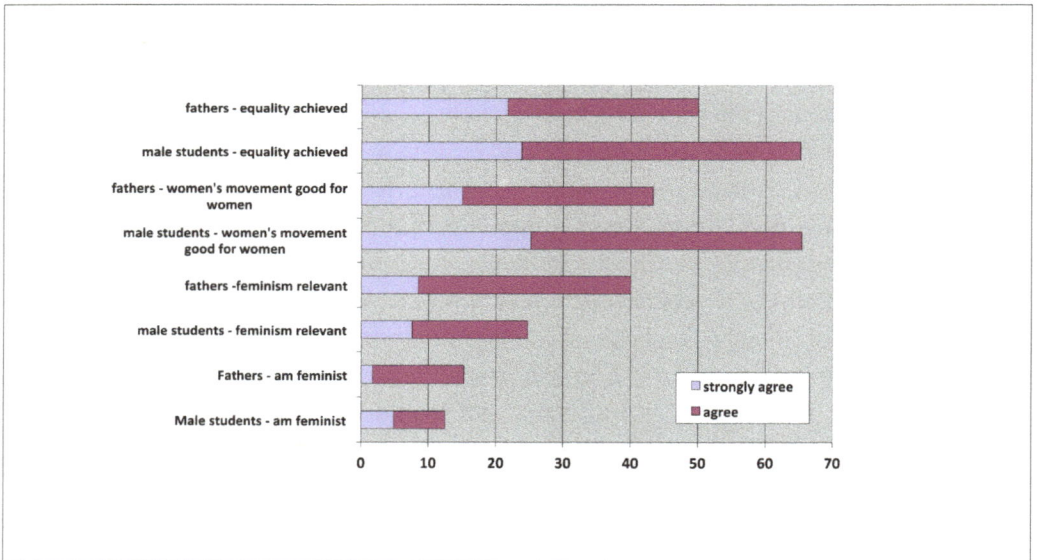

Chart 2.2: School students and their parents compared on attitudes to feminism and the women's movement: Gender by generation: Males

is TV, watching, you know? (Naomi, middle class government high school student, Adelaide)

Following Karl Mannheim (1959), studies of intergenerational responses to feminism suggest that warm attitudes towards feminism belong to the baby-boomer generation who forged women's liberation, rather than to the daughters who inherited the movement, and so garnered feminist understanding from secondary sources. This means less emotional attachment as well as less knowledge (e.g. see Pilcher 1998: 124; Everingham et al. 2007). Kate, an Adelaide high school student, expresses 'respect' for the women who gave her generation of women equal opportunities. But, not having lived through the change, 'we can't really have the same passion about it that perhaps our grandmothers or mothers had'. Chart 2.1 reveals that mothers are more likely to identify as feminist and are less likely to believe equality has been achieved than their daughters. However, both generations have similar attitudes towards the value of the women's movement and the relevance of feminism. Fathers also express a greater closeness to feminism than do young men, in a stronger belief in its relevance to their lives, willingness to define as feminist, and — it could be argued — their stronger apprehension that equality has not been achieved (see Chart 2.2).

Natasha Campo (2009: 7) argues that the media narrative 'composes', both in the sense of intersecting 'collective memory' with personal experience/memory and in offering 'a feeling of composure', allowing 'contradictory aspects of our experience [to] be suppressed'. Campo (2009: 8, 14, 29–56) argues that the 'rise' of feminism in the 1980s offered the successful image of women as career women, whether or not easily combined with motherhood.[6] This positive media construction became more negative with claims concerning a 'generation gap' in which feminism has failed — particularly young women but also full-time mothers. Young women were incited to 'distance themselves from and critique their elders — their foremothers' for their 'failures' and 'false promises', in particular that women could 'have it all': career and motherhood. This narrative became 'common sense' by 2001 (Campo 2009: 111, 182). In fact, the young women in my sample do not express the 'feminism failed me' mantra, perhaps because most of them have not yet had to deal with the tension between career and motherhood (c.f. the young mothers in Everingham et al. 2007: 430–1). The majority did, however, consider feminism redundant and irrelevant, 'outdated' and no longer 'necessary' now that they personally had equal rights, did not experience discrimination, and that 'men/guys [don't] think any less of females' (see Baker 2008; Robinson 2008: 158, 177; Huntley 2006: 42–3 for similar findings concerning young women's belief in the irrelevance of feminism).

The almost universal progressive contention that Australian women are better off than ever is expressed in the large majority of young people (four-fifths of females and two-thirds of males) who believe the women's movement has been good for women. However, less than one in 10 young women unhesitatingly defined themselves as feminist (see Charts 2.1 and 2.2). Instead, they were feminist 'in my own way: I would not, however, call myself a "typical/generalised feminist"'. They rejected what they assumed was a homogenising movement: 'I am a strong female who believes some of the beliefs feminists fight for but I am individual and will not conform to a stereotype.' The 'stereotype' was often a media-constructed image of 'a fanaticized feminism' (Budgeon 2011b: 287): 'pathetic', 'ridiculous', 'bullshit', 'angry', 'militant', 'bra-burning', 'waving the placards and things', in 'boots, overalls and shirts', 'hairy armpit brigade', and 'man-hating' 'extremists'.

Gender inequality: All about male disadvantage

> they [men] have a lot more on their shoulders. Like a son, your dad may expect you to be a doctor or a lawyer, something big, but if you're a girl, they're more easy on you. Even men are not supposed to be crying or expressing their emotions, that's weak of them if they do that … whereas women can go off and cry and do whatever they want. … That's why apparently women live longer than men because they can express their emotions. (Evelyn, girls' middle class government high school student, Sydney)

The mothers in my sample are most aware that gender equality has not been achieved, followed by daughters, fathers and then the sons, two-thirds of whom agree more than disagree with this proposition (see Chart 2.1). When discussing areas of women's inequality, the vast majority cited work (income inequality and occupational segregation) followed by women's under-representation in politics. Several linked these public issues to women's greater obligations for childrearing. Interestingly, however, for my sample men's disadvantage was of more concern, at least in terms of the comments made.

While Michelle, a women's studies university student, saw the need for affirmative action as something that 'created inequality to create equality', more commonly respondents expressed concern about the unfair reverse discrimination men suffered. Eight female respondents (and two males) complained in these sorts of ways: 'I don't see why a woman should get it over a man'; 'It's not about capacity any more'; 'sometimes women are given more of a chance than men'. Proffered examples of feminist excess included assisted reproductive rights for lesbian couples, abortion rights, sexual harassment legislation and government appointments of females.

Much of the identification of male disadvantage was based on the disadvantages of the 'traditional' male role, as suggested by Evelyn, quoted above, noting the negative impact of expectations concerning career success and repressing emotions.

For Lucy, a women's studies student, females have a wider range of choices: 'we can go and wear boys' clothes but boys can't wear girls' clothes'. Jacinta, a Catholic college student, noted that a man who chose to stay at home as a full-time carer would be 'a bit frowned on', even Jacinta finding the image 'very strange' (Jacinta, co-educational Catholic college student, Perth). Respondents do not consider that men's apparently limited choices actually express the structural superiority of being male: women can now dress 'up' whereas men who dress 'down' appear to be embracing an inferior subject position.

Lucy says of men, 'They're actually, as far as I'm concerned more disadvantaged gender-wise than what women are.' Lucy works behind a bar where a male co-worker ('I'm actually stronger than him') suffers discrimination because he is never offered assistance by the stronger men in moving the 'big-arse bucket' full of ice, 'whereas when a chick has to move it, the guys will come up and say, "Do you want me to do it for you?"'. Unlike Lucy's mother, who sees such assistance as patronising, Lucy is quite happy to accept the offer. For her, equality means that stronger workers assist weaker workers, irrespective of gender. Lucy tells another story of the 'gender stereotype ... that it's disadvantaging men in some circumstances rather than women': the different treatment of males and females at the motor vehicle repair shop, where everything is explained to the 'chick' and obscurantist terminology is used on the 'guy', who is going 'I have no idea but I'm not allowed to say that because I'm a man'. Lucy has other examples. A woman can play 'dumb blonde' and avoid a traffic infringement for a faulty headlight. Bouncers are unwilling to remove drunken females from nightclubs because they are concerned that they will fall prey to sexual assault. Men 'walk into a courtroom against a woman, they're instantly wrong', and restraining orders are issued 'at the drop of the hat' but 'it's much harder for a man to get a restraining order'.

Claims that women experience discrimination are exaggerations, according to Lucy: 'I've done sport and been the only chick in the competition and I was never treated any differently.' She turns to her friend, Michelle, who worked in the mines for confirmation. Michelle answers:

> I did get treated differently because I got my truck driving licence ... and I had so many more qualifications, like written qualifications, study qualifications, to work on the mines than a lot of guys, but I would get to the interview stage because they read it all and things like that, see my size and go, wait, no, hang on. (Michelle, women's studies university student, Perth)

This does not faze Lucy, who then argues that a 'big beefy boy' is stereotyped as an 'Aussie brute' or 'a butcher', no-one raising a murmur by contrast with the absolute 'outrage' when women are stereotyped.

Primed no doubt by the rhetoric of some federal politicians and by men's rights groups (e.g. see Henderson 2008: 38), other interviewees noted a major flashpoint in the men's disadvantage discourse, that is, custody of children: 'I mean an immediate thought that the woman is the best person for children to live with, it just doesn't sit with me' (Linda, middle class government high school mother, Perth). As with many people discussing this issue, the example of a friend piques their criticism. Karen has 'friends' 'where the woman gets the children (and that's fine), and the man should pay maintenance (and that's okay)', until the woman remarries, has 'another job', 'a lovely home' and 'a husband that provides for them'. Meanwhile, the husband has remarried and 'is trying to keep a wife — a new wife — a house, and he's also paying ridiculous amounts of maintenance to the children still'. This seems 'totally unfair' because the man 'is supporting two [households]' and the woman has 'got it all', meaning the kids and extra financial support (Karen, Catholic college mother, Adelaide).

While a handful of interviewees and respondents mentioned violence against women when discussing the issue of gender equality, almost as many interviewees echoed the men's rights movement's (false)[7] claims that men are disadvantaged when it comes to domestic violence and rape. Interviewees suggested that women have a better chance of winning sexual harassment cases, that raped men cannot use the rape support services established for women, and that women 'can get a restraining order at the drop of the hat', as Lucy put it. Four young male interviewees complained that employers appoint females on the basis of physical attractiveness or are seduced by the 'can-do' girl image (Harris 2004) to believe that women make better workers.

Lucy claims that men 'need their own revolution' through which they can develop communication skills, express their feelings and work out whether to hold the door open for women. Married men in one study experienced 'Frustration. Despair. Anger. Misery. Resignation' in relation to sex, begging or asking for an experience that clearly was not giving their wives sexual pleasure (Townsend 1994: 109–11). Instead of blaming women or recommending that females willingly and smilingly provide sexual services (Tyler 2008: 367: see also Carpenter 1998: 162), some feminists suggest that males be exposed to a different kind of sex education, one that places men's responsibility for consensual pleasure on them (for example, directing the rape prevention message at males in sex education classes: Maguire 2008: 79), and that explores emotional commitment and responsibility. Such sex education would challenge normative masculinity that the male is meant to make the running, is meant to score: 'you've got to be treating the girls badly' (Powell 2008: 176). Such alternative masculinities can be taught, being more widespread among male Swedish students (Johansson 2007: 3, 80). In Australia, too, there are some limited signs of young Australian men challenging masculinity from a feminist perspective, beyond parodic masculinity. For example, in 2011 a group of teenage boys at Sydney Boys High School chose to tackle the issue of gender inequality in their school presentation to 600 other boys (High Resolves 2011). However, as the next chapter explores, young women's psychic skills and orientations have changed more vis-à-vis their mothers than is the case for males.

Conclusion

> Society will have become less a pain in the arse and something useful and women will have hopefully realised they don't have to be a size 8 with big boobs to be wonderful. (female, youth service client, Adelaide)

Whereas the mothers almost invariably shared a social imaginary of women's intergenerational progress, often linking this with the achievements of the women's movement, the majority of fathers were baffled by my request to compare their lives with that of their fathers and sons. The puzzlement and resistance of fathers mean that their sons are not, on the whole, witnessing new performances of masculinity. Nevertheless, I found some evidence of sons who expressed more awareness of feminism's impact on gender relations than the fathers' generation generally did. Usually, however, parodic masculinity safely distanced this understanding from real questioning of young men's lives and values. As the next chapter explores, comfortable acceptance of gender equality was extremely rare in young men's life stories — for example, as expressed in shared parenting or staying home to raise children.

In the half dozen interviews I undertook with a mother and daughter together, it was like eavesdropping on an ongoing conversation about gender relations and feminism. Mothers and daughters had distinct opinions but there was evidence of 'mentoring each other' in relations that are 'as much about friendship as parent-child connections' (Andres and Wyn 2010: 171). There were no father-son interview pairs in my research, but the individual interviews yielded little evidence of this mutual mentoring, apart from Tony and Keith, who understand gender relations through a feminist lens. This does not mean that children do not learn from observation of their parents, as Kathleen Gerson (2010) found. But I would suggest that the lack of intergenerational conversation and role modelling gender differences from fathers to sons contributes to the emotional muteness of young men. The lack of 'role models', for example, in balancing desires for education, work and parenthood, further leaves young people 'floundering' (Andres and Wyn 2010: 199), not that my respondents have fully realised this just yet, as the next chapter explores.

Notes

[1] When asked if women 'have it better today than they did in the past', 83 per cent of women and 76 per cent of men say better, but only 35 per cent of men and 45 per cent of women say men are better off (Gerson 2010: 189).

[2] Margaret Henderson's (2006: 224–35) review of popular men's books on feminism and gender reveals men's difficulties in 'speaking about the feminist legacy', which they confront in 'stammers and stutters marking historical trauma'. In Helen Townsend's (1994: 2–3, 34, 39) study of 350 Australian men, she was 'startled' to discover 'how little men really know of their fathers', seeing them as 'estranged and indifferent' and 'distant'. The exceptions were most often found in non-Anglo families, where a Dutch father played games and laughed a lot and an Italian father kissed his son every day.

[3] In Canada and Australia, the 'good' (most likely to be successful) sexual assault complainant is 'marked by her/his consistency, rationality and self-discipline', is 'prudent' in not behaving stupidly (Chunn et al. 2007: 22; Gotell 2007: 142, 151–2), and has 'a rational (masculine) demeanor/presentation in giving evidence' (Easteal and Judd 2008: 336, 341–2).

[4] In one study, teenage girls rejected sexualised descriptions of their tight-fitting, low cleavage tops as well as the suggestion that they dressed thus to attract attention, but this did not stop men from 'perving' and 'beeping their horns' (Gleeson and Frith 2004: 107–9).

[5] Male complaints concerned discrimination in job applications and other workplace treatment as well as denial of entry to bars for wearing jewellery (as women do) or because there were too many men inside already (Hammond 2011: 1). For Sue Price, spokeswoman for Men's Rights Agency, 'society had swung too far in favour of women and men were fighting back' (journalist paraphrasing). For Paul Pule, secretary of the WA Men's Advisory Network, the results reflected a generational change and men's increased emotional vocabulary (Hammond 2011: 1).

[6] The 1980s media images were 'upbeat and positive about feminism and the possibilities for fulfilment, pleasure and progress it had brought about' (Campo 2009: 8–9). They constituted the Career Woman (professional women in suits and pearls in their corner offices), the 24 Hour Woman (a full life expressed in consumption of travel, cosmetics, clothing, sports and fitness: Campo 2009: 29–54) and the 'Happy Working Mother', 'who defined herself through her ability to perform multiple roles', not as 'Superwomen' but as normal women (Campo 2009: 56).

[7] A survey of 19,000 Australians in 2001/02 found that 4.8 per cent of men and 21.1 per cent of women had been forced or frightened into unwanted sexual activity, many of them (2.8 per cent of men and 10.3 per cent of women) when they were 16 years of age or under (Australian Research Centre in Sex, Health and Society, circa 2003: 3). By contrast, men are more exposed to (and overwhelmingly the perpetrators of) other forms of violence. Writing of civil war scenarios, Adam Jones (2006a: 201) claims 'the most vulnerable and consistently targeted population group, throughout time and around the world today, is noncombatant men of "battle age", roughly fifteen to fifty-five years old'. This is because an invading or ruling force sees them as the greatest threat, and so they are wounded, killed and tortured; 'eager liberation fighters' or suicide bombers should not be seen as 'asking for it' but as victims of masculine scripts (Jones 2006b: 237).

3

EMOTIONAL LITERACY
AND DOMESTIC RELATIONS

Introduction

> the worlds of men and women appear to be spiralling away from each other.
> (Arnot 2002: 262)

The young women's and men's life stories discussed in Chapter One reveal that, in many relationships, a good deal of emotion work will be needed to connect the female stories of romance to the male stories of sex, before, after and during marriage. These essays also hinted at the unequal distribution of emotional capacities needed to negotiate such complex relationships. Chapter Two explored intergenerational changes, suggesting mothers have bequeathed their daughters a progressive and empowering narrative of changed gender relations but fathers have not prepared their sons in the same way. My claim for a disjunction between expectations in intimate relationships and the emotional literacy brought to the project by each partner is the topic of this chapter. Biographers are more or less self-aware, and more or less reflexive, in assessing the intersection of their ambitions with society's resources and constraints (Adams 2006: 514–6; Adkins 2003: 25).

As the comparison between Anne Summers' essayists and mine revealed, if anything young women today are more committed to marriage and motherhood than their mothers were (see Chart 1.1, Chapter One). The difference is not in the desire to have children but in the desire to combine this with paid work, a challenge for which their parents' experiences provide little modelling (Andres and Wyn 2010: 230). The 'fields' of work and family are misaligned, making it difficult for young women, in particular, to 'inhabit' both (see Andres and Wyn 2010: 21, 236). The young women who achieve so well in the field of education suffer in the field of work, which assumes the habitus of a male lifestyle. Young women rather than young men adjust their lifestyle (Andres and Wyn 2010: 239), for example regretfully delaying marriage and parenting: 'The personal politics of child-rearing have remained highly gendered' (Andres and Wyn 2010: 181, 237). Lacking the parental blueprint of inherited recipes, young people must craft an 'experimental life'. They do not know if they can bring marriage, parenthood, public activity and paid work together (Beck and Beck-Gernsheim 2002: 26).

Marriage, an institution once above the individual, is now 'a product and constraint of the individuals forming it' (Beck and Beck-Gernsheim 2002: 8). In the past, marriage prescribed what the husband and wife could do in terms of work, economic behaviour and sexuality (Beck and Beck-Gernsheim 2002: 9). Today, for example in no-fault divorce based on 'irretrievable breakdown', 'the why, what and how long of marriage are placed entirely in the hands and hearts of those joined in it' (Beck and Beck-Gernsheim 2002: 11). But this imposes the negotiation of contradictory desires and requirements on family members. Custody and child support have become heated flashpoints between men and women.

Anthony Giddens (1991: 94–7) addresses this situation through his concept of the 'pure relationship', grounded in 'mutual trust' and 'intimacy', both of which require psychological 'work' of the sort recommended in self-help manuals. The 'pure relationship' can be terminated at will, is only 'good until further notice' (Giddens 1991: 186–7). Heterosexual couples are no longer bound together by convention, unwanted parenthood or indissoluble marriage bonds. Sustaining the pure relationship requires each partner to achieve 'self-mastery' or 'self-identity' in their reflexive project of the self combined with 'the development of intimacy with the other' through 'reflexive questioning' ('is everything all right?'; Giddens 1991: 91, 97). The pure relationship is mobilised through 'authenticity', to know oneself and reveal that knowledge to the other, potentially putting enormous strains on the relationship (Giddens 1991: 187–8).[1]

Ulrich Beck's terms, 'reciprocal individualization' (Beck and Beck-Gernsheim 2002: 7; Beck 2002: xxi), 'altruistic individualism' (Beck and Beck-Gernsheim 2002: 157), 'self-organized concern for others' (Beck 2002: 213) and 'co-operative or altruistic individualism' (Beck 2002: 212), identify this interlinked necessity to work on the relationship to work on the self and vice versa. Beck and Beck-Gernsheim (2002: xxiii) state that, 'co-operative individualism ... presupposes that each [partner of a couple] has a right to a life of his or her own and that the terms of living together have to be negotiated in each case'. In other words, in intimate relationships, there are now '*three* careers — his, hers, and theirs' (Gerson 2010: 201, emphasis in original), requiring a level of interaction and compromise, which the traditional gender-differentiated household did not. This suite of skills could be described as psychological capital, after Pierre Bourdieu's (1984) construction of cultural capital: the capacity to craft the therapeutic self and its modes of negotiation, to articulate the authentic self and its desires, and do this within the context of other authentic selves with their desires.

Giddens and Beck generally propose gender-neutral descriptions of the 'pure relationship' and 'reciprocal individualization' (but see Giddens 1991: 91; Giddens 1994: 187; Beck and Beck-Gernsheim 2002: 59), in the same way that Charles Lemert and Anthony Elliott (2006: 17) cheerfully conclude their discussion of individualisation by asserting that mutual dependence makes everyone 'remarkably cooperative'. Generally, however, the therapeutic self-help literature, which suggests that *Men are from Mars and Women are from Venus* (John Gray), is closer to the mark. In this literature, the disadvantages of femininity are rebadged as women's superior capacity for 'emotion work' (Murphy 2001). Psychological capital is in fact 'emotional labour', a term coined by Arlie Hochschild (1983) and used by feminists to signal that it is work and an obligation that falls disproportionately on women rather than men (e.g. see review of the literature in Murachver and Janssen 2007). Young women have 'more personalized and more reflexive processes of decision-making' while young men 'cling on to traditional male roles, traditional family structures and local (territorial and community) identities' (Arnot's study cited in McLeod and Yates 2006: 206). Very few of the young men in my sample indicated skills and interest in empathy, responsibility, cooperation and social competence (a result confirmed by other research).[2]

This chapter explores the different 'choices' that young women and men in my research are likely, it appears, to make in their domestic lives. The evidence suggests that the 'half won' gender revolution (Esping-Andersen 2009; Gerson 2010) puts males and females on a collision course. A comparison of young people's subjectivities as implied in their 'I am' statements reveals that young women identify much more in terms of an independent subject who is also connected with significant others than do the young men. The different meanings of 'settling down' in male and female life stories suggest the male breadwinner role is essential to adult masculinity, despite the strong undertow of dreams of freedom from this mundane slavery. Young women's ambivalence does not, in the majority of cases, concern the role of either mother or earner or indeed how to combine the two. Instead, they resolve role conflict with presumed support — both physical and emotional — in the domestic sphere, support that may not be forthcoming. This is revealed both in the life story essays and in a comparison of young men's and women's attitudes to three questionnaire items on domestic democracy: sharing housework and childcare, role reversal and abortion decisions. Not only are young men less committed to domestic democracy than young women are, their discussion of these three issues again exposes the different amounts of psychological capital each gender brings to negotiating differences. The complexities of making abortion decisions where both partners may not agree highlights gender divergent understanding of responsibilities and rights. Young women align the two whereas young men are more likely to assert their right to be part of this decision, whether or not they share responsibility for rearing the unborn child. Again, the gap between what men and women want is exacerbated by their different capacities and willingness to negotiate contradictory expectations.

Emotional literacy: Crafting a choice biography in the company of others

> I know whatever I do I will do it as best as I can. … I know I will make something of myself and I know I will help others to do the same thing. I hope that I have helped at least one person to realise that … they are special & loved & worth being loved over & over again … that no matter what has happened, no matter how bad they feel life has gotten they will reach a time where they can look back on it all & feel strong enough to call it their <u>past</u>, not their present, not an indicator of their future & not who they are. As a survivor of sexual assault, domestic violence, substance abuse, teenage pregnancy and many other common life issues, I feel like I really have an understanding of where people are coming from when they say that life is not worth living. (Siobhan, working class government high school student, Perth)

For all their assertive independence, youthful selves must be lived in conjunction with other selves. Siobhan, the young mother quoted above, encapsulates her life in a set of reciprocal relationships: 'Been a teacher & been taught; Been a lover & been loved … felt immense power & felt powerless'. Carol Smart (2007: 29–30) shifts the emphasis from the 'I' of the DIY biography to the 'me' (to use G.H. Mead's formulation) of 'personal life', which links the 'individual' to the 'social' via the personal. The life story unfolds in a 'time of being-with-others' (Ricoeur 1980: 188). Young people may 'choose' to develop and realise themselves, but it will be in negotiated partnerships and collectives: family, friends, work, and community organisations. The evidence presented in this chapter suggests that young women are more adept than the young men at negotiating intimate partnerships. Given that young middle class women can choose independence rather than settle for less than fulfilling partnerships, at least until they become mothers, they are likely to leave young men puzzled and dissatisfied.

'I am': independent and interdependent?

> I am: Capable of looking after myself, stubborn, willing to listen to other people, not willing to have people tell me what to do or think, selfish when it comes to caring & loving people, caring but guarded, motivated, sociable, the most important person in my son's life, me. (female, young mothers' Christian school student, New South Wales)

> I am: Wanting the best for all my family, not just me to be happy and fulfilled, bitchy and critical at times, a good mum, nurse, free and independent — enjoy being independent, confident with my own company … happy being me. (Chris, co-educational Catholic college mother, Perth)

The above quotations, drawn from 'I am' statements, support the 'detraditionalisation' of gender thesis discussed in the previous chapter: women 'can be individuals now, which they couldn't before' (young woman in Summers 2003: 27). Chris is 'a good mum' and a 'nurse' as well as being 'independent' and 'happy being me'. Similarly the young mother is both 'the most important person in my son's life' and 'me'; she is 'caring but guarded' and won't be told what to think.

While a 'highly honed reflexivity' (McLeod and Yates 2006: 7, 115) was expressed by a handful of middle class male youth in my sample, it was explored much more richly and extensively by the middle class females. Thus my findings echo Jennifer Coates (2003: 76–7), whose English study of all male conversations found 'emotional honesty and openness' was extremely rare. This can be seen in Charts 3.1 and 3.2, which map the 'I am' statements according to independence and interdependence. Young women are more likely than young men to define themselves in terms of their autonomy: individuality ('me', 'unique', 'different', 'important') and independence ('independent', 'a loner', 'my own person', 'selfish', 'competitive'). They are also more likely to define themselves in connection with others, either in terms of a relationship ('loving partner', 'good friend', 'daughter of parents', 'friend of my friends') or dyadic self-descriptions ('friendly', 'caring', 'loyal', 'helpful', 'trustworthy'). Young women have a robust sense of their personhood as a negotiated outcome: 'A people's person but I also need my own space'; 'Self dependant, Respectful of others needs … a happy & supportive friend'. Catholic school females appeared most adept at this, disproportionately defining themselves

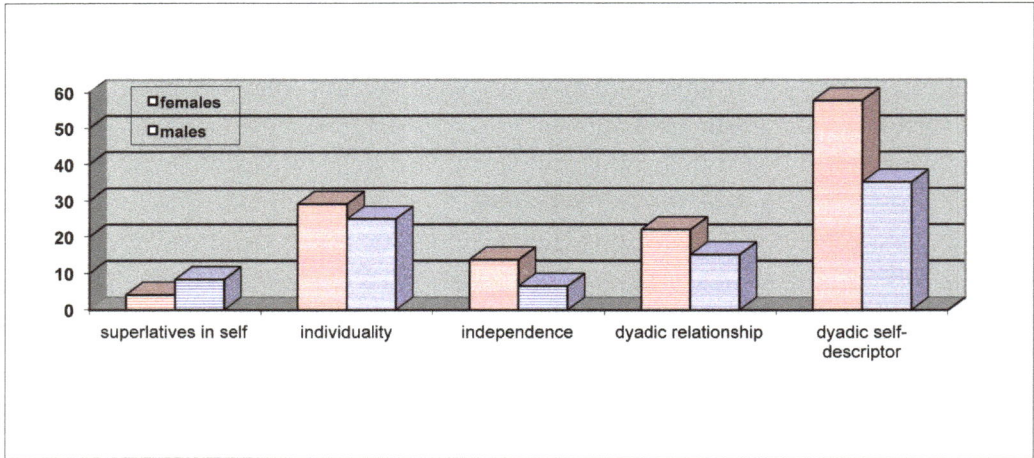

Chart 3.1: A selection of responses to 'I am …': Young people x gender

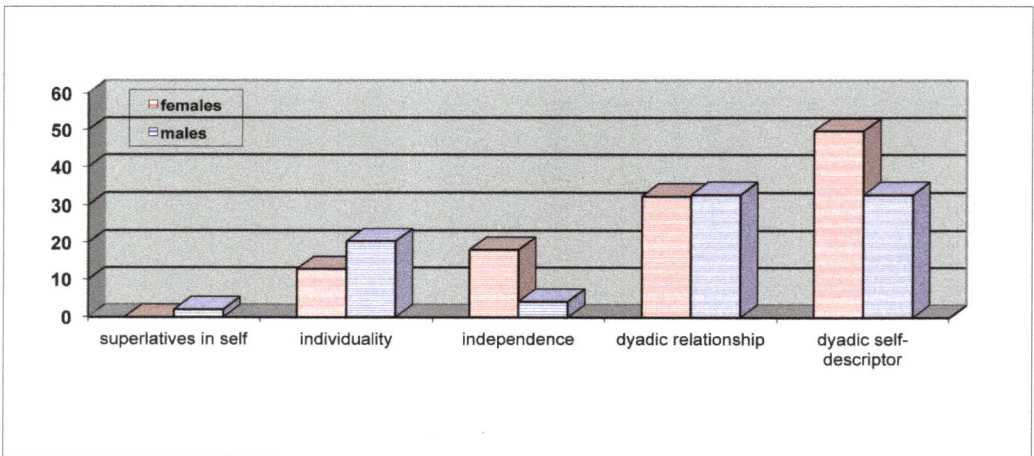

Chart 3.2: A selection of responses to 'I am …': Parents x gender

in terms of individualism and interdependence — on average more than one of their 'I ams' (see Tables A3.7 and A3.8 in Appendix 3).

This compares with the rigid individuality of many young men, expressed in anxious superlatives that make connection and negotiation with others more difficult ('a hero', 'Spiderman', 'deadly', 'amazing', 'invincible', 'great', 'number one', 'fantastic'). The male students attending disadvantaged schools and the clients of disadvantaged youth services (the majority of whom were Aboriginal) were the most likely to use superlatives in their self-descriptions. That this expresses fragile identity is further suggested by a lower recording of 'I ams' indicating a positive self-perception among these groups (see Tables A3.7 and A3.8 in Appendix 3).

The male quest for invincibility is also reflected in some of the life stories. In one class in a private school, a young male — something of a ringleader — expressed initial resistance to completing a life story. I asked him to jot down a few points. Instead he came up with a prototypical male fantasy in which he established 'Jolt Cola', which 'put all other colas out of business' as he amassed 'a hundred billion dollars'. He fought in 'World War 3', winning the 'VC medal', became an 'Aussie icon' and married Linda. His son, Peter the 2nd, became Prime Minister. Linda had an affair and:

> fled to Russia to escape my wrath but Peter the 2nd has launched the nuclear warheads to her exact longitude and latitude location. I just died a happy man in bed with a supermodel, my second wife of two days. Peter the 2nd takes control of the empire. (male, Protestant college student, Adelaide)

His 'I ams' combine assertion of a dominant gender and ethnic identity with superlatives: 'Male, cool, the coolest, 16, me, not you, not a female, white, extremely good looking, your worst nightmare'. A collectively imagined female narrative of world domination by three female friends in a Sydney Catholic college initially appeared to be as merciless as any of the young men's science fiction-like scenarios. One writes: 'I plan to take over the world and rework it, not making it a better place, but a place that generally and honestly suits my own needs and wants.' However, the other two braid their world domination into a tale of interdependence. To reverse overpopulation, they kill a third of the world's population (painlessly, with a biological weapon and genetically engineered crops), 'eradicated indiscriminately all the people who have started wars and enforce unreasonable rules', reduce crime by increasing the price of bullets, and undertake research to eliminate poverty. One of these essayists gives 'lots of money to charity — because there are millions of kids who need my money more than I will'.

In the parent sample, too, mothers 'suture' independence with interdependence in their self-descriptions (see Roseneil's (2007) notion of 'sutured selves' indicating how the psychic self connects to others).[3] However, fathers and mothers are equally likely to identify themselves in dyadic relationships, family being the most important. Only a tiny handful of fathers reach for superlatives; more identify their individuality. But not a single mother describes herself in superlatives.

When the *Sydney Morning Herald* published an opinion piece based on my findings in January 2004, a young father was moved to email me saying that, while his adolescent dreams might have been focused around sex and cars, he was now a responsible man committed to work and family. Lacking longitudinal data, I cannot establish how the young people in my research will change in a decade or two's time. However, Table A3.5 in Appendix 3, comparing selected 'I am' statements for the two generations in my sample, suggests that the father who emailed me was not alone in shifting from youthful preoccupations to the responsible masculinity of fatherhood. Young women and men are more preoccupied by sex, love and romance than their parents, for whom relationship, family and employment are more important. From this we might conclude that when men and women come together in relationships the rough edges of difference are honed in interaction; they move from divergent goals of sex or romance, sports or family, towards a common commitment. While there is some evidence for this, in both generations females define themselves more by their social connections than males do. Females are far more likely to identify in terms of being in a romantic relationship, being a family group member or a friend and, for the mothers, being family-oriented. Family relationships bulk so large in the mothers' identities that on average they mentioned these relationships more than once: often as 'mother' and 'wife', and at almost twice the rate men identify themselves as 'husband', 'father' or other family member.

Where classic liberalism imagined a self-sufficient male who sprang fully formed into the polity, and classical economics imagined a *homo economicus* expressing his preferences without regard to the needs of others, feminists have long argued that this is a fiction of male theory. We are all raised in dependence on adult others; we all live our lives in interaction with others. The imagined female author of the do-it-yourself biography is just as much a fiction of untrammelled autonomy. On the other hand, as Shelley Budgeon (2011a: 153) notes, the 'distinctive value of autonomy [has been] invoked by feminism' as a critique of longstanding feminine dependence. Feminist activism for women's independence from men has contributed to the image of the 'can-do' girl, sometimes posited in media commentary as singularly self-sufficient in the mode of the male of classical political or economic theory. 'Femininity now involves living a tension between exercising the traditional feminine mode of relationality and the exhibition of individualized agency previously associated with masculinity' (Gonick in Budgeon 2011b: 285). Thus, young women express a stronger sense of individuality (although not independence) than their mothers, and even in some senses than young men in my research. But this individuality is not won at the cost of interdependence. Young women situate their own life projects in the context of living with others, negotiating with the life projects of those around them, as a comparison of Vanessa's and Nick's imagined relationships reveals.

Psychological capital

> I see happiness in marriage and I think you have to work for it to attain it so
> I believe that it is achievable. … I would definitely like to have a person that
> I could share my life with so I'm not alone because I am a big people person.
> (Stephanie, Catholic college student, Sydney)

Interdependent independence is 'a relation in which the other is always present'
(Castoriadis in McNay 2000: 153). In the same way that Giddens articulates the
construction of 'self-mastery', autonomy comes from continuously 'regarding,
objectifying, setting at a distance, detaching and finally transforming the discourse
of the Other into the discourse of the subject' (Castoriadis in McNay 2000: 152).
Autonomy is thus desired for both self and others, a proposal that moves beyond 'a
masculine will to transcendence against a feminine will to connection' (McNay 2000:
153; see also Budgeon 2011a: 146–52). Charmaine, who writes 'I am: somebody
who doesn't want to rely on a man to keep me happy', suggests:

> I don't really want to rely on other people much. I want to do things for myself
> and be an individual and that as well. But I want to do things with other
> people at the same time. (Charmaine, middle class government high school,
> Adelaide)

I asked Charmaine how she would achieve this as a mother and her answer
endorses Castoriadis' notion of autonomy: 'I … don't mind people relying on me for
a while. Like, I like helping people to be able to rely on themselves.'

A number of young women understand that constructing the psychic self
through interaction is work, is labour. This labour is both the purpose of relationships
and the guarantee of their success (see Huntley 2006: 80–3): 'I have found one
partner who I shared an honest, true and passionate love with. It has been hard but
completely worth it.' As Stephanie suggests in the quotation above, essayists identify
partnerships as an earned outcome, 'a compromising and loving partnership' in which
the couple must try 'hard to make it work'. Relationships that fail are valuable if they
teach lessons that make subsequent commitments successful (see Hughes 2005: 73).
In this vein, Alannah writes in her life story that she is 'completely heart-broken'
when her relationship ends, but 'I realised that … I had learnt a great lesson in love
that would in the future help me find the person I would finally stay with'. Although
her ultimate relationship also has its 'ups and downs, mainly stresses over money
and our career paths', Alannah learns to work 'out an arrangement that favoured
both our lives' and that 'my life became more about our needs rather than just mine'
(Alannah, middle class government high school student, Perth).

In the extract from Vanessa's interview below, she identifies her individuality (which I have identified with italics), the emotion work she will need to do (underlined), and that expected of her partner (bold):

> I did mention HSC and career. I feel that builds *who you are a lot* of the time. Because if you don't know who you are you can't possibly want to <u>share who you are and what you've done with other people</u>. ... I can imagine the children part because the children are a part of you but finding somebody completely different who you have to be able to **work as a team** <u>and acknowledge each other's positive sides and things that you may not want to accept or may not be able to accept</u>, that is a lot harder. ... I think it is very important for *husband and wife still be their individual*, I am very much *a personal space type of a girl*. To <u>work in a team</u> and know that you are going to become better because of it, not that you are going to be *lumbered down by somebody else*. Or **you're going to have to do all the helping**. Or <u>they're going to have to do all of the helping</u>. You have to be equal and you have to be able to **move forward together**. I think that's the most important thing. ... Hopefully I will find out as I learn a bit more about myself, because you learn something about yourself every day, every second. But I am looking for an achiever, somebody who is motivated. I think once you've found the person who is motivated and who can *achieve in their own right*, **help you achieve** and both of you, as I said, **moving together**. That person will automatically want to be part of anything you are part of. Children and the workload that comes with marriage is part of that. So, when someone is married to a person who they can be friends with as well as be a husband or a wife to, if you can manage to find that state of balance then it should come naturally. That's the image I have in my head anyway. (Vanessa, Catholic college student, Sydney)

Vanessa contrasts 'knowing who you are', being 'able to do the things you want to do' and being an 'individual' with the challenge of 'working in a team' and 'moving forward together'. At first she suggests she has trouble imagining a person who will become her life partner, given the difficulties of 'things that you may not want to accept'. However, she concludes that once she is 'ready', she will find the required 'friend' and they will 'automatically' want to share each other's lives.

In his interview, Nick devoted considerable attention to discussing his relations with the opposite sex: both present and imagined in the future. Compare his discussion of emotion work in the extract below with Vanessa's above. Nick's emotion work comments are underlined and his independence comments are in italics. Vanessa speaks of working on the relationship and moving 'together', of being a 'team'. She links this to achieving in one's own right, a classic instance of 'self-mastery' in Giddens' terms. By contrast, Nick speaks of being 'open' and 'communicating'. He has a barely developed notion of interdependent independence:

When you talk about SNAGS and stuff — sensitive new age guys. That's kind of true. Like we've come a long way from what we used to be like. But umm, now, say we can't hold back our emotions. It's written in the books these days. Guys, don't hold back your emotions. … They'll be <u>more open to themselves, to people like and stuff</u>. That's true — I'm quite an open book to people and umm *I do express when I don't feel right*. And, umm, yeah, it's true — I want to find someone that's actually, umm, that will *care for my children and will also be there for me* and <u>have a really strong relationship as a family that we can both communicate</u>. I don't just want to marry someone because it's just a nice person. It's, I want to find someone who's truly soul mate material. (Nick, Protestant college student, Perth)

Nick sees himself as 'kind of' a new age guy, embodying what Hugh Mackay calls 'new bloke' masculinity (Mackay 2007: 56). He describes himself as loving and egalitarian in his imagined domestic relations. In his 'I ams' he writes that he is:

A loving kind of person to women, a tall and well built bloke, a techno fan, a hard working adolescent, a caring and understanding person, a fan of rugby and a rugby player, money orientated, an actor and artist, a highly respected member of my peers, in control of my life.

In his essay, he writes:

I found my soul mate and married her and we had two kids, I did house working as well and I was the best father I could ever be.

Nick tours as a 'well-known' DJ, has 'many women after him' and becomes a successful fashion designer. Indeed, in 'real life' Nick has designed 'metrosexual' clothing for his mates, including a new rugby jersey for the school team ('the guys fell in love with it'). In his life story, prior to his success with women, he inserts parenthetically a complaint about feminism and demanding girlfriends:

I felt that men had to work harder to win the heart of a woman and I found myself having to call the girls and do everything to keep them happy ending up with getting large phone bills. I also found that feminism had become a problem, lesbian feminists were taking the movement too far and basically I was losing many rights.

Nick further expressed his discomfort with the independence of his female peers in the interview, describing the demands made by the young women he knows — for 'chocolates, flowers', 'rich', good-looking boyfriends:

they'll go through men. It's very, umm, it's very hard, actually for guys. … They're [the girls] just very snobby. They string you along and then cut the string, and you're by yourself again … They're very unique in their own little selves … if they don't find that you're as interesting as they thought originally you were.

While Nick identifies the need for emotional virtuosity, he is more concerned about the unrealistic demands of the 'snobby' young women in his acquaintance (see also Huntley 2006: 124–5, 128–9). He goes on to criticise fellow female workers in supermarkets who will not do the heavy work or clean up when a child 'has urinated in one of the aisles' as well as telling me he had a 'bad brush' with a bisexual girlfriend who dropped him for a female. Nick's awareness of the gender equality discourse is evident when he asserts, 'I'm not putting down the female race and saying they're weak, or anything, no, no, I'm just saying there's a couple of them', then pacifying me with his evenhandedness: 'there's problems with male society and there's also problems with female society'.

Nick becomes almost incoherent in his attempt to balance independence and interdependence when discussing unionism. He notes that the union 'stands up for us' against 'monopoly people just destroying, wiping out people's lives' but:

> we shouldn't always be, we shouldn't always be like having us, having someone to help us, we should always have to help ourselves out in this world. If a democracy has someone to help someone it's good but we have to have our own individuality. We have to stand up for things as well ourselves or we're just nursed, nurtured throughout the whole of our lives which is good but not good.

Similarly, one of Nick's female teachers was, he said, 'very unhelpful', contributing to his low tertiary entrance score, by contrast with a male teacher who understood that 'you have to breast feed' a student. Nick's dramatic swings between claiming independence and yearning for nurture are the most expressive example among my interviewees of young men's difficulties in negotiating the egalitarian companionship forged by two equals, as imagined by Vanessa and other young women.

From her intergenerational study of Australian males, Karina Butera (2008: 268–73) suggests that men in their early twenties express a 'more flexible, emotionally expressive and individualistic style of mateship', a 'neo-mateship' in which they support each other. In my study, too, a handful of male essayists describe themselves as 'caring' or 'loving' or enjoying 'spending time with others'. Because of these attributes a young man, who describes himself as 'half Dutch', wants to study psychology. He desires a wife who is both conventionally attractive and inwardly beautiful:

Helping people will always make my life happier. … I consider myself to be a very loving person and relationships in the future will hold great significance in my life. Although I have to say I am primarily attracted to socially accepted 'beautiful women' I really can't see my relationships lasting in the future unless I can bond and connect with the woman on a more mental and spiritual way. (male, middle class government high school student, Adelaide)

Generally, however, young men describe their life companion in bare snippets, focusing more on what wives will do for them rather than exploring the emotional labour they will bring to the relationship:

I would like to have a girlfriend who loves and respects me. … I would like her to every once in a while give or do little surprises so that I know she loves me. I would also like to have a couple of kids, preferably a boy and a girl because I love kids and playing with them. (male, Catholic college student, Perth)

Thus, the young women in my study appear more comfortable with the nuances and needs of contemporary intimacies. This is not to say, of course, that all young women are reflexive choice biographers, given the capacity of 'Bitch Barbies' to rule playgrounds, functioning as the deputies of bullying males (see Martino and Pallotta-Chiarolli 2005: 138, 106, 87).[4] This dark side of emotional virtuosity surfaced in five young women's interviews, which identified the 'petty, insulting' 'bitchiness' of women. Courtney compared this with the 'sutured selves' (Roseneil 2007) of her rowing team, in which each is aware of the effort put in by others, and each is dependent on the others: 'I love that everyone's there's sort of helping each other push each other along' (Courtney, Protestant college student, Perth). Charmaine suggests:

I've seen girls who are really mean to guys and stuff. Sometimes I do think that part of the problem is women. Like, they let things happen and they do all these things to make other women look bad and whatever. Yeah, it's not all the guys' fault. I think that women need to, I don't know, look out for each other a bit more as well. (Charmaine, middle class government high school student, South Australia)

Many life stories, including a good proportion of female stories, contained evidence of limited reflexivity by contrast with the considerable negotiation, sometimes across almost mutually incomprehensible positions, required as biographers are torn between desires for oneself and cleaving to others. Furthermore, while some young middle class women are preparing themselves for narratives of interdependent independence, they do not seem to have considered that their partners may lack similar psychological capital or the same commitment to domestic equality, an issue explored below after considering why young men embrace 'settling down' with less ambivalence than young women.

A meeting of minds? His and her imagined relationships

> Loving people and being loved by people is such a great thing. Even though I would like a career, I don't want to cut out other people from my life at all. Finding that elusive balance between them is something that I'm going to have to work on. … If I find someone who makes my life fuller in some way and I can visualise myself being able to pursue what I want and also being happy helping them get what they want, then I wouldn't have a problem with it but marriage isn't something I feel like I need to be a fuller person. It's just something that might happen if I find it along the way. … Also, I think that one of the ways that you can sort of leave your mark on the world is by having children and imparting them with lessons that you have learned along the way as well. … I think in myself I am a bit selfish. For me, I want to travel, I want the career and where I am at the moment I know that I am not ready to make the sacrifices for somebody else. (Kathryn, middle class government girls' high school student, Sydney)

Kathryn writes in her essay that 'children would have frankly been a cramp on my lifestyle' of travel and tertiary study. In the interview extracted above, she ponders the tension between 'furthering myself' through individual agency and 'finding someone who will make my life fuller'. Lara, the feminist-trained interviewer, queries Kathryn's use of the adjective 'selfish' to describe her desire for travel and career. Kathryn responds with the reciprocal individualisation common as middle class young women describe their emotional labour:

> It's not just related to children, it's related to other people as well. I want what I want for me and there are occasions where I am going to pursue what I want regardless of how it affects other people. Not that I am saying that I am willing to hurt people on the way up but I am going to pursue what I want and I really don't want to let other people get in the way of that.

Kathryn concludes that she would 'tone down' her career goals if necessary when she has children: 'People are the most important thing. That's all there is basically, that's all that makes the world different from anything else.' She hopes for a partner who will work 'equally hard' on parenting, although contributing differently (Kathryn, middle class government high school student, Sydney).

The male stories canvassed in this section suggest that Kathryn may hope in vain. Only three young men identified children as the 'best decision' or 'proudest achievement' in their lives, one referring his proudest achievement back to himself:

'I can see my son growing up exactly like me' (male, Catholic college student, Perth). The most effusive male statement comes from Scott, raised by a feminist single mother:

> The most important thing in my life has been family; I would do anything for them. They have been the people that have moulded me into the person I am today. I will always love them for that. My respect for my wife and children is endless; being with them is the true success story of my life. (male, Catholic college student, Perth)

Anne Summers' (1970: 53) essayists did not struggle with the career-family balance that Kathryn ponders. Their 'main function is to bear children and to look after the family', measuring 'their happiness almost solely in terms of the material splendour of their homes' (Summers 1970: 87–8). 'Only a few girls showed any awareness that housework might be demanding' or dreary (Summers 1970: 87–8), generally riposting that their children or loving husband was the antidote (Summers 1970: 87–8, 92). One essayist 'felt a duty' to love her daughter, who 'took from me my right to be myself, my freedom and my love for my husband' (Summers 1970: 97). Another essayist reprimanded herself for being 'too lazy' to study hard enough to get into university and instead finding herself 'chained to my kitchen sink', 'trapped' in 'one of those duplicated shells that make up suburbia'. She upbraids herself for being too 'afraid' to 'break out of this cage', concluding with a discussion of alternative suicide measures, settling on sleeping tablets: 'goodbye cruel world'. According to Summers, this is the only essayist who 'showed any real understanding' of the inadequacy many women felt as 'just a' housewife and mother (Summers 1970: 88–91).

Very few young women in my millennium sample write simply of 'marrying a millionaire', a 'rich pom who has the personality of Jim Carrey' or a 'rich businessman' (and killing him 'if he was mean'):

> When I leave school finally, I would like to become rich by marrying a rich guy so I can have everything I want. His name would be Shannon and we would have four children, two girls and two boys. We would have all sorts of animals, from cats to turtles and we would live to be about ninety or so. (total life story; female, working class government high school student, Adelaide)

Another handful wrote that their husband's wealth allowed them to stay home caring for the children: 'I'm not fussed on having my own career, as long as my husband could support our loving family, I will be happy.' Most luxuriously, a third essayist stays 'at home in my huge mansion' with 'a maid to help out, whilst my husband brings home the money'. Only two per cent of females explicitly write that they do not return to work after having their children (while a quarter do, see Table A3.1 in Appendix 3). Even the essayist who marries 'a rich pom' also studies for a double degree at university and works as an early childhood teacher and then as a youth worker, along with raising eight children!

Kathleen Gerson explains her research with young adults on the grounds that 'This generation lived through a natural social experiment', being reared in households where domestic arrangements were often volatile — for example, when mothers returned to work or when fathers deserted their families (Gerson 2010: 4–6). The interviewees (80 per cent of the females and 70 per cent of the males; Gerson 2010: 105) responded to this uncertainty with a belief, not in a particular family structure, but in a 'quality' relationship: 'a flexible, egalitarian partnership with considerable room for personal autonomy' (Gerson 2010: 11), one that allows them 'to strike a personal balance between earning and caregiving' (Gerson 2010: 104). Both women and men drew lessons from their parents and others about the perils of clinging to strict gender roles, eschewing these. But men 'focused on the burdens of sole breadwinning, while women worried more about the dangers of domesticity and the difficulties of doing it all' (2010: 96). If the companionate marriage eluded them, young men's fallback position was a focus on their careers, supported by a partner who did 'the lion's share of the caregiving'. Young women preferred economic 'self-reliance', 'emotional and economic autonomy', either with or without children, if they could not find a partner committed to their egalitarian ideals (Gerson 2010: 11). Young women chose their fallback position as an expression of self-reliance, even as mothers. Thus, young men and women are on a collision course in their 'practically grounded actions and plans' (Gerson 2010: 235). Chiming with my results, Gerson also discovered young women who imagine independence forged in connection and young men who construct their autonomy in isolation. The next section explores how the young men and women in my sample write about their lives together in their life story essays.

'Settling down': Breadwinning and childraising

> Alex and I were just in different places I guess, he wanted to settle down, but I wasn't ready. It was the same story with Michael and Jeremy. I wanted to focus more on my career. I was only 21 at this time. It was one New Year's Eve that I met Jack. We got engaged 3 months later when I found out I was pregnant. 3 kids, divorced at 53, got PhD. (female, Protestant College student, Perth)

> I will never get married, unless I get a pre-nuptial agreement, because women will try and take advantage of me because I am a very wealthy man. I will be an electrical/instrument fitter and work for a mining company up north. I will

go fishing all the time. Have a lot of women. Have my best mate, boxer dog called 'Rocket'. And be a happy man. (male, Protestant college student, Perth)

The young man quoted above is among the small sample of male essayists who reject marriage and fatherhood, fearing faithless 'gold-diggers' (see Winchester 1999 on separated fathers' discourses) like a 'supermodel' who takes 'all my money, the house, and the cars'; a 'stunning, brilliant and easy to manipulate' woman who 'takes half' the male writer's assets; 'a cheap floozy' who 'took me to the cleaners and I lost all my assets because women are favoured over men so feminists should shut up and stop trying to draw attention to their otherwise dull and miserable existences'. Several essayists avoid this outrage by explicitly rejecting the breadwinner role, never 'working a day', instead living on the dole and surfing, or drinking and smoking with 'a few mates to talk to'.

Others start to write of breadwinning fatherhood only to reject the life of the 'mindless tax payer. I will marry and have 2.4 children. My children will eat weet-bix & [I] will die when I am about 80'. This male essayist crossed this out and wrote instead of 'living it up': making the nationals in swimming, touring the world and in particular having 'sex at least 10,000 times before marriage' (male, Protestant college student, Perth). A self-defined 'Indian Punjabi' male's routine renders him finally 'unable to be the man you can':

> You begin working and realise that being a doctor isn't what it should be. You're not out there saving lives, you're doing the mundane. You see 40 people a day and it's more like a factory with people coming and going. … You no longer care about saving people, only seeing your 40 patients a day and getting all the money you can. Marriage is inevitable. I already know what kind of woman I will marry — a nice educated Indian girl. … It will be interesting to see how long it takes for the novelty to wear off and the boredom to sink in. … Then the kids come. They seem so cute until they vomit, and poo, and begin to walk. Then they grow up and reach their teenage years. They lose their respect. … And slowly you get older. … You lose your movement, your independence. Till finally you're bedridden, crapping your pants, unable to be the man you can. (male, Indian Punjabi, middle class government high school student, Perth)

Marriage refusal was also expressed in the only item in relation to marriage and children on which young men were more likely to write than young women: the divorce or death of their loved ones. Among this six per cent of male essayists, the flight from commitment was often described in bizarre circumstances, almost as though women were being punished for aspiring to marriage. Several killed fiancées and wives before or shortly after marriage. A fiancée was shot by a mugger while shopping 'for a wedding dress'. Two wives died on the honeymoon, one 'eaten by a shark while snorkling. … A better girl came along'. Another wife survived to the age of 42, when 'the dryer fell on her head and killed her'. Another essayist's wife met 'a cold and lonely death in the front seat of a weird car'. As discussed above, in the most elaborate scenario, an unfaithful wife is punished by a warhead aimed at her.

Allon Uhlmann (2006: 157) found that many men in his Newcastle study describe two 'bosses': 'Men work for their families. They also work for their bosses', this 'homology' emerging in some conversations. This negates the male breadwinner role as a performance of masculinity, instead making it a denial of autonomy. For many men — young or old — this tension must mark their working lives. If family obligations require long hours or undesirable jobs, not only is their loss of autonomy at work, their wife might also be experienced as another regulating 'boss'. On the other hand, as disadvantaged youth without access to paid work fully know, adult masculinity is so firmly premised on a wage sufficient to support a family (even if with the assistance of a second income) that few males can imagine eschewing this aspect of adult masculinity. Without employment, young men feel they cannot become fathers, have a public face or share their life with the blokes (see Wierenga 2009: 109). A frontier of masculine performance, then, concerns men's willingness to do any job, including jobs marked as feminine with their 'shit wages and a shit job', rather than remain unemployed and/or take on the caring role or doing voluntary work (Peel 2005: 27–9 and McLeod and Yates 2006: 211 for Australia; Walkerdine 2008 for a south Wales mining community).

So, like the dependent wife, the unattached male only featured in a handful of essays. Much more often than its refusal, the role of male breadwinning was presumed or embraced, even if the rupture with the former carefree life of 'Clubs, drugs pubs and parties', 'numerous girlfriends' or sporting success is momentarily regretted. Male essays express 'a ballistic model' in which individuals mature as they prepare for work, consolidate their masculine success in employment, 'settle down' into a successful career that supports their family, and then experience 'physical and functional decline in retirement' (Howard 2007: 33):

> After a couple of years, I found one girlfriend and settled down with her, as I had finished my degree and had a steady income to support us comfortably. … [B]y the time I was sixty and my wife was 59 I had retired, prosperous and having earned enough money for a happy retirement, with enough in reserve to help out my other family members if they ever needed it. (male, co-educational Protestant college student, Adelaide)

Male essayists are more likely to write of their business success and five times more likely than the female essayists to imagine extreme wealth, an extravagant hallmark of breadwinning masculinity (see Table A3.1 in Appendix 3). They found Nike, put nicotine in a soft drink, speculate in the stock or property markets, or make 'mega millions' as a director in multimedia or arts. They make their fortune in music, sports, and occasionally crime, such as hit man or drug runner. One writer is clear that his objective is wealth, by whatever means:

> I have no particular goals or ambitions. I don't know what I want to be, where I want to live, or anything like that. My main ambition is to be rich, not your everyday well off kind of rich but filthy, stinking, more income than Spain rich. (male, co-educational Catholic college student, Perth)

More realistically, a 'real job', 'a nice house and car', 'enough money to support my family' are prerequisites before they can 'search for the woman of my dreams' or find 'the lady that I thought was the greatest thing that had ever happened to me'. Having sorted out the financial necessities, males write of readily 'obtaining' the 'right partner' along with a car, house and children to live 'happily ever after'. While wives are accumulated with little thought, several young men attend to their children's future, sending them to 'a great school to receive a great education' or projecting their financial support into their children's and even grandchildren's lives as they pass on family law firms or businesses.

For many female essayists the significance of motherhood is so self-evident that they confine themselves to a phrase or sentence of hyperbole: the 'best part of my life', 'the most rewarding thing of all', 'the best thing I ever did, better than any qualification', 'the greatest joy in my life. The love I feel for her [daughter] is never ending', 'the moment I think I will cherish forever'. A handful expressed a hyperbolic motherhood in a similar fashion to male expression of excessive masculinity in extreme wealth. While twins were relatively common, some young women wrote of much larger families, such as eight children ('four of each'), 'ten kids' or fourteen children (essayists at a working class government school, Perth). At other schools are mothers of five (a Catholic college) and six children (Middle Eastern essayist, government school Sydney). An essayist at the Protestant college in Perth regrets her decision:

> I decided I wanted children so my new husband Lane & I had octuplets called Stacy, Tracy, Lacy, Masy, Kacy, Dacy & Chacy [sic: only seven children are named]. After a year I decided children weren't for me & fled the UK back to the US.[5]

Very rarely do young women refuse motherhood, although some young women write of mothering as something that comes after you've 'done everything you want to do in your life' (Alannah, co-educational Catholic college student,

South Australia). These writers pursued their own 'experiences' and 'lived my life first', either 'as a young "carefree" adult with no major responsibilities' or a woman who has her 'career in sights'. Only when her life is going 'downhill' would a young woman accept being 'struck down with the responsibility' of children. Given that 'fun' and 'my life' are on one side and 'responsibility' and 'commitment' are on the other, some female writers are not sure that they do want to 'just settle down and have kids'. Carina imagines that she might either be the 'modern woman' who adjusts 'my plans to those of my partner', has a 'career and then children' or her marriage might break up and she will live in Europe, following the 'Bohemian life' of her mother who studied in Berlin:

> See there are two pathways. Either I'll be straight and narrow and I'll get married and I'll have a really good career and then I'll have a couple of children. And then, yeah. Or if probably, maybe, hopefully not, my marriage goes to bits, I'll go off and be my own wonderful little self. (Carina, middle class government high school student, Perth)

On the whole, then, among the millennium essayists motherhood itself is expressed with the same unqualified enthusiasm as it was for Summers' essayists. The issue is not, generally, the value of motherhood but the institution, as Adrienne Rich (1976) drew the distinction: how to realise motherhood in a world of unforgiving workplaces and non-sharing partners. As the British 'Inventing Adulthoods' study found, 'Settling down' 'can be more easily realised by young men within a traditional framework, but for young women it is more problematic' (Henderson et al. 2007: 25). While the young men in my study take or reject the fork in the road to normative adult masculinity, they rarely weigh its costs and benefits. More young women struggle for a resolution, a compromise, between their desire for motherhood and their anxieties concerning its costs. Like the female writer at the head of this sub-section, they sometimes parry boyfriends who are ready for a family. This is not only because femininity trains in negotiation. It is also because of the different signifiers of adult sexuality for each gender: supporting a family for males and raising a family for females. Males readily clip the family onto their stellar careers, and at almost any point in their lives. Some females write in the same vein, but most must know that children and husband are not merely add-ons to a career. Furthermore, they cannot delay motherhood indefinitely, running the risk of becoming 'circumstantially childless' (Cannold 2005: 20). The 'opportunity cost' of full-time mothering (the mother's foregone income while out of the labour force) increases as women gain access to the labour market. The expectations, and hence costs, of raising children have also risen, but parental nurturing remains largely unpaid — and undervalued — in market economies (Pocock 2001: 88; de Vaus 2004: 272–4). Women must plot and plan if they are to achieve this difficult juggling act (see similar findings in Huntley 2006: 51).

The 'neo-traditional' family: A compromise between his and her relationships

> I got married at the age of 28, after much searching for a soul-mate. Of course it was a bit 'rocky' at first but after a while me and my wife adapted to our new life. I worked full time earned around 110 thousand a year in a career of my choice. My wife pursued her career to a certain extent until she was pregnant. During this time I worked whilst she stayed at home and looked after our child for two years. (male, Protestant college student, Perth)

By contrast with the tight coupling of masculinity and breadwinning in the young men's stories, most of the young men barely discuss how fatherhood changes their lives, perhaps because they imagine it hardly will.[6] While very few male essayists considered domestic arrangements in their essays (five per cent), a greater proportion of young women (a little over 20 per cent) wrote about this issue (see Table A3.1 in Appendix 3). Furthermore, young men and women imagine different domestic arrangements, as Table 3.1 shows. Only one-quarter of the female essayists imagine no caring role for their partners while this is the preferred option of half the male essayists, in line with other surveys indicating that many young men expect childcare to be primarily their partners' responsibility (Flood 2005: 4; Pocock 2006: 129–31). Male essayists expressed most support for the fallback position identified by Gerson (2010), in which they focus on their careers. Expressed as the 'neo-traditional' '1.5 breadwinner' family, this is the dominant arrangement in Australia today (see last column in Table 3.1). The writer quoted above quickly dispatches emotional difficulties through 'adaptation' rather than emotion work, after which he settles into a comfortable neo-traditional arrangement, justified by his wife's lesser commitment to her career (which she pursues 'to a certain extent').

The young men in favour of the traditional gendered division of labour wrote that they wanted to 'support the family' or 'be the prominent source of income' and their wives would not 'work' but 'stayed home and cooked dinner and done the washing as they did in the 1960s' (male, Protestant college student, Perth). The gendered dichotomy in expectations is most evident in a comparison of Henry and Kristie. Henry, a Chinese Indonesian, told me he will 'prohibit' his wife from working, instancing the negative impact of working mothers on his friends who 'keep on slacking school' (Henry, co-educational Catholic college student, Perth). Where Henry talks and writes about himself as a man in an intergenerational chain of filial duties (passing his business onto his son), Kristie, of Hong Kong Chinese

Percentage of essayists who discuss work and childcare arrangements			Australian data: work and childcare arrangements for mothers of children 0-15 years old where fathers are employed or full-time carers*	
Life story item	Females	Males		%
Mother returns quickly to full-time work *(number)*	38 *(35)*	31 *(5)*	Full-time paid working mother; paid working father	23
Traditional gendered division of labour *(number)*	28 *(26)*	51 *(8)*	Mother at home; paid working father	27
Mother takes part-time work after some years *(number)*	25 *(23)*	5 *(1)*	Part-time paid working mother; Full-time working father	46
Father is full-time carer *(number)*	10 *(9)*	13 *(2)*	Father at home	4~
Percentage of all essays	22.9	5.5		100

Table 3.1: Percentage of female and male high school essayists who mention various work and childcare arrangements

* These figures are approximate as they relate to different years: Australian Bureau of Statistics 2006; Australian Bureau of Statistics 2009.
~ for 2003, and showing percentage of couple families where the husband was not in the labour force while the wife is (Australian Bureau of Statistics 2005).

background at a middle class Adelaide high school, seeks escape from gendered domestic relations. Kristie is certain that she will not have any children:

> it costs so much to raise the children. … [Y]ou have to depend on your husband. You take most of the responsibilities for the children, of course. Everyone expects the woman to stay home and all that. And I don't like this. … I have to get my career and I have to, you know, support myself, my life.

Like the independently-minded young women in Gerson's study, Kristie wants 'to be independent' and 'to get power' with a 'good job', rather than 'carry all the housework and all that'. A Muslim Indian-Fijian female is critical of gender inequality, apparently drawing on her own experience, but sees no way to resist it. She and her husband 'both worked full time' but she:

> had to cook, clean and raise the children. … [M]y whole life I've been taught that the women cook, clean and raise the kids and the men just work but in my culture all women do the same. (female, Catholic college student, Sydney)

Apart from asserting that their wife will *not* work, male essayists rarely mention their partner's working arrangements. Unusual, then, is the male essayist writing as an Air Force officer who, with his wife, works part-time once their son is born, 'so someone would be home to look after our child'. Similarly unusual is the male essayist writing as an environmental manager who 'would share housework and childcare with my wife. … Write books in my own time and cook a lot'. Nick, as discussed above, albeit critical of feminism, nevertheless marries his 'soul-mate' and shares in the 'housework'.

Only two male essayists write of being full-time carers:

Sarah my wife went off to work while I stayed at home and looked after the boys. It was great, I cleaned and cooked. (male, Catholic college student, Perth)

After his professional basketball career with the 'Cleveland Cavaliers in America', an Aboriginal youth service client retires and cares for his family in Brisbane. Several others grappled with the tension between fatherhood as earning a family income and fatherhood as being there for one's children: 'I've given my family the best I could by taking every time off I could to spend with them and I could still offer them the best money can buy.' One young man becomes a senior associate in his law firm before proposing to his girlfriend. He finally hits on the perfect solution to allow him to 'be there for my children': politics. As a senator, 'I only had to be working in parliament for 1/3 of the year, giving me a chance to be with my kids too' (male, Catholic college student, Perth). Early retirement from his athletic career allows another essayist to 'stay at home helping my wife. I see my kids growing older and older over the years'. Gerson (2010: 174) also found that some men envisage 'delaying' fathering by working hard in the early years of their marriage and taking time off for children later. More often, fabulous wealth allows young men who retire early to party and holiday, rather than spend more time with their families.

Given that most young women presume and desire motherhood and few imagine depending entirely on their husband's incomes, balancing paid work and motherhood is perhaps the major routine challenge young women will face. Very, very few of these young women resolve the collision between career and motherhood with either full-time full-life housewifery or remaining childfree. Most dance their complicated dreams, their self-reflexive negotiation of self and partner, around equal parenting, taking some time off work or reducing their working hours. A brave few are superwomen doing it all, stitching their family's stretched emotions back together with 'quality time' on family holidays. Their putative male partners, the male essayists in my research, are vague about parenting arrangements, apart from noting that they become fathers. These attitudes suggest that parenting will remain a major challenge for female DIY biographers, whether or not they embark on this journey with a male. The next section explores the 'acrobatics' (Beck-Gernsheim 2002: 9) by which many young women, but not all, yearn for some kind of equality in domestic relations, while many young men envisage a more traditional arrangement but continue to expect an (almost) equal say in an imagined abortion decision.

Equality at the limits: Sharing the caring

> My children have been our most greatest achievement. After our children were
> in school I decided to begin work once again as a health worker. I decided to
> study at adult education and after 2 years I was qualified to work. This time
> of my life was a difficult one, the pressure of my partner and I both working
> fulltime to pay off our home was stressful almost leading to our separation. We
> decided that we could afford to have one of us not work and stay at home. My
> partner knew how much my job meant to me so he stayed home during the
> day taking care of our kids. … Until I was 37 we were able to have luxuries of
> a nice car and to take the kids away to see the family. … I have never regreted
> anything in my life. I just hope I can spend as much time with my family as I
> can. (Caitlin, Aboriginal services client, Victoria)

'It's their choice' was often said in accepting abortion (and homosexual relations),
less frequently in relation to role reversal in the household and rarely in relation
to sharing housework and childcare. This suggests that 'equality' in housework has
achieved widespread normative endorsement as 'fair', and that personal preferences
are not an acceptable retort to hegemonic beliefs. Nevertheless, as study after study
confirms, the reality enforced by structures such as unequal salaries is that couples
rarely practise an equality based on sameness, each doing a similar amount of paid
and unpaid work,[7] even when couples claim they 'share' (McMahon 1999: 86; de
Vaus 2004: 287–8; Lindsay and Dempsey 2009: 172). Discursive contortions paper
over inequality, for example among young male entrepreneurs working 24/7 who
nevertheless claim they 'do all the work' for the family as 'the ultimate thing' or
see themselves as active and engaged, 'hands-on', 'fantastic' (if not equal) partners
(Bowman 2007: 393, 395; see also Connell 2008). In another study, the young women
were keen to present their relationships as equal 'despite the evident contradictions':
in one case a young woman described sharing the cooking as 'We decide what to
cook and then I cook it' (Maher and Singleton in Lindsay and Dempsey 2009: 171).

There are several explanations for this 'pseudomutuality' (Bittman and
Pixley 1997: 155), endorsing egalitarianism but rarely practising equality. First,
egalitarian does not mean equality — 'a rigidly organized division of everything all
the time' (Gerson 2010: 106) — according to Gerson's interviewees, but 'a long-
term commitment to equitable, flexible, and mutual support in domestic tasks
and workplace ties' (Gerson 2010: 107). This means that 'his' and 'her' notions of
egalitarian relationships are not always aligned. Second, in few households do men
and women have the same hours in paid work, so equality as sameness would be
rarely practised. Thirdly, young women desire equality in the relationship, not just

in the housework, more so than young men. And they are willing to deploy their psychological capital to think through the balance between rights and responsibilities in a way that young men show less interest in, at least when discussing abortion decisions, an example I use to explore this issue.

Equality and egalitarianism in housework and childcare

> if the man is willing to help or jumps in and does it himself, well then let him do it. But if you can't get them to do it, then there's no point trying 'cos you're not going to get anywhere. (Kelly, working class government high school student, South Australia)

Chilla: What about you guys? Are you thinking of staying home with your kids at all, or are you gonna have this beaut wife that's just going to do it?

Barry: No. I reckon not.

Ross: We'll share. I'm not gonna stay home two-thirds of the day, but we'll share.

Chilla: Okay. So you'll be also working, but you'll share.

Casey: What, she has them during the day and you have them at night?

Ross: No. Whenever we can.

Casey: Night is the best time to have them 'cos you don't have to get up to them.

Ross: We'll share the children equally. …

Adam: I'm not gonna have kids, man. I'm gonna get a hysterectomy or whatever they call it.

Casey: [laughs] You can't have a hysterectomy. (focus group, working class government high school students, Adelaide)

Study after study confirms that the idealised marriage has shifted from distinct gender roles to a partnership or companionship based on 'equality', 'respect' and 'understanding' (Scott et al. 1996: 482, 484–5; Ciabattari 2001: 5 and Gerson 2002: 16 for the US; Lewis 2001: 57 and Pilcher 1998: 11–12, 24, 135 for the United Kingdom; Probert 2002: 8–11; Everingham et al. 2007: 424–6 and McCalman 1993: 208–10, 250–4 for Australia). In their questionnaire responses the young women and men in my research also expressed this ideal of equality, perhaps surprisingly given the divergences in their imagined life stories. Chart 3.3 reveals that young women and men support shared housework and childcare when both partners undertake equal hours of paid work, although the young women endorse this statement more strongly. The young women take domestic democracy for granted, justifying their support with claims of equality and fairness.

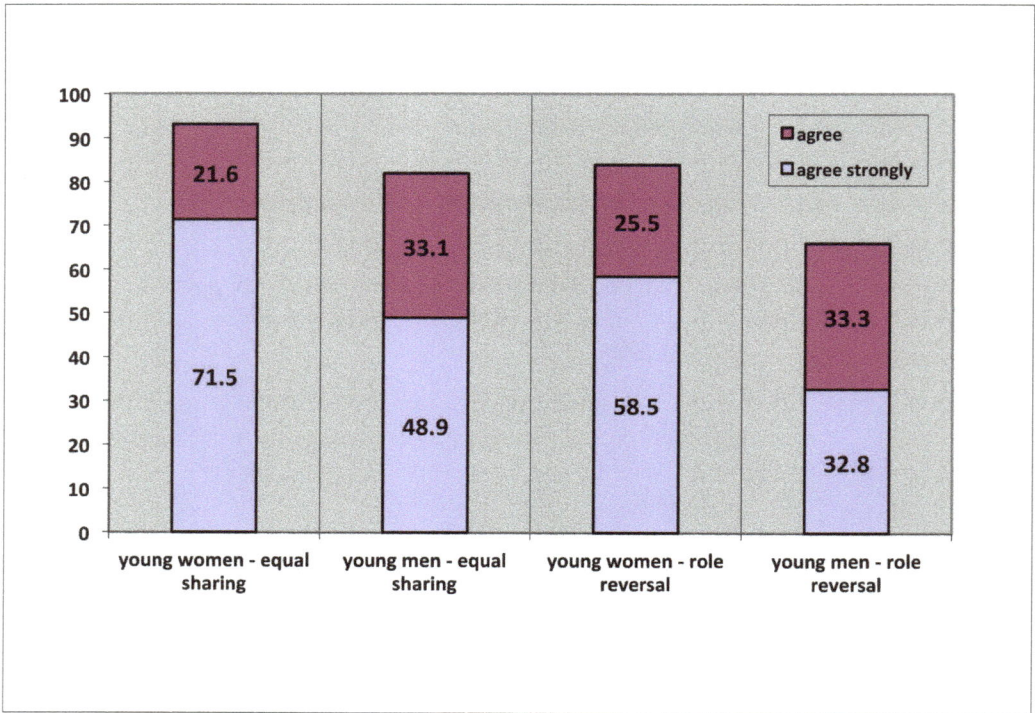

Chart 3.3: Young people's responses to domestic democracy questions

'If both partners in a household are working the same number of paid hours, they should share housework and childcare equally'.

'It is fine in a marriage or relationship for the man to stay at home and do the housework and look after the children, if there are any; and for the woman to go out and work full time'.

Note: A national random survey of Australians in 1996, 'Negotiating the Life Course Survey', found that 95 per cent of men and women aged 18–54 years agreed with the first statement ('If both the husband and the wife work, they should share equally in the housework and care of the children') (McDonald 2000: 8).

Young men and women's opinions are more divergent when it comes to role reversal, or men staying home and doing full-time parenting. Whereas the young women see these items as being similar, young men mobilise individual choice to suggest that other couples can practise this if they wish to do so, but it is certainly not what the respondent desires for himself. The one-third of young men who reject role reversal often do so on the basis of 'traditional' claims, such as presumed biological sexual differences or the patriarchal division of labour (one in five of the male comments compared with only one in 10 female comments). As one young man wrote, 'I think proving your worth can only be done by providing for your family' (see commentary after Table A3.10 in Appendix 3 for a discussion of gender vocabularies). Around the time I began my research, a national survey found that a third of young men see males as the 'head of the household' (Office of the Status of Women 2004: 94).

Edward's interview offers some insight into the mechanisms of 'pseudomutuality'. Edward ruminates on the balance between a job one enjoys and the obligation to support a family. While willing to share housework, Edward expresses two reservations about role reversal. First, with men in the top reaches of business and politics, they are 'obviously getting more money'. As Gerson (2010: 172) notes of similar findings in her study, market realities often lend 'an air of inevitability to men's reliance on women's caretaking'. 'Equal, but different' is explained as due to 'circumstances beyond their control' (Gerson 2010: 178). Second, Edward would 'rather be in a good job where I could exercise my talent. I don't sort of hang out for housecleaning as it goes'. Indeed, given he understands his job will occupy '6 out of 7 days per week', it is unlikely Edward will have much time to share housework and childcare. Similarly, while Nick writes about sharing housework in his life story, he endorses different roles for mothers and fathers based on a popularised version of object relations theory. Prior to the age of ten or eleven, boys should 'grow up with their mothers', but after that masculinity (Nick says 'maturity') is forged by separation from the mother and connection with the father.

In the interview extract above, Ross and Barry assert they will 'share' at the same time as they hedge these statements. Kelly's scepticism was echoed by other respondents whose experience of partners 'sharing' or reversing roles was disappointing. In her interview, Karen told me her husband took their children half the time, *and* the supporting parent's pension, until illness forced Karen out of paid work. When she asked for her share of the pension, 'he said "Oh, if you want that you may as well have the kids"' (Karen, middle class government high school mature age student, Adelaide). In line with national statistics,[8] mothers told many stories suggesting that the younger generation will not necessarily be different. Their 'really disheartening' 'constant struggle' with sons over housework involved pleas to participate in the community that is the family, to learn important life skills for independence or that sharing is only fair. James asserts that he does a lot of housework, which his mother 'doesn't see', but then he trails off:

> I vacuum, I clean the toilet and the bathroom and stuff. I clean my own room, I do the windows when they really need it and stuff … [when] my mum notices them and tells me to do it. … She does a lot of work as well so she probably doesn't see what we do as much because she vacuums a lot more because I'm at school and stuff. ('James', Catholic college student, Perth)

Housework remains a 'performance of femininity' (Natalier 2003), young mothers struggling with their male partners who 'freak out' when asked to do housework (see also Baker 2008: 56):

> look at most girls: they've got to work and they've got to come home … and they've got to cook and then clean and look after everyone else and then the next day they've got to get up and do exactly the same thing. And then when you finally get to rest someone ends up saying, 'Oh, can you do this for me, can you do that for me', so they pick up and do that. So basically always going all the time and it doesn't give you any time to rest; the only time you do get to rest is when you close your eyes. … [I]f your mates come up they're going to see you hanging the washing out and they're going to laugh, but if they see a woman doing it they don't say nothing. It's like, 'Oh yeah, you're supposed to be hanging out the washing'. ('Elise', young mothers' Christian school student, New South Wales)

Only one single mother in my sample identified a partner (a trucker) who 'helps around the house', commenting 'I don't want my kids to think only women cook and clean and stay home etc — both can do it equally' (female, middle class government high school student, Adelaide).

Pioneers of new domestic relations experience personal anxiety, from the discomfort of being the only man at playgroup to nigh on 'open derision': 'extradited … you loser, you should have a job'. Pina's husband became the full-time carer so that Pina could continue teaching, making Pina proud but challenging friendships: 'For a male Italian to do that is really quite … we actually lost friends because of that, Italian male friends' ('Pina', working class high school mother, Adelaide). Nettie's partner took twelve months off to care for their son and then wanted to work part-time: 'his employer said, "Well you have a choice, either you work full time or you stop working"' ('Nettie', Catholic college parent, Perth). A manager at Vanessa's accountancy firm has been 'standing his ground' and 'fighting' to spend more time at home with his newborn child but he has been 'railroaded so much'. Vanessa has watched this situation with a keen interest, as she and her partner wish to share parenting equally (Vanessa, gender studies university student, Adelaide).

Wives had to struggle with their own presumptions when husbands took on full-time parenting. Theresa and her husband, Tim, took turns in full-time working and full-time parenting but Theresa remembers her 'constant struggle' to allow Tim into the domestic domain that she experienced as 'her responsibility':

> you learn to live with that sort of tension, but I do wonder then what happens with the girls of Kate's generation. Are they going to go through a similar

thing? … Is it going to be easier or harder for them? (Theresa, Catholic college mother, Adelaide)

Indicative of the potency of this issue, sex and domestic service were constant themes in the parodic masculinity essays discussed in Chapter Two. The 'sex god' who becomes PM legislates against men doing 'any housework what so ever' while his friend writes that 'women belong in the kitchen'. Others write 'where's my wife, I need my dinner cooked and my shirts ironed' or 'I prefer to have women cleaning than me'. The most pervasive complaint wives voice against husbands is lack of support in housework and childcare, even to the extent of divorcing them (Dempsey 2001: 62) or not having children by them (Cannold 2005: 203), thereby adopting the fallback position of independence.

For many women, 'sharing the caring' is an expression of companionship as much as it is of equality. In households where men contribute significantly, couples often do things together rather than follow a strictly 'efficient' division of labour (Esping-Andersen 2009: 47–9, 143). Throughout their essays, the young women in my sample linked 'respect', 'equality' and 'sharing'. Zoe has struggled with the meaning of an 'equal relationship'. Initially she thought it was a compliment when a man she went out with called her 'princess', but came to realise:

> It puts you in a position where you're no longer a person, you're just some*thing*, I don't know, the trophy girlfriend kind of thing. … [T]hey don't care what you think. (Zoe, middle class government high school student, Adelaide)

Nonetheless, Zoe says 'it's hard to tell' what makes an equal heterosexual relationship, deploying the template of female friendships with their 'easy back and forth conversation and they really listen to you': 'you can just tell that they care', for example by sharing and helping 'each other out'. Similarly, with some 'male friends', 'you can just talk to them about anything, rather than you are up on a pedestal, and you can't feel comfortable'. When pushed, Zoe admits that she doesn't talk with her male friends 'about anything', self-censoring discussion of feminist issues, books written by Virginia Woolf and so on. In defining feminism, Zoe again connects 'equality' to 'sharing':

> It's probably to do with getting equality and maintaining it. … [E]quality and maybe some political issues like getting, what's the word, just paid maternity leave, just having things in place so that if you have children then your career's not affected and your life isn't too badly affected, so it's sort of about sharing responsibilities I guess as well. I mean, getting equality and sharing. … [M]aybe it's not until socially everyone can treat each other equally we'll actually have equality.

Three essayists link 'equal' sharing of domestic labour with 'respect' and shared 'interests'. One of them writes:

> My husband is still with me, although we have separated twice. I love him because he respects me and my decisions and understands that I am a worker as well as him. We did equal amounts of housework and childcare. We share the same interests and the same thrill of living life as if it was our [unclear] last. (female, Protestant college student, Perth)

Female essayists, more so than males, imagine companionate marriages in which they share leisure activities or work together:

> We are both caring and loving and there is always humour! We both do martial arts and train regularly. After two years when we could finance everything we opened a law firm together. We did a lot of stuff together. (female, Protestant college student, who describes herself as 'a black belt')

The scripts of romance and sex are available to young people in Mills and Boon or Penthouse; the scripts for 'new' parenthood are little more than a generation old, still unfamiliar and far from hegemonic. Optimists suggest that 'pseudomutuality' and other disjunctions between ideals and practice are unstable. On the one hand, the 'regulative tradition' of 'lifelong internally stratified marriage' crumbles due to cohabitation, divorce and wives in paid work (Gross 2005: 286, 288). On the other hand, the more resistant 'meaning constitutive traditions' or 'patterns of sense making', which influence 'the thinkability of particular acts and projects' endure (Gross 2005: 296), including the male as primary breadwinner and female as primary nurturer (Gross 2005: 299) — as was revealed in many young men's essays. Furthermore, 'the gendered imaginary behind sex', 'according to which tough and hard men penetrate soft and passive women', has shifted little (Gross 2005: 300). However, young women now have the economic means to deflect the patriarchal bargain. The reality of the 'modified breadwinner model' invokes its partner, the 'modified maternalist culture of care' (Maher, Lindsay and Bardoel 2009). In exchange for female contribution to household income, women expect men to participate more in childcare. This tension is expressed also when comparing respondents' attitudes to abortion decisions.

Emotional literacy at the limits: Abortion decisions

> 'cos I'm on the pill. I had arguments with my Mum about it, but now she's like, I'm actually quite glad we went on it. ... We actually sat down and counted how many girls haven't had sex in our year, 'cos we're in Year 12. And I think it was about five or six [of] ... I'd say about forty girls. ... [M]ost of the time

it's actually the girls putting pressure on the guys. ... [M]ost people find it hard to talk to their parents about that stage of their lives because the parents always want their little kids to stay little. You know, they don't want them to grow up that fast. ... You can go out and buy condoms, but that can be very embarrassing and most of my friends won't do that. I know my boyfriend won't. (Anneka, co-educational Catholic college student, South Australia)

Anneka suggests that sexual abstinence is unusual by year 12 and that contraception is women's responsibility, in this case Anneka's and her mother's ('*we* went on it [the pill]', added emphasis). Anneka represents young men as neither in charge of contraceptive decisions nor of decisions concerning sexual activity. While Anneka's options are sorely limited in her own mind, they are vast compared with 40 years ago. Only three of the 117 essays Summers (1970: 92–4) analysed referred to reproductive choices, including one girl who had test-tube babies, avoiding the necessity to marry. The boyfriend of another 'used a contraceptive' while the third had 'an operation' at age 33 so she would have no more children. On the other hand, 'a good many assume

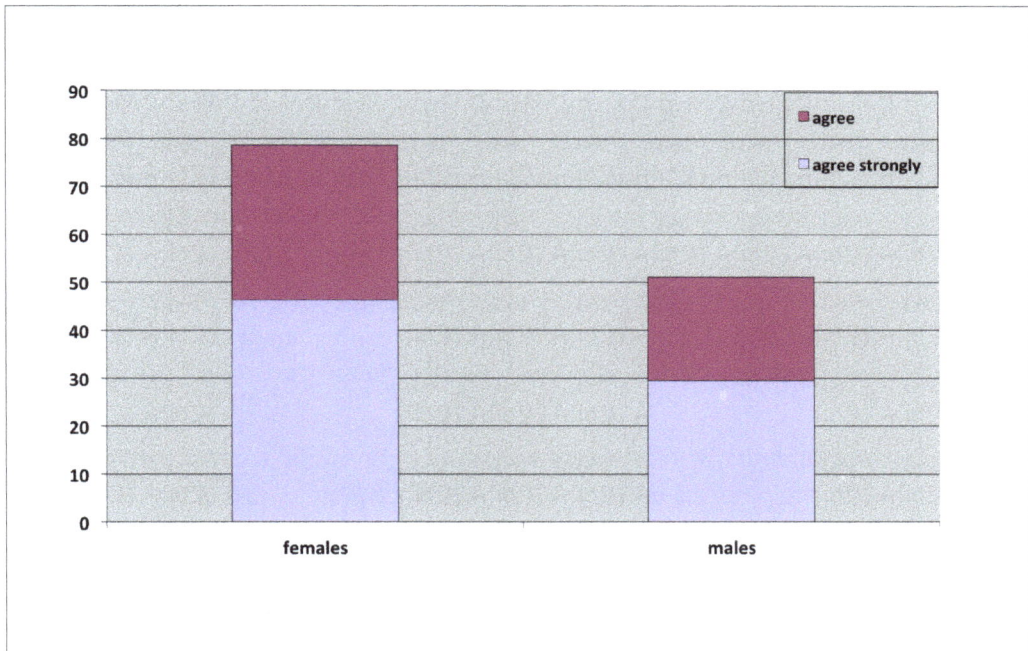

Chart 3.4. It should be the pregnant woman's right to choose whether or not she has an abortion: Young people x sex

Note: For youth service clients, the item was 'Do you think a pregnant woman should be able to choose whether or not she has an abortion?'

family planning in that they space their children' but provide no details of how they achieve this (Summers 1970: 93). Access to contraceptive freedom underwrites entry into paid work, the leitmotif of women's intergenerational progress according to my interviewees (see Chapter Two). Abortion is a significant issue for my young respondents, with half of them commenting on their answer (52 per cent of young women and 48 per cent of young men), making abortion the item that attracted the greatest number of comments (see Table A3.6 in Appendix 3).[9] Several young women had engaged politically with the issue, Kathryn, for example, 'writing letters to newspapers and trying to make more people my age aware' (Kathryn, girls' middle class government high school student, Sydney).

As Chart 3.4 reveals, young women support a woman's right to choose an abortion at almost twice the rate of young men (similar to national results, e.g. see Evans and Gray 2005: 22). A woman's choice because it is her body or her responsibility for the child was self-evident to one-third of the young women who made comments, with an additional 14 per cent framing the issue in terms of rights: 'It is her body and no-one else can tell her what to do with it.'

By contrast, the young men were more likely to express lukewarm support for or rejection of the statement, claiming that the pregnant woman should discuss her decision with the putative father (a proposal that many female respondents also endorsed). Comments were along the lines of 'both partners should decide', 'come to an agreement', 'decide on a strategy' 'work it out, not just the individual' and 'it should be a joint decision, discussed thoroughly. It is unfair on the baby that it must live on account of one person's decision.' Michelle felt that the putative father's emotional needs are often not considered:

> If they're in a relationship together, it's exactly the same situation. He should
> be getting just as much support, they should be talking about it, it's just as
> much their decision I think. (Michelle, women's studies university student,
> Perth)

Those respondents who advocate a woman's unfettered right to decide either did not mention the putative father at all or described him as 'the man'. Those who argued for discussion wrote of the 'father' of the foetus, or the 'partner' or 'husband' of the pregnant woman. Of course, there are semantic reasons for this difference — comments focusing on a woman's choice are less likely to mention either a 'man' or a 'partner'. But a good number of comments explicitly claimed that men earned their right to negotiation by sharing responsibility for the child:

> but if the bloke wants to keep the baby, help bring it up, stay with the woman,
> she should at least consider it. (male, gender studies university student,
> Adelaide)

Men who have 'left her for dead', raped the woman or otherwise reneged on their fathering responsibilities have no rights in relation to the foetus. Fourteen respondents explicitly noted that fathers are often 'unreliable', don't 'stick around' or 'run off'. The tension, as one respondent put it, is 'it's "her" body but "their" child'. No one had ready answers for the situation where he wanted her to keep the baby but she did not:

> both should have equal say but this obviously wouldn't work. (male, Protestant college student, Perth)

After talking it through, Charmaine concludes that the woman should have the baby if the father wants it and will care for it:

> if she wants it and he doesn't, then it's too bad. She's having it. But thinking the other way around, I still think that if he really wants it I'd sort of lean towards her having it and if he wants to look after it he can look after it. It depends, yeah, 'cos it's not fair if she can have it when he doesn't want it, [but] he can't have it if she doesn't want it. (Charmaine, middle class government high school student, South Australia)

I asked Nick, Matthew and Edward, students at a Protestant college in Perth, how they would respond if they were the putative father and disagreed with their partner. Matthew felt that the 'final decision' remained hers, but that discussion was better than her secretly having an abortion:

> that would be an issue in the relationship for them to resolve, such as if he wants to get a car and she wants to get a, something else, a microwave or something, I can't think of an example.

Edward could not 'say for sure' until in the situation, but ultimately would accept the decision as hers:

> depending on what sort of situation I was in, umm, where you know say I was able to support her, a child, if we were married, not married, something like that, I would argue against it but ultimately I would say that decision would be hers, particularly if it's not something that you've talked about and agreed to. Yeah. So looking at the accident side rather than intended pregnancy.

Nick understands that the woman 'has the power' 'to say yes or no' to the putative father's wishes, but would rather she listen to his objections, a story made more acute by the experience of a friend who is now a young father:

> his girlfriend didn't tell him until five months after that she was pregnant and that's kind of stupid because it doesn't give him a right to say 'have an abortion', or to think about it. … So they have a child now, so it's very upsetting because

now he has to worry about bringing up a kid. … [N]ot only are you effing up your own life but you're doing the same with another person. And you're bringing this, you're making this kid's life a nightmare. … [K]ids cost like a million a year to look after during its, staying up all nights … but it always should be a, yeah, it should always be a strong choice between a male and a female, but if the guy says like 'seriously I don't believe we should; … listen to what I feel about this and please take it on board because you know this will stuff up your life and my life'. … Like you, umm, you see a lot of people with kids struggling, families struggling. … [H]is parents might be the loveliest parents in the world but if he's going to have a hard time financially. … and we do call them white trash because they just don't know what they're doing.

Nick appears to believe that men have the right of veto when their life will be 'effed up' by unwanted fatherhood, giving the example of a man he saw on the news who beat his wife because 'she wouldn't listen'.

Azleena's partner demonstrated his lack of psychological capital when Azleena chose to terminate her second unexpected pregnancy:

We were always friends, we'd been friends since we were about 15, I think, and we only sort of became a couple when I was 17 and when I became pregnant. … [B]ecause I wanted to breastfeed, he wanted me to express milk so he could feed him. After a couple of weeks of actually having the baby he kind of didn't really want to do that anymore, but he is a good father. But when I became pregnant the second time, he didn't want to know. We were already sort of really rocky because he didn't really want to give up his lifestyle. … He plays football and he has to train three days a week and all day Saturday he's at the games. … I felt he needed to stay home with us a bit more and so there was quite a lot of friction there. And then when I became pregnant … he didn't want to know about it. I would try to talk to him about how I was feeling. … I actually told him and he's like, 'Well you can't keep [it]' and I said, 'Well, I know… but I just don't like being told'.

Azleena's boyfriend did not accompany her when she had her pre-operation counselling, nor when she had the abortion: 'he went to football that night'. Neither did he want to discuss her experience when Azleena came home from 'having it':

And now he's saying that it hurt him too much and that gets me angry because I didn't have a choice whether or not to sort of be involved but he thinks that he should have a choice to just stand back. ('Azleena', gender studies university student, Adelaide)

Azleena's story suggests that many young women's ideal of 'sutured selves' (Roseneil 2007), of men understanding women's stake and experience in pregnancy via extensive discussion and deep bonding with children, may be far from realised in real lives. Women's responsibility for the baby as well as the bathwater denies them the same freedom as men have around abortion and housework decisions. However, there is a difference between the baby and the bathwater. In relation to abortion decisions, males in my sample were more likely to argue for negotiation and females for the woman's individual right or choice. By contrast, although the differences are not as great, females were more likely to deploy negotiation — as well as masculine duty — to make claims concerning men's involvement in childcare and housework.[10] This suggests that negotiation skills or psychological capital are a 'weapon of the weak' (Scott 1987). Women deploy emotional labour to cajole men into housework. When it comes to reproductive decisions, men assert women should also exercise their emotional skills and listen to men's desires, rather than act unilaterally from their stronger bargaining position. In fact, my findings suggest men who wish to have more influence on abortion decisions, as well as successful partnerships, would do well to improve their emotional literacy and participate more equally in 'suturing selves'.

Changing institutions as well as women's desires

> I've just done my major research for social studies and that was looking at the relationship between working mothers and stay-at-home mums. It was really interesting to see what facilities, workplaces, actually offer, and looking at how much they offer locally, I know that it would be very hard to try and have your children and a career at the same time. I think that's really what's made me sit back and say to avoid a lot of stress I think it would just be easier if I concentrate on having a family and then having a career. … If your career's going to change anyway, you might as well have a family and raise these people that are going to stick around in the world longer than the things that you do in a career. (Catherine, co-educational Catholic college, South Australia)

> I guess I'd have to take out some time to look after the kids (laughs). Oh, maybe I'd have a partner or somebody there to help, or my mother. 'Cos, yeah, I haven't really thought about it. ('Anne', co-educational Protestant college student, Adelaide)

Summers (1970: 65) concluded from her analysis of the high school girls' essays, 'It has been seen that women's two major designations — wife and mother — are uneasily combined. When a third is added, the psychic conflict is likely to be great.' Summers (1970: 43–8, 62) was alluding to the loneliness of suburban housewifery and the difficulties of returning untrained and ill-prepared to the workforce. Today feminist researchers write about the struggle to find work-life balance (e.g. Pocock

2003). Esping-Andersen (2009: 54) claims that 'one of the greatest tensions in modern society has to do with the reconciliation of careers and motherhood', his study identifying the lack of institutional supports to allow women to exercise this choice. Kathleen Gerson (2010: 12, 104) suggests that the largely shared ideals for egalitarian relationships stumble against economic and social obstacles, in particular a vulnerable job market exacting long working hours, 'pressures to parent intensively, and rising standards for a fulfilling relationship'. JaneMaree Maher (2005: 19) suggests a more positive negotiation of the work-life dilemma, respondents redefining the 'good mother' as 'someone who can get that balance right, of their own stuff and the stuff they need to do with their children' (Esme in Maher 2005: 25), in other words forging interdependent independence in their relations with their children.

As with Anne, quoted above, many young women in my research 'haven't really thought about' this 'greatest tension'. Others, like Catherine quoted above, when faced with institutional constraints, more or less happily give up or suspend their careers, rather than thinking about how they might change social supports. A lack of fit between habitus and field or disjunctions across fields does not always strike women with 'the lucidity of the excluded' (McNay 2000: 69 citing Bourdieu). Rather, they might, like Catherine, lower their expectations or rethink their priorities. Catherine's classmate, Anneka, suggests that working mothers are an inconvenience to their co-workers. Anneka commences by affirming it is good for 'we' women to have careers and a family and also work with 'the men'. Anneka then outlines the difficulties for 'the men' when mothers refuse to take an equal load, at which point women become 'they':

> Women come through this revolution and say they want all these things and they want to be equal. And then there are some things where they … say, 'Oh, we want equal opportunities for all the jobs'. Then when it comes down to it and the hard work and they get pregnant and go on leave and then they come back and the kid's sick all the time. Then they say, 'Well, you're not treating me equally'. 'Well, if you've gone and had kids, and now you're not working properly 'cos this kid's always on your mind'. Like, there are some things that women might need to face up to. Like, they can't work all the time because they've got to have a family. It's a bit hard sometimes.

Trapped in the male model of the ideal worker, Anneka and Catherine readily impose handicaps on their own dreams of combining career and motherhood. They endorse the widespread belief that household relations are largely a private matter, indeed the mother's responsibility (Probert 2002: 14; Bryson and Mackinnon 2000: 4; McDonald 2000: 8; Pusey 2003: 84; Maher 2008a: 268). Changes in the contribution of fathers, the demands of employers, or government legislation supporting paid parental leave and the right to part-time careers do not feature in their scenarios.

We might take some comfort from Laura Dales' (2005: 148) notion of 'agency by consequence', in which the accumulation of individual self-centred decisions can challenge social structures. As Gerson (2010: 196) suggests, 'because these desires are wide and deep, they are an emerging force for change', Gerson (2010: 198–205) positing workplace reform allowing parents a succession of jobs, work from home and flexible hours. However, this sounds like making a virtue of structural necessity: 'closing the gap between male "careers" and female "jobs"' (Gerson 2010: 200). A comparison of Canadian and Australian data suggests that the policies of the Howard government years, such as Work Choices and lack of parental leave arrangements, influenced the lower fertility rate among young Australian women (Andres and Wyn 2010: 181, 232). In the Victorian Life Patterns study, young people struggled to achieve the work-life balance, blaming themselves for 'failing' to do so (Andres and Wyn 2010: 81, 185, 199, 224, 230). As interviewees revealed, only a privileged few have the bargaining power to negotiate parental needs with their employers.

Conclusion

The first three chapters in this book have focused on continuities and discontinuities, difference and sameness across the generations in women's and men's experiences and imagined futures. While respondents generally endorsed gender equality as a way of valuing people and as a claim about the 'good society' that Australia now is, there is little evidence of gender equality in practice or even in the imaginations of young people. Their essays are insistently gender coded, with young women accumulating psychological capital through friendships, romance, travel, and thus preparing themselves for the egalitarian relationship based on communication, sharing, equality and respect. For their part, young men are engaged with 'objects' — sports, cars, sex — and are preparing themselves for the traditional role of the breadwinner, extravagantly imagined in some essays via fame and fortune. Young women are much more likely to imagine higher education and careers than their mothers did, but on the whole they still envisage a narrow band of lesser paid female-coded jobs and professions. Young men parry gender change with a parodic masculinity far more often than they write about the possibility of role reversal — staying at home to raise their children — or even the less revolutionary idea of sharing the caring.

When comparing the (scant) male stories that deal with domestic arrangements and the one in five female stories, the former's preference for traditional arrangements and the latter's for egalitarian companionship suggests tension in future households. This does not prevent many young men claiming a role in abortion decisions. In this test of emotional literacy, the young women are more sensitive to the feelings of the putative father and the requirement to talk the issue through while the young men are more likely to assert their rights without attention to reciprocal obligations, either to care for the unborn child or to negotiate a mutually agreed decision with their partners.

Interdependent independence is based on continuing critical consideration, both of one's own needs and desires and of the needs and desires of those around us, posing selves not yet in existence or always under construction (Budgeon 2011a: 149). In order to find and express our 'authentic' choices, we must have the kinds of relationships that make choice possible. Our choices, and those of our partners in life, then have reciprocal effects on the relations in which we and our choices are embedded (Budgeon 2011a: 21). My results suggest that, far from achieving gender equality and harmony in a 'postfeminist age', young Australian men and women are bound for conflict in the domestic sphere as their ideas of responsibility and choice, and of equality and difference, continue to diverge.

The weight of the voices in this chapter has been from young middle class respondents. They are generally optimistic concerning their friendships, their leisure pursuits, their careers, their family life, and their negotiation of these. They seem largely unaware of institutional limitations on the free expression of their choices. By contrast, as revealed in Chapter One, the stories told by disadvantaged young people indicate horizons of hope cramped by negative experiences, limited options and few resources, material or personal. The next chapter explores another 'pseudomutuality': increasing income inequality combined with declining sociological literacy, producing negligible capacity (or willingness) on the part of almost all respondents to talk about class relations that connect wealth to poverty.

Notes

[1]   Where theorists criticise Bourdieu's habitus as being over-deterministic and leaving actors with almost no reflexivity, they criticise Giddens' self-reflexivity thesis for assuming too much autonomy for actors (Adams 2006: 514–5; Adkins 2003: 25).

[2]   The Australian Temperament project found gender differences emerge from late childhood. There were no gender differences in terms of self-control, but females achieved higher empathy, responsibility, cooperation and overall social competence scores, while being weaker in terms of assertion (Smart and Sanson 2003: 8, 6). Michael Flood (2005) found that men are lonelier than women and have fewer social engagements. Some of Townsend's (1994: 88–9) sample of 350 men decried women's greater emotional literacy as 'manipulative power', portraying themselves

as 'hapless victims', or jealous that they lacked the language or skills to read emotional cues. McLeod and Yates (2006: 7, 115) compare their findings of 'a relentless self-scrutiny of seeing the self through the eyes of others', most common among middle class female youth, with the way many young men 'cling on to traditional male roles, traditional family structures and local (territorial and community) identities' (as Arnot put it, cited in McLeod and Yates 2006: 206; see also Budgeon 2003: 146–7 for England).

3   Roseneil's study suggests that friendships beyond the heterosexual sexual/love relationship are often the strongest source of suturing, not only for those self-defining as gay (Roseneil 2007: 122, 129–30), further suggesting that my biographers, who rely largely on marriage as a source of connection and friendship, may be heading for disappointment.

4   A study in 400 schools revealed that most sexual harassment was carried out by boys with their targets being a small group of boys who are intensively harassed and a larger group of girls who are less intensively harassed. However, while boys are the main perpetrators, girls also harass (Collins 1999: 19).

5   By contrast with the average family size of 2.5 children in 1970, 42 per cent of Summers' essayists wrote of having three or more children. Eight bore twins (two having two sets), while a third essayist had two sets of triplets (Summers 1970: 94, Tables 1 to 4, between pages 75 and 76).

6   Although a survey in 2001 found that 30 per cent of fathers — by comparison with 70 per cent of mothers — had changed their working arrangements to accommodate childcare needs. The main family-work arrangements were flexible hours, part-time work, shift work, working from home, and job sharing (Campbell and Charlesworth 2004, citing an ABS survey). In 2006, only 6 per cent of fathers worked part-time (Australian Bureau of Statistics 2006).

7   Between 1992 and 2006, the average time men spent on household work rose by an hour and 25 minutes to 18 hours and 20 minutes a week. The time men spent in paid work remained steady at an average of around 31 hours and 50 minutes a week. In 2006 women still did around two-thirds of household work, while men did two-thirds of paid work, women spending 58 hours a week on these activities combined, compared with 54 hours and 20 minutes for men (Australian Bureau of Statistics 2009). When only primary activities are counted, in 2000, men did 55 hours (46 paid and 9 unpaid) and women did 47 hours (but only 23 were paid, and 23.6 were unpaid) (Baxter et al. 2008: 264). There is low availability and low take up of paternity leave while divorced men undertake more domestic labour than any other group of Australian men (Baxter in Maher and Franzway 2008: 551). However, a study of divorced couples who shared parenting found that children's present and future needs are in their mothers' minds whether or not children are with them so that they never experienced themselves as free of responsibility, while only one father had this encompassing approach and had changed his work patterns to fit in with his parenting (Lacroix 2006: 186–8, 192–5). In 2007, 35 per cent of men and 42 per cent of women described themselves as always feeling rushed (Australian Bureau of Statistics 2011).

8   Males living at home with their parents did 5 hours and 22 minutes of domestic work per week, compared with 7 hours and 28 minutes for females. When purchasing activities are included, the time is 8:45 and 13:25 (Australian Bureau of Statistics 2009).

9   The Catholic Education Office in Victoria did not allow inclusion of the abortion and homosexuality items in the questionnaire, although none of the other Catholic state offices or schools demurred. Female Catholic school students supported a woman's right to an abortion at about the same rate as other young women; only one third of Catholic male students did, compared with around two-thirds of the males in the other school categories.

10   In their comments, 3.3 per cent of females and 1.4 per cent of males support discussion and negotiation to achieve shared housework and childcare, while 6.2 per cent of females and 2.6 per cent of males do so in relation to role reversal. In relation to abortion decisions, 12.9 per cent of males and 8.8 per cent of females support discussion and negotiation.

4

GLOBAL VISIONS AND CRAMPED HORIZONS: STORIES OF CLASS

Introduction

> As a Tax Officer I was able to help the government take other people's hard earned money and learn for the future the interesting loop holes which allow the rich to avoid paying as much tax as they possibly can. In other words I got my training for my next job … [as an accountant with] a large corporation to assist their shareholders in tax avoidance schemes. (Matthew, Protestant college student, Perth, a 'member of the Liberal Party' who is 'against the greens and Socialist alliance parties')

> I once knew a guy called Paul who thought that he was pretty cool. Now, however he is homeless, and sleeps with aboriginals in the park. (male, Catholic College student, Perth)

The puzzle Beck sets out to address with his notion of *Risk Society* is why 'the structure of social inequality in the developed societies displays a surprising stability', yet 'the living conditions of the population have changed dramatically' (Beck in Woodman 2009: 248) and 'questions concerning inequality are no longer perceived and politically handled as class questions' (Beck and Beck-Gernsheim 2002: 30).

In the 1950s and 1960s the family wage brought the Australian dream within the reach of working class as well as middle class men. Most could be 'workers, fathers, sportsmen, beer drinkers, home handymen', although women's role was confined to 'full-time housewives and mothers' (White 1992: 165). Today the working class is more fragmented into those who might still dream but have little chance of owning a house and car, and the aspirationals whose scramble into prosperity requires large mortgages and two incomes. A more uncertain social world, in particular a much more precarious labour market but also more unstable family forms, intersects with scaling back of the institutional and collective supports that protected the baby-boomer generation. This makes work and love more challenging projects nowadays. The demolition of the welfare state, which once delivered (generally) good public education, health care and sufficient social security; the dislocation of families with single parenthood, divorce, remarriage and FIFO (fly-in fly-out, for example to mining sites) employment, and; the loss of friendships and communities through geographical mobility as people pursue education and work have thrown individuals back onto our own resources.

At the same time, neoliberalism has become a pervasive ideology, dominating not only our understanding of economics but also social relations, and almost completely occluding from people's consciousness any idea of structural forces and factors shaping their lives and opportunities. Peter Kelly (2006: 18) suggests the 'entrepreneurial self' is the response to the uncertainties of a neoliberal economy. The 'entrepreneurial self' is presumed to be rational, prudent and autonomous. Individualising logics mean that people no longer share experiences as members of the same social class, and so lose this sense of identity and ground for politics. Instead, 'social problems can be directly turned into psychological dispositions: into guilt feelings and anxieties' leading to 'broken down biographies' (Beck and Beck-Gernsheim in Woodman 2010: 741) for those who fail to craft an 'entrepreneurial self'. Ultimately, 'how one lives becomes a biographical solution to systemic contradictions' (Bauman 2001: 47). Loneliness is a failure of personability, unemployment a failure to acquire the necessary skills, and illness to follow the health regime.

The pressures and stresses of the struggle against uncertainty create a surprising degree of downward envy — for example, callous rejection of 'dole bludgers' — and little upward envy — for example, of the almost unbelievable expansion of top corporate salaries.[1] Only two of my respondents named people like Kerry Packer as tax cheats, echoing national opinion in their greater outrage at dole cheats (Evans and Kelley 2004: 254). Matthew, quote above, actually has an unusually clear grasp of the philosophies of the two major political parties, from the conservative perspective of being a young Liberal. His disassociation from the collective obligations we express in paying taxes is such that he endorses tax avoidance as a desirable strategy.

Despite their scant ability to understand structural patterns conferring opportunities on some people as a result of reducing the life chances of others, my respondents were not so blind as to be unaware of poverty or unemployment, or to know who is most disadvantaged in society, as the second essayist quoted above reveals. Interviewees struggled to explain social inequalities in ways that did not denigrate the poor or social security recipients. Those respondents who were poor or in receipt of social security themselves rejected the 'abject' subject of 'dole bludger', finely parsing the differences between their position and that of others on welfare. The first part of this chapter reveals the capacity of most of my interviewees to describe socio-economic differences in considerable detail. Following this I turn to attitudes concerning the welfare state, revealing a degree of empathy with those in poverty and more support for publicly funded education as a gateway out of poverty.

The hidden injuries of class

Chantah: They [rich people] get everything. Like, you know, you get the better education, the better car, the better boyfriends.

Mariah: Oh yeah.

Chantah: Because, you know how there's something where rich people date rich people, sort of thing?

Mariah: Yeah. But I think it depends on the person — what you see as yourself is better off. I think, to me, money doesn't matter to me. I reckon friends and family is — 'cos I've got so much of it — I reckon I'm better off, not in like a snobby way, to girls that go to other places — more richer girls.

Chantah: That's what the rich boys love, anyway.

Mariah: They look down on you just because you don't go to the private schools sort of thing. That's how it is. It really is like that.

Latecomer to group: That's Mr Pizzi [a teacher] — he's changing to the Heights [another government school] 'cos we're not good enough for him. …

Chilla to Adriana: And what about you? What do you reckon?

Adriana: Um [long pause]. Yeah.

Chantah: See, she's richer.

Mariah: That's why it's hard for her to say. (focus group with students at girls' working class government high school, Adelaide)

The young women cited above, with perhaps the exception of Adriana, who is not given much of a chance to express her opinion, understand that economic inequality ('rich', 'the better car') is linked with life chances ('private schools', 'a better education') and cultural capital (who you date, what you study). They also understand these differences to be hierarchical: 'rich people' have 'better' lives and 'look down on' others. On the other hand, Mariah believes that she is 'better off, not in like a snobby way', because she has 'so much' of 'friends and family'. The notion that 'money can't buy you love' is one reason why many young people in my research reject a class lens to understand inequality in Australian society. This was reinforced by a male teacher who entered the open space where our focus group was being conducted. He told me and my researcher that his definition of poverty had changed as a result of talking to the girls at this school. A family on an annual income of $100,000 but in debt was 'in poverty' while a single parent earning a third of that, but 'getting by … they're not in poverty': 'As long as they're living within those means', 'as long as everything that they need is got, it's not poverty'. This casts poverty in individualistic terms: 'what you see as yourself', as Mariah puts it, an idea far removed from Henderson's 'objective' poverty line.[2] These students are defensive about having less (describing one of their teachers moving to another school 'cos we're not good enough for him') but they also reject the presumed superiority of those with more (who are 'snobby' and 'look down' on others).

The privileged interviewees in my sample also find the hierarchy of class discomforting, describing themselves as a 'bit different' (see Kenway 1987: 398, 648 for similar responses among privileged school students):

> our kids are lucky enough to go to, well, I'm not saying that they are getting a better education but they are getting a different education and definitely single sex schooling for girls is fantastic. … In this area, people are privileged enough, I mean, it's a standard joke. They roll up in the European car in the gym gear and drop the kids at school then go off and have coffee with their friends and then, I mean, it's not all like that but it's a bit different to out in the mortgage world where people have two incomes and might work in a bank or in retail. ('Aviva', Protestant college mother, Perth)

In their 'I ams', some private school students described themselves as 'privileged', 'fortunate' and/or 'grateful', Edward asserting in his interview that this did not make him 'snobby or stuck-up to anybody'. Edward can, he says, 'communicate a lot better with people of the same sort of stature', defining this in terms of income. He quickly adds that this 'is obviously nothing down to me' but a result of his parents' efforts. Furthermore, Edward has 'friends, good friends' whose parents have a little less money, although he points out 'we didn't sit down and have long conversations about what our parents earn and things like that. Yeah, that's a great way to make friends!'

Only one per cent of the respondents (12 out of 1240) mention 'class' in their 'I ams' or life stories, sometimes using the term in non-sociological ways. The two self-defined 'working class' young people have fathers who are 'Equipment manager for TNT Australia' and 'Lieutenant Commander in the Royal Australian Navy', this father having deserted his family (her mother is a librarian). One university student describing herself as middle class is the daughter of a bricklayer and full-time homemaker. Even occupational identity, perhaps a surrogate for class, does not feature heavily in young respondents' 'I ams', although 'student' was second only to gender in social affiliations. Although a good many young people are in casual employment,[3] less than one in 20 school students in my sample indicated they were in paid work. Compared with their parents for whom occupation (combined with 'working' status and class) was second only to family group membership as aspects of their self-identity (see Table A3.5 in Appendix 3), part-time work is not salient to young people's identities, in part because many imagine a career trajectory elsewhere.

The upper class are accused of snobbery or prejudice ('stuck up sort of snobby richy people'), undermining the Australian notion of mateship and liberal tolerance. Emerald, a young mother, asserts, 'I think there is no class at all, we're all the same, but just some people have more money and some people don't and the people that have money just think they're better.' Catherine also suggests, 'I think class can also be the way that people view themselves'. The self-defined upper class 'view themselves as the leaders and popular, in control', whereas those 'in the middle' 'get along with everyone' (Catherine, co-educational Catholic college student, South Australia). By contrast with the snobby rich, my interviewees assert 'I don't like to think in terms of higher and lower'. Other respondents deploy individualism to stress that they do not think in terms of categories: 'I make judgements on people's opinion and people's values. I try to judge people as an individual and not group them' (Kathryn, girls' middle class government high school student, Sydney).

Even so, my respondents did not deny that income inequality exists in Australia. Indeed, many could elaborate minute socio-economic distinctions signalled by suburbs of residence (an 'industrial area' compared with suburbs with amenities and higher house prices), parents' occupations, and the insignia of consumption, which included a salad for lunch rather than a sandwich, 'what sort of music you listen to', cars and 'two-storey houses'. Political orientation also counted, Courtney describing her location in a 'pretty privileged environment … a very Liberal politics kind of a society'. Similarly, in the Life Patterns study, despite lack of awareness of the 'operation of classed processes', young people are 'aware of the uneven distribution of resources' (Andres and Wyn 2010: 37).

A common route out of this apparent paradox was to reduce class to culture, thereby replacing structure with prejudice. Fraser explains 'class disadvantage' by comparing 'people in Asia, dying every day' with Australia. When pressed to discuss inequalities within Australia, he shifts to a notion of 'status' or how people are treated: 'Most people usually get along but there's always certain differences', such as those that led to the Cronulla Riots.[4] Vanessa is 'getting goose bumps' just thinking about the 'extraordinary amount of money' spent on unnecessary things, which is 'almost an insult' to those 'fighting to survive every day': 'It isn't fair!' Rather than pursuing this line of analysis, she segues into ethnic discrimination: 'Class differentiation. Discrimination because of it. … [R]efugees and immigrants … with limited opportunity'. Vanessa then comforts herself with her school's 'multicultural policy' that gives everyone 'equal time', a notion of equality of opportunity (Vanessa, Catholic college student, Sydney). Melissa is wheelchair-bound and has been treated as though she is 'really dumb' or 'deaf'. She suggests that class inequality is unfair for the same reason: 'people just see them for what they look like and not their abilities'. Annabel also psychologises and racialises class:

> I think it is based on race, gender and socio-economic status. With race you see the class differences. For example, in selective high schools there are many Asian students. Their parents started in the lower classes and then have worked hard and push their children to work harder and to enter selective high schools so that they can have a better life. (Annabel, girls' middle class [that is 'selective'] government high school, Sydney)

Katrina initially responds to the question about class by discussing racist aggression by 'the stereotype of the white Australian' against Sudanese families. When asked whether there are any 'differences in wealth or life opportunities for people in Australia or in the town', Katrina asks perplexedly, 'Are there different opportunities?' She then describes kids in Wendouree West as 'trapped' in underfunded schools where 'it's going to take years, not like five years, probably thirty years to fix it' (Katrina, sexuality youth service client, Victoria). Elise's first response to how she understands class is 'school' but she then slides into 'different languages, different coloured people'. Of course, ethnicity and class are interrelated, glaringly so in the case of Aboriginal people, but the invisibility of and the discomfort with class is a persistent theme.

Furthermore, the solution for economic inequality is minimised to the liberal solution for racial intolerance: educating people out of their prejudiced views. Like so many other respondents, Stephanie says, 'I don't really agree with class structure because that only creates divisions in society', divisions that at her school are due to nothing more than ignorance: 'that creates a barricade because the lower person can't understand the higher person. The higher person probably can't understand the lower person' (Stephanie, Catholic college student, Sydney).

Judith Brett and Anthony Moran's (2006: 276, 279, 326) interviewees were also reluctant to discuss differences attributed to 'social categories' such as race or poverty, quickly sliding to personal characteristics such as lack of information, unwillingness to improve oneself, not caring enough about one's children to make an effort, or cheating on welfare. In my study, too, individual differences were deployed to make low income possible to overcome, which means that high income is 'deserved'. Casey says 'If you're poor, you can always turn to be rich. You've just got to wait. You know?' (Casey, working class government high school student, Adelaide). Anne knows that the rich have 'better opportunities', 'more money', which means 'better teachers, more facilities', as well as 'Mum or Dad helping them along'. Having said that, 'if you really want to work hard, if you really set your mind to it and you're not that rich, you can get to a high position' ('Anne', co-educational Protestant college student, Adelaide). Niki does not think income inequality is 'fair at all', 'but then I believe that people put themselves in their own situations'. She goes on to suggest that girls like her are better off because her parents 'are just proud that you're going to school' and doing 'what you want to do', while middle class parents pressure their kids into high status occupations (Niki, girls' working class government high school student, Adelaide).

Even when they accepted that people have different opportunities, interviewees still argued that personal persistence could triumph:

> Everyone's got different opportunities. But, they can use skills that they have learnt. Some of my friends can speak second languages quite fluently because like their parents can't really speak English. … [For the rich] the work ain't going to get any easier for them just because they have money. … So they have to work just as hard as what we do to get to the same place, even though their financial situation when they get there might be a bit different than what ours might be. (Robbie (male), working class government high school student, South Australia)

Larelle, a youth worker, suggests 'the starkest experience I have as a [youth] worker with class inequality is … a lot of young people get bullied' because they lack mobile phones, email accounts, or brand clothing. Nevertheless, she believes young people from 'lower classes … can achieve the same', even if family background influences this capacity, because 'they need to believe in themselves':

> Day to day we have young people come in here that have absolutely no goals and no aspirations for the future because they've never had those seeds planted. So often they have parents that live in maybe poor housing conditions that don't have employment, have never finished school or gained any further qualifications themselves. … A lot of young people come through and they

don't have those aspirations and they don't get that you need to work for money and those sorts of things. … They can achieve the same, but it's going to be a bit more challenging for them because they need to believe in themselves before they can go and get there. (Larelle, sexuality youth service worker, Victoria)

'Determination to succeed' explains different life circumstances. But success is also individually evaluated: 'everyone has their own ideas'. Both ideas express the 'non-class character of individualized inequalities' (Beck and Beck-Gernsheim 2002: xxiv). Just as commenting on gender-based differences in terms of better or worse is understood to be an expression of sex discrimination, so do these individualistically oriented students believe that noticing class differences in anything like a pejorative sense is also an expression of discrimination.

A personal experience has given Amanda a handle on class, responding to the question with 'Like upper class, lower class, middle class?' She then asserts that class inequalities 'very much exist, as much as people claim they don't and gloss over the fact'. She illustrates with 'my little story', a friend who moved houses and sent a résumé with the previous 'lower class area' address as well as with her new 'upper class area' address: 'she got an acceptance in the upper class area and a refusal for the lower class area. And it was exactly the same résumé'. Amanda, however, does not 'like to admit it personally', linking class with judging people 'on their appearances', rather than intrinsic characteristics like 'intelligence'. She hints at a materialist understanding, however, when she stresses the need to 'look past appearances' to the 'reasons for those appearances', such as 'an awful home life. They have no money' (Amanda, co-educational Catholic college student, South Australia).

With the contemporary precariousness of the labour market (White and Wyn 2004: 135, 173; Dwyer and Wyn 2001: 188–9), researchers argue that meaning-making has shifted from production (occupation as one's calling card) to lifestyle or consumption (Walkerdine 2005: 51–4; see also Klein 2000: 332, 340; Marsh et al. 2007: 134–8). This embraces clothes, music, style, even body shaping, following Bourdieu's (1984) concept of cultural capital (e.g. see Wyn 2009: 81; Martens et al. 2004: 163). Many young people are sophisticated at reading such insignia displayed on one's body or about one's person, even though less than seven per cent of my sample identified with commodified society in their 'I ams': for example, 'loving' shopping, being 'obsessed with' clothes, fashionable, 'a consumer', 'a victim of advertising' (see Table A3.5 in Appendix 3 for the most popular self-identifications). My interviewees readily understood school friendship networks to be an expression of money as well as leisure activities.

Consuming class

> Having a free dress day [at school] was really challenging for some young people because that was your opportunity to showcase your best clothes. A lot of young people didn't have those sorts of things which I think would be a really uncomfortable experience for those young people that didn't. The guys that did probably didn't understand how the others would feel. That's where bullying and those sorts of things come from. ... [T]hey use that ammunition freely between each other. (Larelle, sexuality youth service worker, Victoria, who reports in her 'I ams' that she is 'nuts for op shopping')

What Larelle has seen, most of my interviewees were reluctant to discuss, despite the popularisation of the Queen Bee and her retinue of 'mean girls' lording it over the wannabes.[5] Only a handful of interviewees note the need to 'conform' or 'impress' other students with brand names or a particular style like 'rap'. The rules for 'impressing' female students are complicated by the need to avoid being labelled a slut (while being 'cool' is a shifting identity in male groups: Imms 2008: 39). Showing 'cleavage' and a 'belly button' or wearing a 'really short skirt' cause comment in some schools, while failing to act 'like a female' is also criticised:

> I believe that a group of women, or anyone, men or women, are allowed to wear what they want to and not be judged, so I personally didn't judge. But I know there was judgment. ... [P]eople would just be like, 'How could you wear something like that with major cleavage and showing the belly button and wearing barely anything?' ... I think that's just through advertising and just the view that you have to be cool to wear a specific brand. ... [Of those who failed to wear the brands:] they were pretty badly — were teased; emotionally abused. ... Some were teased because of clothes. ... you'd get girls that would kind of act like males in a sense, and they would obviously be teased because they weren't female, or they weren't acting like a female. (Niki, girls' working class government high school student, Adelaide)

Incorrect sartorial display leads to 'teasing', 'emotional abuse', being 'snubbed off', called a 'dickhead' or getting 'paid out'.

These students express the contradiction of 'mass individualisation', as Norbert Elias (1991: 127, 55) put it 60-odd years ago. An Australian student more recently described this pressure as *Being Normal is the Only Way to Be* (Martino and Pallotta-Chiarolli 2005 adopting the comment for the title of their book). The scope for nonconformity 'in dress, in values and behaviour required for group acceptance' is quite limited (McLeod and Yates 2006: 122). Several mothers battle 'extreme consumerism', while not wanting their children to be 'reviled' as 'weird', waging the war product by product. David, at a Catholic college in Perth, asks his parents to buy a slightly more expensive jumper ('like $2 or $4 difference') if the brand name means 'I don't get further into inviting unpopularity just so that I can just live at school in peace without people coming up and talking to you and insulting you and abusing you'.

Not surprisingly, none of my interviewees admit that they pressured others to wear designer label clothing. The closest to this position was Nick, whose psychological capital was dissected in Chapter Three, and who plans to become a fashion designer. He submits that expressing an individual style, with 'guidance' from advertising, consumer 'experts' and so on, is a required task in the reflexive project of the self (see Martens et al. 2004: 168), along with 'character', 'personality' and 'knowing what you're talking about'. Clothes sense builds self-esteem, helping wearers 'be cool':

> guys will go, 'Okay well I'm not that good looking, maybe if I have that stuff I can get myself to be like that. I could try and create myself.' ... [U]nfortunately it's we've lost ourselves, we don't know who we are anymore. ... [P]eople do definitely want to look their best, and so ... weight loss and stuff. ... I don't want to be second, what was it, Australia to be the second fattest in the world, it's not cool. (Nick, Protestant college student, Perth)

Nick is an example of what Rebecca Huntley (2006: 19, 156) calls 'notoriously enthusiastic and indefatigable consumers' who draw cultural capital from being 'conscious of brands but not loyal to them' and believing they determine what is 'cool' in the marketplace. Huntley (2006: 19, 156–8) found this most common among the Gen Ys she interviewed, by contrast with the anti-brand minority, although respondents were also concerned about 'the pursuit of "stuff"' that threatens the friendships in which they invest 'an almost romantic belief' and commitment (Huntley 2006: 81, 151–3; see also Pocock 2006: 64–5, 197–203, 209).

It was usually at other schools, in other friendship groups, at other ages, among other ethnicities or among the other gender where hierarchical evaluation on the basis of consumption was identified. One interviewee described her friends as more 'mature' and as people who 'appreciate' originality, 'especially if you're ethnic, heaps more than Australian girls'. Amanda went to a public school where students threw food at the 'scabs', but this does not happen at the Catholic college she now attends where students are not from 'the lower, lower side' and wear a uniform. Catherine looks back across a vast distance to her former year 8 or year 9 self, in the younger 'more competitive grades' where students sought to fit the 'class' groupings, by contrast with her contemporary individualist capacity to find and express her authentic inner self:

we're a lot more comfortable now with who we are and how our friendships sit with people within the grade. I know that last time we had a casual clothes days, people just came in trackies and ugg boots and just what was comfortable for them. So I think that, as you grow older and you become more aware of who you are and how you feel, definitely the issue of class, it changes because you're less likely to look at class and more likely to look at who you are. (Catherine, co-educational Catholic college student, South Australia)

Catherine's friends resist the dominant scripts by 'queering' them (Martens et al. 2004: 172), dressing in track suits and ugg boots. Others, like Larelle quoted at the head of this sub-section, celebrate op shop clothes that reveal the wearers as 'very individual and very intelligent people'. Even more interventionist against the bullying associated with income inequalities, Alex's class protested one casual clothes day by wearing 'the rattiest t-shirt we could find and a pair of track pants'. Anne suggests that 'often really popular people go out of their way to wear goofy clothes just to try and be funny'. Naomi refuses brand names for the very reason that they are associated with snobbishness ('she thinks she's better').

Other respondents place themselves in the golden mean between the 'bitchy' girls who wear expensive fashionable clothes on mufti days and the derided girls who are so poor they have to wear the same clothes every mufti day. Stephanie does not spend too much on her dress for the formal (but a 'considerable amount'), does her makeup and hair nicely at home (not at the hairdresser's) and shares a hire car with her friends, but not 'to the extent of, "Look at me, look at me" sort of thing'. Justin does not dress like a 'dero', 'goth' or 'punk' because 'people can't take them seriously', but neither is he obsessed about 'the latest shoes and the latest shirts' 'because I know how to impress when I'm myself'.

Aware of the critique of 'mass individualisation', a number of interviewees assert that they are 'individuals' who judge others as 'individuals'. This distinguishes them from the 'popular group' who are judged on their looks, dedicated to consumption, and who talk only about sports and clothes or boys and clothes, depending on their gender. David and his friends are not interested in sports 'and that's why we were shunned into the runt of unpopularity' by the 'popular group'. David's group retorts with 'we have no interest in what they do', 'we think they're stupid' and that they 'haven't really grown up since year 9': still deriding people as 'bogans', 'throwing paper around the [class]room' and so on. David takes pride in his marginalisation — 'I know that's kind of weird, I don't enjoy being bullied or, but I enjoy the popular group hating me' (David, Catholic college student, Perth) — and embraces the nerd label, which so many studies have found leads to boys' rejection in Australian schools (see Kenway 1987: 682; Martino 1999; Martino and Pallotta-Chiarolli 2005; Mills et al. 2007).

Carina, like David, eschews the popular group, describing her group of six females and six males as 'funny' and doing 'the craziest things', like inventing feast days when they 'dress up and haunt the streets' or writing scripts for their own radio station. Dorothea, Carina's mother, suggests the group consists of 'creative' 'nerds'. Zoe, a classmate at Carina's middle class government school and in the same friendship group, describes her group as 'academic', by contrast with the 'sporty people', the 'bitchy girls or the prostitots',[6] 'driven by their social obedience and point of dress' and the 'giant group of boys who are absolute deros'. Zoe describes this as the 'little class system in our school'. She pauses and then rejects the 'class system' descriptor by saying that groups are based on 'interests' rather than class, because 'we're not a strongly class-based school. We are all quite on the same level a lot of the time' (Zoe, middle class government high school student, Perth). Zoe, like so many other respondents, can clearly distinguish her school groups on the basis of an intersection of educational opportunities and income, but is unwilling to call this class.

The 'zombie' category of class

> Michael (interviewer): What does class inequality mean to you?
> Dominic: That would be the fact that the labourers or the lower class go out and work for the men in management. To me class inequality I always relate back to business terms. Workers versus management, you know lower class versus upper class. … [T]hey make a lot of money versus those that go out and work for those who make a lot of money. … I don't see us in Australia as having a big class difference. … I think lower class people are much less motivated to pursue their own hopes and dreams. I think that they're very satisfied to inherit dad's butcher shop or work with … a tradesperson. … [I]n my own personal experience life is what you make it and I think anybody in this world, regardless of whether you're disabled, female, male, Asian, African, it doesn't really matter to me in Australia. I think everybody's got the same opportunity if they put the same effort … in. I don't think you deserve a job just based on a minority fact. I think you deserve a job or a place in a tertiary institution like this for working your butt off, and it doesn't matter what background you come from. (Dominic, sociology university student, Melbourne)

Even students in a university sociology class slipped from sociological to psychological explanations. Dominic is capable of reproducing the Marxist mantra, but he rejects its explanatory role. Instead he offers the evidence of his 'personal experience' in which 'everybody's got the same opportunity' as long as they 'work their butt off'.

Alex, studying sociology in the same class as Dominic, asserts that unequal opportunities are passed from generation to generation, but, like many interviewees quoted above, shifts to the more comfortable ground of race as the cover for class differences:

> You don't necessarily see poor parents with children in high school ... becoming rich and famous; it usually carries on throughout the generations. ... They don't have the opportunity to go to university, they don't have the opportunity to maybe drive or earn a car to drive to the job that they wish to do, and own a house in the city so that they can work in the city. ... (T)here's definitely the higher class compared to the lower class, especially when it comes to race as well. Like the Aboriginals are classified as living in a third world country, you know, they're living in Australia. (Alex (female), sociology university student, Melbourne)

Few of my respondents, then, have a 'theoretical analysis of society' in Raewyn Connell's (1971: 92) terms. This is a reasonably coherent ideology based on knowledge of social dynamics, and in which largely consistent opinions fit together. Only two teenagers in Connell's sample achieved such a schema (Connell 1971: 212–27). Only two of Brett and Moran's (2006: 195, 307–14) adult interviewees could readily mobilise class distinctions without either envy or fearful rejection of abject victimhood. One was a social sciences university graduate and the other self-defined as working class in a collective sense.

Respondents may well be able to describe the stigmata of poverty and have a sense of unfairness about this, but they do not explain it as *causally* created by the wealthiest in society, by the owners of capitalist firms. As Melanie Bush found in her research with US university students, this means respondents endorse the 'right to be rich' (Bush 2004: 177–90; see also Bettie 2000: 14). Although they could relate statistics of inequality, Bush's participants implied that 'all grievances are equal': 'My parents worked two jobs, so do I, and so do my friends. Everybody is pissed and feeling screwed' (Bush 2004: 231, 181, 185). This is what Beck means when he calls class a 'zombie category' (Beck 2002: 202–3). Class — along with other social or categorical affiliations — is still alive to sociologists but has little resonance for social participants (see also White and Wyn 2004: 19; Andres and Wyn 2010: 21 and Budgeon 2003: 9 for young people in two studies) and no longer functions as a useful basis for social policy development and application.

These 'living-dead categories' blind sociologists 'to the realities and contradictions of globalizing and individualizing modernities' (Beck and Beck-Gernsheim 2002: xxiv). This is particularly paradoxical in the case of the welfare state, a triumph of the class-based collective struggles of early modernity. Yet its institutions increasingly apply the principle of individual assignment of claims and contributions (Woodman 2009: 250). The welfare state, won by collective class action, now contributes to the declassification of individuals, hailed in contradictory ways by a range of state authorities, for example as recipients of benefits or subjects of regulations, and charging them to act proactively to improve a situation they can often control partially at best (Beck and Beck-Gernsheim 2002: 23; see Woodman 2009: 250). Woodman (2010: 744) suggests that a 'non-unitary habitus' expresses the contradictory institutional pressures by which individuals are increasingly forced to 'shape their biography': to negotiate and to manage the greater uncertainty and risk in our lives arising from 'individualising structural logics' (Beck's terminology), and to resolve, as far as possible, the contradictions arising in different fields. The next two sections explore respondents' perceptions of the role of the welfare state in redressing poverty and offering equality of opportunity.

Addressing class differences: Abject social services recipients and the welfare state

Chilla:	And you don't think we should pay any taxes?
Claire:	None at all, none. [unclear] You sit there and you think the queen in England, she can make like 50 million dollars, give everybody a million dollars and not pay tax ... there's still povo [poor] people in the street. ... There should be no taxes, but they should give poor people benefits so they don't live in poverty.
Chilla:	Where are they going to get the money from to give them? ...
Hannah:	They can make plenty of other money, just photocopy it. (Claire and Hannah, working class government high school students, Adelaide)

Zygmunt Bauman argues that in recent decades welfare has shifted from something that is 'ours' and 'our right', to something that 'we' give to 'others', an 'altruistic burden'. Most recently social security has become something 'we cannot afford' (Bauman in Bonnett 2000: 43). When the majority are self-sufficient, even if a minority are enormously wealthy, it is easier to convince the desperate minority to accept 'personal responsibility for socially determined circumstances' (Seabrook 2008: 3). But most humans are also compassionate and connect with others in their daily encounters. Connection with those who are suffering at the hands of neoliberal policies, causing the breakdown of family, community and society (Taylor 2009: 1; DeKeseredy et al. 2003: 12, 83–9), causes cognitive dissonance (Bunting 2009 for England citing a study by the Joseph Rowntree Association; Mackay 2007: 1 for Australia), sometimes resolved by arguing the poor must work harder and sometimes by suggesting mechanisms to assist them out of poverty, particularly education.

Speaking of the unemployed people living in the suburb where she grew up, a parent in my research, Cheryl, expresses contradictory ideas as a punitive neoliberal discourse jostles against concern for fellow Australians. Cheryl expresses both empathy ('really sad') and downward envy ('I have to pay for six people that are unemployed', 'they have to tax the fewer people more'). She suggests both structural explanations ('they're closing' places and jobs are going overseas, 'a vicious cycle') as well as blaming the victim ('They're not encouraged to have pride in anything, 'cos everything's given to them'). Cheryl's solution is Keynesian (and akin to the Australian government's response to the global financial crisis): reinstil self-worth with jobs, whether or not they are necessary:

> I spent my whole entire life in that area, and it's really sad to see the way that it has deteriorated. I grew up in Housing Trust homes because my father was in the army. But everybody that was there was there because that was a cheap, affordable type of housing. But it didn't mean they didn't have any pride in it. They all looked after their gardens. They all kept their houses spotlessly clean. They were all nice people. … People don't have pride any more in anything. … But why don't they have pride? They're not encouraged to have pride in anything, 'cos everything's given to them. 'If you don't give it to me, well I'll get it anyway.' Well, somehow or other — stealing, whatever. … I've got a job. I have to pay for six people that are unemployed. … And they're closing places. They're closing jobs down and they're taking things elsewhere or whatever. That's putting more people on welfare. So they have to tax the fewer people more, and it's not going anywhere. It's just — they should just stop and think about things and maybe keep these places open so that these people are at least contributing something for their own self-worth and for the community's. 'Cos if you think you're useful, even if you're not really, but if you think you're useful and you're made to feel useful, well then you're contributing something. (Cheryl, working class government high school mother, Adelaide)

The most common response in my research — among those who accepted the trade-off between social security and taxes, which Claire and Hannah quoted above do not — was to see welfare as something that a select group of others needed but that many 'undeserving' people received, and that ultimately would not completely eliminate poverty and income inequality (see Bush 2004: 177 for this approach among US university students; Mackay 2007: 85 for Australia). One in five school students and two in five parents commented in individualist terms, identifying poverty as the fault of the poor, generally because of their unwillingness to work, but also in terms of consumption choices, such as wasting money on 'beer, wine and smokes'. Another one in five high school students and one third of the parents distinguished between the 'deserving' and 'undeserving' poor.

A muted sense of 'threat' also shadowed the sample's responses. One threat was to respondents' own income from redistribution. As Cheryl worried, young people in my sample agreed that 'we' suffer due to the 'multitude' of demands on the welfare state: 'we'll just become a broken down country', a 'poor economy'. The other concern was becoming too closely aligned with abject recipients of welfare.

Rejecting the social security subject position

Chilla: Maybe I didn't ask questions about the things that really matter to you in your life. Maybe, so let's talk about the things that really concern you.

Paul: Like, the question 'Should people who work pay more taxes?' I think no-one should get pensions.

General astonishment with Chilla asking: No-one should get pensions?

Paul: Well, it's a bit of a dodgy issue, because it's like, it's like people who are kicked out on the streets certainly need money.

Gareth: I need money to get smokes so don't tell the government not to give us our pensions [unclear].

Paul: It's like in a way people should look for a job instead of sitting on their arse. In other words, people that are on [support?] can't get jobs, but then again it's their own position, they need money to go to pay their rent —

Gareth: They need money to go to school or TAFE so you can't get the government to cut their pensions.

Paul: So in a way it is —

Gareth: You do need the pension.

Paul: In a way you *do* need it and in a way you don't really need —

Gareth: You do need it if you are going to buy supplies and stuff and food until you do get a job.

Paul: But you don't really need it if you're kind of just sitting on your arse. … the only thing is because we've been lazy. It's not always, it's not always that we've been lazy.

Mark: … My stepmother … can't always watch me or help me out and I have to find my own place, find my own job and that. … this place, [name of] Youth Service, this place where, they got me a place to stay and also helped me out with budgeting and how to do this. But money is still not enough. (focus group, disadvantaged youth service clients, Adelaide)

that's where dole bludgers come in. I think that that sort of life is so wrong and so self pitying that it's just like why should someone help you if you're not willing to help yourself? (Courtney, Protestant college student, Perth)

In my focus group with youth service clients, Paul causes general astonishment when he asserts that 'no-one should get the pension', but backs down on this 'dodgy issue' by admitting people 'kicked out on the streets certainly need money'. Gareth needs money for his cigarettes, but later contributes more 'acceptable' reasons for pension payments: 'to go to school or TAFE'. As Beck claims, 'risk and wealth are in inverse proportion' (Threadgold and Nilan 2009: 61). Not only do the disadvantaged have less financial and cultural capital with which to negotiate risk, as the exchange above suggests, they are also more exposed to the contradictory demands of institutions of the state (Woodman 2010: 742–3; Threadgold and Nilan 2009: 48). Beck calls this 'institutional individualization': the 'life of one's own is completely dependent on institutions' as the legal norms of the welfare state make individuals (not groups) recipients of benefits or targets of administration (Beck in Beck and Beck-Gernsheim 2002: 23). Systems that cannot cope with the emerging uncertainties suddenly deem people 'mature and responsible', forcing on each person a reflexive life, responsibility for 'self-organization', 'self-realization and self-determination' (Beck and Beck-Gernsheim 2002: 28). As Paul's struggle with the idea suggests, 'self-responsibility' may be an example of false consciousness but individuals have no choice (Beck and Beck-Gernsheim 2002: 23).

Significant intrusion of institutional demands in disadvantaged youth's lives was experienced by other welfare recipients in my sample. At the youth service where I spoke with Paul, Gareth and Mark, the youth worker, Karen Walters, added an item to the questionnaire for disadvantaged youth service clients: 'If you've ever thought you've been treated unfairly, what did you do to change that?' (see Appendix 1). A number of respondents replied, 'nothing', 'because there's nothing I could do' or because 'no one believed me'. Others responded with aggression: 'bashed them', 'got angry and curse them', 'knock them out so they get their senses right'. Others spoke of unfair treatment by institutions of the state:

Centrelink, and I couldn't do nothing to change that. Being labelled by the community because I was a street kid at 12 to now and I couldn't change that either. (female, disadvantaged youth service client, Adelaide)

I was not given the dole even though I'm transients so I took it further to an appeals court. (male, sexuality youth service client, Adelaide)

I have gone through many people and groups like counsellors, youth action groups, councils, police etc. (male, Aboriginal youth service client, Adelaide)

This version of the questionnaire found its way into the hands of some middle class respondents, who either wrote that they had not experienced unfair treatment or, if they had, usually experienced it at the hands of school friends, boyfriends and in one case an employer. In the first case, they spoke to the person concerned to resolve the situation. If necessary, they took their complaint to authorities, such as teachers or a complaints tribunal:

I went to the person and spoke about what was happening and we sorted out our differences. (male, other youth service client, Adelaide)

I did something to change it. If I was the shit kicker at work, I proved I was capable of more. I thought my parents didn't understand me and how I needed to be treated — so I moved out. A guy sexually assaulted me because I was merely female, so I showed him what a few years of taekwando teaches you and chased him down. (female, other youth service client, Adelaide)

I have never put myself in a position where I could be victimised. Also I come from a white middle class background which generally doesn't suffer any sort of discrimination or unfair treatment. (female, other youth service client, Adelaide)

As a comparison of these quotations reveals, if reflexivity, or the capacity to understand and respond to demands across fields, is also a resource, disadvantaged youth 'are marginalized by a social structure which empowers reflexivity in others' (Adams in Threadgold and Nilan 2009: 61).[7]

Like Courtney quoted at the head of this sub-section, in their rejection of victimhood, Joanne Baker's (2008: 58, 60) sample showed 'a chilling lack of empathy' towards others in similar situations, holding people personally liable for failing to muster the resources necessary to triumph. The stigmata of poverty repelled Paul and many of the young mothers in my sample from the subject position of welfare recipient. They either rejected this identity or drew a distinction between their legitimate needs and the laziness or immorality of others. 'Others' might be undeserving migrants who are not true Australians yet get government housing before a respondent's supporting mother, Centrelink clients who are rude and abusive, dole bludgers 'sitting on their arse' rather than seeking work, or students who receive 'Abstudy and Austudy' but 'just drop out of school and stuff'. Justin receives a youth allowance to support him in his school studies but criticises those on the dole who are not studying but who 'get more money'.

Single mother Kristy, who explains class in terms of 'money', 'clothes and where they live, jobs', points to the ways people 'get teased if they come from a lower class family: "She can't even wear shoes"; "They can't afford to buy bread"'. Little wonder Kristy refuses this identity:

> I live by myself now and I don't have that much money but I don't think of myself as poor and I still have nice clothes and my daughter's always clothed and has shoes on and we have a nice house and that sort of thing, so I don't think of myself as lower class in any way, so I still think I'm up there [laughs]. ('Kristy', young mothers' Christian school student, New South Wales)

A classmate of Kristy's, Elise, describes her three-generation household struggling on occasional work and pension support. But rich families also struggle in their own way:

> my dad … does on and off council work and my mum's a full time housewife, because my grandparents are living there too and my Nan's … just had to learn how to do everything again because she got severely bashed and raped. … She was in a coma for three months. … My brother and my sister, they live at home, and Dad because he suffers from anxiety stress so he has to do something to keep himself motivated. He's rebuilt his own car. … Most people can't brag about their money because everyone stresses. ('Elise', young mothers' Christian school student, New South Wales)

It is the small rather than large — and therefore perhaps inconceivable — inequalities that prey on Elise's mind. Elise has twins, which means less disposable income. Her single mother friends 'brag' about their spending power and 'tease' Elise with their 'shopping sprees'. Elise distinguishes herself as putting her children first:

> they're rubbing it in and everything. … Other people are just worried about their money before their kids, but I do my kids before anything else.

Emerald, another single mother at the same school, initially describes her family as 'strugglers' and then as 'the comfortable class'. Her mother is 'happy go lucky' in their Housing Commission home, although 'it would be nice' 'to have enough money just not to worry' about how the rent, electricity and telephone bills will be paid each fortnight:

> There was someone in Centrelink the other day … and I had to stand behind them and I was embarrassed because they were swearing their heads off. … Social security … isn't enough to live if you've got children, but what about people just spending that money on drugs and not giving their children what they need or not paying their rent … like it's so easy to cheat the dole that

people do it. ('Emerald', young mothers' Christian school student, New South Wales)

The justifications offered by these young mothers reveal how little space there is for the disadvantaged who embrace the obligation to craft DIY biographies and yet are so regulated by their involvement with state institutions and philanthropic organisations. To avoid being a victim or a loser, they squeeze a wafer-thin difference between their situation and single mothers or dole bludgers, grasping at shreds of possibility to craft a story of self-improvement. They can be aggressive in their rejection of others in need as they repress their own ambivalence and self-criticism concerning their present position, swallow their envy of those with privilege and express anxiety towards others competing for the same scarce social security resources (e.g. see Luttrell's 2005 study of working class women in the US; Brett and Moran 2006: 308).

The poor are always with us

Daniela (interviewer): Do you think it's fair that there are rich and poor people, or different classes in society?

Annette: No, I don't. Because I mean, sometimes there are people who worked really hard and so they're rich. And there are some people that don't work really hard so they're poor. But I mean, the divisions between them is just too big at the moment. … Whereas some other people … have it given to them kind of thing, are still, you know, abusing that privilege, I guess. …

Daniela: Do you think that kids from poor and rich families have the same opportunities?

Annette: Excuse me for saying this, but like the rich people are given like certain opportunities basically. You know, they can have whatever they want in whatever, basically. I mean, the poor people, they do work and they do get some opportunities, but just not to the extent that the rich do.

Daniela: And how do you think these inequalities can be fixed or addressed?

Annette: I'm really not sure, but I mean if you work hard — if you try to improve it — . I mean, I guess the tax system could affect like, you know, the rich. But I'm really not sure. ('Annette', Catholic college student, Adelaide)

Annette's grandmother worked 'something like three jobs' and her grandfather two jobs to support their family. From this, Annette draws a stout critique of class inequality. Nonetheless, she is not sure how to redress the situation, alluding first to individual effort and then to the tax system.

Kate accepts that there are people living in poverty who are hard workers but, like other respondents, resorts to the unassailable claim of TINA, 'there is no alternative'. Poverty is 'inevitable':

> Like, it sort of just seems the way society is. Like, ever since the dawn of, you know — since human civilisation started, we've always had paupers and we've always had rich people and people in the middle. ... I don't think it's realistic that we could ever eradicate poverty. The truth is not all that many people want to. The rich are quite happy where they are. (Kate, co-educational Protestant college student, Adelaide)

Kathryn endorses 'occasional' taxation contributions to the commonweal because this is the 'responsibility of being a citizen' but claims individuals have 'a right to their earnings' in a 'free nation' and 'should be able to keep as much of it as is possible' (Kathryn, middle class government girls' high school student, Sydney). Other respondents agree that income inequality is a desirable aspect of Australian society, proof that we live in a democracy rather than a communist state 'where everyone has no money and there are just certain schools'. Even Penelope, self-defining as working class and 'a socialist', agrees that 'because we're a democratic society, there will always be people who have more than others. It's certainly not fair'. A lone voice retorted 'we're a rich nation and I won't bore you with my bolshy, communist philosophy'. His was one of six per cent of young respondents who made comments that recognised structural disadvantage or, more frequently, the desirability of greater income equality.

Around 20 per cent of young people in my research accepted the need for social security to avoid poverty because they identified with the poor and/or saw this as a social obligation. The respondents who expressed empathy, like Cheryl quoted above, often noted that they had been discouraged job seekers, had a friend on social security, grew up in a poor suburb, used a public hospital or went to a state school: they realised that misfortune could also strike them. They were also more likely to be students at the working class government schools than the other schools.

More commonly, however, respondents echoed the phrase in the question that 'no-one should live in poverty' but went on to add a caveat, 'but ...', which individualised fault for poverty. The caveat condemned welfare cheats and 'dole bludgers', required people to work for their social security, or take responsibility for themselves, in particular learning to manage their budget and not waste money on 'beer, wine and smokes':

> no body should live in poverty esp. in a developed country such as Aust. However social security should also catch those deceitful people who work the system. (female, Catholic college student, Sydney)

Edward stoutly asserts, 'definitely nobody deserves to live in poverty, whether it's out of their control or within their control', but then qualifies his statement in relation to those who 'have the opportunity to work and they just don't take it'. Fraser is similarly ambivalent, moving from the inevitability of poverty ('There's always going to be the people who live on the streets and the people who live in … mansions') to suggest, although tentatively, that most poor people have the 'choice' to avoid living on the streets: 'It's probably wrong to say, but they probably had the choice whether to — yeah. There's probably certain situations where they didn't have a choice' (Fraser, sexuality youth service client, Victoria).

In her interviews concerning the US welfare system, Claudia Strauss 'found that *work* was a keyword' (Strauss 2005: 205–6, emphasis in original). The term was used in two senses: paid employment and the 'work ethic', meaning something 'hard' that could be applied to any task involving regular responsibilities. Work is thus linked to capitalism, responsibility and morality, but it is in tension with the pleasures of hedonism and advertising constantly beguiling us to have fun (see Wilson et al. 2005: 113 for Australia). As one essayist wrote, 'I work hard and know that the world is my oyster.' Dominic admonishes more sternly in his interview: 'work your butt off', 'work hard' and 'put in the hard yards' to surmount 'obstacles'. Caitlin rejects unemployed people who are 'comfortable' in their refusal of the work ethic:

> a lot of money is being pumped into people that are unemployed and aren't looking for a job and they don't want a job, they're comfortable — it doesn't matter what race you are or whatever class — they're comfortable in what they're doing. (Caitlin, Aboriginal service client, Victoria)

By contrast with punitive work for the dole schemes, Larelle, who works in community services, notes that a properly resourced scheme that effectively trains people for long-term employment is more expensive than present arrangements (see d'Ercole 2005: 49), and is therefore 'very utopian' (Larelle, sexuality youth service worker, Victoria).

In the British 'Inventing Adulthoods' study, 'critical moments' or turning points are both positive (university entrance, marriage) and negative (ill-health, drugs, family violence, mental illness). Negative critical moments are confronted more often by disadvantaged youth and they have fewer resources to deal with these troubles (Thomson et al. 2004: 226–9; Henderson et al. 2007: 20–3, 98). University entrance is much more the lot of the privileged, as the next section explores.

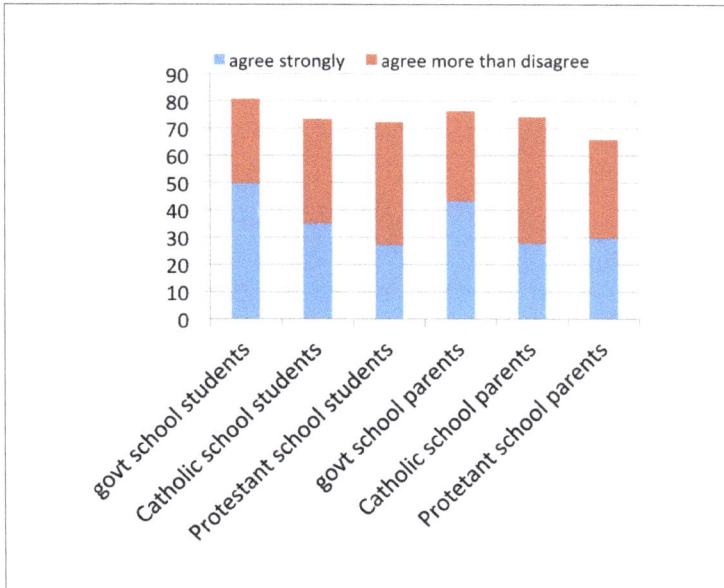

Chart 4.1: The Australian government should provide sufficient social security benefits so that no-one lives in poverty in Australia: School type

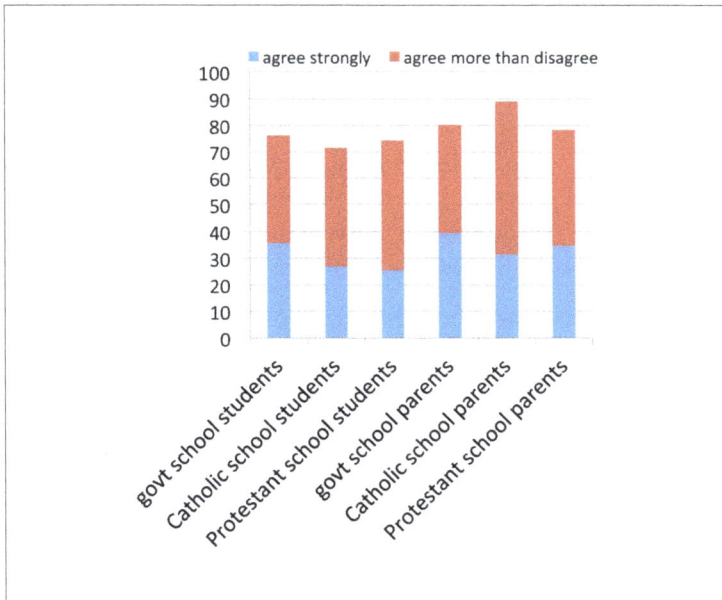

Chart 4.2: Good schools, hospitals and welfare benefits are more important than low rates of income taxation: School type

'Education generation': Equality of opportunity?

> In each of the chapters we arrive at the conclusion that young men from low
> socio-economic backgrounds — and especially those who have not participated
> in post-secondary studies — have fared the worst of any group. (Andres and
> Wyn 2010: 230)

The 'education generation' (Andres and Wyn 2010: 64) born just after 1970 pioneered 'mass post-secondary education' that is now the experience of subsequent cohorts, even as the stress of a HECS debt adds to financial insecurity and anxiety (Andres and Wyn 2010: 235). Attempts to extend access to those excluded from mass education have met with only patchy success. Working class boys without post-secondary education are a 'structurally dislocated' 'new underclass' of '*outsiders* who feel a lack of satisfaction about what they have been able to achieve' (Andres and Wyn 2010: 91–2, emphasis in original). This section explores varying access to educational opportunity among my respondents, and the effects of this on future employment imagined by the essayists in my sample.

Education is the most radical formulation for reducing inequality on offer by the two largest Australian political parties. This expression of (some) equality of opportunity suppresses evidence of massive structural inequality, offering education and then employment as the vehicles for self-improvement. This is echoed by respondents who see education as the magic bullet: a panacea for healthcare, social security and single motherhood:

> money for education should be a priority. More money for education would
> mean less needed for hospitals as health education would stop the swamp
> of people needing hospitalisation for preventable diseases. Better education
> would reduce welfare benefits to people on disability pensions caused from
> insufficient work place safety education, to single mothers who could have had
> better sex education and choices education. (Protestant college mother, Perth)

There is another reason why good schools and hospitals are more acceptable to 'middle class' respondents than social security benefits: all Australian schools receive considerable government funding. The disenfranchised young people in government schools express the most fellow feeling for those in poverty. Support for social security benefits, particularly at the strongly agree level, declines as the advantage of respondents increases (see Chart 4.1). By contrast, approval of public spending on education and health is generally higher — particularly among the parents. While support at the 'strongly agree' level still declines as advantage increases, this correlation is not found when this is combined with the 'agree more than disagree level' (Chart 4.2). One interpretation is that many young people, and their parents, in working class government schools know that they will rely on social security benefits in the face of an education that is not delivering good job prospects. By contrast, those in private schools, particularly parents, can see the benefits flowing from public funding of so-called 'private' services. However, it is noteworthy (and cheering) that at least two-thirds of every sub-sample supports the welfare state on both counts, at least to the extent of agreeing more than disagreeing.

Comparing educational pathways in the life stories

> I will have finished my HSC, with a fantastic HSC/UAI result i.e. above 95. … I will be able to find a successful, well-paid, rewarding job/career. … I will have married the 'man of my dreams' and we will have successful careers, a successful marriage. We will have two sets of twins, 2 girls and 2 boys: Alessandra, Sonja, Jack and Nathan. We will (no matter how materialistic it sounds), have a beautiful house, cars, our children will go to good schools and be the best people they can be. (Vanessa, Catholic college student, Sydney)

Most of my interviewees were aware that educational opportunities are not equal, although they were rarely exposed to the contrasts I perceived as I went from school to school. The leafy shades, sweeping playing fields and flag-stoned courtyards formed a backdrop to the polite neatly uniformed students in the Protestant colleges, where government funding is supplemented with private fees and endowments. In the government schools, broken asphalt pathways and crowded grounds cramped between shabby buildings heaved under the periodic overflow of motley-garbed students, noisily moving between their classes. While completing my questionnaire, the working class government school students chattered among themselves or interrupted the teacher as they lolled in their seats or on the floor. The academically oriented middle class government students were spirited in their interactions with me and their teacher, but they pursued themes relevant to completing the questionnaire. As Jane, a mother in my sample, tersely put it: 'opportunity is still something to some extent that you buy'. Parents buy better behaviour — middle class comportment and self-restraint (McLeod and Yates 2006: 55) — as much as extensive facilities or smaller class sizes (Kenway 1987: 659–60). My interviewees rendered this as 'more discipline', teaching 'manners' and refusing to accept racism and bullying.

As Charts 4.3 and 4.4 demonstrate, expectations of further education (as revealed in life stories) reflect the educational resources available in these different schools. Apart from males at the middle class school, students at private colleges are the most likely to write of attending university. Students at the working class government schools, the disadvantaged youth and the Aboriginal respondents are the least likely to imagine they will study at university, although they are more likely

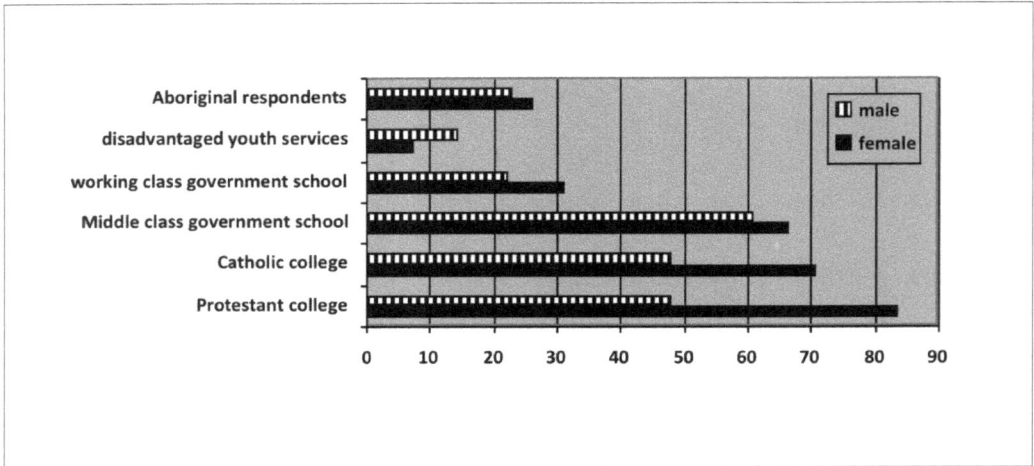

Chart 4.3: Percentage mentioning attending university in life stories x gender and 'class'

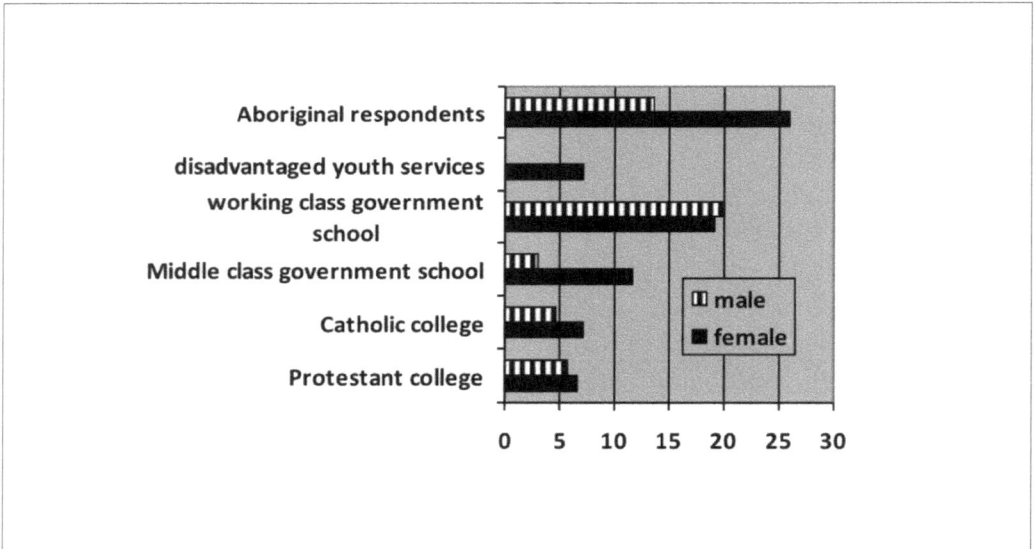

Chart 4.4: Percentage mentioning further education in life stories x gender and 'class'

to write of trade or other training as an alternative. In their 'I ams', the students at working class schools were most likely to define themselves through negative intellectual descriptors. They are 'not smart', write '[I am] stupid' over and over again or are 'fat and stupid, fat' (see Tables A3.7 and A3.8 in Appendix 3).

Although female essayists are more likely than the male essayists to mention further education or university entrance, young men have more lucrative alternative options than young women do. Young men can enter a trade (plumbing paying a great deal more than hairdressing), can dream of sporting success (that statistically will pay males better than females) or can imagine themselves as entrepreneurs of Microsoft and other mega-million dollar corporations. Many disadvantaged young women find only part-time jobs or join the 'spectacular increase in welfare support' (Mackinnon and Bullen 2005: 39, citing Bob Gregory's findings; Harris 2004: 51–2). As Tables A3.3 and A3.4 in Appendix 3 reveal, the young essayists imagine occupations that will cement Australia as one of the most sex-segregated economies in the OECD (House of Representatives 2009: 46). Young women work in a 'narrow band of occupations' in which wages are lower on average compared with their male counterparts (Andres and Wyn 2010: 38). There were scattered hints that male harassment directed some women away from non-traditional careers. Two of the female college students who write of entering engineering do so despite opposition from 'male chauvinists' and 'morons'. In real life, Larelle was discouraged by the barriers she encountered. She became a youth worker because of the harassment she experienced at school doing woodwork: 'I wish I had been braver and I wish that there had been a little bit more support to do something like that' (Larelle, sexuality youth service worker, Victoria).

Nettie, a mother, is one of the few respondents in my research to note the intersection of class and gender. She suggests that 'upper middle class and middle class' girls are outshining their male contemporaries, 'taking more than half the places in universities', which, along with being 'more socially adept' and 'more assertive', means they 'have more opportunities for professional employment'. By contrast, she 'suspects' that in the 'lower socio-economic groups' males are paid more than females.

While the large-limbed boys are cramped and fidgeting behind their school desks, dreaming of hurtling and tackling across the playing fields, the middle class girls are studiously aware that their path to a well-paid career lies through one portal: post-secondary education.[8] Studying the 'suicide five' 'to finish year 12 with a killer TER', young middle class females are aiming for medicine, dentistry, law-commerce, and occasionally engineering. While young men also write of achieving the desired tertiary entrance score, they quickly pass on to the reward of 'leavers' week' 'where I socialised 24/7 until I passed out from a lack of sleep on the third day'. At university, they recapture their 'deferred youth' (see Henderson et al. 2007: 227) and write of 'partying hard' and 'getting trashed a lot' with 'good mates'. The young women in my study are more likely to go on deferring their youth by working hard at university, 'spending countless hours in the library' or 'extending my knowledge and completing my degree'. Some do 'theatre productions with youth theatre companies, and do uni exchanges', or join 'almost every committee possible, getting involved in UNYA and Amnesty and continuing my rowing'.

The middle class Protestant college girls' study horizons encompass the world: 'a 4 year specialisation in haematology' at 'Colombia University (or maybe Oxford)', psychiatry at Oxford University where she 'formed a string quartet which earned me a bit of money', 'my Cordon Bleu course in France', 'Parsons School of Design in New York', 'Harvard Business School', 'the Sorbonne University in Paris' (see Chart 1.6 in Chapter One; other studies also finding that geographical mobility associated with study and employment is an option for the privileged — e.g. see Threadgold and Nilan 2009; Wierenga 2009). A Protestant college student in my study, Courtney, wants the 'basic' things: 'I want to live in a big house, meet a nice man, get married and have my son go to a good school and things like that.' She comments on her life story:

> I want to go international, which it's true I do, that would be a really very cool goal, yes, like dream. The biggest bank in America would be a nice goal, but I don't think I would really fit in, so yes, just one of those nice big busy, stereotypical like New Yorkish sort of apartment things. I mean, you would have to have a lot of like money and sort of make the right choices and things like that. I would like to do like honours or something at a really prestigious, like Cornell or Harvard or — that would be nice. That would be a dream as well, so I guess I was being a little optimistic with the scenario. (Courtney, Protestant college student, Perth)

Courtney's father has provided 'little incentives' to keep her on track for her dreams. For example, he has offered her an 'apartment at Bondi' if she is able to get into law at the University of Melbourne.

In her life story extracted above, Vanessa describes a successful life, premised on the success of her high school certificate score. This allows her to canvass an array of career options. Vanessa toys with the status of a medical career (but you have to 'be prepared to spend 10 years studying'), the non-traditional excitement of becoming a pilot ('I have actually had flying lessons and been to the university. It is really exciting'), and the nurturing profession of teaching from which she imagines progressing to school principal ('I teach piano now to children and have been involved in tutoring and stuff'; Vanessa, Catholic college student, Sydney). Threadgold and Nilan (2009: 58) found that the middle class respondents were the most likely to entertain 'six or seven careers', changing their ideas from week to week. When they said they 'take life as it comes', this was an assurance that derives from their belief that they can manage risk, given their quality education and parental support:

> Both of my parents are very supportive of allowing me to do whatever I want in my life and whatever makes me happy. My mother … always [says] 'I'd like you to go do your work' or 'I'd like you to work really hard' and that sort of gave me the work ethic. … She said to me 'Your job in the family is to do your schooling and to get a good education so that you can do what you want with your life.' (Stephanie, Catholic college student, Sydney)

In the 'Inventing Adulthoods' study, too, middle class interviewees presumed family support for their career goals as their entitlement. By contrast, a number of young women from disadvantaged families had significant care responsibilities for siblings or parents and this disrupted their own educational efforts and perhaps contributed to their path into early motherhood (Thomson et al. 2004: 226–9).

Life stories not only display different degrees of discursive capital (see McDermott 2004: 185; Giddens 1991: 6), they also reflect differing financial and interpersonal resources based on class: whether or not your parents can afford to send you to university (and offer you a flat in Bondi as a 'little incentive'); whether or not you have someone in your parents' social network to give advice about future careers that may be beyond your ken (see Andres and Wyn 2010: 109; Henderson et al. 2007), and; whether or not your parents can provide you with flying lessons. Esping-Andersen (2009: 122–8) identifies three aspects of the correlation between parental income and children's educational outcomes: the 'money effect' (income influences educational outcome), the 'time investment effect' (parental time with children influences educational outcomes) and the 'learning culture' effect (indicated, for example, by the number of books in the house, and which overpowers socioeconomic status in accounting for educational outcomes). Many disadvantaged students demonstrated a lack of the school grades and knowledge required to achieve their career aspirations as doctors, pilots or fashion designers (see Wierenga 2009; Mackinnon et al. 2010). They often had only vague ideas of what is available at university, for example completing 'certificates', or studying for two years to gain degrees. One Aboriginal male wrote of graduating as a doctor after only three years at college, while another intending doctor at the same youth centre writes of saving her 'first pashent'. One working class government high school student chooses pharmacy 'because I enjoy studying about chemistry' although given 'my other favourite thing is make-up and hair', she might become a beautician. Without the intellectual capital to achieve their goals, disadvantaged youth write 'wandering' stories (Wierenga 2009: 49, 57–67, 136, 109), unrealistic dreams of glamorous jobs, often prompted by the mass media.

In their wandering stories, disadvantaged males became a 'well paid rich guy', a general who will 'invade enemy countries and send hundreds of troops to war' or an astronaut who ascends to 'NASA high command'. In 'settling' stories, knowing 'how hard [it is] to find a job', disadvantaged youth ask only for a 'good job', a 'full-time job' (young men) or to 'Have money saved in my account for future needs, Whatever future … just as long as I am happy' (young woman). In Threadgold and Nilan's (2009) study, working class respondents also identified limited (blue collar jobs) or vague and unlikely ambitions ('make it' in sports, 'become an engineer and earn lots of money'). Andres and Wyn (2010: 145) found that early school-leaving young men are the least likely to have work plans, either in high school or seven years later. By contrast, several middle class respondents in Threadgold and Nilan's (2009: 55–6) study named very specific professional pursuits ('Curator for the Museum of Contemporary Art at The Rocks in Sydney').

In my sample, the most common 'wandering' escape from dreary prospects was via sporting success, with information technology also appealing to those in working class schools (see Table A3.3 and A3.4 in Appendix 3). One writer takes over the World Wrestling Federation, 'earning 8.5 million dollars a year' and retires 'a sixty year old multi-millionaire, happily married with children'. Playing 'for the Lakers in the NBA' while also becoming 'a computer genius', renders a working class high school student in Adelaide 'famous', 'rich, irrasistable and very very cool'. Sitting next to him, Adam copies this phrasing in his life story, to become 'famous', 'rich, irrasistable, and very very cool' as a graphic designer. In the focus group, Adam describes his story as 'What I'd like to happen' and he believes that some of it will happen (Adam, working class government high school student, Adelaide). In the same class, Barry reads out his story to the focus group:

> Become a fashion designer. Would like to get married. Would like to have one to three children. Would like to travel the world. Would like to become a soccer star. Would like to have a happy life. Take care of my grandchildren and be rich.

When he reads, 'would like to become a soccer star', Barry comments self-deprecatingly 'yeah, right'. Barry believes he will become a fashion designer, but 'That rich bit — I would like to be rich, but who knows? Umm but the rest is probably — and soccer star, that's probably hanging my goals too high, but you never know.' While some disadvantaged essayists do not have a firm grip on their prospects, Barry can distinguish between the more and less likely, the more and less within his remit. However, like the disadvantaged males in Wierenga's (2009) study, Barry has limited resources with which to achieve his goals.[9]

In the 'elite Protestant' boys' colleges, students are trained to run the country and corporations (McCalman 1993: 281–2). Privileged male essayists in my sample write of entering legal and managerial occupations, or become politicians and prime ministers. Privileged female writers imagine entering the caring professions.[10] Working class female essayists write of entering the caring sub-professions or the low-paid insecure hospitality and service sector. They often choose 'traditional' female occupations like beautician, nurse, flight attendant (to 'travel the world'), or jobs in the hospitality industry. Middle class government school male essayists disproportionately convert their intellectual capital into traditional male professions. Working class male writers are the most likely to write of traditional blue-collar occupations, and the disadvantaged youth of sporting careers (in part due to the high proportion of Aboriginal essayists in this sub-sample). Some young men (although more so the females) from disadvantaged background mobilise their 'caring capital' (c.f. Skeggs 1997: 82–3, 109–10), for example their own experience as troubled youth (Probert and Macdonald 1999: 144–5), to imagine themselves as youth workers. An Aboriginal youth service client suggests, 'I have trouble learning so I would not mind any job like a carer, like a care giver with looking after elderly, young, people with disabilities' (see Tables A3.3 and A3.4 in Appendix 3).

Young mothers becoming 'can-do' girls?

> the thing I wont the most in life is for ma baba growing up noing that mumma and dadda love them very much. (female, young mothers' Christian school student, New South Wales)

The 'can-do' girls represent that small minority of middle class girls who will achieve high educational outcomes and careers, be successful consumers and 'ambassadors' for their nations (Harris 2004: 10, 14, 19), although almost all of them will be denied the heights of corporate control and largesse. The image of the 'can-do' career oriented girl casts teen mothers as their obverse, 'at-risk girls' who as 'incontinent mothers' (Reekie 1998: 180) have abandoned their futures to be a drain on the taxpayers' purse (Walkerdine et al. 2001: 209). They are represented as unworthy, and so there is a 'lack of fit between their gendered habitus and the world with which they must engage' (Andres and Wyn 2010: 39):

> When I was pregnant, I noticed it. ... You get comments from people, like all my friends have still got their sort of normal lifestyle and they sit there and say,

'Ugh, I'd hate to have children, it'd be the worst thing in the world'. And I'm sitting there. And you get, the child welfare and health … and they're 'How old are you?' … When my mother would introduce me to people when I was pregnant, she'd say, 'Oh, but she's going back to uni'. So I had to be redeemed, I wasn't just a young mother, I was going to redeem myself by going back to university. … I don't even think it's the fact that I wasn't married, I think it was just that I was young. … I mean, I even do it, I even do it, like I'll go down the street and I'll see a mother and I think, 'Ugh', and I shouldn't be like that because I'm one of them. ('Azleena', gender studies university student, Adelaide)

Azleena's parents are teachers and they have supported her to raise her baby at home while 'redeeming' herself with tertiary education. Anneka is dismissive of teen mothers who have 'already put themselves in the kitchen before they've left school' (Anneka, co-educational Catholic college student, South Australia).

Alex, a young mother at sixteen as a result of rape, shares in the condemnation of young mothers, criticising twelve-year-old girls 'running amok on the streets and getting themselves bashed, raped and injured' or 'shooting up and getting pregnant' (Alex, disadvantaged youth service client, Adelaide). Alex distinguishes herself as 'being there for' her son and 'not letting [him] down'. In this way she both speaks back to and reproduces mainstream society's critique of welfare dependent mothers whose babies are 'unplanned' or 'a mistake' (see Luttrell's 2003: 92, 94 study of largely African-American pregnant teenagers in the US for this subject position).

While young mothers bulk larger in the social imagination than social reality,[11] year 12 programs offer an escape from stigmatisation (de Vaus 2004: 202) and an opportunity for economic self-sufficiency.[12] In my study, young mothers are grateful for this second chance offered by their 'excellent', 'beautiful' school, 'the greatest place 4 me'. Kristy praises 'our mums' school', which has assisted her to develop life goals, expressed in her essay as 'a beautiful house in an exotic location' and studying 'to be a psychologist'. Elise writes of a 'good job' as a bar attendant: 'I wont to do my bar cors to get a good job to get my drive lisants to go travelling places that I have wont to go to.' Several link their career and study with their motherhood role. Elise is at school because she doesn't want her twins to grow up 'thinking, oh, Mum's dumb, she's stupid'. Emerald writes of becoming a police officer and establishing a global fashion label 'Jaydo'. In the interview she canvasses her 'interests' that might become jobs: 'fashion design', 'photography' because 'I've got my own camera' and 'Beauty therapy … like waxing and nails and all that'.

Middle class respondents, particularly in the Protestant schools, have life plans: they link university education with a career in the professions or management.

The students at working class schools, and more particularly those who have left school before completing high school, have cramped horizons, both longitudinally and laterally. They cannot see far ahead and what they can see is often less than a handful of options.

Conclusion

> I reckon that classes will become more distinct and that 'cos I think the government will probably try to wipe out poor people. Or like not wipe them out but shift them away ... sort of like I sort of imagine like *Titanic*, you know how you have the lower class on the bottom and the upper class on the top. ('Monique', girls' middle class government high school student, Adelaide)

On the whole, not having yet experienced workforce unpredictability, most of my middle class essayists were sanguine about their working lives and technological changes. They imagined a path from educational success to workforce achievement. Unusual was the dystopian scenario of ever-longer work hours ('Work hours are 8am–10pm'), which eliminate family life, 'and as usual, the rich get richer while the poor get poorer'. Another writer suggests a future where teachers are replaced by giant screens: 'Too bad if your kid is sick and falls behind.' Despite the cheerful optimism of many essayists, this chapter echoes other sociological studies in confirming the persistence, and indeed increased significance, of class in determining life chances. Young adults bear the brunt of rising inequality: precarious employment, erosion of relative wages, and higher unemployment (e.g. see Esping-Andersen 2009: 57). Young Victorians in the Life Patterns project scaled back their aspirations from earning a lot of money or having a career to finding 'steady work' (Andres and Wyn 2010: 79–80).

Individualisation undercuts the ties of social connection. Empathy for the poor jostles with anxiety concerning the stress on the social and economic fabric. With the increasing division of services into (well-resourced) private and (poor) public schools, hospitals, even workplaces, members of the middle class today rarely rub shoulders with the working class. Gone is the capacity for empathy founded in knowing people on the other side of the class divide (McCalman 1993: 300). Monique, at a middle class government school, graphically captures this 'apartness' when she suggests that the government wants to hide or 'shift' poor people away, like the working class in steerage in the *Titanic*. It is an apt metaphor for most Australians' understanding of the ship of state: it contains both the very rich and the poor. The poor are more exposed to the consequences of misfortune than are the rich, but people on *Titanic Australia* are differentiated largely on the basis of lifestyle and consumption. The workers who build ships and the sailors who sail them are not represented as contributing to the wealth of those who own shipping lines. Even the sociology students in my sample, although they might be able to repeat what their lecturers have told them about class relations, were reluctant to endorse these as the explanation of inequality in Australia.

As a result, because working for low wages is a sign of failure rather than making the most important national contribution (as in the old cartoons of bloated capitalists living off the sweating workers), respondents distinguished themselves from the abject identity of 'welfare bludger', 'low income earner' at the same time as they dismissed the unwarranted superiority of the better off. They knew of and admitted socio-economic differences but they had no affirming language for locating themselves anywhere except as 'the same' as everyone else. The middle class interviewees tiptoed just as anxiously around their 'privilege' as the working class interviewees endorsed their own contentment with family and friends.

Without a sociological understanding of class, it is difficult to conceive the equity or distributive goals of unions, social security support for the disadvantaged or public education and health care as the right of all. The next chapter explores in more detail the arena beyond the intimacy of the family, the polity. I argue that young people imagine civic engagement in intimate terms: expressed in philanthropy and personal contact rather than impersonal 'big P' politics.

Notes

[1] At the start of the twenty-first century, the income share of the richest 1 per cent of Australians was higher than it had been since 1951, according to a study by Sir Anthony Atkinson and Professor Andrew Leigh. In the decade to 2002, CEO salaries of the top 50 companies rocketed from 27 times average earnings to 98 times, compared with top public servants who earned five times average earnings in 2002, High Court judges who earned eight times and politicians who earned 2.7 times. A study by John Shields showed the 51 listed companies whose CEOs are members of the Business Council of Australia had given their chiefs a 564 per cent pay rise between 1989–90 and 2004–5, their regular cash earnings rising from $514,000 to $3.4 million (Garnaut 2006; AAP, 2006).

[2] The Henderson enquiry, published in 1976, established a poverty line that has been used subsequently, although not without contention, to measure the percentage of Australians in poverty (e.g. see Daniels 2002). See Brett and Moran (2006:2, 162, 179, 309–11) and Bettie (2000) for popular interpretation of structural inequality in individualist terms, Brett and Moran also finding that respondents were quite capable of classifying people according to their paid work.

3   In the late 1990s, between 30 and 50 per cent of working age Australian school students held a part-time job, more than twice the OECD average (Pocock 2006: 204). Around half the young South Australians in an ABS survey worked in part-time jobs (Department of Education, Training and Employment 2000: 1).

4   The 'Cronulla riots' erupted in December 2005 after incidents between Lebanese and Anglo-Australian youth over the use of Cronulla Beach: see Lattas (2007) for a discussion of the complex race and gender issues.

5   Wiseman (2002) popularised these ideas, but see also Hey (1997) for a study of girls' friendships and Aapola et al. (2005: 49) for a list of other texts. Tamsin and Kaitlin discuss 'the new girl' who dyed her hair blonde in an attempt to be accepted in the 'popular group'. Kaitlin concludes that groups are much more fluid than the film *Mean Girls* (based on Wiseman's book) suggests ('Kaitlin', Protestant college student, Perth, interviewed with her mother, 'Tamsin').

6   Apparently used in a *Newsweek* article discussing Hilton, Spears and Lohan (Maguire 2010: 19).

7   Sociological theorists conceptualise reflexivity along a spectrum from 'the everyday reproduction of social structures rather than transcending them' through a 'habituated form of regulatory pseudoawareness' and 'knowing reflection' upon the social field through to purposive action (or inaction) to effect 'transformative social change' (Adams 2006: 516).

8   Since the 1970s, females have been outpacing males in year 12 retention rates, although low participation in apprenticeships, particularly the lucrative ones associated with the building industry, has not markedly improved, despite 30 years of gender equality programs. In 1990, year 12 apparent retention rates (number of students in year 12 divided by number of students in first year high school) was 70 per cent for girls and 58 per cent for boys; in 2003 it was 81 per cent and 70 per cent (Office of the Status of Women 2004: 92). In 2002, 36 per cent of apprentices and trainees were female, up from 20 per cent in 1996, but much of this due to changing definitions to include other than traditional trades (Office of the Status of Women 2004: 95). Across the OECD countries young women now have higher educational expectations than young men (OECD 2003).

9   Many studies confirm that young people's career aspirations are often a 'potent fantasy' (Walkerdine 2005: 54) that does not match either the present distribution of occupations in the workforce or, for those achieving at lower academic levels, what they can realistically hope for (Wicks and Mishra 1998: 93; Beavis et al. 2005: 6–7 for Australia; Schneider and Stevenson 1999: 3–5 for the USA; Walkerdine et al. 2001: 205 and Henderson et al. 2007: 6 for Britain). Put succinctly, 'Forty per cent of school leavers believe they will end up in the top ten per cent of incomes' (Rundle 2005: 45).

10 For example, female Protestant college students constitute almost half the essayists who wrote of entering the caring professions (largely the medical field: 19 of the 47 essayists who wrote of these careers).

11 Eighty-seven per cent of children born in 2000 were born to a couple, married or cohabiting (16 per cent to cohabiting couples), with 12 per cent born to single women, and 1.4 per cent to widowed, separated or divorced women (de Vaus 2004: 202). The teenage pregnancy rate in Australia is 17.6, 'the lowest in the industrialised English-speaking world' (Summers 2003: 29).

12 Young men and women without children experience very similar labour force participation rates, but 94 per cent of young men with children are in the labour force compared with 38 per cent of young women; 33 per cent of young women without children participate in education while 8 per cent of young women and 13 per cent of young men with dependents do so (Probert and Macdonald 1999: 135).

5

'INTIMATE' CITIZENSHIP?

Introduction

> I am very lucky within my group of friends because we can discuss issues like
> this. They're all amazingly intelligent people. I mean, we do talk about T.V,
> make-up, typical teenage things but we can also sit down and we can have a
> serious discussion about politics, about religion, about the state of the world.
> (Kathryn, girls' middle class government high school student, Sydney)

A number of Brett and Moran's (2006: 325) younger interviewees did not see
Australia as a 'national community where bonds between people mattered'.
Dora, living in the bohemian inner city on unemployment benefits, had neither
a sense of entitlement nor of obligation, because she had no sense of society as a
set of reciprocal obligations: 'Dora simply saw being unemployed as an option for
individuals to consider, a choice living in Australia made available' (Brett and Moran
2006: 226–9). People identified with their breastfeeding or mothers' group, their
nightclub or sporting club, as a 'community' that would look after its own (Brett and
Moran 2006: 275–6, 164, 130).

Those trained in political philosophy and sociology, or who have merely spent
their adult lives being 'good citizens' by following current affairs, making informed
voting decisions and perhaps being members of a political party, sometimes despair
at such a lack of social connection and political awareness. This chapter seeks a more

positive reading, hopeful of finding potentially new engagements in politics (broadly defined) — more fleeting, more local, more intimate (although sometimes more global) — and based on individual freedoms or abstract ideals rather than ingrained responses to the 'totem' issues that divide the baby-boomer generation. Mark Latham identified these 'totem' issues as 'patriotism, national identity … asylum seekers and attitudes to our history, including the past and present treatment of Aborigines' (Simons 2005: 24, 28). Totem issues refer to fairness and nationhood, us and them, and to who belongs and who does not, with mutual distrust or anger expressed by those on either side of the debate. A price on pollution (the so-called 'carbon tax'), mandatory poker machine limits and asylum seekers were totem issues in 2011 and 2012, those on the side of 'reason' and 'evidence' stunned by the vehemence and fear of those who believe that proposed changes will kill their community and/or limit their freedom.

The chapter explores young respondents' attitudes to mainstream politics, comparing the few who write of becoming politicians with the greater number who engage in 'celanthropy', celebrity philanthropy. I then compare 'caring' for the environment with 'caring' for disadvantaged others, contrast enthusiasm for multiculturalism with greater reluctance concerning Aboriginal reconciliation. I analyse the effect of personal contact with Aborigines and migrants in shaping opinions and interventions. While there is evidence of 'paranoid nationalism' or worrying that pits our insecurities against each other (Hage 2003), many young Australians, both at the centre and the margins of presently constructed political discourse, work with generous, inclusive, optimistic categories to imagine their lives within the context of the lives of others (see Huntley 2006: 21). However, rather than imagining their interventions in the vein of 'big P' politics, defined by theorists in an age before the internet, mass communications and media celebrities, much of their focus is on 'intimate citizenship': personal actions in relation to friends and family as well as philanthropic interventions to 'do good' or 'make a difference', the 'important' work that means they 'won't be forgotten' as essayists put it (see Hamilton 2008: 239–40 for a discussion of an outwardly focussed 'meaningful life').

Playing at politics

> when I first saw those papers, it was like rolled out so much, then I thought …
> I had to ask the lady, how do you do it because I've never done it before and
> they said, 'Well, out of these hundred or so boxes you only have to tick one',
> and I thought, 'Rightio'. … And then they had another questionnaire thing,

1 to 7, we had to read that and that had all the politics stuff on it and that, all the ministers, we had to mark that from 1 to 7. But I did that all right. That all worked out. ('Elise', young mothers' Christian school student, New South Wales)

I've signed petitions, umm, I've like, I've sent letters and you know how you can get postcards that have got like it written in and you've just got to write your name and the address and send it off, I've done those for Amnesty and battery hens. … And also the one thing that I'm really interested in is the government cutting funding to public libraries. That's one of my big things because I love libraries. … I've signed petitions and I've like written a letter but that's about it. (Naomi, working class government high school student, Adelaide)

Robert Putnam's (2000) claim that people are 'bowling alone' pithily captures his argument for an erosion of social capital over recent years and from generation to generation. Building on Putnam's analysis, the 'civics deficit' thesis bemoans young people's lack of engagement in conventional political activities, like voting and political party participation — for example, the 'routine observation' that more people vote in the television reality show *Big Brother* than in local, European or UK general elections (Marsh et al. 2007: 91). Instead of blaming young people, other commentators blame mainstream politics: it fails to 'hail' young people, whatever their gender, class and ethnicity. Attempts to 'include' youth via forums, leadership positions and so on are experienced as tokenistic (Vromen 2009; see also Manning 2006: 49; Saha et al. 2005: 25; Harris 2004: 160–1; Marsh et al. 2007: 98, 211, 216). This argument understands participation in voting for *Big Brother* as a preference for direct democracy rather than a refusal of engagement in politics (e.g. see Huntley 2006: 108).

Chart 5.1 shows that political involvement is generally lower among young people than their parents, although parents have had longer lives in which to engage in these activities. One third ticked none of the political activity boxes in the questionnaire (see Appendix 1), suggesting that they had not even signed a petition (other research finds that only a handful of young people engage in 'mainstream' politics, e.g. see Harris et al. 2007: 24–5). In line with other studies, self-definition as politically oriented was related to socio-economic status: lowest amongst the disadvantaged working class government school students and youth services clients (Bean 2005: 136; Saha 2000; Saha et al. 2005: 8; see Table A3.7 and A3.8 in Appendix 3). University students are more involved than the other young respondents in almost every activity shown in Chart 5.1, several indicating a wide range of involvements, for example a university student in Adelaide wrote 'Student association, labour club, NOWSA Conference, International Woman's Day March, work experience in a union, research project on female membership and campaign for safety in workplace.' Michelle, a women's studies university student in Perth and one of the most politically active respondents, founded a successful youth group, 'Youth on Health'. With a budget of 'a couple of hundred thousand dollars each year', it promotes healthy messages, discussing topics such as youth suicide, drug use and AIDS. In seeking support from 'local members of government' and so on, Michelle comments, without rancour, that not she but a male lawyer talks to the male politicians as this brings more success.

Almost nine per cent of school students and 10 per cent of university students — unprompted — in their 'I ams' identify their membership of a political party or activist group, or express an orientation towards politics, such as being a 'good citizen', 'political' or 'politically aware'. However, for most high school sub-samples, sporting engagement outweighs politics in their 'I ams', by four or five to one in most cases (see Tables A3.7 and A3.8 in Appendix 3). Of course, sporting passions can become campaigns. For example, in a regional South Australian town, Robbie lobbied the local council to build a BMX track.

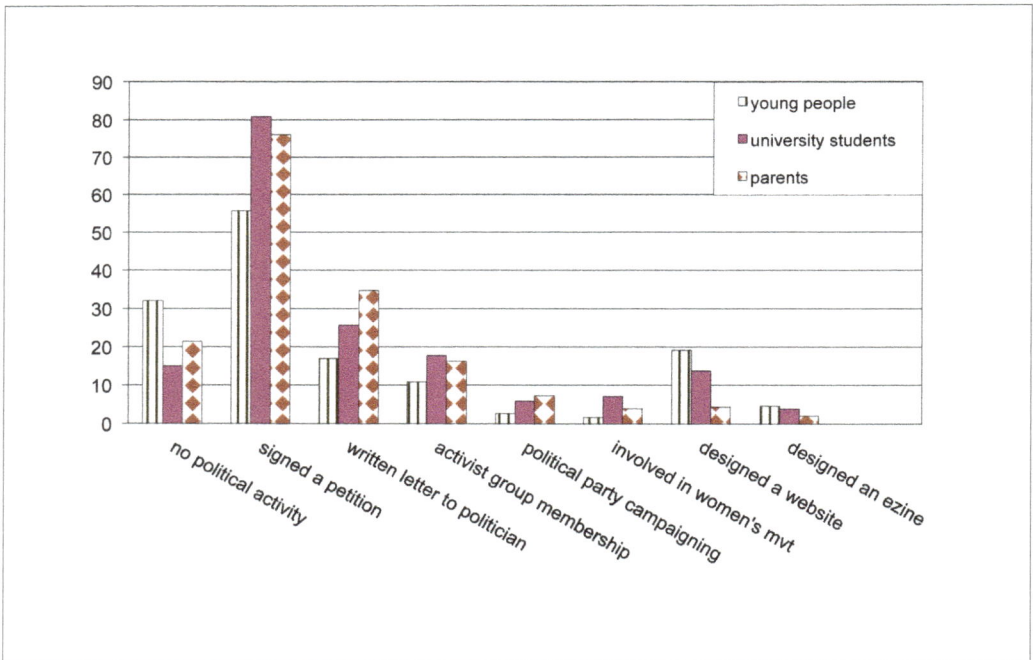

Chart 5.1: Political involvement x respondent type (% ever involved in each activity)

Despite the claims that young people are 'netizens' (see Willis and Tranter 2006: 51 for statistics on greater internet usage among the young), citizens of a cyber-community such as Facebook (which 'likes to describe itself as the world's sixth biggest country': Schultz 2009: 9), GetUp (although only one third of its supporters are under 34 years old: Coombs 2009: 108), YouTube or underground 'girl zines'[1] discussing women's issues like violence, unemployment and sexuality (Harris 2001: 134), there is little evidence of cyber-activity among the young people in my study. Naomi suggests of most Internet communication, 'there's not really much deep thought into anything' (Naomi, working class government high school student, Adelaide). Thus, while other young people outpolled university students in designing a website and writing an ezine, the nature of their websites was rarely 'political' in the conventional sense — for example, several advertised goods such as fashions and Aboriginal crafts. Some respondents stretched the definition of politics to include attempts to change people's behaviour or to pass on information:

> it is something me and my friend set up to just … it's just jokes and funny stuff on it and stories and stuff. [Asked whether this website was political:] I suppose it could be because it's basically me and my close friends in a way putting our views across, but it's not widespread, I suppose [does not reach a lot of people]. ('Sam', middle class government high school student, Perth)

Most of the young interviewees defined 'politics' as the government, that is, politicians, political parties and political institutions:

> I don't know if I could define it [politics], but I could say like you know how they, the Prime Minister and Treasurer and all that, then you've got your State Parliaments and you vote every once in a while. (Eleanor, working class government high school student, Western Australia)

Conventional politics was often criticised as 'boring' or irrelevant ('it doesn't affect me') and politicians condemned as self-centred and corrupt (see also Huntley 2006: 104):

> Political for me is, you know, the bigwigs sitting in Canberra and laughing at each other. Because when I was in Year 10, we went to Canberra for a school trip and … they were in session and we could listen in. And Bronwyn Bishop, I think it was, was talking and all the Opposition was doing was laughing at her. You know, you could hear them sniggering and all that kind of stuff. And the lady that was showing us around, she just goes 'I don't think we'll listen to that anymore' [laughs]. … They get paid more than what anybody else does, and they still complain that they don't have enough, and they get all the tidbits that go with it, and they just — I don't know. It just doesn't seem right. (Kelly, working class government high school student, South Australia)

Kelly's cynicism chimes with an English study in which middle class respondents defined political in the accepted academic sense, as about government. Young people on welfare to work schemes understood politics more broadly, and knew how much their daily experiences were shaped by politics, but in a context of very low levels of 'political efficacy'. They felt there was little they could do to change things, this explaining their alienation from politics (Marsh et al. 2007: 211, 217). In this formulation, young people 'practise a highly political disavowal of politicians' (Beck and Beck-Gernsheim 2002: 158).

Charmaine, the only female to write of entering politics in her imagined life story, describes herself in her 'I ams' as 'somebody who wants to make a difference, somebody who wants to help people, somebody who doesn't want to rely on a man to keep me happy ... disgusted with the way man sees woman, a feminist, somebody'. In the interview she notes that her political career is not about self-aggrandisement: 'I'd be happy if it was someone else who was Prime Minister or whatever. ... Like, it doesn't have to be me.' As the youngest prime minister in Australia, at the age of 25, Charmaine:

> made pornography illegal, put an end to all worries concerning the Murray River, increased the popularity of country schools, banned cosmetic surgery and made sure that Australia provided absolute equal opportunities for men and women. As a result of my solving the problem of illegal immigration to Australia I was elected President of all countries where people were previously fleeing persecution or unbearable living conditions. I turned these countries into a safer and happier environments than Australia had been in the 1990s, putting an end to the worldwide problems of illegal immigration.

In her interview, Charmaine self-mockingly laughed about her prime ministerial ambitions: 'I'll get out of uni and work a couple of years. ... They'll see me for my great talent, I won't have to like work for years and years in a local branch [laughs]' (Charmaine, middle class government high school student, Adelaide). Another committed politician will be sitting opposite Charmaine in the House. He writes that 'I will have sat in Parliament for a period and contributed to society in a positive manner', explaining elsewhere in his questionnaire that he is 'against lesbian feminist communists' who have 'destroyed the moral fibre of Australian society'.

Four other essayists write of entering parliament but appear to put the 'lifestyle' or the 'profession' ahead of 'serving the nation', even if they also amended a few 'minor things'. One prime minister felt 'insignificant at being classed as only a film actor'. Although he created a 'perfect' 'socialist state', 'I of course retain my wealth and return to film acting at 58'. Another young man became 'the youngest, longest serving Prime Minister in which I introduced several successful reforms', before retiring to coach 'the Perth Wildcats to 5 successive NBL championships'. Perhaps these narratives are expressions of Henrik Bang's (2005: 168) 'everyday makers', who desire their politics to be both 'fun' and 'necessary', and 'to get something out of it yourself' as they engage in localised politics (see also Marsh et al. 2007: 193). Young people want 'fun' — 'fun sports, fun music, fun consumption, fun life' — so it is little wonder they seek 'fun politics' (Beck and Beck-Gernsheim 2002: 159). It took an expression of politics more aligned with my own for me to see that having fun while doing good does not necessarily undercut the political impetus: 'I wish to also do something about the illegalisation of rainforests. … My life will be happy and hopefully benefit people in the future' (female, Catholic college student, Adelaide).

A young essayist from Chile is drawn to anarchy and communism as 'alternatives to capitalism' and its 'war-mongering'. He combines a career in the music industry (perhaps 'an underground record label') with his politics:

> I believe in equal rights for all people and I believe in preserving the environment. Hopefully sometime during my life I will be able to express these views. … I do plan on having children and I would like a world free of oppression for them, and for all children. … [I]n other words I want my life to be worth something. And I also want to have fun, lots of fun. (male, Chilean, middle class government high school student, Perth)

According to Robert Putnam (2000: 129, 265), the only hopeful sign against the widespread loss of involvement in community and politics is the increase in volunteerism by high school and university students (see also Gold and Villari 2000: 147; and Wilkinson 1994: 43 for Britain). I turn to young people's philanthropic engagement.

Celanthropy: Money buys love

> We were taken in on the Warped Tour and toured all over America. We had a great deal of success through the tour and got in top ten rock charts. Once we returned home we did a spot of local gigs and sold out a number of shows. With the success I started a charity which raised money for numerous groups. (male, Catholic college student, Melbourne, 'a guitar player', 'a black belt (I really am)')

> By 25 I was head designer of my own label. I eventually became CEO of the conglomerate I was part of. I was also the fashion editor of British Vogue for 5 years & I was a patron of 15 charities & a UN ambassador. (female, Protestant college student, Perth)

Where working class respondents are motivated by income in their job choices, middle class respondents have the 'luxury' to consider philanthropy as a career motivation, even if combined with fame and fortune (see Chart 1.7 in Chapter One; Threadgold and Nilan 2009: 55–6; see also Huppatz 2010 for a study of nurses). In my sample, compared with the four in five female essayists and around two in three male essayists who married, parented and had a career, only one in 10 engaged in philanthropy of some sort (see Andres and Wyn 2010: 81, 90 for similar results). The females were more likely to write of charitable involvement (13 per cent compared with eight per cent of the males) while the males wrote of fame (11 per cent compared with six per cent of the females; see Table A3.1 in Appendix 3). The gender difference suggests that volunteerism jibes with middle class forms of femininity that focus on being 'nice', 'blending in' and 'getting along with everyone' (Aapola et al. 2005: 117). The school environment might also encourage young women 'to add stories about caring for the less fortunate to a narrative primarily about hopes for a glamorous and successful future' (McLeod and Yates 2006: 167).

As with the wider population, religion and education influence philanthropy (Evans and Kelley 2004: 21–2), although only 6.2 per cent of the sample identified themselves in terms of religious affiliation in their 'I ams'. Such identification can require courage, at least in the government schools. Zoe has experienced discrimination, a friend saying, 'Oh, you think you're so good. Like you think you're superior to us.' As a result, at her government school Zoe 'suppresses a lot' of her religious interest. Another essayist assures the reader that she is 'a Christian (not a traditional, dull faced, mass going, bored, judgemental, down looking hard hearted person)' (female, Catholic college student, Adelaide). Just as Zoe plans to be an engineer or missionary in the third world, other self-identified religious essayists sought to 'serve others', for example 'Ministering to unsaved people. Preaching and prophecy' or assisting in projects in 'third world countries'.

Other protagonists write of becoming aware of their own good fortune as they 'help the less fortunate' in 'poverty-stricken' India and Africa. An 'Asian on the outside, but white on the inside' becomes a doctor whose 'greatest joy' was 'to visit third world countries and the gratitude received when I successfully treated patients'. A young 'Chinese' woman writes:

> The world has tempted us to live the easy life but I encourage all to take those chances, reach out to meet neighbour, give other a hand. Through that we learn & accept & appreciate rather than complain & become frustrated with life. ... [In Africa] I tended to sick children & spoke (with a translator) to helpless mothers who longed for the welfare of their children. In seeing the everyday blessing that I often experienced at home taken away from these

people it showed me how much more well off I was. … I lived there amongst my friends in Africa waking up to the scorching heat of the country & sleeping to the fading stars of the night sky. I gained friendships that were cross-cultural & despite language barriers I maintain them now. (female, girls' middle class government high school student, Sydney)

Noblesse oblige was a strong theme among the essayists at private schools, writing that their 'privilege' induces them to express 'community awareness': 'We shouldn't be selfish you know. We should help those who are needy and some people are very, very needy.' Courtney suggests that such civic service is an antidote to guilt and being 'depressed' about one's privilege: 'They [the school] just want you to put things in perspective and realise that you are in a position that could strongly advantage the rest.' Vanessa's work around 'drugs' 'is something you can put back into your own community', in return for being 'blessed' by 'a wonderful school' and living in an area that 'has nurtured who I am'. Like the religious cloak of Christianity, which rested unquestioned and almost invisible on so many mainstream shoulders up to the 1950s, this service orientation is meant to provide a counterweight to self-obsession. Janet McCalman (1993: 113, 300) wonders if this is effective within very unequal relations, suggesting that those who give but have never learned to take 'unconsciously resent the takers', an emotion likely to be amplified by the rhetoric of individualism and hard-headed self-reliance. Only one of my essayists was troubled by the potential for smug self-satisfaction in the unequal relations that philanthropy in Africa or India produces:

> I … worked as a volunteer … [i]n South Africa, and stayed there for nearly eight years. I worked in hospitals for children, and the dying and worked in poverty stricken countries helping them to grow good food and build better living standards. I came back to Australia and worked with a protest group about the devastating deterioration of the environment. … Travelled again, Asia this time where I adopted a little girl, who was orphaned and was blind in one eye. We stayed in Cambodia for 4 years working with communities and I taught English at a local school. … I don't mean to sound snobby or self-centred about all my 'good deeds' but I do hope that somehow all these things (not literally these things) will somehow fit into my life. I find them really important. (female, Catholic college student, Adelaide)

None of the essayists use the terms 'celanthropy' or 'philanthrocapitalism', coined to identify the philanthropy of celebrities and capitalists: Bill Gates combating AIDS in India, Oprah Winfrey building a school in Soweto, Bob Geldof working to 'Make poverty history' (Chandler 2006; see Marsh et al. 2007: 101 for the impact of celebrities on democracy and political activism). Even so, interviewees commend this behaviour and essayists describe moments where this is exactly what they do, such as the essayists quoted at the head of this sub-section. Naomi argues that inequality 'can't be solved by politicians. It's got to be solved by … the adhesion of society', by which she means privileged people willingly giving generously. Larelle applauds the local owner of 'a fitness club' who raised $40,000 for homeless people after 'spending a night out on the streets in Ballarat at minus two degrees with a homeless person'. Only one of the interviewees advocated corporate sector philanthropy as an obligation rather than a 'choice'.

At the imaginative level, a 'gun guitarist and songwriter … saved the world'. An Olympic gold winner 'stopped environmental change, saved all world wildlife'. A 'world famous artist … ended hunger, made world peace and love'. The 'best soccer player you can find' opens 'small high schools in Africa and also a hospital … Even now if I go near the village in Wikati you will see the soccer ground'. Other essayists articulate a close connection between their paid work and good works, several even becoming 'philanthrocapitalists'. The owner of 'a conglomeration of the best companies in each field of business' supplies 'financial aid to small business and donate[s] supplies to developing countries'. An Environmental Manager is committed to helping 'the world became a cleaner, better place'. Other essayists design environmentally friendly cars or nanotechs that 'benefit mankind' or use their millions to promote peace or 'the struggle for equality'. A successful handbag, jewellery and baby toys designer opens community centres around the world while also making a film that spoke to teenagers:

> Yah! It was HUGE, and people said they loved it because it was real and it showed them how to live for themselves and to love and keep peace!! … I then opened a whole line of community centres in Brooklyn, Melbourne, Brazil and SO many more places. It contained a dance class, gym, basketball court, lounging area and much more! It was free of course! But the most important thing in my life was my husband (who I met at 25). And my four beautiful babies! What a life I've led! Wooo! (female, middle class government high school student, Melbourne)

Others express a philanthropic impulse unconnected with fame or fortune: 'I help in charities and work to increase the standard of living throughout Australia' or 'I want to support a child from a poor country, eg 40 hour famine etc. also I want to donate blood until I'm not physically able to.' A young mother imagines volunteering in her retirement:

> I hope two be still with my partner happily living in a beautiful home with beauful grandchildren, a dog and living close 2 the beach in one of those retirement village carvan parks volentering at a day care center so, I can be

around lot of buitful, baby's & children and in the past own a cocktail Bar on some tropical Island and it very popular. (female, young mothers' Christian school student, New South Wales)

Given 'our celebrity-obsessed culture' (Caterson 2005: 57; see also Hopkins 2002), it is not surprising that young people's imagined route into politics is so often via boardrooms and television sets rather than the backrooms of political parties or activist movements (see Bang 2005). Compared with many second wave feminists, who took to the streets in hippy clothes and attacked capitalism as well as patriarchy, young third wave feminists claim there is no sin in attracting or giving money — indeed, it is essential. 'Feminist … philanthropy … is itself a form of activism', the 'women's funding movement' linking those with money to those with ideas and needs (Labaton and Martin, 2004: 287–8). However, most life stories do not venture beyond the rim of personal relationships: the 'majority' 'whose lives were never touched from my presence … doesn't concern me'; 'I'm pretty much indifferent to ppl I don't associate with, but will always be there 4 the ones who count.' In fact, the young Australians in my sample were more inclined to express empathy for the environment than for people they did not know.

Planet earth needs our love and protection

> Everything will be destroyed. Australia will fall in economy because of politics. Politics will destroy Australia. Food will be low. Water will be salt water. We'll all die. (total life story, male, middle class government high school student, Adelaide)

Among the themes Summers' essayists' addressed and which I listed in the instructions for writing the life story, was 'world crises or technological changes that would affect their lives'. My essayists write of war (often World War III), technological change and environmental disaster. Females often write as mothers, worried for the safe return of their enlisted children from the front, although one writer travels as a paramedic with her husband 'to the Middle East to help out the over worked paramedics' in a war precipitated by US anti-communism. Males more often fight, for example as a 'sharpshooter (sniper) in the Ukrainian alps' or 'in 2017 against North Korea … my home town was bombed and all my loved ones died'.

In relation to climate change, some imagine a dystopian scenario in which technological innovation is impotent against climate change:

> My life would have been full of technological changes, flying cars and mobile phones the size of eyes of needles would have been and gone. The latest transport would be done telekinetically and aliens would become servants to

mankind. Food won't have to be consumed thanks to an injection that never makes you hungry. ... Even though technology hasn't reached the stage of cheating death I'll be better off dying thanks to the pollution. (Justin, co-educational Catholic college student, Perth)

The young woman who goes as a paramedic to the Middle East also writes that the world becomes 'too horrendous' for her to contemplate children. Another writes: 'I will not make it to seventy — the world will be lucky if it survives to 2054' (total life story, Allan, Catholic college student, Adelaide, who talks in his interview of becoming an environmental engineer). Young Aboriginal essayists write about 'less plant life' and 'no more good environment'.

More optimistically, bleak scenarios are solved by a technological fix: 'The scientists made it all good' with fast-growing trees, hydrogen or other renewable energy sources:

All the currents changed and took the good weather with it. Almost continual storms reduce plane travel and places which was once prime land now is flooded, or blown arid, while severe coastal storms hammer beaches and stop offshore drilling. Without nearly any oil, you'd be amazed how quickly governments got their scientists to provide viable alternative energy sources. (male, Catholic college student, Perth)

An 'Australian born Chinese', as an environmental peacekeeper responding to the effects of global warming, assists in 'producing mini-cities which were 10kms tall ... to counter the rising sea levels and various natural disasters. ... Note: Think Day After Tomorrow plus 2001 Space Odysee'. A youth service client parodies such science fantasy solutions, writing that he and his girlfriend save the world when they 'some-how come across a vortex into another world, which is just like Earth, surprise-surprise!' A lone essayist produces a social, as opposed to the more common technological, solution when 'we ran out of fossil fuels' and global currents had almost ceased: 'I ... helped people understand their lives weren't going to be the same', although another essayist noted that 'reworking our social structures' is much harder than technological innovation.

As in other research (Vromen 2003: 89; Harris et al. 2007: 24–5), the strongest political engagements of the young people in my research are around the environment and human rights: 'I believe in equal rights for all people and I believe in preserving the environment.' However, only a minority are actively involved (in line with the population at large). Niki, a working class government high school student in Adelaide, is a member of Greenpeace, 'such a big and helpful organisation'. Jasmine, a university student in Perth, was a member of her local environmental group, which revegetates and gets 'the rubbish out of reefs'. Anne, a member of World Wide Fund for Nature and Greenpeace, wrote of becoming a greenie, studying 'environmental science' and living a 'hard' life for the environment 'in a hut':

> I would work tirelessly to find better ways of treating the environment and more sustainable practices. In my spare time I would paint and play the guitar. After uni I would buy a small bit of land, plant lots of native trees and build a small stone hut where I would live with my dog, my goat and my duck. I would campaign for organisations like Greenpeace and WWF and devote my time to educating people about the environment. I would have little time for relationships, especially children although looking back I wish I had had a daughter, maybe I will have. She will share my beliefs because I will raise her to see that they are good beliefs, she will be her own person though. She will respect me, herself, others and the environment. She will help me around the house looking after it and helping me to grow vegetables and to become self-sufficient. I will take her on environmental campaigns and we will be best friends. … My life will have been hard, people will have not always seen or shared my beliefs and that will be hard for me. I will always work towards a better planet and future for not only my daughter but for every living thing on the planet. To the day I die I will live in my hut in the bush. ('Anne', co-educational Protestant college student, Adelaide)

In the interview, Anne laughs as Daniela, the interviewer, reads out sections of her life story, but Anne confirms that she 'hopes' for and will work towards such a life, 'definitely' studying 'something to do with environmental issues or science'. Of living in her hut, Anne says 'I like the idea of becoming self-sufficient', avoiding 'mass produced' goods 'and also I'd like to get away from the city'. Environmental work is more important than a relationship: the environment is 'something I'm going to work towards', whereas 'I'm not going to work towards getting married to someone or forming a long-term relationship'. Anne realised 'about mid-way' through writing her story that she would 'like to have a daughter' after all, and so wrote one in.

Lacking Anne's Spartan convictions, other young respondents express an ambivalent relationship with consumerism: 'You kind of get obsessed with money sometimes'; we must 'stop needing to be constantly thinking about money'. One essayist is concerned that melting ice caps and rising temperatures make South Australia a 'drought area', blaming 'politicians and industrialists' for not preventing these changes. In her 'I ams' she writes both that she is 'interested in dolphins and their protection' and that she is 'a person who loves spending money' (see Langer and Farrer 2003 on children's attitudes to consumerism and citizenship).

In our commodified world, money means status, as explored in the previous chapter in relation to brand names and other insignia of class. Money also paves access to friends, sports, leisure and travel. Expenditure on children is a sign of love, and thus difficult to resist. Four young respondents identified parental love at least partly in these terms. One said, 'Our parents work hard to give us joy and happiness', although three of them also distance themselves from excessive materialism. Linh's mother 'tries her hardest to give us everything we want', which Linh would like to do for her children, although 'not like stupid things' (Linh (female), Vietnamese father, youth service client, Victoria). Vanessa's parents 'give me basically anything that I need' or which 'make life a little bit easier', although she points out 'we try in our family not to focus on [material things]' (Vanessa, Catholic college student, Sydney). Scott is wary of putting financial pressure on his supporting mother, 'but she — if I truly want something, she would do the best in her ability to go out and get it for me' (Scott, Catholic college student, Perth).

Theresa and her husband are 'downshifters' (see Hamilton and Mail 2003) who both work part-time to spend more time with their children. Their children return the compliment by asking, 'Why can't we be rich like' families with a 'flash' car, pool and so on? As Theresa says, 'if we didn't have the view of your worth is tied up with your income', it would be easier to leave 'a good and fine earth … not just for our kids, but just for the earth's sake itself' (Theresa, Catholic college mother, Adelaide). The distance between today's young generation and their baby-boomer parents is also captured in this segment from Katrina's life story:

> I fell in love with a man who was caring and loving but he came from a selfish family … ruled by material things and money. He had a daughter with a lady with no morals. She was an alcoholic hippy. She believed that what belonged to others was hers to have and use and give to her horrible children. … She did not see her father (my partner) as a father but rather as a bank. But I looked after him and we had a boy. Unlike his girl, I insisted our son called him dad and not by his 1st name! (Katrina, sexuality youth service client, Victoria)

Katrina knows that hippies were/are libertarian (hippy children call their parents by their first names) but she cannot conceive that they are/were also anti-materialist. Katrina's unassailable presumption is that everyone wants 'stuff', including hippies, which transforms their anti-materialism into bludging. Anti-materialism was a barely used vocabulary, only four per cent of comments questioning unfettered economic progress (see Table A3.10 in Appendix 3).[2] While respondents were generally unwilling to engage with the possible contradiction between consumption and environmental preservation, they cherished the environment, even more than they expressed concern for Aboriginal people, migrants, or the unemployed.

The three issues that young people endorsed most strongly were multiculturalism, sharing housework and sustainable development (for the questionnaire items see Appendix 1). By contrast, welfare for migrants, land rights or compensation and saying sorry to Indigenous people invoked a zero-sum response — 'their' welfare benefits come at the cost of 'our' resources or 'our' taxes; 'their' land rights mean 'we' lose our land (our homes, farms, beaches and so on). This is not, of course, the import of the High Court decisions in *Mabo* and *Wik* but respondents wrote that 'We may end up paying for the whole of Australia' or 'we [the white Australians] would have to leave Australia' (see Table A3.6 in Appendix 3). If there is 'an existential gulf' (Elias (1991[1987]: 198) between us and others, we lack a moral compass beyond ourselves (Beck and Beck-Gernsheim 2002: 38). Connections between Australians were narrowly fenced by respondents who claimed 'we' are only responsible for the children or land 'we' stole, for the migrants 'we' invite to Australia, for the foetuses 'we' want to become our children. Sometimes 'others' were divided into the 'deserving' and the 'undeserving': 'good' migrants are willing to assimilate; 'honest' social security recipients are willing to work; 'authentic' Aborigines practise traditional customs. The anxiety caused by economic precariousness was turned not against CEOs accumulating massive salary packages or governments failing to redistribute this wealth to low income wage-earners but against those marked as 'other': 'third world looking' migrants and refugees, Aborigines, single mothers and homosexuals.

As Chart 5.2 reveals, environmental sustainability and multiculturalism most often attracted the 'ethics of care' vocabulary (Gilligan 1982). This vocabulary covered three main sentiments: the strongest being the empathetic 'we are like them' identification, the second being the 'we care for them' maternalistic/paternalistic expression, and the third being a declaration of 'tolerance' towards others. Tolerance was mobilised by respondents only in relation to multiculturalism. The universalist empathetic identification was mobilised most commonly in relation to supporting social security so no-one lived in poverty (although only seven per cent of young women and 10 per cent of young men expressed this identification). The expression of care towards others was most commonly mobilised in relation to the environment, around 20 per cent of young women and 15 per cent of young men identifying this sense of stewardship. Combining the universalist identification and the ethics of care approaches, Chart 5.2 reveals that lower levels of empathy were expressed towards those in poverty, migrants to Australia and Aboriginal people than towards the environment (see questionnaires in Appendix 1 for wording of the items).

Not only did the environment need 'protecting', 'preserving', being 'looked after', 'treasured' and 'cherished', there was some suggestion of misanthropy towards humanity: 'a parasite' 'feeding off mother nature', bringing 'this pox upon itself', 'destroying' the planet (see Franklin 1999: 3, 194). Others expressed a need to care for our 'dying', 'sick' mother earth, which 'cannot defend itself', 'cannot fend for

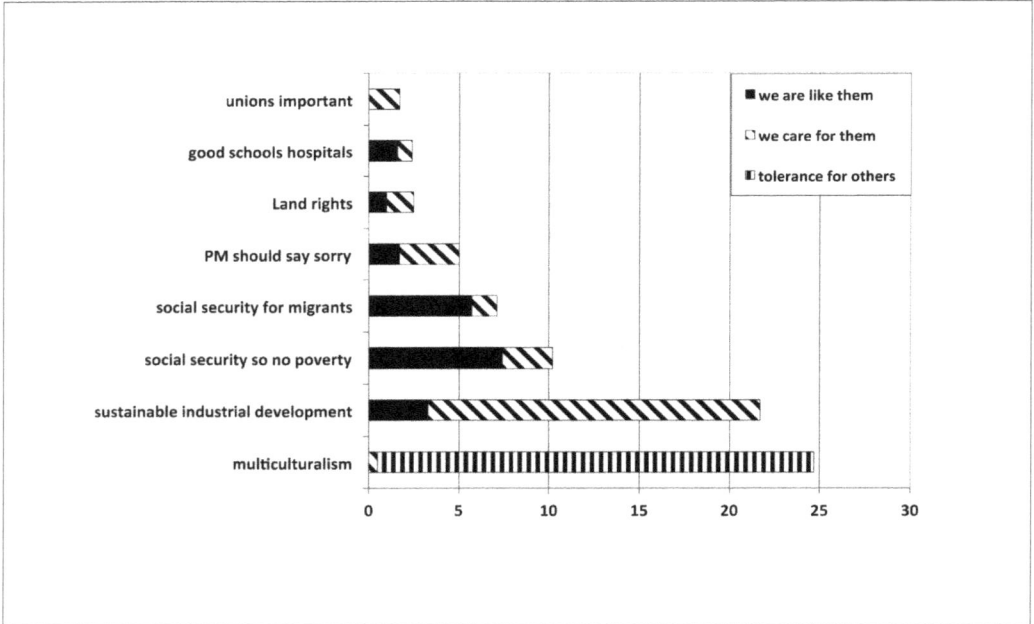

Chart 5.2A: Young women's use of the 'ethics of care' vocabulary: Selected items

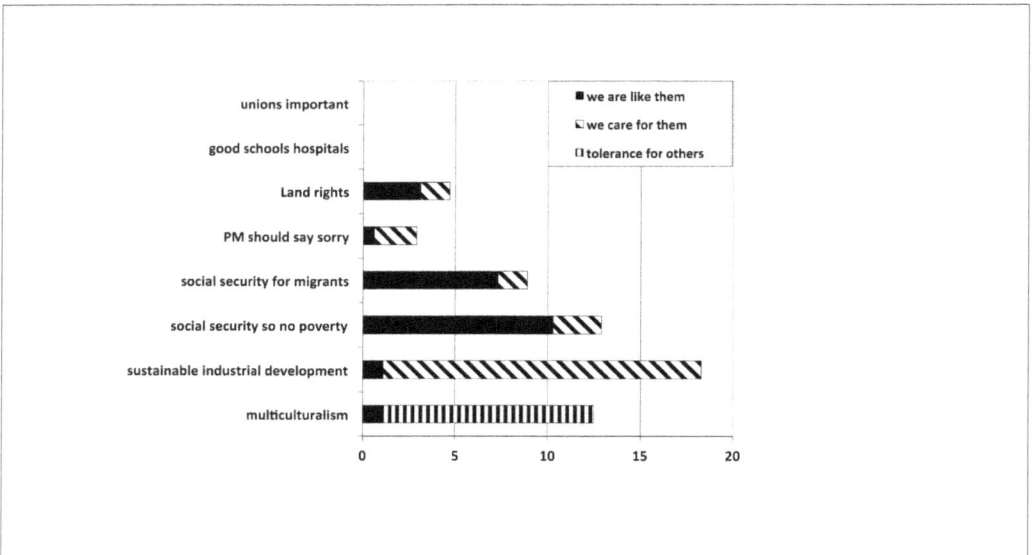

Chart 5.2B: Young men's use of the 'ethics of care' vocabulary: Selected items

itself'. Several cast this in an eco-feminist frame of 'raping': 'man's rape of female nature' or 'commercial rape of the environment'. Leila, a Perth Protestant college respondent, and Kathryn, a Sydney girls' middle class government high school student respondent, both vegetarians, go further to pose an oceanic connection of humanity and the rest of nature: 'humans and the planet are one thing' and 'We are part of the planet not owners of it … humans are not necessarily better than anything else on the planet'. A very few proposed a 'green and red-neck alliance' (Morris 1998: 219) or 'eco-nationalism' to express racism disguised as environmental concern (e.g. see Franklin 2006: 197, 238; Hage 1998: 164ff): 'I do think that the numbers of immigrants allowed into the country should be more limited c.f. unsustainable (environment)'; 'We need to look after our sustainability. But so does the rest of the world eg CHINA.'

I was surprised to find more empathetic connection with animals and trees than with migrants, workers, the unemployed or even Aboriginal children taken from their mothers. Respondents' ideas of living together in difference stumble against concerns about 'our' resources and needs as well as 'their' differences, sometimes framed as undesirable (for example, the sexism of Muslim men that threatens 'our' tolerance and egalitarianism) and sometimes as pitiable (for example, the alcoholism of Aboriginal people, their 'bleating' or 'whingeing' — like little children). The next section explores how Anglo-Australian respondents drew their boundaries around 'us' and 'them', focusing on intimate or small-scale interactions.

Beyond 'yeah, whatever': The potential for individualised citizenship

> I do think it's a problem when people start casting off all that's gone before just for the sake of individuality. … Individuality is great and wonderful, but you have to respect the other things and the other people especially, that's what it comes down to. I don't know how much respect people have for each other anymore. (Zoe, middle class government high school student, Perth)

> I think the word political to me just means how much of our life is determined by the individual and how much is determined by the controls of society, spoken or unspoken. (Kathryn, girls' middle class government high school student, Sydney)

> I'd say it [song lyrics] would have to be pretty powerful to actually make me go and do something. Usually you hear it and go, 'Oh yeah, whatever'. ('Florence', girls' middle class government high school student, Adelaide)

According to Ulrich Beck, politics as usual is inadequate to managing a society based on risk and individualisation. The sweeping reforms required in relation to insecure employment and ecological change are all totally beyond national politics (Beck in Beck and Beck-Gernsheim 2002: 29, 158), as climate change, asylum seekers and the continuing global financial crisis continue to remind us. Political parties and trade unions become increasingly irrelevant (Beck and Beck-Gernsheim 2002: 28) along with national politics, because the nation becomes both too large and too small. National politics addresses superseded collective identities in a top-down fashion rather than hailing people as equal citizens, a form of engagement that requires more localised actions (Beck and Beck-Gernsheim 2002: 28).

There is some evidence that young people's politics is either global or local (see Huntley 2006: 16, 113–5; Barlow and Clarke 2001: 26; Klein 2000). As Katrina notes, 'You can't change the world but you can change your neighbourhood absolutely and if everyone changed their neighbourhood, you know ...'. Nettie's sons have an international orientation, keen to see *Bowling for Columbine* and *Fahrenheit 9/11*, and 'value highly social justice', but consider the ABC news and current affairs as 'the driest and boring stuff'. Carina also has no interest in 'the Australian [political] system' although she and her mother went to the anti-Iraq war demonstration: 'I do have a pretty strong international picture because of my dad. ... [H]e writes me these long nine page letters about the current world situation'.

Nettie, a mother, suggests that many young people are motivated by a moral impulse, which they do not recognise in national politics (see also Saha et al. 2005: 13). Vanessa, citing discrimination and injustice, defines politics as 'taking a stand away from your life ... about something that you feel can make a difference' 'and making the right choices as well'. In 2003, Courtney observed a protest against the Iraq war. She did not join the protest because she felt she was too ignorant to have an opinion, but she 'wanted to see why other people were so passionate about the cause'. Courtney took away a 'moral' rather than a 'political' message, finding it 'very empowering' that people can be concerned for the well-being of those beyond our personal ken: 'It just shows that people are quite considerate of each other which is quite absent in today's sort of internationally' (Courtney, Protestant college student, Perth).

Citizenship and political engagement are no longer experienced as a duty to a national collective expressed in hierarchical organisations like business associations, political parties, trade unions (with their falling membership),[3] or even philanthropic societies like Rotary and the Women's Christian Temperance Union (associations in which the well-off work for the betterment of the less advantaged). The 'public realm no longer has anything to do with collective decisions' (Beck and Beck-Gernsheim 2002: 26). Instead people are mobilised by a more fluid involvement in horizontal networks, akin to mutual support groups or leisure-oriented clubs (Giddens 1994:

193). Instead of dividing the helpful and the helpless, new social movements are loose and egalitarian, based on 'mutual helplessness' (Beck and Beck-Gernsheim 2002: 18, 46, 160), although my research suggests solidarity around 'mutual helpfulness' might be the more appropriate expression, given the rejection of any hint of 'victim' status. The notions of 'network', 'serial community' or 'randomly formed queue' as the guest book on a website has been called (Sartre's distinction applied by Reid-Walsh and Mitchell 2004: 177), perhaps even 'dinner party' (Baumgardner and Richards 2000: 49), suggest 'co-operative or altruistic individualism' (Beck and Beck-Gernsheim 2002: 162) or 'self-organized concern for others' (Beck 2002: 213). A 'seeking, experimenting morality … ties together things that seem mutually exclusive: egoism and altruism, self-realization and active compassion, self-realization as active compassion' (Beck and Beck-Gernsheim 2002: 159). For example, one working class high school student refugee writes that he hopes to complete university and 'get a good job trying helping with poor poor people' (see also Peel 2003: 164 for 'shared responsibilities' binding those in disadvantaged communities together).

Can the 'tribal' support between friends (Mackay 2007: 288–91) be extended into 'good citizenship' and an 'ethic of care' between citizens? Writers have coined the terms 'sexual citizenship' (Evans) or 'intimate citizenship' (Plummer) to claim the extension of intimate concerns and sensibilities into the political domain (Roseneil 2009; Giddens 1992: 182). Self-help can become philanthropic volunteerism (Cimino and Lattin 1998: 131–3; Kaminer 1999: 145) or lead to group actions and 'the assertion of an identity in public life' (Rupp and Taylor 1999: 365; Maddison 2002). Several of my interviewees offered stories of personal difficulties motivating social interventions. For example, experiencing anorexia prompted the desire to improve mental institutions ('it's made me care about people a whole lot more'); gay sexual identity led to promotional work in 'how we can protect ourselves from sexual diseases', and; surviving sexual abuse stimulated 'a Support Group for male victims of sexual abuse'. Personal actions knit together personal and public activities (some imagined, some real): anti-globalisation protests and buying fair trade coffee; being a vegetarian and campaigning for the reduction in greenhouse gas emissions; reading women's magazines and writing letters to their editors condemning their sexist content; playing in bands and reforming the music industry; extending one's passion for acting to assisting youth to develop and perform plays. Tash subscribes to the 'McSpotlight' website (which criticises McDonalds) and tries to convince school friends to reduce their patronage. She reports to little avail, her classmates replying, 'Oh, we eat Maccers 'cos we eat Maccers' (Tash, working class government high school student, Adelaide).

However, the students at a girls' middle class government school who were encouraged to participate in a Fair Wear protest against the use of sweated labour to manufacture Nike shoes did not conclude that they should make different choices when buying shoes. Florence was excited but also 'frightened' by her engagement, while Monique and Tiffany decided that 'other things were more important' or they had 'better things to do with my time':

> We went to a Fair Wear march down on Rundle Mall and that was pretty damn scary. ... I was involved in some chanting, 'Nike make shoes that have no souls.' ... I was kind of scared because it was huge, because I didn't want to get arrested that day. ... [T]hey had made this papier-mâché shoe. And it was choice! It was good. Like, that was the first *real* political thing I've ever been involved in. ('Florence', girls' middle class government high school student, Adelaide, emphasis in original)

> You know how some things you think 'Oh my god, that's terrible', and you want to just do something about it. With this, you think, 'Yeah that's really bad', but you forget about it and it doesn't really bother you. Whereas other things to me, like, I don't know, other issues are more important to me in other ways. ... People's lifestyle and suicide and things ... interests me more. All that psychological stuff. ... I'm really interested in disabled, like helping people with disabilities and things like that. ('Monique', girls' middle class government high school student, Adelaide)

> I was into it when I first started the assignment but I think I've got better things to do with my time. I know that sounds a bit horrible ... I do find it horrible that people aren't getting paid properly for the long hours they work, but ... I wonder how my input could help. ('Tiffany', girls' middle class government high school student, Adelaide)

This section explores some of those 'better things', the forms in which young people expressed shared community in the coinage of neighbourly exchange. These cover the personal practice of feminism such as putting pressure on recalcitrant boyfriends, the response of Whyalla residents to the Baxter detention centre for refugees and interactions between Indigenous and non-Indigenous Australians.

Gender relations: 'my feminism'

> I see it [feminism] as being more a lifestyle and you just making sure that you do what you have to do to be equal and to have your life how you want it to be and make the choices that you want to make, as opposed to always having to be as somebody else wants you. ('Daria', women's studies university student, Perth)

Recent books by young feminists (e.g. for Australia see Dux and Zimic 2008; Maguire 2008; for the UK see Redfern and Aune 2010) attest that contemporary women's activism encompasses different values, goals, and strategies from previous women's movements, even if some of the issues remain stubbornly the same. In particular, these books claim that today's do-it-yourself feminism or 'girl power' represents a shift away from the presumed collective identification of the older 'second wave' feminists based on their gender (their 'group identification'). Instead, young DIY feminists define themselves by their 'individual practice' (their 'personal challenges', their passions like publishing fanzines or ezines; e.g. see Bail 1996: 6). Young women in my sample equated feminism with 'I support my own rights and those relevant to me' or 'I fight for my own rights', a point made by Daria in the quotation above.

In standing up for her rights, Siobhan, a young mother, started charging her male housemates for the cooking and cleaning that she does for them: 'the money helps me out. They get used to the idea that it's actually valuable'. Jane claims that as a result of studying women's studies, 'I think I stick up for a lot of females more than I ever have before now.' For example, when her boyfriend's friends are deriding a girl, Jane is 'very quick to say, you know, "I don't want to hear about this, like don't sort of, yeah, put these women down in front of me"' (Jane, women's studies university student, Perth).

Mobilisations around the self in terms of tastes, interests, the body, sexuality (Beck 2002: 213) might be just as challenging as attending a rally against the war in Iraq or against sweatshop labour. Young women who wear daggy clothes on school mufti days in solidarity with schoolmates who cannot afford designer labels are thumbing their noses at the increasing sexualisation of women's bodies (e.g. Levy 2005; Walter 2010). Kathleen describes her daughter's courageous stand:

> My daughter has a confidence about her in things to do with the body that I may not have had. … For example, she decided she wouldn't shave her armpits and her legs. … She's dark, so the dark hairs on her legs made a very strong statement at her school and she had to put up with a lot of, you know, flack, because it's a co-ed school, naturally particularly from boys. … I can remember that she had some quite hard emotional things to face about that but she decided to and she did it and that showed me what a strong will she has. And it was probably in some ways one of her first political acts. (Kathleen, middle class government high school mother, Adelaide)

Several other young interviewees engaged politically-personally on this battleground. Jane has 'done quite a bit of modelling'. She asserts individual choice in pursuing this work, and argues that the dangers of girls desiring to be unrealistically slim is 'exactly the same' as young boys who role-model sporting heroes in their 'drinking … drugs or adultery and things like that'. Similarly, the media is a 'fantasy world' in which airbrushed photographs of models are just a small instance. Jane applauds 'Cleo and Cosmo [who] have started using a lot more larger sized models' and do 'fashion editorials' with 'real women', discussing the look achieved by a range of outfits. Jane begins confidently with the assertion that a reader just needs 'individual confidence' to feel 'all right' with themselves, knowing that the 'girls were airbrushed'. However, she goes on to admit 'it can sort of play on your mind … "gawd she's beautiful", you know, "I'd give anything to look like her"'. Thus, young women can understand that images are not real *and* still have a problem with their bodies (see Budgeon 2003: 89).

Charmaine suggests that cosmetic surgery is on a 'continuum' with 'putting your hair up in the morning'. 'People' are seduced by the desire 'to look heaps good' while also being aware 'that it's wrong as well', unable, it appears, to resist internalising looks as a measure of identity in a society that judges 'people' on their looks. Lucy became starkly aware of the obsession with body image on returning from two months 'down south cutting pines':

> It felt great. Get back up here and it's like, diet, diet, diet, must be skinny, must be this. It filters in all the time, it really does. … It's like breathing, you breathe these ideas in. (Lucy, women's studies university student, Perth)

Males are the major consumers of pornography (see Johansson 2007: 39–56 for Sweden; Flood 2007 for Australia) and are much more in favour of it than women (in my sample 40 per cent of young men strongly approved female nudity in magazines by comparison with 11 per cent of young women). While some young men are aware of the feminist objection to pornography ('I know it gives a very bad image to females in general'; 'males will have higher expectations in woman and view outer beauty stronger than inner beauty'), individualism generally trumps these concerns: 'People should do what they want to their bodies/selves. It is called freedom of expression.' Some young men were upfront about their stake in the question: 'to be honest with you, I like to see those naked bodies'.

In contrast with physical or sexual violence against women, the use of pornography is more widespread, its normalisation almost complete but expressive of the tensions between desire, power and sex. There is a relationship between viewing porn films and practising oral and anal sex (Johansson 2007: 58). Young Australian women describe men who mimic porn movies, such as hitting nipples or commenting in surprised disgust on seeing girlfriends' pubic hair, as 'porn watchers' (Maguire 2008: 154–5). Ariel Levy (2005) urges young women to refuse to engage in 'raunch culture', refuse to be sexualised. Amy Dobson suggests this is no longer possible, that the 'debate for girls today is perhaps not so much about a choice as to *whether or not* to participate in the image economy, but about how one will best survive and thrive in it', choosing to objectify oneself before being objectified by others (Dobson 2008: 145, emphasis in original). Opposition to pornography is thus an 'unhappy performative' (see Raddeker 2006). In my sample, many women's gut feelings are that pornography is 'offensive', 'humiliating' and 'exploiting'. They were 'angry' or 'really uncomfortable' with it. They feel that pornography portrays women as sexual objects, even when feminist teachers or mothers tell them otherwise. Jane, a former women's studies academic, claims it is impossible to apply universal notions of exploitation and degradation. Her daughter, Verity, can see Jane's point but still dislikes pornography. After rejecting the objectification of women, Nettie pauses in reflective confusion: 'I just sound like an awful prude'. Nettie regains her confidence by adopting a gender-equality rhetoric to defeat individualism, at least in relation to scenarios like bondage: 'I'm coming from the assumption that intimate relationships … are on an equal footing' ('Nettie', Catholic college mother, Perth). Azleena worries whether she dislikes pornography because she is 'jealous' or because 'I just don't think women should be treated like that, as just an object' rather than as a daughter, sister or mother ('Azleena', gender studies university student, Adelaide).

In their intimate relations, three young women strive for 'disidentification' with idealised pornographic body ideals (see Heyes 2007: 67) by regulating boyfriends' behaviour. One respondent includes her boyfriend in the 'we' who will not be involved in pornography: 'As long as it isn't viewed around me or my partner.' Vanessa, a gender studies student, criticises her male friends for visiting strip clubs. Azleena warned her then boyfriend that if he went to the 'schnitz and tits' night with his football mates, where topless waiters served the schnitzels, 'well you see that, you won't see anything when you get home'. At the imagined public level, Charmaine supports these small-scale interventions. In her life story, when she becomes Prime Minister, she illegalises pornography.

Some young women reject feminism because its 'petty' issues — 'getting more or less pay than guys' or 'only men are allowed to play football' — do not compare with the pressing issues: 'the ozone layer, there's less jobs … there's the economy collapsing, we're on the verge of a world war again' (Naomi, working class government high school student, Adelaide). Courtney believes that compared with 'abortion', 'equal pay' and other struggles, feminists today are concerned only with 'small things', that 'if you really want to, you can create it yourself, like they created women's soccer when people really wanted it'.

Other respondents suggest that the women's movement's focus on gender is too limited: 'I believe that although the Women's Movement is important, so are other movements concerning the disadvantaged' (female, Catholic college student, Adelaide); 'feminism doesn't take account of men who are oppressed i.e. indigenous men, poor, white uneducated men — they also deserve social justice' (Aboriginal, mother).[4] In reply, several respondents were aware of debates within feminism, which have produced a wider embrace of social justice issues:

> I think if a girl my age called herself a feminist, you would, I would assume that she would be caring about the environment. Would want refugees to come to Australia. Would be anti-Bush, anti-war. So I think there is a lot of those sorts of things that would just go with being a feminist which is probably not true for everyone, but it's sort of an assumption. It's not so much an appearance thing anymore, like you know, should have a shaved head and wear overalls. (Jasmine, women's studies university student, Perth)

As Leila notes, 'I don't want inequality to happen with me, so why should I want it to happen with other people' ('Leila', Protestant college student, Perth). Rebecca Walker (2004: xiv) captures this by comparing the '"I'm not a feminist but …" girls who don't have a clue' with 'the rest of us, who are feminist but not Feminists'. Second wave feminists carved out a space for third wave women to make this different claim: 'I *am* a feminist *but* that is not all I am' (Rice and Swift 1995: 195, emphasis in original) or 'I'm a feminist and I'm a peace activist; I'm a feminist and I'm an environmentalist; I'm a feminist and I'm an international NGO worker' (e.g. see contributors to Labaton and Martin 2004).

Refugees: Good neighbours

> I think Australia's great with multicultural … like the more people, many races live together, you have to be tolerant to each other … a lot of respect has to be put forward. … I think Australia is a great country. You know, you've got your vast land, you've got your natural bush land which a lot of countries just envy, got so many, many resources. And also, with the multicultural, you've got diversity of food, of culture. … It's not like if you go to Thailand, it's just only Thai culture. … [in Australia] Every citizen enjoys the same things and life is more interesting with a lot of things happening. (Sunhy, Chinese Thai, middle class government high school mother, Melbourne)

> THERE WAS <u>NO</u> WAR!! AND … REFUGEES IN AUSTRALIA WERE <u>FINALLY</u> LET OUT AND GIVEN THE RIGHTS TO LIVE A HAPPY LIFE IN AUSTRALIA AS THEY RIGHTFULLY DESERVE!! (female, co-educational Catholic college student, South Australia)

The environment and multiculturalism command support in a strongly affective register, a national survey noting the link between feeling close to one's nation and pride in it (Evans and Kelley 2004: 313). Like Sunhy quoted above, my respondents were 'proud' of and 'loved' a 'strong' and 'beautiful' multicultural Australia. Multiculturalism makes us 'unique', 'special', 'a great country', 'more interesting', 'welcoming, laid back, relaxed', and 'a good example to other countries that there are so many nations living here in peace'. Sunhy's paean to Australia enfolds respect for difference, cultural diversity, democracy and natural wonders and resources (see also Brett and Moran 2006: 317–8 for similar expressions from their interviewees). However, as a 'coloured person', Sunhy has experienced 'Racist remarks towards me sometimes. When I speak my own language, they'll just turn around: "Speak English, you're in Australia now."'

The ideal of good neighbourliness, 'the touchstone of Australianness as it has been imagined traditionally by the white Australian community' (Rutherford 2000: 70), is one expression of 'everyday multiculturalism' (Wise 2010). Respondents suggested that we are 'welcoming': 'we should all share' and show 'common courtesy' to 'visitors' as 'we all need help sometimes'. The presumption of good neighbourliness was a powerful motivator for political action in the widespread grassroots movement to free refugees, particularly children, from detention. The campaign stretched beyond the 'do gooders' of NGOs, lawyers, church people, human rights advocates and welfare workers, to embrace concrete tolerance from rural communities and dissenting Liberal backbenchers: a 'range and level of activity ... unprecedented in Australian history' (Reynolds 2004: 4). Like the women's movement, the refugee support movement linked engagement at the personal level (small personal gestures) with the wider remit of political campaigning (Gosden 2006). Furthermore, the campaign linked human compassion with national pride in our neighbourliness. Those who became activists reported being 'ashamed', 'beside myself', 'outraged', and felt they 'had to do something' (Reynolds 2004: 9; see also O'Doherty and Augoustinos 2007: 241 for letters to the editor in which 'we' despair that the actions of the government make us 'a coward and a bully'). Activists in this campaign claimed that to be the Australians we believe we are, we must treat asylum seekers with humanity. I found this understanding echoed most particularly by interviewees in Whyalla where the Baxter detention centre was located:

> I wish our Prime Minister [then John Howard — but it hardly seems to matter who is Prime Minister] would appreciate it [Australian multiculturalism]. And understand it. Which he doesn't. And he's turned us from what was a good, wonderful country into a racist, segregated, awful — He's divided our country. ... I just think it's an absolute disgrace, what we've done. And how our country — I just think back to Cathy Freeman, when she lit that Olympic flame, and

since that time I just think we have lost all our credibility in the world. (Lyn, co-educational Catholic college mother and member of parliament, South Australia)

Nancy Margaret's egalitarianism is based on her religious beliefs: in heaven 'we're all going to be boxed up together'. Three of her church's congregation worked at Baxter and 'they will say, "Can we pray for these kids because they're really suffering emotionally because they've been separated from their parents"' ('Nancy Margaret', co-educational Catholic college mother, South Australia).

When I conducted interviews in 2003, a group of 10 students at St John's College were 'bringing' detention centre children out for sports, discos and suchlike. Anneka laughingly reports 'we took them to Hungry Jack's. Welcome to Australia — have American fast food'. Anneka's experience has made it clear to her that detaining 'kids' is not right and has also challenged her to think about the gender values and educational aspirations of refugees:

> I don't think it's right that they're keeping kids there. I really don't like that because these kids — actually, from the visits over time you can see them changing. ... You know how you see little kids running around. They just have energy, bundles and bundles of energy. ... Over time they get less and less interested and you can almost see the hope kind of being taken, like sucked out of them. ... The teenagers are very emotionally disturbed. ... It's like, 'How are we gonna cheer you up this time?' They're very, very down all the time. It's hard. ... They're very ambitious. Most of them want to do medicine. They go to school in Port Augusta, I think. Yeah. And they're like, we're the brightest in our class, and all go like that. ... I think they've had some very bad experiences. 'Cos I was talking to one boy. ... 'Your school's really different to ours because at our school we learn to fight'. ... Instead of, you know, how we have PE ... the teachers taught them to fight. ... One of them was very interesting. ... I was playing sports and he was like, 'You can't [play] 'cos you're a girl'. So I tackled him; ... it was really funny.

By contrast with Anneka's direct response ('So I tackled him'), others speak more abstractly about the intersection of gender egalitarianism and the perception of Islam (e.g. see Ho 2007: 290). Australia 'is freedom country', 'more equal than say Arab countries' 'where the women have to stay at home and they have their husbands chosen for them'. In her questionnaire, Anna wrote 'women in Middle East are treated like crap'. She elaborated in the interview:

> there are other countries where there's all the honour killings and they're purely exploited just simply because they're women and I think that in western nations we do have the power to really make a difference in protecting those

women and I think — in that area it's an issue that we should really address.
(Anna, working class government high school student, Sydney)

These respondents are correct about the status of many women in many countries, as migrants to Australia from some of these countries confirm, both in my sample (e.g. 'My father is very sexist as we are Arabs, but Christian': from Syria) and other research. In one study, gender egalitarianism is the defining difference of Australian culture for respondents of Turkish and South American origin (Zevallos 2005: 45–6). It is the rhetorical manoeuvre that makes the comparison with women elsewhere racist rather than, say, feminist. Sunhy responds to otherness with 'world travelling' (Maria Lugones in Gunning 1992), comparing an alien practice with a similar one we take for granted:

> [we] need to respect what their traditional culture, even though we think it might be stupid that the female has to put a veil on, but that's their way of life. Just like the white women wear mini skirts and then the Muslim woman thinks that's ridiculous. Like, you just have to give and take. (Sunhy, Chinese Thai, middle class government high school mother, Melbourne)

Lucy is also clear that wearing the hijab is not a sign of oppression any more than wearing a bikini is: being feminist, she claims, is wearing what you want to wear. Alternatively, instead of imagining homogenous others, Jasmine, another women's studies student, says we should avoid caricature:

> When I did Japanese I was the only like Caucasian girl in about a group of fifteen like male and female Asians. Even saying 'Asians' I feel bad now because I don't even, I don't even know how to describe them anymore. It is true that a lot of them are quiet but I think it's not because of their, that's their feminine trait is being quiet and submissive, it's just a communication thing. (Lucy, women's studies university student, Perth)

In Whyalla, daily interactions with refugees were proffered as counter-stories to those told by political leaders or the media. Amanda compares the knowledge Whyalla residents like herself gain of the 'human side of what goes on there' with 'the political side' on the news: 'You see the politicians and they never actually meet the people. They never actually hear the stories' but receive a 'glossed over version'. As a result of hearing 'hellish life stories' about those refugees who have been refused asylum and sent back, Amanda had been 'writing letters, getting involved with drama groups that go down there'. Amanda aligns her involvement with 'helping people' rather than 'radical political' intervention, such as picket lines:

> the thing that drew me to psychology was I have a huge desire to help people.
> So if I can help people I will in any way I can, but not so much — nothing

radical political. (Amanda, co-educational Catholic college student, South Australia)

Not everyone imagines themselves as the welcoming host, some worrying that we might become an overstretched host (see Moloney 2007: 69–70): 'getting on top of our line in front of us so they can be helped out' or 'we must have a big sign above us that we can't see, please come here, we will help you'. The opponents of immigration express fears concerning 'ant-like' immigrants who, like insects, are out of place in 'our' homes (Hage 1998: 38): 'too many' 'slopes', 'the whole lower class of a country', an 'uncontrollable flood' 'taking over', 'overtaking', 'overrunning' us, 'feeding off' and 'sapping the country':

> now there is too many wogs, Chinese here and none of our own people. People think they can come over here in boatloads. (female, middle class government high school student, Adelaide)

> the Asian boat people think they can just come to our country and live here like it's theirs it makes me very angry. (male, co-educational Protestant college student, Adelaide)

> Immigrant[s] can go get fucked and stay in their own fucking country. (male, Aboriginal, working class government high school student, Adelaide)

Furthermore, these respondents suggest, migrants should be 'grateful' for our hospitality and adapt to some of our 'table manners', such as speaking English in public and not congregating together in ghettoes, which deprive mainstream Australians of the opportunity to demonstrate tolerance (Ahmed 2004a: 134, 137; Smith and Phillips 2001: 326; Brett and Moran 2006: 321, 171; Hage 1998: 216–7). Nick labels as 'un-Australian' illegal immigrants, gay couples who wish to marry, politicised individuals who disrupt *Big Brother* with a message about asylum seekers, and people who drive fast cars, target elderly people or do not speak English. Despite his commitment to 'authenticity', Nick does not accord these groups the right of 'being themselves'. While aware of white Australians' tenuous foothold gained by dispossession, he concludes by asking why we should add other bad migrants to our nation:

> they're like, 'Well we have rights too'. It's like, 'You do have rights but you don't do this. ... You're not trying to be Australian, you're trying to be yourself'. ... I'm not trying to be racist here, I'm not trying to say it's bad that we have Asians and African Americans, but it's a problem. ... It's not like we don't have bad people in Australia already, the white people aren't many good ones. I mean like the blending of the Aboriginal race to try to make them whiter that wasn't really smart. (Nick, Protestant college student, Perth)

Nick's denial of racism ('I am not racist, but …') is ubiquitous. In this 'new racism' apparently racist comments are proposed as rational expressions of unfavourable traits that characterise 'others'. Australia's religious tolerance, peaceableness and cultural openness forged in multiculturalism, democracy and gender egalitarianism is contrasted with the perception of undesirable migrants who have 'gangs', 'crime', 'drugs', religious wars and ethnic hatreds. They 'bring their own troubles with them', including 'their Holy Wars and stuff'. Mainstream Australians' notion of tolerance derives from the governing ideology of liberal individualism, allowing each person the choice to follow their own desires. Western defined freedom — of speech, for example — is sometimes compared with the constraints imposed by other discourses, for example Islam (see Taylor 1994: 59–66). Matthew, a private college student in Perth, suggests that 'Australia usually changes an awful lot to accept new people except a lot of these people won't change in the slightest to accept Australian conditions.' Cheryl, a mother, claims that if she went to 'their country' and demanded '"I want, I want, I want", I'd be shot out of the country'. In this vein, the equality argument is deployed to claim that 'we' are unfairly treated and are the 'real' victims of prejudice, 'affirmative action' and official decisions such as the prohibition of Christmas celebrations. By contrast, minority groups who complain of racism are 'over-sensitive' (Augoustinos and Every 2007: 239–43).

In pondering the analogy between a headscarf and a bikini, Lucy is rethinking 'otherness' in the context of academic study. For some respondents in my sample, personal interactions with those marked as other were mobilised to explain their attitudes. For these interactions to be positive, they were usually premised on hearing or seeing things that were not too different from the interviewee's pre-existing values.

Reconciliation: Us and them and its quotidian expression

> there are a lot of people out there that want to help out Aboriginal people to be treated fairly and to have the same opportunities as others but as a young Aboriginal person and experiencing everyday life I'll have to say NO — Aboriginal people are not treated fairly. (female, Aboriginal youth service client, Adelaide)

In line with the tertiary educated nationally,[5] the social sciences and humanities students in my sample express much greater support for the issues of immigration, asylum seekers, the new histories and policies that recognise past and present treatment of Aborigines. These cosmopolitan attitudes often align with a rejection of patriotism and an embrace of global cultural diversity. Edward likens multicultural Australia to international travel, allowing those of us who stay home to 'get that taste of other people' and see that 'Australia is not the whole world'. This approach is puzzling to locals who are proud of Australia's Anglo-heritage (Simons 2005: 24, 28; see also Calcutt et al. 2009 and Gillespie 1995: 21–2 for a discussion of cosmopolitanism). Cosmopolitans are secure in their intellectual and cultural capital by contrast with locals whose fear for their future financial security is expressed in 'worrying' (Hage 2003) about cultural others.

Cosmopolitans acquire an 'empathic imagination' — via religious commitment, philosophy or the arts — that can enfold people who are 'other' and unmet. Their 'moral universe [is] defined by complex compounds of private conscience and global concern' (Burchell 2005: 123, 131, 118–9; see also Wise 2005: 182). Cosmopolitans can also identify themselves as 'objective observers', for example of Aboriginal-white history, and place themselves in a position to pass judgment on Aboriginal people (Augoustinos and Riggs 2007: 123–5). Locals empathise with people they meet and know: family, friends and neighbours. They respond to issues less because of reason than emotion. Fiona explains the change of heart when her in-laws overcame their racism to welcome a Burmese daughter-in-law: 'once you experience it, you can imagine it' (Fiona, working class government high school mother, Western Australia). Mark Peel (2003: 152) suggests:

> I think we can distinguish this combination of concrete tolerance and abstract intolerance from another version of multiculturalism, in which abstract tolerance — such as temporarily enjoying someone else's culture and cuisine — exists alongside a very concrete intolerance.

It was largely in the small coinage of daily exchange that respondents learned to think positively about different others, whether they were homosexuals (see Flood and Hamilton 2008: 22), refugees or Aborigines. Young straight respondents knew gay people who were good standard bearers for homosexuality, potentially loving parents, caring of their own kin and partners: 'the same as us', as Daria puts it, speaking of her two gay friends at school in country Geraldton. Interviewees in the parents' generation were more wary, describing gay acquaintances who were 'odd', 'strange', 'funny', 'arty', 'violent' or 'exploitative' (of the young), although they usually sympathised with gay people's lack of acceptance by their family or society. The different reaction of young people and their parents suggests that a predisposition to acceptance no doubt colours or contextualises the personal experience (young people being two to three times more likely to strongly support gay sexual relations than their parents: see Chart 1.4 in Chapter One), just as personal interaction with Aboriginal people worked to confirm stereotypes as well as to challenge them.

Around half the non-Indigenous interviewees mentioned a close or casual personal relationship with an Aboriginal person, ranging from school friends among the rural respondents to Joyce's husband discovering he was a member of the Stolen Generations. Joyce, somewhat jokingly, notes his attitude swiftly shifted from telling racist jokes to 'G'day, brother'. Joyce and her husband have given up their jobs to become foster parents. Dorothea believes that while an apology is a necessary acknowledgement, a more important acknowledgement is for individuals to 'be friends' with Aboriginal people: 'we can make something that, you know, acknowledges this Aboriginal person, as a person'. Dorothea describes this as 'education of the heart, not just go there and patronise them with education'. Carina, her daughter, adds in 'comradeship'.

Dorothea, Gloria (both mothers), Carina, Anneka and Siobhan (young women) reported conversations that allow them to draw distinctions between different kinds of Aboriginal people. They compare those who 'are trying to do something for themselves', who are 'of some substance to have a vision' as Dorothea puts it, who take responsibility for their situation, with the 'no-hopers', 'sponging' off other Aboriginal people, 'trashing the house' or blaming colonial history and contemporary racism as an 'excuse to stuff up their lives' or steal cars. Gloria has argued the issue of compensation over the kitchen table with an Aboriginal activist: 'I've known people from the stolen generation of Aboriginals, some have used it as a positive in their lives and others have used it as an excuse and this is what worries me.' Anneka's family friend 'from the stolen generation … wouldn't want anyone to say sorry to him' and 'wouldn't blame any of us for it', but Anneka can understand his desire for land rights: 'We have our house here. This house means a lot to us.'

Siobhan gets quite heated: 'what more do they want, is what I want to ask them. Like they've had the whole of Australia say sorry, they've had people marching across the Sydney Harbour Bridge with big banners saying sorry'. But she also criticises stereotyping (like 'saying well I had a fight with a white person one day so I'm off whites') and advocates individual assessment ('every person is an individual'), regretting our fear of the unfamiliar, which creates racism. Despite her apparent racism, Siobhan supports an instance of affirmative action, her working class government school's sports program exclusively for Aboriginal students. However, she misunderstands the difference between discrimination and affirmative action when she likens the sports program for Aboriginal students with a 'specialised soccer program for boys, you shouldn't be kicking up a fuss that girls aren't allowed to be in it'. Furthermore, Siobhan falls into the stereotypes she elsewhere rejects when she describes the hoped-for outcome: 'at least they're still in school making an effort, learning something at least not just wandering around aimlessly doing nothing other than making the place look untidy'.

Cheryl grew up with two Aboriginal cousins and an aunt who were stolen. Cheryl's mother often joked that she would happily have swapped Cheryl at birth for the 'absolutely beautiful' Aboriginal twins born at the same time as Cheryl. Cheryl worked as a cook in Alice Springs for a construction company 'building the houses that the Aboriginals didn't want in the first place', and which therefore became 'derelict' in three months. Such Aborigines were so ruined by white culture, she believed, that they 'just want money so they can buy booze and kill themselves'. 'Farther' away are Aborigines who 'live on the land, they're fine. … They don't expect handouts … And they're happy'. Cheryl does not approve of affirmative action, which she describes as an 'unfair' advantage, citing an Aboriginal friend who wanted something for her children and used the pretext of discrimination to extract it from the relevant authority. Laura, Cheryl's daughter, corrects her mother if she says something derogatory to the 'derros around', Cheryl adding 'white and black'. Cheryl says in her defence, 'it's not nice but it's probably true' (Cheryl, working class government high school mother, Adelaide).

As these comments attest, personal relationships did not displace an assimilationist belief that Aboriginal people, like non-Aboriginal people, will be best served with individualism, procedural fairness, responsibility, hard work and motivation. Courtney struggles not to sound racist when she makes this point: 'society is so dominated by white or like Caucasian' and 'Aboriginal people' are 'not as — educated', not 'as — high in society'. Courtney then realises 'that's a horrible thing to say but like, economically, and so you can't mix those two communities until you've got some sort of, got some even playing field kind of'. Indeed, Courtney is right that 'money whitens' (Frankenberg 1997: 8), meaning those who do not succeed economically look more abject.

A number of respondents exempted traditionally-living rural Aborigines from the proposed assimilation. Thus, Cheryl applauds Aboriginal communities untouched by misplaced white intervention. However, the price of their exemption is that 'authentic' Aborigines are criticised when apparently pursuing land rights for monetary gain. Matthew, whose life story includes assisting clients in tax avoidance, condemns Aboriginal people who 'sell it [their land] for money' as opposed to 'help their tribe or help set their family up for life'. One Aboriginal respondent in my study sternly recommends:

> Aboriginals need to stop finding excuses for unacceptable behaviour, accept the past and move on. The world has changed and it is [not] going back. (female, Aboriginal legal service client, Victoria; see also Pearson 2002)

Another Indigenous respondent, Caitlin, is worried that an apology should be directed only to those who were stolen and is concerned that 'people can kind of try and get money out of it, which is not what it's there for'.

Three interviewees comment that Aboriginal shoppers are presumptively treated as shoplifters, for example tailed by floorwalkers. Michael adds that in Whyalla, at least, this is a response to the reality that Aboriginal kids invariably *are* the shoplifters ('I can't even remember one white kid stealing'). Michael, a student at a Catholic college in regional South Australia, at first explains this as, 'It's just the way they were born.' Lara, the interviewer, asks him to clarify what he means and Michael says, 'It's the way they were brought up.' Still concerned that he sounds 'racist', Michael adds, 'In Adelaide I think there's probably more bad white kids than black kids.' Michael does not explain the different incidence of shoplifting in structural terms — in terms of different economic opportunities — but rather in biological and then family morality terms. Francesca also feels uncomfortable that she stereotypes Aboriginal strangers on the street as potentially drunk or violent ('it's not fair, because maybe one in twenty is drunk or one in a hundred'), yet Francesca's daughter was verbally attacked for no immediate reason by a group of Aboriginal girls. Francesca is aware, however, that Aboriginal people have a legitimate sense of grievance and entitlement:

> I think that, you know, if it was your land and it belonged to your great-great-great-grandfather and they took it from them, well, you would think that you were entitled to something, and I think that, yes, you know, they should be entitled to something, too. (Francesca, Italian background, middle class government high school mother, Adelaide)

Carol confronts and accepts her racism, evidenced in her negative attitudes born of nursing drunk and abusive Aboriginal patients. Carol genuinely anguishes over her emotional reaction. While offering various reasons why 'it is not their fault' that they drink, suffer burns, and are abusive to hospital staff, while also feeling guilty to realise she is racist, Carol staunchly concludes 'I have made my judgment on what I have experienced':

> I have looked after some really foul people and that's the only way that I can describe it. I hate being racist and whatever, but this lady, she'd, in the burns unit, had been taking methylated spirits and rolled in a fire. She had all these burns all over her back. She called us every name under the sun mainly because of all the booze. … And I'm there all night looking after her. She was the only patient. She smelt, I smelt. I had gloves on. I couldn't wait to get home.

I couldn't get rid of the smell. I felt bad because I felt guilty and I thought, 'it's not her making' but I have made my judgement based on what I have experienced. Another man, he went on the booze for three days, woke up, a dog had chewed his leg off. Maggots and things like that. Now these are the things that stick in my mind because we have to look after these people. … It's not their fault. ('Carol', co-educational Catholic college mother, Perth)

Fiona, an educator, grapples with how to respond to Aboriginal students truanting and sniffing petrol on the streets of Kalgoorlie. On the one hand, she criticises the ignorant whites with 'no concept of the economic deprivation' that has determined the 'slot that they've ended up in', but:

I can say they're not going to school, but I can't help them individually in any other way. All I can see for them is either death or gaol because they will get into strife, not being at school and lack of education. Their literacy skills are nil. I just don't know what we can do. (Fiona, working class government high school mother, Western Australia)

Given the racist society in which we all live, anti-racist speech *in a racist world* is an 'unhappy performative': the conditions are not in place that would allow such 'saying' to 'do' what it 'says' (Ahmed 2004b: 11). The italics are mine, focusing on the point that the saying cannot overcome the structures in which saying occurs, whereas speaking racism conforms to racist structures.

It appears to be a positive sign that so many of my white respondents have conversations across the colour line. Australia is no longer an apartheid society in which only white rural dwellers knew they knew Aboriginal people. However, the yawning silence in my respondents' discourse, even for those who try to think across difference as a potentially rewarding challenge, is reluctance to voice the complicated power relations that magnetise the force field of interaction. Wendy Brown argues, 'a tolerant attitude or ethos' 'reduces political action and justice projects to sensitivity training. … A justice project is replaced with a therapeutic or behavioral one' (in Bray 2008: 325). My interviewees focus on the need for liberal tolerance: avoid stereotyping all people based on the characteristics of one person, and ensure 'they' have the same opportunities to achieve as 'we' have. The limits to 'everyday multiculturalism' might be called the persistence of 'everyday race relations'.

In everyday multiculturalism, people celebrate or enjoy difference, consuming it without questioning to any significant degree their own valued practices. By contrast, conversations and actions across the colour bar are fraught with potential misunderstanding, snag on racial stereotypes and are liable to founder on the rocks of structural inequality. Living with difference as inequality, or 'everyday race relations', means really having to negotiate another practice as not one's own, and to confront difference mediated through power (discursive, material, and so on). The upshot may require shifting from personal expressions of hybridity that are interesting, or enriching, to the more profound challenges involved when we have to do something differently that we do not want to do differently. Such examples include not wearing bikinis on beaches to avoid giving offence, or not celebrating Christmas. From the other direction, perhaps, not wearing a headscarf as it disguises one from police detection. The costs to the privileged of 'restorative justice' are expressed in Linh's ambivalence (see Ahmed 2004a: 197; Maddison 2009: 60, 236–7):

> People should realise that Aboriginals, like it's their country, give it back — not give it back to them, but they should have as much right in their own country as we do in their country. … They should get, well not exactly what they want, but they should have an equal opportunity to what they want and what we have. (Linh (female), Vietnamese father, youth service client, Victoria)

The young Aboriginal woman quoted at the head of this sub-section does not believe Indigenous people are treated fairly. In their life stories, Aboriginal respondents become elders, Aboriginal legal aid lawyers or social workers and 'fight for land rights'. By contrast with non-Indigenous respondents, Aboriginal respondents were more likely to evaluate land rights and saying sorry in terms of the potential for a collective or shared identity (with added emphases): 'so we can *all* move on to the future'; 'We want to be treated equally, recognised for our culture as aboriginal people. *Want to share it and live it peacefully*'; '*we are all human* and we all have rights'; 'we *all* get along now'; 'More cultural awareness, people will respect and learn more because *we all* live and are in more contact with each other'. As a number of non-Indigenous respondents similarly understood, the apology was also valuable for white people: 'It's not just for the Aboriginals' or 'we can move on to an Australia that we all can share and live in with equity'. Dispossession of land, culture and family did not only produce 'them' (Aboriginal people) but these griefs also created 'us', a shared history that caused all of us to be as we are and to believe the things we believe (see Morris-Suzuki in Mackie 2005: 214). But it caused us in different investments in the relationship, so that white Australians' pride in our apology may crowd out the capacity to hear the other's testimony and so make it impossible for Indigenous Australians to participate in loving the nation (Ahmed 2004a: 108–13).

Lacking sociological literacy in an age of individualism

> I think some Aborigines do the same as some feminists. They get on their high horse about everything possible, umm, and it just puts a bad light on all Aborigines then. Everyone says, 'Oh, you're another whingeing Aborigine.'

Whereas, you know, some of them are very genuine cases, and you look at those. But, you know, to claim just all the choice bits [of land] is just not fair. There are a lot of other people to consider these days than just the Aborigines. (Karen, Catholic college mother, Adelaide)

My focus as a sociologist is on the gender, class and ethnicity of the young people in my research and how such identities have (or have not) shifted from their parents' generation. In many of the respondents' minds, however, class is the rich and the poor, unconnected by relations of production or exploitation. Gender is a mismatch of categorical difference and personally achieved equality. Ethnicity is certainly visible, and appropriated by those of non-English speaking background, although far fewer of the Anglo respondents saw themselves as white, or connected their whiteness with their racism, or their opposition to reconciliation, immigration and so on. Rather than bemoan the limitations of an individualist sensibility, here I seek to identify the cracks in the discourse, those locations where experience and ideology are particularly discordant and can, perhaps, be split open with the right theoretical or rhetorical wedges. Such wedges, which deploy individualism against itself, can be the Trojan horses for structural literacy, for explanations that move beyond individual agency to identify the continuing structural barriers that must be understood as the counterpart to the liberating prospects of imagined lives in which self-determination delivers the goods.

Whether discussing gender, race or class issues, there were moments when young people expressed discomfort in speaking about difference. The command to be tolerant, to treat everyone equally, is a liberal discourse of individualism that stops our minds and mouths when it comes to speaking difference. To notice and talk about difference becomes an expression of discrimination. This fear is expressed most clearly when young people talk about Aboriginal disadvantage, but it also marks statements about gender and class differences. The new landscape of class disguised by the conceits of individualisation is often expressed through a discourse of individual choices (instead of structural inequalities), 'cultural' differences (instead of racial and economic inequality), 'gender blindness' (instead of noticing gender inequality) or displacement ('anti-elitism', which attacks feminists, Aboriginal activists and so on as the 'elite' rather than corporate CEOs; see Sawer and Hindess (eds) 2004).

McLeod and Yates (2006: 64) explain such confusion as arising from the failure to hold a 'political view of gender'. A US study found that feminists are more likely to deploy structural explanations for gender disadvantage and non-feminists to apply biological or psychological explanations for gender difference (McCabe 2005: 494, 501–2). This suggests that the disappearance of feminist discourse in public life is correlated with the disappearance of knowledge concerning women's disadvantage as a structural issue. Indigenous respondents in my research are aware of the structural barriers that fence their options, a number proposing to work in their Aboriginal communities, for examples as 'an elder'. Among the non-Indigenous there is less support for land rights or compensation than the other social and gender issues (apart from female nudity in advertising, the low result due to low female support for this issue: see Table A3.6 in Appendix 3).

Individualism is a powerful discourse not only because it is hegemonic. As tempered by feminists, it has been combined with liberalism to advocate tolerance of difference, for example of gay people, of a variety of cultural practices, and of different performances of gender, as Zoe's example of her male friends who are not 'blokes' suggests. But, I argue, personal agency must be leavened by sociological literacy, captured by Shelley Budgeon's (2011a: 130–43) notion of 'reflexive choice'. Feminist theorists believe, on the one hand, that not all choices are equally 'nourishing' or 'affirming' for women but, on the other hand, realise how debatable is a 'normative' account of 'what women need' (Budgeon 2011a: 151). As social theorists or feminist activists, we can seek to expand the strategies women have for interrogating their apparently 'authentic' choices (Budgeon 2011a: 135); we can 'facilitate an *evaluation* of those choices and of all the associated ramifications' (Budgeon 2011a: 136, emphasis in original). Shelley Budgeon (2011a: 131, 148) argues that we need to evaluate *why* particular choices are made, which choices are socially possible and which are socially favoured (Budgeon 2011a: 131, 148). We should give particular attention to the 'choices' women make that appear to lead to less rewarding outcomes, in terms of income, power, or autonomy, or appear to amount to 'following fashion' (Budgeon 2011a: 134). This same argument can be applied *mutatis mutandis*, to also providing young men with the tools to expose the taken-for-granted bases to the 'choices' they make. In this way, young people who do not achieve their dreams because they are placed behind the eight ball can learn to recognise the eight balls rather than blame their playing skills.

I am enough of an old sociologist to worry about the limitations of an individualised engagement. A workshop with young people summarised their proposed actions as 'Don't litter, don't be prejudiced, have shorter showers'. These were 'micro' solutions that paled before the 'macro' problems they had identified: ecological destruction, war, water (Wierenga in Eckersley et al. 2007: 41). Thus, 'young people are growing up in a context that individualises responsibility, but offers few clear answers to the big picture challenges' (Eckersley et al. 2007: 7, 16). In this vein, Carina has 'lost interest' and 'given up' ('yeah, whatever') on local actions, which are inadequate against the enormity of environmental damage. Or, as with Catherine discussed in Chapter Four, young people give up their written dream of an uninterrupted career when they discover the real impediments to combining work and motherhood. Some of the changes that will support shared parenting must occur at a social level, as discussed by Esping-Andersen (2009), rather than young people blaming themselves — or feminists (Everingham et al. 2007: 431) — because they cannot, for example, 'do it all', that is, successfully combine career and parenting for example (Andres and Wyn 2010: 185).

As Beck and Beck-Gernsheim (2002: xxiv) warn, even they do not really know how the 'contradictory processes of individualization and denationalization can be cast into new democratic forms of organisation'. The political landscape — from major parties to voluntary groups — is still bereft of a compelling new narrative that expands the small change of neighbourliness into the international currency of actions that are required to meet Australia's challenges. How can the longing for self-determination be brought into harmony with the equally important longing for shared community? How can one simultaneously be individualistic and merge with the group? How are we to achieve cosmopolitan recognition, 'recognition of the diversity' of others as not (so) like ourselves? Some institutional changes are easy to imagine and have been partially implemented elsewhere, such as quality public education and strong institutional support for equal parenting in Scandinavia. Other solutions are imaginable but not readily to hand. For example, Charmaine's solution to the refugee dilemma is to be elected world leader and to make all countries 'safer and happier environments than Australia had been in the 1990s'.

Woodman (2010: 741) suggests Beck is sturdily committed to understanding social action in terms of universals, Beck hypothesising a new 'contextual universal class' that is delineated along the lines between 'the global "decision makers" and the individuals onto whom dangers are shifted either intentionally or unintentionally by this group'. Beck hopes that those excluded from global decision-making and exposed to the risks and dangers produced by the elite will be the source of a new politics (Woodman 2010: 741). Commentators on the left took hope from the anti-globalisation protests of a few years ago, and are now taking hope from the 'Occupy' movement, originating with the idea of 'Occupy Wall Street' but spreading globally. One slogan captures Beck's proposition, addressing those who were largely responsible for the global financial crisis but who have emerged unscathed and propped up by governments, governments that instead of increasing taxes reduce social security. The sloganeers claim their numerical weight: 'we are the 99%'.

Collective actions can occur at many levels, perhaps even at the level of the family. But certainly local governments are becoming engaged in activities to minimise climate change, local communities in freeing children from detention, and

Indigenous corporations in trialling alternatives to welfare dependency, as pioneered by Noel Pearson (2002). In this way, neighbourliness is mobilised as a framework for action, sometimes linking those who share the same position (for example, climate change) and sometimes those who have apparently different investments but share the same values (for example, the movement to release asylum seekers from detention).

Conclusion

> you're sort of out of the norm. You get out and get involved in that topic 'cos you want to make a difference, sort of thing. (definition of politics by Sallyanne, middle class government high school student, Adelaide)

This chapter has explored the evidence for new forms of citizenship among young people, such as 'celanthropy' combining fame and philanthropy, or 'intimate citizenship', social engagements that are based on personal interests, experiences and connections. The clearest example of this was the engagement of Whyalla interviewees in activities linked to the Baxter Detention Centre, some distinguishing their social concern for the detained children from the oppositional or empty rhetoric of politicians. In their philanthropic intentions, many imagine 'helping' in 'third world' nations. Those who plan to help at home more often discuss individually oriented psychological support than collective action. They write and talk of the desire to increase young people's self-esteem and overcome youth suicide, drug abuse and so on, but less often of working in unions to improve the situation of low-paid workers or in the women's movement against rape and domestic violence.

In Raewyn Connell's (1971: 20–9) study, as children came to see politicians as authority figures, extrapolating from known examples such as parents and teachers, they identified two main roles: to 'help people' and to 'tell them what to do'. Some teenagers understood the Vietnam War in terms of a 'threat' schema, which drew on the emotional intensity of their childish distinction between 'goodies' and 'baddies' (Connell 1971: 98–100). Against this, although not explicitly identified by Connell, I would argue, is a 'fairness' schema. Thus, one child in the study, Veronica, claims poverty is 'unfair' for poor people in Australia and the Vietnam War is 'unfair' because of poverty in Asia (Connell 1971: 186, 190, 192). Morality, like psychology, mobilises young people in their approach to civic issues. Thus, their concern for the environment is framed in terms of an ethics of care. Many interviewees struggle to balance discomfort with 'racism' and behaviour that seemed to justify it: criticism of Muslims because of Islam's treatment of women or accusing Aboriginal people of drunkenness, shoplifting and violence. They were pleased to have met Aboriginal people who presented a different image — in the process, however, being comforted by assimilation of the other to an acceptable variant of the self.

The young respondents conclude that activism does not need to involve parliaments and 'men with pot-bellies', as one young woman described politicians. Like Sallyanne, quoted above, Annabel entertains an expansive definition of politics: as 'something controversial', including stereotyping ('label someone as black or talk about women in a derogatory way') 'that will affect a wide range of people'. These young people know that we do politics with our whole bodies and minds; we do it at home and at work and in parliament. As we do it, we potentially change ourselves (our identities and our actions) as well as changing others (see Manning 2006).

Notes

1.   Zines are noncommercial often homemade publications usually devoted to specialized subject matter, for example 'girl zines', 'punk zines'. Ezines are the electronic version.

2.   This might change when they become adults. Offered two positive scenarios of Australia's future — one focused on individual wealth, economic growth and efficiency, and enjoying 'the good life', the other on community, family, equality and environmental sustainability — 63 per cent in a 1995 workshop expected the former but 81 per cent preferred the latter. In 2005, the gap between expectations and desires had widened, 77 per cent expected the former but 89 per cent preferred the latter (Eckersley et al. 2007: 17–18).

3.   Union membership has declined consistently over the last two decades, from 43 per cent for male workers and 35 per cent for female workers in 1992 to 18 per cent for both sexes in 2011 (Australian Bureau of Statistics 2011b). By the age of 16 over half of young people are in some form of employment, but only ten per cent of young employees are union members (Hannan 2008: 1). The membership of the Australian Labor Party was around 370,000 in the 1930s and 1940s; in the mid 1990s it was around 56,000. Liberal Party membership has declined from around 340,000 in the 1940s to 63,500 in 2000 (Marsh 2000: 131–2). In the face of falling membership, the major political parties are reluctant to release more recent data.

4.   Due to the difficulty of securing Aboriginal respondents, I asked an Aboriginal colleague to promote the survey through her networks. A handful of questionnaires were secured in this way, and so do not have data on a school or youth service source.

5.   Tertiary education is the most significant predictor of attitudes to immigration, treatment of Aborigines and social security support (e.g. see Pusey 2004: 200; Marsh et al. 2005: 243–4 and Goot and Watson 2005 for analyses of the Australian National University's 2003 Australian Survey of Social Attitudes).

CONCLUSION: EQUALITY IN THE RHETORIC, DIFFERENCE IN REALITY

> in terms of this book and everything with young people I think that it should really be taken into account, into what we do have to say, because we are the new generation coming through and we hold the future … that's what our nation's going to be like tomorrow. (Anna, working class government high school student, Sydney)

Young Australians express a discourse of equality or sameness, for example in relation to gender, class and — to a lesser extent — culture and sexuality, while experiencing and living material realities of difference deriving from these structural factors. Young people claim to live in a world of gender equality, even as they continue to cherish performances of gender difference. They (and indeed their parents) do not understand the world in terms of class relations, but proclaim that everyone is 'the same', even as they are aware of fine distinctions in economic resources and cultural capital. Race and ethnic-based disadvantage is explained as either intolerance on the part of the mainstream and/or individual failure on the part of the marginalised.

These findings, concerning the tensions between a discourse of equality and a reality of difference, arose out of my project to explore changes in young people's experience and understanding of gender relations in the light of changes won in part by feminist activism and circumscribed in the main by globalising economies and neoliberal polities. Based on a comparison of Anne Summers' study of young women in 1970 with my sample of young people in 2000–2006, my first comparison was intergenerational. Most young women today believe they will work most of their lives and thus pay attention to both post-school university education and their chosen careers. Only a few young women, and only among the working class area school students and other disadvantaged respondents, chose what Summers' essayists almost universally focused on: to marry and have children as their only destiny. Whereas a few of Summers' essayists became teachers or air hostesses or hairdressers, young women today imagine careers ranging across the caring professions, including medical specialisations, law and even engineering. On the other hand, as a comparison with young men's imagined careers made clear, aspirations still remain distinctly gendered, with young women aspiring to the lower paid professions and sub-professions rather than imagining themselves as plumbers and engineers or managers and CEOs in the same proportions as male essayists.

In contrast with their mothers and grandmothers, young women today assert their equality — and young men agree with them. The rhetoric of equality is expressed in the promotion of the 'can-do' girl and the idea that the 'future is female'. This equality is underlined by comparison with previous times and with benighted women in less advanced nations. Gender equality has been coupled with progress and modernity. To question the equality of Australian women means to be a whingeing victim, to be unpatriotic. Young people in my research reproduce this discourse, well aware of gender inequality elsewhere, less aware of it at home.

Unlike the progressive story women told about generational change, most of the fathers and sons in my sample were unable to articulate any differences between themselves and their son/father, apart from individual characteristics such as personality and interests. Only two fathers told a progressive story for men, and they understood these changes through a feminist lens. Thus it would appear that few fathers are mentoring their sons to live with women who expect gender equality to be realised in an egalitarian domestic relationship. By contrast, I found some evidence of a 'postfeminist', 'parodic' masculinity forged in retort to the feminist critique. The public narrative concerning intergenerational changes in masculinity was the discourse of 'male disadvantage', preoccupying interviewees more than the evidence for women's disadvantage. When it comes to any discrimination they have personally experienced, young women appear more wary than young men of being defined as whingeing victims.

In comparing women's lives in previous generations with the prospects for young women today, significant positive changes are claimed for women. These discursive proclamations, or beliefs, contrast with the evidence, suggesting that gender is a revolution only half won. There are persistent pervasive indicia of women's ongoing material inequality. Furthermore, despite their abstract claims concerning gender equality, young people in their life story essays cleaved to gender differences. The life stories written by the young men suggest that their interests and goals remain focused around hegemonic masculinity (for example, sex, sports, cars and fame) while the young women focused on social interactions (for example, romance, friends, motherhood). At one level, the life story essay is an unreliable device: clearly eighteen-year-olds cannot predict their futures with any accuracy. At another level, the task of essay writing encouraged the expression of more unguarded attitudes to gender. In their essays, with their attention focused on their apparently unique personal biography, writers expressed the 'resurgence of ideas of natural sexual difference', largely unaware of the tension with their professed commitment to gender equality in the relevant questionnaire items (see Gill and Scharff 2011: 8). Although they 'knew' that they should proclaim Australia as a gender equal country, young men did not apply this knowledge to crafting life stories that would produce egalitarian domestic relationships.

Neil Gross (2005) distinguishes between 'regulative traditions' and 'meaning constitutive traditions'. The regulative traditions of the family have crumbled with cohabitation, divorce, women combining career and motherhood. Gross (2005: 296) claims that 'meaning constitutive traditions' or 'patterns of sense making' have filled the gap. Young women are more likely to envisage an equal companionate relationship, which is a continuing work in progress based on negotiation between the partners. Young men reveal less enthusiasm and capacity for such 'reflexive projects' of the relationship. In their 'I ams', in the interviews and in their attitudes to making difficult joint decisions, such as having an abortion, young women exhibited a higher degree of interdependent independence, of the psychological capital required to negotiate a relationship in which two choice biographers are joined. Young women presumed in their putative partners the same capacities and investment in sharing desires and opinions to produce a solid shared relationship.

Furthermore, young men were somewhat less likely to approve and a great deal less likely to write about equal relationships. They expressed more enthusiasm for either the traditional family form, in which they were the sole breadwinner, or the neo-traditional family form, in which the wife was still the major care-giver although she supplemented the family income. Whereas young women write of an equal companionate relationship, growing together through constant negotiation, young men's imagined lives are studded with an accumulation of possessions and accolades: there are large differences between 'his' and 'hers' dreams.

These systemic tensions will arise as the young middle class women in my research pursue their careers even more assiduously than their mothers in a field of limited institutional responsiveness as well as limited male responsiveness to young women's desires. Andres and Wyn (2010) identify the impact of an increasingly uncertain labour market and greater time and commitment demands made on young people attempting to find a work-life balance, young women in particular delaying motherhood in the face of this institutional challenge. Even if the young women in my sample achieve their dreamed-of careers, given the gendered nature of their choices they will on average earn less than men. This will add another argument, pragmatism, to the argument of tradition, in placing pressure on them, rather than their partner, to give up work to look after children.

Many young middle class women step out of their wedding dresses into a business suit; a few exchange their veil for a hard hat. Some young men seek fulfilment in marriage and children, a handful even contemplating careers that will be shaped to fit the needs of partners and offspring. However, their life stories, their attitudes to sharing housework and role reversal, the failure of most fathers to role model changed masculinities and the despairing witness of their mothers, all reveal that the majority of young men imagine a gender differentiated family in which fathers are the primary breadwinner and mothers the primary domestic figure. This suggests tense flashpoints are likely in future families. The young middle class women preparing themselves for narratives of reciprocal individualisation do not seem to have considered that their partners may lack similar levels of emotional literacy or the same commitment to domestic equality. Even in the compromise of the neo-traditional family form, or the 'modified breadwinner model', young heterosexual couples are bound for conflict. Young women have the right to expect a 'modified maternalist culture of care' (Maher, Lindsay and Bardoel 2009): in exchange for female contribution to household income, women expect men to participate more in childcare.

Skills of reflexivity are required, not only in the intimacy of the family but also in negotiations in the workplace, community and with state authorities; with employers, work colleagues, Centrelink officers and police officers. Their life stories painfully reveal the exclusion of many disadvantaged young people, particularly young men who are not completing high school, from jobs requiring these self-crafting skills. Even when disadvantaged youth deploy the terms of the reflexive do-it-yourself biography, they do it as a vague and hollow gesture. They lack the resources to give the gesture substance, but also lack alternative discourses with which to tell their tales, apart from the handful who wrote in terms of 'parodic disadvantage', expressing the inequity of class relations in their imagined misfortunes. Obstacles are approached with the weariness of those who have confronted hurdles and failed rather than the enthusiasm of the middle class respondents reaching out for valuable learning experiences. The realistic best the early school leavers can hope for is 'settling' — a steady job based on acquiring some relevant TAFE skills. When they dream far afield, their 'wandering' stories are built on the shifting sands of ignorance or inadequate skills. Privileged essayists see farther afield, and are armed with the financial and social resources to achieve their goals.

Just as class-based difference marked their life stories, so too were the interviewees clearly aware of income differences and their expression in cultural capital. However, almost universally, they were unwilling or unable to apply a class analysis to explaining economic inequality. In their assertion of discursive equality, they slid from class to race-based differences, from structures to personal attributes such as prejudice, the ability or desire to work hard, or into claiming that economic differences were of little significance in relation to the most important things, such as happiness or family. Ultimately, and despite their attempts to avoid this position, economic difference did become an individual attribute — producing both implied blame of the disadvantaged, who did not try hard enough, and reinvoking a hierarchy based on income. Rich people were condemned for their snobbishness just as much as people on benefits were rejected as abject dole bludgers. While class may be something Australians cannot talk about and do not understand, class divides us more than it ever did. Class inequalities are exacerbated by intergenerational inequalities arising from a more insecure labour market, the growing differential in wealth and income between the rich and poor and rolling back the welfare state in times when more people need its support.

Young people imagined their civic engagements in 'intimate citizenship'. Most eschewed mainstream politics, although some wrote of becoming politicians, as often for lifestyle reasons as to bring about social change. National politics did not resonate with their concern for moral or personally relevant issues. Instead, their life stories canvassed philanthropy and even 'celanthropy', where they combined generosity towards others with personal fame and fortune. There was also evidence of a commitment to 'mutual helpfulness', to community actions based on the writer's own personal experiences, rather than fair wear campaigns or the war in Iraq.

They advocate for equal rights of speech and tolerance of the practice of others, but then are stumped (as many in liberal societies are) by provocation at the limits of tolerance: dealing with cultural differences that challenge our own values. The dominant public discourses provided unsatisfactory resolution to the challenges of difference in terms of gender, race or ethnicity. Some young women deployed a DIY feminism to challenge the behaviour of boyfriends, but few connected this with any sense of the need for wider social action around gender issues. Non-Indigenous interviewees reported affirming interactions only with those Aboriginal people who were the 'same' as the interviewee, assimilating to mainstream Australian values of economic independence and setting aside complaints based on dispossession or race discrimination. Interactions with Aboriginal people who shoplifted, were admitted to hospital drunkenly out of control or truanted school posed an anguished challenge to non-Indigenous interviewees' attempts to avoid racism and yet speak the realities of glaring suffering and lost chances. Some respondents rejected refugees in the abstract for their presumed cultural difference from 'Australian' values, including sexism, violence and so on. By contrast, those who worked with refugees negotiated these differences. For example, Anneka challenged a refugee's claim that girls could not play soccer, in a playful manner by tackling him. Even so, there is no widely accepted public discourse that allows Australia and Australians to combine good neighbourly humane treatment of asylum seekers with government regulation of immigration.

Lacking sociological literacy, the young people in my research find it hard to discuss inequality without falling into the unwanted traps of 'victimhood' or 'intolerance'. Their response, on the whole, is to deny the differences that so patently exist in our lives. This produces a cognitive dissonance that can only be avoided by strategies like asserting equality in one's intimate relationship even if it does not exist (pseudomutuality), having little to do with people from different cultural or socio-economic backgrounds (ignorance) or limiting engagements beyond the familiar circle to those who share one's values if not one's ethnicity or class. Via sociological literacy, young people can unpack the contradictions produced by a discourse of equality that jars with the experience of continuing material inequality. New ways to intervene around the causes of global inequality are emerging, for example in the Occupy movement.

Lucy's suggestion that raped men should be granted access to rape crisis centres set up for raped women is premised on placing the individual's experience and characteristics ahead of their gender. Second wave feminists, with their focus on the structures of gender, find such suggestions wrong-headed. But Lucy's proposition set me thinking: perhaps raped men do share a situation with raped women, which would allow for productive mutual helpfulness. Given the complexity and contradictions of gender today, and the widespread purchase of individualism, perhaps it is time that offices of gender relations replaced our present offices of women's affairs. Men must be encouraged and allowed to take on more childcare if more women are to take on running our nation. If we are going to perform our individuality ahead of our gender, masculinity and femininity must cease to be antithetical opposites pinned invariably to bodies marked in irreconcilable gender difference. A gender relations office would express 'reciprocal individualisation' between males and females, tap into the humanism and individualism that Lucy and many other interviewees express, a belief in our common humanity and the equal worth of individuals whatever our gender. At the same time, the office would identify those situations where we must notice gender disadvantage — whether male or female — because it is about subordination. In fact, as a step in this direction, the Gillard government introduced a Bill to revise and rename the *Equal Opportunity for Women in the Workplace Act 1999* as the *Workplace Gender Equality Act 2012*

(Cth). The proposed Act, introduced into parliament in 2012, covers women, as the previous legislation did, and men 'particularly in relation to caring responsibilities'. The proposed Act thus highlights that enabling men's equal involvement in caring is central to the achievement of gender equality (Department of Housing, Community Services and Indigenous Affairs 2012).

The great challenges facing young Australians require innovative solutions. They will demand personal resources and the capacity to intervene collectively, belief in the value of every individual as well as comprehension of social structures. As Anna suggests, young people 'hold the future' and reveal 'what our nation's going to be like tomorrow'.

Appendix 1: The questionnaires

The first questionnaire was used for the school sample and, without the life story, for the university students and parents. Question 3.1a 'What does "feminism" mean to you?' was added in 2005, as I became increasingly aware of a widespread lack of knowledge concerning feminism, either negatively or positively imagined. In those schools where students asked me what feminism was, I answered that there were many definitions but a popular one was 'people who believe that men and women should have the same opportunities or be treated the same/equally'. Although minor problems had emerged with other questions (for example, many parents in particular noted 'books' as a major source of feminist ideas), I decided not to revise the standard questionnaire, thus retaining consistency across the samples.

The second questionnaire was adapted from the original version in consultation with Karen Walters of Inner City Youth Services, specifically for the early school leavers who are clients of youth services. This questionnaire was used for all the South Australian youth services samples, which included questionnaires distributed to sexuality youth services and by word of mouth. Where the standard questionnaire had a four point scale, from agree strongly to disagree strongly (with a 'no opinion/don't know' option), the youth services questionnaire only has 'yes', 'no' and 'don't know'. As the alternative version reduced comparability across samples and I received criticisms from some respondents who felt the questions were too colloquial, I reverted to the original questionnaire for subsequent youth service samples (in Victoria), without apparent problems with comprehension.

I omitted the life story from the university samples to allow completion of the questionnaire in a final 20-minute slot in a lecture. It was omitted from the parent sample as the topic is inappropriate for someone well into their life journey (as indicated by one mature age university student who was given the wrong questionnaire by mistake) and because parents were asked to complete the questionnaire at home in their own time and post it back to me, rendering it unlikely that they would write a life story.

THE QUESTIONNAIRE:
<u>STUDENT</u>

.... SCHOOL

Finding Feminism: The impact of generation, class and feminism on young women's and men's experiences and values.

Thank you very much for agreeing to complete this questionnaire. It is divided into four sections. The first section asks you to reflect on your self-identity by completing an 'I am ….' Statement. The second section asks for your attitudes to a range of social issues. The third section asks for your attitudes to the women's movement. The fourth section asks about your political involvements. In many of these questions there is room for comments, if you wish to make them – but you do not have to. The fifth section asks for some details about you, including your contact details if you are willing to be interviewed.

PART 1: I AM ….
Please complete the following statement as many times as you can easily, up to 10 times. Do not spend more than 30 seconds or so trying to think of any of the 'I am' answers:

1.1. I am ……………………………………………………………………………

1.2. I am ……………………………………………………………………………

1.3. I am ……………………………………………………………………………

1.4. I am ……………………………………………………………………………

1.5. I am ……………………………………………………………………………

1.6. I am ……………………………………………………………………………

1.7. I am ……………………………………………………………………………

1.8. I am ……………………………………………………………………………

1.9. I am ……………………………………………………………………………

1.10. I am ……………………………………………………………………………

PART 2: ATTITUDES TO SOCIAL ISSUES

Indicate in the boxes whether you strongly agree, agree more than you disagree, disagree more than you agree, or strongly disagree to each of the statements below. There is also room if you want to comment on any of your answers.

2.1 It is fine in a marriage or relationship for the man to stay at home and do the housework and look after the children, if there are any; and for the woman to go out and work full time

☐ Agree   ☐ Agree more   ☐ Disagree more   ☐ Disagree   ☐ No opinion/
strongly   than disagree   than agree   strongly   Don't know

Any comments you wish to make:

....

....

....

2.2. If both partners in a household are working the same number of paid hours, they should share housework and childcare equally.

☐ Agree   ☐ Agree more   ☐ Disagree more   ☐ Disagree   ☐ No opinion/
strongly   than disagree   than agree   strongly   Don't know

Any comments you wish to make:

....

....

....

2.3. Men and women have equal opportunities in Australia today. They have the same chances and are treated equally.

☐ Agree   ☐ Agree more   ☐ Disagree more   ☐ Disagree   ☐ No opinion/
strongly   than disagree   than agree   strongly   Don't know

Any comments you wish to make:

....

....

....

2.4. It should be the pregnant woman's right to choose whether or not she has an abortion.

☐ Agree
strongly

☐ Agree more
than disagree

☐ Disagree more
than agree

☐ Disagree
strongly

☐ No opinion/
Don't know

Any comments you wish to make:

....
....
....

2.5 Sexual relations between people over the age of 16 of the same sex are acceptable.

☐ Agree
strongly

☐ Agree more
than disagree

☐ Disagree more
than agree

☐ Disagree
strongly

☐ No opinion/
Don't know

Any comments you wish to make:

....
....
....

2.6 It is acceptable to show women's near naked bodies in advertising or in magazines like *Playboy*

☐ Agree
strongly

☐ Agree more
than disagree

☐ Disagree more
than agree

☐ Disagree
strongly

☐ No opinion/
Don't know

Any comments you wish to make:

....
....
....

2.7 The Prime Minister should say 'sorry' to Aboriginal people because of the stolen generations

☐ Agree
strongly

☐ Agree more
than disagree

☐ Disagree more
than agree

☐ Disagree
strongly

☐ No opinion/
Don't know

Any comments you wish to make:

....
....
....

2.8 Aboriginal people who have lost their land should have access to land rights or to compensation.

☐ Agree
strongly

☐ Agree more
than disagree

☐ Disagree more
than agree

☐ Disagree
strongly

☐ No opinion/
Don't know

Any comments you wish to make:

....

....

....

2.9 Industrial development in Australia should be limited to what is environmentally sustainable, that is to what can be done without damaging the environment.

☐ Agree
strongly

☐ Agree more
than disagree

☐ Disagree more
than agree

☐ Disagree
strongly

☐ No opinion/
Don't know

Any comments you wish to make:

....

....

....

2.10 Jobs for the unemployed are more important than preserving the environment.

☐ Agree
strongly

☐ Agree more
than disagree

☐ Disagree more
than agree

☐ Disagree
strongly

☐ No opinion/
Don't know

Any comments you wish to make:

....

....

....

2.11 Unions are important because they protect the rights and conditions of workers.

☐ Agree
strongly

☐ Agree more
than disagree

☐ Disagree more
than agree

☐ Disagree
strongly

☐ No opinion/
Don't know

Any comments you wish to make:

....

....

2.12 It is better for each worker to reach an individual wages and conditions agreement with the employer than for unions to bargain with employers on behalf of workers

☐ Agree strongly   ☐ Agree more than disagree   ☐ Disagree more than agree   ☐ Disagree strongly   ☐ No opinion/ Don't know

Any comments you wish to make:
....
....
....

2.13 It is good that Australia is a multicultural nation.

☐ Agree strongly   ☐ Agree more than disagree   ☐ Disagree more than agree   ☐ Disagree strongly   ☐ No opinion/ Don't know

Any comments you wish to make:
....
....
....

2.14 Immigrants should have access to the same welfare benefits as people born in Australia.

☐ Agree strongly   ☐ Agree more than disagree   ☐ Disagree more than agree   ☐ Disagree strongly   ☐ No opinion/ Don't know

Any comments you wish to make:
....
....
....

2.15 The Australian government should provide sufficient social security benefits so that no-one lives in poverty in Australia.

☐ Agree strongly   ☐ Agree more than disagree   ☐ Disagree more than agree   ☐ Disagree strongly   ☐ No opinion/ Don't know

Any comments you wish to make:
....
....

2.16 Good schools, hospitals and welfare benefits are more important than low rates of income taxation.

☐ Agree
strongly

☐ Agree more
than disagree

☐ Disagree more
than agree

☐ Disagree
strongly

☐ No opinion/
Don't know

Any comments you wish to make:

....

....

....

ATTITUDES TO FEMINISM AND THE WOMEN'S MOVEMENT

3.1a. What does 'feminism' mean to you? (What do you think feminism is? How do you feel about it?)

....

....

....

....

3.1b. Feminism today is relevant to me personally.

☐ Agree
strongly

☐ Agree more
than disagree

☐ Disagree more
than agree

☐ Disagree
strongly

☐ No opinion/
Don't know

Any comments you wish to make:

....

....

....

3.2 Feminists share my values.

☐ Agree
strongly

☐ Agree more
than disagree

☐ Disagree more
than agree

☐ Disagree
strongly

☐ No opinion/
Don't know

Any comments you wish to make:

....

....

3.3 I would call myself a feminist.

☐ Agree
strongly

☐ Agree more
than disagree

☐ Disagree more
than agree

☐ Disagree
strongly

☐ No opinion/
Don't know

Any comments you wish to make:

....

....

....

3.4 The women's movement has achieved good things for Australian women.

☐ Agree
strongly

☐ Agree more
than disagree

☐ Disagree more
than agree

☐ Disagree
strongly

☐ No opinion/
Don't know

Any comments you wish to make:

....

....

....

3.5 The women's movement has achieved good things for Australian men.

☐ Agree
strongly

☐ Agree more
than disagree

☐ Disagree more
than agree

☐ Disagree
strongly

☐ No opinion/
Don't know

Any comments you wish to make:

....

....

....

3.6 Do the following describe feminists (please tick either the 'yes' or 'no' box)?

	Work for equal rights	Work for equal pay	Work against sexual harassment	Support abortion rights	Work for affordable child care	Don't respect stay-at-home mothers	Don't like most men
yes							
no							

3.7 Where do you get most of your ideas about feminism and the women's movement? Tick the three most important sources.

☐ television   ☐ newspapers

☐ school classes   ☐ my female friends

☐ my male friends   ☐ the internet

☐ my mother   ☐ my father

☐ other family members   ☐ films

☐ Other please specify..

POLITICAL INVOLVEMENT

4.1 Please tick the box if you have ever been or are now involved in that 'political' activity.

☐ signing a petition   ☐ writing a letter to a politician

☐ writing a letter to the editor of a newspaper   ☐ designing your own website

☐ been involved in writing a magazine, e.g. an 'ezine' - electronic magazine published on the net

☐ been or are a member of a political party

☐ been or are a member of an activist group, e.g. environmental group, neighbourhood group, please

specify..

☐ been or are involved in a political party campaign

☐ been or are involved in the women's movement in any way, please specify: ....

....

☐ other, please specify ....

....

SOCIO-ECONOMIC CHARACTERISTICS

5.1   Your sex: ☐ female   ☐ male   5.2   Your age: .... Years

5.3   Were you born in: ☐ Australia   ☐ elsewhere, please specify ....

Please mark the appropriate box if you identify as :   ☐ Aboriginal   ☐ Torres Strait Islander

5.4. Was your father born in ☐ Australia   ☐ elsewhere, please specify ....

5.5. Was your mother born in ☐ Australia   ☐ elsewhere, please specify ....

5.6 Your most recent paid work was or is:

☐ none   ☐ casual

☐ part-time   ☐ full-time

5.6a Please name or describe briefly your most recent or present paid job:

....

5.7 Your highest level of education achieved:

☐ left school before completing the high school certificate (or equivalent)

☐ high school certificate

☐ TAFE qualification

☐ university degree

☐ still at school

5.8 Your mother's highest level of education achieved:

☐ left school before completing the high school certificate (or equivalent)

☐ high school certificate

☐ TAFE qualification

☐ university degree

5.9 Your father's highest level of education achieved:

☐ left school before completing the high school certificate (or equivalent)

☐ high school certificate

☐ TAFE qualification

☐ university degree

5.10 Your mother's major occupation was or is:

☐ home duties ☐ unemployed

☐ part-time ☐ full-time

5.10a Please name or describe briefly your mother's major paid job (if any):

....

5.11 Your father's major occupation was or is:

☐ home duties ☐ unemployed

☐ part-time ☐ full-time

5.11a Please name or describe briefly your father's major paid job (if any):

....

6.1. The last section of the questionnaire is a short essay, 2 to 4 handwritten pages (although you can add more pages if you like!). Imagine you are 70 or 80 years old and reflecting back on your life. Describe your life experiences (more details below).

But before writing your short essay: ARE YOU WILLING TO PARTICIPATE IN AN INTERVIEW ON THE ISSUES RAISED IN THIS QUESTIONNAIRE? If so, please give your name and contact details (please print):

Name: ....

Address:..

:...

Telephone:...Email: ....

MANY   MANY   THANKS   FOR   YOUR   PARTICIPATION   !!!

Imagine you are 70 or 80 years old and reflecting back on your life. Describe your life as you think or imagine it will be.

When Anne Summers asked high school girls in 1970 to write this essay, they discussed:

- romance, marriage and children,
- paid work or a career
- further education
- travel
- personal crises, for example accidents and deaths to loved ones
- sexual experiences, before, during and after marriage
- world crises or technological changes that would affect their lives.

For those who worked, they talked about why they chose the jobs or careers that they did. For those who married, they talked about whether or not their marriage was happy and why. For those who talked of having children, they discussed what being a mother[2] meant to them.

But you write your own story! What does life hold in store for you?

[2] For the NSW and Victorian school samples this was changed to 'parent' as one of the teachers at a boys's school felt it excluded boys from attending to this issue.

....
....
....
....
....
....
....
....
....
....
....
....
....
....
....
....
....
....

....
....
....
....
....
....
....
....
....
....
....
....
....
....
....
....
....
....
....
....
....
....
....
....
....
....
....
....

THANKS AGAIN FOR YOUR PARTICIPATION

QUESTIONNAIRE: YOUNG PEOPLE: YOUTH SERVICES

Thank you very much for agreeing to complete this questionnaire. It is divided into four sections:

- Me, now
- What do you think?
- What can you do?
- Facts about you

There's space for comments when you want to say something about your answers - but you can just tick the boxes if you like.

PART 1: ME, NOW
Please complete the following statement as many times as you can easily, up to 10 times. Do not spend more than 30 seconds or so trying to think of any of the 'I am .... ' answers:

1.1. I am ....

1.2. I am ....

1.3. I am ....

1.4. I am ....

1.5. I am ....

1.7. I am ....

1.7. I am ....

1.8. I am ....

1.9. I am ....

1.10. I am ....

PART 2: WHAT DO YOU THINK?

Tick the 'yes' or 'no' box, depending on your answer to the following questions. There is also room if you want to comment on any of your answers.

2.1 Is it okay in a marriage or a relationship for the man to stay at home and do the housework and look after the children, if there are any; and for the woman to go out and work full time?

☐ Yes   ☐ No   ☐ Don't Know

Why? ....
....
....
....

2.2. Do you think if both partners in a household are working the same number of paid hours, they should share housework and childcare equally?

☐ Yes   ☐ No   ☐ Don't Know

Why? ....
....
....
....

2.3. Do men and women have the same chances in Australia? Are they treated equally?

☐ Yes   ☐ No   ☐ Don't Know

Why? ....
....
....
....

2.4. Do you think a pregnant woman should be able to choose whether or not she has an abortion?

☐ Yes   ☐ No   ☐ Don't Know

Why? ....

....

....

2.5 Do you think sexual relations between people of the same sex who are over the age of 16 is okay?

☐ Yes   ☐ No   ☐ Don't Know

Why? ....

....

....

2.6. Do you think it is okay to show women's near naked bodies in advertising or in magazines like *Playboy*

☐ Yes   ☐ No   ☐ Don't Know

Why? ....

....

....

2.7 Do you think the Prime Minister should say 'sorry' to Aboriginal people because of the stolen generations?

☐ Yes   ☐ No   ☐ Don't Know

Why? ....

....

....

2.8 Do you think Aboriginal people are treated fairly?

☐ Yes   ☐ No   ☐ Don't Know

Why? ....
....
....
....

2.9 [2.10] Do you think jobs for the unemployed are more important than saving the environment?

☐ Yes   ☐ No   ☐ Don't Know

Why? ....
....
....
....

2.10 [n.m.]Do you know what a union is?

☐ Yes   ☐ No   ☐ Don't Know

2.11 If yes, do you think unions are important?

☐ Yes   ☐ No   ☐ Don't Know

Why? ....
....
....
....

2.12 [2.14] Do you think that people who come to Australia should have the same stuff as everyone else?

☐ Yes ☐ No ☐ Don't Know

Why? ....

....

....

....

2.11 [2.15] Do you think you should be paid more social security so you can live better?

☐ Yes ☐ No ☐ Don't Know

Why? ....

....

....

....

2.13 [2.16] Do you think people who work should pay more taxes to the government so you can get more social security?

☐ Yes ☐ No ☐ Don't Know

Why? ....

....

....

....

3.1 [n.m.] Do you know what feminism is?

☐ Yes   ☐ No

If yes, what is it?...

....

....

....

3.2 Some people think that feminism means men and women should be treated equally. Do you agree that men and women should be treated equally?

☐ Yes   ☐ No   ☐ Don't Know

Why? ....

....

....

....

3.3. [3.4] Do girls have the same opportunities as guys? Are girls treated as well as guys?

☐ Yes   ☐ No   ☐ Don't Know

Why? ....

....

....

....

3.4. [3.5] Do guys have the same opportunities as girls? Are guys treated as well as girls?

☐ Yes ☐ No ☐ Don't Know

Why? ....

....

....

....

3.5 Would you have the same opportunities if you were the opposite sex?

☐ Yes ☐ No ☐ Don't Know

Why? ....

....

....

....

3.6 [n.m] Where do you get most of your ideas about where you fit in the community?
....

....

....

....

3.5 [3.7] Where do you get most of your ideas about relationships and about the differences between guys and girls from?

....

....

WHAT CAN YOU DO?

4.1 If you've ever thought you've been treated unfairly, what did you do to change that?

....

....

....

....

....

....

....

....

4.2 If you couldn't do anything, what stopped you?

....

....

....

....

....

....

....

....

....

FACTS ABOUT YOU

5.1　Your sex:　☐ female　　☐ male　　　　5.2　Your age: .... Years

5.3　Were you born in:　☐ Australia　　☐ elsewhere, Where? ....

Are you　☐ Aboriginal　or　☐ Torres Strait Islander?

5.4. Was your father born in ☐ Australia　　☐ elsewhere, Where? ....

5.5. Was your mother born in ☐ Australia　　☐ elsewhere, Where? ....

5.6　What was your last job?

☐ none

☐ casual, please describe the job: ....

☐ part-time, please describe the job: ....

☐ full-time, please describe the job: ....

5.7 How far did you go in school/TAFE?

☐ left school before completing the high school certificate (or equivalent)

☐ high school certificate

☐ TAFE qualification

☐ university degree

5.8 How far did your mother go in school/education?

☐ left school before completing the high school certificate (or equivalent)

☐ high school certificate

☐ TAFE qualification

☐ university degree

5.9 How far did your father go in school/education?

☐ left school before completing the high school certificate (or equivalent)

☐ high school certificate

☐ TAFE qualification

☐ university degree

5.10 What does your mother do for a job?

☐ home duties   ☐ unemployed

☐ part-time   ☐ full-time

5.10a Please name or describe briefly your mother's major paid job (if any):

....

5.11 What does your father do for a job?

☐ home duties   ☐ unemployed

☐ part-time   ☐ full-time

5.11a Please name or describe briefly your father's major paid job (if any):

....

The last section asks you to write a story about your life.

When you have finished writing your story, please contact me so that I can get your questionnaire and give you $20. You can post the questionnaire to me, or we can meet at the youth centre - or anywhere else that suits you. Or I can leave the money with a youth worker for you to pick up. Give me a ring or send me an email and we'll sort it out:

CHILLA BULBECK,
SOCIAL INQUIRY, UNIVERSITY OF ADELAIDE, SA, 5005
Phone: (08) 83034864
email: chilla.bulbeck@adelaide.edu.au

Don't forget to write your story!

ESSAY COMPETITION

Your name:.......................................(so your essay can be put with your questionnaire - first name is okay)

The essay topic: 'My dream and what is stopping me from getting it, or what has stopped me from getting it'.

(For the voucher, you must fill this page and the next page, but you can write more if you want to. Then give your essay back to a worker).

....
....
....
....
....
....
....
....
....
....
....
....
....
....
....
....
....
....
....
....
....

....
....
....
....
....
....
....
....
....
....
....
....
....
....
....
....
....
....
....
....
....
....
....
....
....
....
....
....

(You can stop here and get the voucher, but please keep going if you have more to say!)

....
....
....
....
....
....
....
....
....
....
....
....
....
....
....
....
....
....
....
....
....
....
....
....
....

THANKS AGAIN FOR YOUR PARTICIPATION

APPENDIX 2: THE SAMPLE

Table A2.1: Source of respondent questionnaires x gender

	High school students			University students			Youth service clients*			parents			TOTAL		
	F (%)	M (%)	total (N)	F (%)	M (%)	total	F (%)	M (%)	total	F (%)	M (%)	total	F (%)	M (%)	% of total
SA % N	62.5	37.5	357	85.7	14.3	77	57.7	42.3	83	69.1	30.9	135	66.4	33.6	**52.6** (652)
WA - % N	49.3	50.7	215	95.1	4.9	41	0	0	0	80.4	19.6	51	60.6	39.4	**24.9** (307)
NSW % N	72.8	27.2	117	100	0	4	0	0	0	83.3	16.7	27	75.2	24.8	**11.9** (148)
Vic - % N	26.9	73.1	54	81.8	18.2	22	56.5	43.5	44	76.9	23.1	13	51.3	48.7	**10.6** (133)
% of respondent type*	57.5	42.5	**59.5**	85.5	14.5	**12.3**	58.3	41.7	**9.6**	73.9	26.1	**18.9**	64.2	35.8	**100**
TOTAL (N)	427	316	743	125	19	144	67	50	127	170	59	226	792	443	1240

* Of the youth services clients, 63 were secured through Indigenous youth services and contacts, 13 were early school leavers, 34 were secured through sexuality youth services, 6 were secured through regional youth services and 11 questionnaires arrived in response to advertisements placed in a number of youth services.

Table A2.2: Source of high school respondents: school type x gender

	Protestant (7 schools~)			Catholic (9 schools)			Middle class government (7 schools)			Working class government (8 schools)#			TOTAL (31 schools)		
ICSEA* average	1131			1045			1052			922			1038		
ICSEA range	1058-1172			976-1147			1022-1129			875-955			875-1172		
students	F (%)	M (%)	total (N)	F (%)	M (%)	total	F (%)	M (%)	total	F (%)	M (%)	total	F (%)	M (%)	% of tot. by state
SA %	51.2	48.8		51.8	48.2		80.7	19.3		71.7	28.3		62.1	37.9	48.3
N			82			112			57			106			(357)
WA - %	57.5	42.5		16.1	83.9		71.1	28.9		64.3	35.7		48.8	52.1	29.2
N			87			62			38			28			(215)
NSW %	0	100		100	0		100	0		60.0	40.0		71.9	28.1	15.5
N			13			33			20			50			(116)
Vic - %	0	0	0	0	100	19	42.4	57.6	33	0	0	0	26.9	73.1	7.0
N															(52)
% of school type	50.5	49.5	**24.6**	44.7	55.3	**30.5**	72.3	27.7	**20.0**	67.4	32.6	**24.9**	57.3	42.7	100
Total students(N)!	92	90	182	101	125	226	107	41	148	124	60	184	423	316	740
parents															
% of school type	72.2	27.8	**15.9**	57.8	42.2	**28.7**	84.6	15.4	**29.1**	81.0	19.0	**26.0**	74.0	26.0	
Total parents (N)!	26	10	36	37	27	64	55	10	65	47	11	58	165	58	223
TOTAL %	54.1	45.9	**22.6**	47.6	52.4	**30.1**	76.1	23.9	**22.1**	70.7	29.3	**25.1**	61.2	38.8	100
TOTAL (N)	118	100	218	138	152	290	162	51	213	171	71	242	589	374	963

* ICSEA: Developed for My schools website, ICSEA is based on areas where students live, percentage of students who are indigenous, rural and remote and so on. The average ICSEA value is 1000. Most schools have an ICSEA score between 900 and 1100. According to the website, the ICSEA should be interpreted with the assistance of the 'About ICSEA Fact Sheet', 'ICSEA Technical Paper' and relevant FAQs. (My schools website: <http://www.myschool.edu.au>, accessed 2 April 2010).

Due to disadvantaged background of students, a Christian school for young mothers (which had no ICSEA rating in April 2010) was included in this sample; one of the working class area schools was closed before the My schools website had been established (and so has no ICSEA).

~ Including the small sample of students recruited from both government and non-government schools into a project at UWA to extend high-achieving students (no ICSEA available).

! Totals do not match those in Table A2.1 because several respondents did not identify their gender, and are excluded from Table A2.2.

Note: In 2006, 60.2 per cent of senior secondary students were in government schools, 21.5 per cent in Catholic schools and 18.3 per cent in independent (largely Protestant) schools (Independent Schools Council of Australia, 'Independent schooling in Australia 2007 snapshot', using figures from the ABS, DEST and other government departments, <http://www.isca.edu.au/html/PDF/Snapshot/SnapshotMay07.pdf>, accessed 16 January 2008).

Table A2.3: Percentage of students who wrote life story essays x 'class' (school type) and gender

	Protestant college	Catholic college	Middle class government school	Working class government school	Disadvantaged youth service	Total
Female (N)	98.9% (91/92)	97.0% (98/101)	88.8% (95/107)	81.5% (101/124)	78.8% (26/33)	89.9 (411/457)
Male (N)	95.6% (86/90)	85.6% (107/125)	82.9% (34/41)	73.3% (44/60)	80.0% (24/30)	85.3 (295/346)
Total (N)	97.3% (177/182)	90.7% (205/226)	87.2% (129/148)	78.8% (145/184)	79.4% (50/63)	87.9 (706/803)

Note: A total of 766 essays were written. Of the 60 essays not shown in the table above, 15 were written by university students who received the wrong questionnaire and 45 by youth services clients at sexuality, regional and other youth services not focused on servicing disadvantaged youth.

Table A2.4: Source of interviews x gender

	High school students			University students*			Youth service clients			Parents			TOTAL		
	F (%)	M (%)	%#	F (%)	M (%)	%#	F (%)	M (%)	%#	F (%)	M (%)	%#	F (%)	M (%)	
	79.5	20.5	53.1	85.7	14.3	9.5	50	50	6.8	84.4	15.6	30.6	79.6	20.4	**100**
Total (N)	62	16	**78**	12	2	**14**	5	5	**10**	38	7	**45**	117	30	**147**

* A high percentage is female because two women's studies classes are in this sample.
# percentage of total interviewees.

APPENDIX 3: SURVEY STATISTICS

Table A3.1: Content of life story essays: Percentage of those who wrote essay by respondent type mentioning each issue (organised in descending order of importance as mentioned by female high school students)

	All young essayists		High school students		Youth services clients*	
	Female	Male	Female	Male	Female	Male
Income-generating work	**85.8**	**79.2**	**87.4**	**80.1**	**67.6**	**66.7**
Females: returned to work after having children	24.6	-	26.1	-	8.1	-
Became a parent	**74.5**	**58.6**	**76.6**	**60.5**	**51.4**	**38.1**
Number of children identified	53.7	42.7	55.7	44.8	32.4	19.0
Parenting important	10.2	2.6	10.8	2.6	2.7	0
How raised children	12.2	3.9	11.5	3.9	8.1	0
Non-nuclear family important (e.g. uncles, aunts)	15.6	4.2	15.8	3.5	13.5	14.3
Became a grandparent	23.5	10.7	24.4	11.2	13.5	9.5
Children's careers discussed	10.6	10.4	11.1	10.8	5.4	4.8
Marriage	**71.8**	**64.2**	**74.6**	**67.5**	**40.5**	**23.8**
Age at marriage identified	24.6	12.1	26.4	12.9	8.1	0
Named partner	13.8	8.5	14.5	8.7	5.4	4.8
Noted occupation of partner	13.3	5.5	14.5	5.9	0	0
Partner divorced or died	3.6	5.9	3.9	6.3	0	0
Long term partnership not marriage	3.4	2.0	3.4	2.1	2.7	0
Further education	**68.2**	**49.8**	**70.4**	**50.7**	**43.2**	**38.1**
University attendance	56.2	41.7	59.1	43.4	24.3	19.0
Further education (not university)	12.0	8.1	11.3	7.3	18.9	19.0
Travel	**63.4**	**44.3**	**65.0**	**44.8**	**45.9**	**38.1**
Resided overseas	16.7	12.4	17.7	12.9	5.4	4.8
Friendship	**32.5**	**21.5**	**33.5**	**23.1**	**21.6**	**0**
Romance or love	**26.6**	**14.0**	**28.3**	**15.0**	**8.1**	**0**
Boyfriend or girlfriend	21.9	16.0	23.2	16.1	8.1	14.3
Sex	9.7	20.2	11.8	16.4	2.7	0

Owned home/described home	28.2	26.4	27.8	26.6	32.4	23.8
Work & childcare arrangements	**20.9**	**5.5**	**22.9**	**5.5**	**8.4**	**4.5**
Woman returns quickly to full-time work	7.9	1.6	8.6	1.7	5.4	0
Traditional gendered division of labour	5.6	2.9	6.4	2.8	0	4.8
After some years woman does part-time work	5.4	.3	5.7	.3	2.7	0
Man is full-time carer	2.0	.7	2.2	.7	0	0
Material comfort	**19.9**	**27.0**	**20.4**	**28.0**	**13.5**	**14.3**
Extreme wealth	1.8	11.4	2.0	12.2	0	4.8
Hobbies, leisure activities (other than music, writing, cars, sports)	**17.9**	**23.6**	**19.0**	**24.1**	**5.4**	**19.0**
Music/writing (including as paid work)	11.6	10.2	12.3	10.8	5.4	4.8
Cars	6.9	16.0	6.7	16.4	10.8	9.5
Sports	6.3	21.4	5.4	22.4	16.2	14.3
Pets	6.3	3.8	6.4	3.8	2.7	0
Illnesses/accidents of others causing grief (not relatives dying of old age)	**17.6**	**12.1**	**18.5**	**11.9**	**10.8**	**14.3**
Personal crises faced by writer	6.8	6.5	6.4	11.5	21.6	14.3
Technological change, world war etc	12.9	17.3	11.8	16.4	24.3	28.6
Charity and philanthropy	**13.1**	**8.1**	**13.5**	**8.4**	**13.5**	**4.8**
Famous, well-known	6.1	11.4	6.4	11.5	2.7	9.5
Contented with life	**43.3**	**31.6**	**45.8**	**34.3**	**18.9**	**4.8**
Discontented with life	4.7	9.1	4.7	9.1	5.4	9.5
Mentioned gender relations or feminism	**6.5**	**4.6**	**6.9**	**4.9**	**2.7**	**0**
Number	443	307	406	286	37	21

* South Australian youth services clients (30 females and 20 males) wrote an essay entitled 'my dream and what is stopping me from getting it'. A further seven females and one male recruited through youth services are included in this sample (the second questionnaire shown in Appendix 1 was only distributed to the South Australian sample). High school students wrote an essay on 'my life' imagined from being 70 to 80 years old.

It could be argued that the percentages in the most popular items were influenced by the advice from Michael Darley, the sponsoring teacher in the first participating school. He requested that I include a list of the themes Summers discovered (see Appendix 1). This no doubt 'normalised' accounts to conform with a scripted pattern (see Henderson 2006: 44). Several students responded diligently to the listed topics, for example, a student who itemised the following dot points:

- I hope to have had many girlfriends then choose the sexiest one and then marry her, and had two kids.
- I was working as a chef, hired killer and ended up as a computer scientist.
- Went to uni.
- Went to Greece and Europe three times.
- NONE [personal crises].
- I was very sexually active before my marriage
- no [world crises or technological] changes. (male, Protestant college student, Adelaide).

However, issues not on the list drawn from Summers' findings, such as friendship, love, home ownership and material comfort, were also mentioned by a good minority. Male essayists in particular felt obliged to supplement Summers' list with issues they found important. For example, one male essayist made a special heading of 'automobiles' alongside 'marriage' and 'career'. Summers did not invent the essay topic list. Her young respondents generated it, and young people in other studies canvass similar concerns (e.g. see Dwyer and Wyn 2001: 18, 31, Wicks and Mishra 1998: 93 and Summers 2003: 22 for Australia; Smart and Sanson 2003: 7, Budgeon 2003: 61 and Thomson et al. 2004: 226-9 for Britain; Lobenstine et al. 2004: 260-1 for the US). For example, Dwyer and Wyn's (2001: 190, 105) survey of 1600 school leavers identified as their adult goals 'financial security' (96 per cent of females and 93 per cent of males), a 'special relationship with someone' (94 per cent of females and 90 per cent of males), 'care and provide for a family' (82 per cent and 75 per cent), 'working for a better society' (68 and 60 per cent), 'make a lot of money' (48 per cent and 57 per cent) and 'help people who are in need' (56 per cent and 42 per cent). Furthermore, the youth services clients in my study were not given a list of items to consider (Karen Walters, the youth worker at the first youth service I worked with, recommended the topic: 'My dream and what is stopping me from getting it'), but also discussed similar themes (see Table A3.2).

Table A3.2: Most frequently mentioned items: Youth services clients and high school students compared (percentage mentioning each item in brackets)

Rank	Females		Males	
	Youth services clients	High school students	Youth services clients	High school students
1	Paid work (67.6)	Paid work (87.4)	Paid work (66.7)	Paid work (80.1)
2	Parenting (51.4)	Parenting (76.6)	Parenting (38.1)	Marriage (67.5)
3	Travel (45.9)	Marriage (74.6)	Travel (38.1)	Parenting (60.5)
4	Further education (43.2)	Further education (70.4)	Further education (38.1)	Further education (50.7)
5	Marriage (40.5)	Travel (65.0)	Technological change (28.6)	Travel (44.8)
6	#Owned home (32.4)	#Contented with life (45.8)	Marriage (23.8)	#Contented with life (34.3)
7	Technological change (24.3)	#Friendship (33.5)	#Owned home (23.8)	#Material comfort (28.0)
8	Personal crises (21.6)	Romance/ love (28.3)	#Material comfort (14.3)	#Owned home (26.6)
9	#Friendship (21.6)	#Owned home (27.8)	#Sports (14.3)	#Friendship (23.1)
10	#Contented with life (18.9)	#Work and childcare arrangements (22.9)	Personal crises (14.3)	#Sports (22.4)

Not in list of topics for high school essay writers.

Table A3.3: Occupational choices in life stories: Industry categories x gender and 'class' (% responses)

		Caring and related professions#	Caring sub-professions#	Legal, managerial	Small, family business owner~	Entertainment and info inds	Hospitality, travel, other service industries	Traditionally male professions	Traditionally male skilled, unskilled	Sports professionals, other sports industries	N
Protestant college	F	13.3	15.4	10.5	12.6	19.6	11.9	8.4	1.4	3.5	143
	M	3.5	2.7	15.9	10.7	15.0	8.8	15.9	9.7	15.0	113
Catholic college	F	7.3	22.6	11.3	9.1	19.4	11.3	8.1	3.2	4.0	124
	M	4.1	7.4	13.9	15.0	11.5	4.1	20.5	13.1	8.2	122
Middle class government	F	4.9	17.1	12.2	10.6	23.6	13.8	10.6	2.4	1.6	123
	M	5.4	16.2	2.7	10.8	24.3	2.7	32.4	2.7	2.7	37
Working class government	F	0	33.9	5.5	10.2	9.2	26.6	1.8	6.4	.9	109
	M	0	9.8	4.9	11.1	9.8	2.4	19.5	24.4	12.2	41
Disadvantaged youth services^	F	0	0	4.8	11.5	9.5	19.0	0	0	9.5	21
	M	0	9.1	13.6	8.3	9.1	0	9.1	18.2	22.7	22
TOTAL&	F	6.1	23.6	9.1	10.5	17.8	15.5	7.0	3.1	2.9	556
	M	3.7	7.4	11.9	12.3	14.2	5.1	19.0	12.8	11.1	352
total		5.2	17.3	10.7	11.2	16.4	11.5	11.7	6.8	6.1	

Professions defined as four year degree or more, sub-professions as three year degree or less.
~ E.g. café, restaurant owner, farmer, viticulturist, skilled trades business.
^ Most of these respondents are clients of Aboriginal youth services.
& Totals include all youth services not just those defined as disadvantaged.

Table A3.4: Selected popular occupations x gender and class (% of respondents identifying an occupation)

	Protestant colleges		Catholic colleges		Middle class government schools		Working class government schools		Disadvantaged youth services	
	female	male	female	male	female	male	female	male	female	male
N (number of respondents)	87	76	85	81	93	28	81	31	22	18
Caring professions, para-professions										
Doctor	16.1	3.9	8.2	4.9	5.7	7.4	0	0	0	11.8
Nurse	4.6	0	8.2	0	5.7	0	9.2	0	9.5	0
Psychologist	9.2	0	3.5	1.2	2.3	3.7	3.9	0	0	0
Teacher	1.1	3.9	10.6	2.5	8.0	7.4	9.2	3.4	0	0
Social work	0	0	3.5	0	3.4	0	6.6	3.4	19.0	5.9
Traditionally female occupations										
Model	1.1	1.3	1.2	1.2	1.1	0	2.6	0	9.5	0
Childcare	1.1	0	1.2	0	1.1	0	9.2	3.4	14.3	5.9
Hairdresser, beautician	0	0	1.2	0	2.3	0	7.9	0	14.3	0
Writer, playwright etc	3.4	0	4.7	1.2	8.0	0	2.6	0	0	0
Traditionally male professions, admin										
CEO, large business owner	2.3	7.9	2.4	7.4	1.1	3.7	0	3.4	0	5.9
Engineer	3.4	7.9	3.5	12.3	3.4	7.4	0	6.9	0	5.9
Defence forces	1.1	2.6	3.5	9.9	1.1	3.7	1.3	6.9	0	11.8
Information technology	3.4	5.3	3.5	7.4	0	11.1	2.6	13.8	0	5.9
Scientist	2.3	6.6	1.2	3.7	5.7	3.7	0	0	0	0
Football player	0	0	0	2.5	1.1	0	0	6.9	0	11.8
Musician	4.6	10.5	0	8.6	6.9	11.1	1.3	3.4	0	5.9
Traditionally male occupations										
Small family business owner	21.8	17.1	14.1	23.5	16.1	14.8	15.8	17.2	14.3	11.8
Mechanic and other skilled trades	0	3.9	0	5.0	0	0	1.3	17.2	0	11.8
Other										
Lawyer	8.0	2.6	4.7	7.4	4.6	0	1.3	3.4	4.8	5.9
Actor	2.3	0	5.9	1.2	1.1	3.6	0	0	0	0
Public relations, advertising etc.	4.6	5.3		2.4	3.4	0	0	0	0	0

Table A3.5: Percentage of respondents identifying selected 'I am' descriptors

'I am' category	Young people		Parents	
	Female	Male	Female	Male
Sexual orientation	2.5	5.9	0	0
Sexually desirable	2.1	11.5	0	0
In love, romance	7.1	7.1	1.9	2.0
In a relationship (boyfriend, wife etc.)	5.5	1.6	39.9	25.5
Family group membership (mother, father, sister etc.)	37.6	9.9	115.8*	62.7
Family oriented	3.0	3.3	19.6	15.7
Friend, friendship noted	13.7	6.9	13.9	3.9
Work, occupation	6.2	7.4	48.1	51.0

* Sums to more than 100% because mothers on average mentioned this more than once in their 'I ams'.

Table A3.6: Summary of questionnaire item responses

Questionnaire item	Young people				Whole sample			
	% agree strongly	% agree~	% no opinion/ don't know	% making comment	% agree strongly	% agree~	% no opinion/ don't know	% making comment
Role reversal	48.5	76.9	5.6	45.5	48.7	79.6	4.5	42.3
Sharing housework	62.7	89.0	3.7	30.7	64.1	90.1	3.2	29.5
Gender equality (disagree in brackets)	17.8 (8.3)	53.0 (40.8)	6.1	40.3	14.9 (10.2)	49.3 (45.2)	5.5	38.8
Abortion	39.8	68.1	5.4	50.7	40.3	70.1	5.0	47.9
Homosexuality	31.0	57.7	12.5	39.2	28.3	55.7	9.9	37.0
Female nudity in advertising	22.6	52.1	11.3	46.8	20.4	50.8	10.0	44.6
Average for gender issues questions	37.1	66.1	7.4	42.2	36.1	65.9	6.4	40.0
Prime Minister should say sorry	32.6	52.9	13.5	47.3	31.5	52.0	12.2	43.4
Land rights or compensation*	22.5	57.4	17.9	30.9	21.8	56.0	16.2	31.3
Sustainable industrial development#	47.9	85.3	7.8	26.0	48.5	86.3	6.7	24.0
Jobs for unemployed more important than the environment (disagree in brackets)	4.6 (22.9)	19.7 (61.3)	19.1	36.4	5.2 (23.3)	20.5 (62.8)	16.9	34.2
Unions are important	38.4	78.0	14.2	20.1	36.8	77.3	12.7	19.7
Individual wages agreements#	11.0	38.9	32.2	21.6	10.9	37.9	29.0	21.2
Multiculturalism is good#	63.1	90.3	3.5	30.6	61.1	90.0	3.0	27.4
Immigrants should have same welfare	28.4	59.0	15.0	33.3	29.0	59.7	13.6	31.8
Social security to avoid poverty*	41.4	78.0	8.5	31.3	40.5	77.6	8.2	31.7
Good schools, hospitals welfare more important than low taxation*	31.5	74.1	17.0	19.7	32.8	76.1	15.4	20.3
Average for social issues questions	32.2	63.5	14.9	29.7	31.8	63.3	13.4	28.5
Feminism personally relevant*	18.0	48.8	21.9	20.6	18.0	49.6	20.9	18.4
Feminists share my values*	8.4	44.3	29.9	19.8	7.5	43.3	28.0	19.5
I would call myself a feminist*	8.1	28.5	22.1	19.3	8.6	29.9	20.7	16.3
Women's movement is good for women*	37.3	77.9	16.9	17.9	36.2	78.8	15.7	18.4
Women's movement is good for men*	14.0	44.4	37.2	20.6	12.9	43.9	33.9	19.9
Average for feminism questions	17.3	49.3	25.6	19.6	16.6	49.1	23.8	18.5

~ Agree strongly + agree more than disagree.

* The SA youth services clients, who answered a substantially different question, were excluded (the percentages vary by 1-2 points when the SA youth services sample is included).

Youth services sample in South Australia (around 70 respondents) did not answer this question.

Table A3.7: Responses to 'I am ...': Young women by 'class' (source of respondent)

School	Protestant colleges	Catholic colleges	Middle class government	Working class government	Disadvantaged youth services
Interdependent adjectives	71.7	76.0	37.5	45.3	15.2
Relationship	18.5	30.0	23.1	16.2	12.1
DYADIC	**90.2**	**106.0**	**60.6**	**61.5**	**27.3**
Individuality	26.1	40.0	22.1	27.4	9.1
Independence	7.6	18.0	20.2	11.1	6.1
Strong sense of self	1.1	4.0	3.8	1.7	3.0
INDIVIDUALISM	**43.0**	**62.0**	**46.1**	**40.2**	**18.2**
SUPERLATIVES IN SELF	**3.3**	**7.0**	**1.0**	**2.6**	**0**
Positive self-perception	98.9	106.0	88.5	80.3	78.8
Negative self-perception	27.2	13.0	23.1	9.4	6.1
Positive intellectual attributes	15.2	20.0	22.1	19.7	21.1
Negative intellectual attributes	5.4	2.9	2.9	10.3	6.1
Positive/Neutral physical attributes	4.3/35.9	3.0/17.0	1.9/23.1	9.4/17.1	21.2/18.2
Negative physical attributes	1.1	2.0	3.8	7.7	9.1
Plays sport	28.3	9.0	18.3	5.1	39.4
Hobbies/Interests	13.0	13.0	15.4	15.4	3.0
Political orientation	3.3	7.0	13.5	1.7	0
Number of respondents	92	100	104	117	33

Table A3.8: Responses to 'I am ...': Young men by 'class' (source of respondent)

	MALES				
School	Protestant colleges	Catholic colleges	Middle class government	Working class government	Disadvantaged youth services
Interdependent adjectives	27.0	50.8	27.5	20.0	36.7
Relationship	13.5	12.9	30.0	12.7	16.7
DYADIC	**40.5**	**63.7**	**57.5**	**32.7**	**53.4**
Individuality	20.2	35.5	27.5	7.3	0
Independence	5.6	8.9	7.5	3.6	6.7
Strong sense of self	4.5	2.4	5.0	0	3.3
INDIVIDUALISM	**30.3**	**46.8**	**40.0**	**10.9**	**10.0**
SUPERLATIVES IN SELF	**4.5**	**8.9**	**7.5**	**16.4**	**16.7**
Positive self-perception	83.1	135.5	125.0	50.9	73.3
Negative self-perception	9.0	16.1	10.0	9.1	13.3
Positive intellectual attributes	24.7	40.3	30.0	29.1	30.8
Negative intellectual attributes	9.0	0	0	14.5	0
Positive/ neutral physical attributes	9.0/30.3	2.4/15.3	17.5/17.5	9.1/7.3	10.6/10.0
Negative physical attributes	4.5	2.4	2.5	1.8	3.3
Plays sport	49.4	53.2	20.0	63.6	63.3
Hobbies/ Interests	20.2	33.9	27.5	18.2	30.0
Political orientation	12.4	17.7	7.5	5.5	3.3
Number of respondents	89	124	40	55	30

Table A3.9: Responses to 'I am …': Social affiliation and other identities

	School students#	Parents	Young people F	M	Parents F	M	CALD	ESB	Aboriginal respondts	total
Gender	40.4	43.6	45.4	39.9	45.8	36.7	42.7	43.3	41.3	43.1
Family group member	21.5	104.4	37.6	9.9	116.8	65.3	36.0	43.3	45.3	39.8
Nationality	13.9	5.9	14.0	13.0	4.5	10.2	14.0	12.0	5.3	12.4
Ethnicity/Aboriginality	16.6	9.8	15.7	21.1	9.1	18.3	31.1*	14.3*	68.0*	17.0
Religion	5.4	9.3	4.9	6.1	7.7	14.3	9.1	5.7	5.3	6.2
Student	31.2	2.0	35.6	28.2	1.9	2.0	34.1	26.3	37.3	27.3
Occupation/working/class	4.6	49.0	6.2	7.4	47.7	53.1	14.0	14.3	9.3	14.0
Reflects living in commodified society	5.0	8.8	6.0	6.9	9.7	6.1	4.9	7.0	1.3	6.6
Age	40.7	27.5	40.3	37.4	23.9	38.8	37.2	38.7	57.3	38.5
Contented, enjoying life	29.0	33.3	335	17.8	35.5	26.5	25.0	29.0	17.3	28.5
Positive self-perception (e.g. 'a good person', 'understanding')	100.4	84.3	97.3	105.6	91.6	61.2	75.6	97.0	81.3	94.7
N	762	204	630	393	155	49	164	1005	78	1241

* 31.1% of CALD (Cultural and Linguistic Diversity) respondents identified their ethnicity; 10.2% of ESB (English-speaking background, born in countries where English is official language, including Australian-born) respondents identified their ethnicity, the remainder their Indigeneity; 64% of Aboriginal and Torres Strait Islanders identified their Indigeneity.

\# Youth services clients who are school students are included in this column.

Note: Categorical affiliations were far less common than individual characteristics, which were psychological ('friendly', 'insecure'), physical ('tall', 'fat', 'blonde'), intellectual ('clever', 'stupid'), related to skills and interests ('good at sports', 'Crows fan', 'play the piano'). They were negative or positive, the table revealing that on average each student identified at least one positive self-perception.

Table A3.10: Vocabularies* used by respondents in relation to social issues: Total sample ('other', i.e. non-classified, comments not shown)

Vocabulary item	Elements of vocabulary	%
Individualism	Responsibility, personal characteristics, effort	16.5
Structuralism	Measure required to redress wrong, racism or economic inequality recognised	13.0
'We' reject 'them'	Zero sum, stereotypes other, they get too much	10.8
Un/deserving	'Legal' asylum seeker, 'legitimate'/'thrifty' social security recipient, 'authentic' Aborigine, 'responsible' union	9.6
Nationalism	Measure either aids or impedes national unity/development	8.9
Equality	Endorses equality; uses equality rhetoric to oppose measure such as 'positive' discrimination; rights (.8%)	8.3
Practicality	Pragmatic c.f. utopian measures; cannot turn clock back; government should not waste money	8.1
Duty, obligation	Our duty to others; social security accepted; duty of government to citizens	8.0
Ethics of care	'We' care for others; 'we' are like them; tolerance achieved	7.3
Economics	Economic progress endorsed; economic progress increases redistribution	5.3
Anti-materialism	Humans need environment; anti-materialist sentiments	4.0

* Adapting Pilcher's (1998) notion of 'gender vocabularies' as an example of 'socially approved vocabularies' (Antaki in Anderson and Doherty 2008: 86), I coded the comments made on the gender and feminism items into 'gender vocabularies' and those on the social issues into 'social contract vocabularies'. Vocabularies are somewhat akin to Foucault's concept of discourse, but draw more heavily for operationalisation on Potter and Wetherell's (1987: 148-57) 'analytic notion' of culturally shared 'interpretative repertoires' or 'frames'. Some frames, in particular individualism as the antonym of 'sociological literacy' or apprehension of the role of social structures in creating inequality, are 'naturalised' as normal and therefore exclude other ways of seeing (Mills 2004: 6-7).

The vocabularies, or codes, have been devised using the so-called 'abductive research strategy', which 'reflects the way in which theory is generated side by side with data collection and analysis', and 'is said to more satisfactorily describe the method used by qualitative researchers than either of deductive or inductive reasoning' (Davies 2007: 235-6). The process consisted of a triangulation of sociological and feminist theory, vocabulary items found in relevant secondary sources (which for example dissect terms like 'liberalism', 'sameness', 'difference', and 'national development') and the 500-odd pages of comments made by respondents in their questionnaires. When all the data had been collected, the comments were again reviewed to produce the final vocabulary charts, which were then used to recode all the comments (see Liamputtong and Ezzy 2005: 269 and Ezzy 2002: 93 for discussion of this procedure).

'Theoretical coding' (Ezzy 2002: 92) seeks a central or core code 'that provides a theoretical point of integration for the study' (Liamputtong and Ezzy 2005: 268). The spine for my codes or vocabularies consists of the sociologist's obsession with the distinction between individual and collective, an issue central also to the individualisation thesis, discussed in the Introduction. The other major organising axis for the gender vocabularies was advancing women's interests as opposed to hindering women's interests. This gave me oppositions between feminist and traditionalist (supporting unequal gender relations based on religion, biology, tradition) vocabularies, rights versus duties, equality versus difference, as well as individualism and love/sharing.

For the social contract vocabularies, the second major organising axis concerned support for or opposition to redistribution to 'others' (the disadvantaged or less well off in society). The most popular social contract vocabulary was individualist, for example the claim that effort determines reward (16.5 per cent of comments). However, the second most common vocabulary was loosely 'structuralist', respondents supporting a measure to right wrongs (for example land rights because of dispossession or unions to counter the power imbalance between workers and employers) or understood Australian society to be prejudiced or economically unequal (13 per cent of comments). One in 10 comments contrasted 'us' and 'them', either outright rejecting the latter or moderating their position via the deserving/undeserving recipients' vocabulary. In particular, 'legal' 'hard-working' migrants were approved, but also 'thrifty' and 'legitimate' social security recipients, 'authentic' Aborigines and 'responsible' unions (responsible to their workers). Slightly less common (garnering around eight per cent of comments) were the vocabularies of 'nationalism' (for example, an apology makes us a stronger nation), 'equality and rights', 'pragmatism' (for example rejecting land rights because we cannot turn the clock back) and 'duty' (our duty to each other or the government's duty to its citizens).

References

AAP 2006 'Average CEO salary is $3.4m: study', *Sydney Morning Herald* 27 January 2006, http://www.smh.com.au/news/national/average-ceo-salary-is-34m-study/2006/01/27/1138319435398.html, accessed 23 March 2011

Aapola, Sinikka, Marnina Gonick, and Anita Harris 2005. *Young Femininity: Girlhood, Power and Social Change*, Houndmills and New York: Palgrave Macmillan.

Adams, Matthew 2006. 'Hybridizing habitus and reflexivity: towards an understanding of contemporary identity?', *Sociology* 40 (3): 511–528.

Adkins, Lisa 2002. *Revisions: Gender and Sexuality in Late Modernity*, Buckingham: Open University Press.

Adkins, Lisa 2003. 'Reflexivity: Freedom or habit of gender?', *Theory, Culture & Society* 20 (6): 21–42.

Ahmed, Sara 2004a. *The Cultural Politics of Emotion*, Edinburgh: Edinburgh University Press.

Ahmed, Sara 2004b. 'Declarations of whiteness: The non-performativity of anti-racism', *Borderlands, e-journal* 3 (2): no page numbers.

Anderson, Irina and Kathy Doherty 2008. *Accounting for Rape: Psychology, Feminism and Discourse Analysis in the Study of Sexual Violence*, Hove: Routledge.

Andres, Lesley and Johanna Wyn 2010. *The Making of a Generation: Children of the 1970s in Adulthood*, Toronto: University of Toronto Press.

Arndt, Bettina 2009. *The Sex Diaries: Why Women Go Off Sex and Other Bedroom Battles*, Carlton: Melbourne University Press.

Arnot, Madeleine 2002. *Reproducing Gender? Essays on Educational Theory and Feminist Politics*, Routledge: London.

Augoustinos, Martha and Danielle Every 2007. 'Contemporary racist discourse: Taboos against racism and racist accusations', in Ann Weatherall, Bernadette

Watson and Cindy Gallois (eds), *Language, Discourse and Social Psychology*, Houndmills, Basingstoke: Palgrave Macmillan, pp. 233–254.

Augoustinos, Martha and Damien Riggs 2007. 'Representing "us" and "them": Constructing white identities in everyday talk', in Gail Moloney and Iain Walker (eds), *Social Representations and Identity*, New York: Palgrave Macmillan, pp. 109–130.

Austin, S., T. Jefferson, A. Preston and R. Seymour 2008. 'Gender Pay Differentials in Low-Paid Employment', Women in Social & Economic Research (WiSER), Curtin University of Technology, Report commissioned by the Australian Fair Pay Commission, 2008, <http://www.fairpay.gov.au/NR/rdonlyres/8069770B-0427-4FE8-B629-6A29FA75A62C/0/Gender_Pay_Differentials_in_lowpaid_employment.pdf>, accessed 14 September 2009

Australian Bureau of Statistics 2000. 'Australian Social Trends, 4102.0', <http://www.abs.gov.au/AUSSTATS/abs@.nsf/2f762f95845417aeca25706c00834efa/24331db49dae9bb4ca2570ec000e4155!OpenDocument>, accessed 7 April 2008

Australian Bureau of Statistics 2005. '6105.0: Australian Labour Market Statistics, Jan 2005', <http://www.abs.gov.au/AUSSTATS/abs@.nsf/94713ad445ff1425ca25682000192af2/30cb19068ccde510ca256f81007761a9!OpenDocument#10>, accessed 10 May 2010.

Australian Bureau of Statistics 2006. '4102.0 — Australian Social Trends, <http://www.abs.gov.au/ausstats/abs@.NSF/bb8db737e2af84b8ca2571780015701e/acf29854f8c8509eca2571b00010329b!OpenDocument>, accessed 10 May 2010.

Australian Bureau of Statistics 2009. '4102.0 — Australian Social Trends', Canberra: Australian Bureau of Statistics, <http://www.abs.gov.au/AUSSTATS/abs@.nsf/Lookup/4102.0Main+Features40March%202009>, accessed 4 June 2010

Australian Bureau of Statistics 2011a. '4125.0 — Gender Indicators, Australia', <http://www.abs.gov.au/ausstats/abs@.nsf/mf/4125.0>, accessed 14 September 2011.

Australian Bureau of Statistics 2011b. '6310.0 — Employee Earnings, Benefits and Trade Union Membership, Australia, August 2011', <http://www.abs.gov.au/ausstats/abs@.nsf/Latestproducts/6310.0Main%20Features3August%202011?opendocument&tabname=Summary&prodno=6310.0&issue=August%202011&num=&view=>, accessed 10 June 2012.

Australian Bureau of Statistics 2012. '4125.0 — Gender Indicators, Australia', <http://www.abs.gov.au/ausstats/abs@.nsf/Lookup/by%20Subject/4125.0~Jan%202012~Main%20Features~Non-school%20qualification~2220>, accessed 10

June 2012.

Australian Research Centre in Sex, Health and Society circa 2003. 'Sex in Australia: Summary findings of the Australian study of health and relationships', Latrobe: Latrobe University, <http://www.latrobe.edu.au/ashr/Sex%20In%20 Australia%20Summary.pdf>, accessed October 2006.

Bacchi, Carol and Joan Eveline 2010. *Mainstreaming Politics: Gendering Practices and Feminist Theory*, Adelaide: University of Adelaide Press.

Badinter, Elisabeth 2006. *Dead End Feminism*, Cambridge: Polity, translated by Julia Borossa, first published 2003 as *Fausse route*.

Bail, Kathy 1996. 'Introduction', in Kathy Bail (ed.), *DIY Feminism,* St Leonards: Allen and Unwin, pp. 3–17.

Baird, Barbara 2009. 'Men behaving badly: The moral politics of white hegemonic masculinity in Australia', in Tanja Dreher and Christina Ho (eds), *Beyond the Hijab: New Conversations on Gender, Race and Religion*, Newcastle upon Tyne: Cambridge Scholars Publishing, pp. 90–104.

Baker, Joanne 2008. 'The ideology of choice. Overstating progress and hiding injustice in the lives of young women: Findings from a study in North Queensland, Australia', *Women's Studies International Forum* 31 (1): 53–64.

Bang, Henrik 2005. 'Among everyday makers and expert citizens', in Janet Newman (ed.), *Remaking Governance: Peoples, Politics and the Public Sphere*, Bristol: Policy Press, pp. 159–179.

Barber, Kristen 2008. 'The well-coiffed man: Class, race and heterosexual masculinity in the hair salon', *Gender & Society*, 22 (4): 455–476.

Barlow, Maude and Tony Clarke 2001. *Global Showdown: How the New Activists are Fighting Global Corporate Rule*, Toronto: Stoddart.

Bartholomaeus, Clare 2012. 'Rethinking Masculinities and Young Age: Primary school students constructing gender', Thesis submitted for the degree of Doctor of Philosophy in Faculty of Humanities and Social Sciences, University of Adelaide.

Bauman, Zygmunt 2001. *The Individualized Society*, Cambridge: Polity.

Baumgardner, Jennifer and Amy Richards 2000. *Manifesta: Young Women, Feminism, and the Future*, New York: Farrar, Straus and Giroux.

Baxter, Janine, Belinda Hewitt and Michelle Haynes 2008. 'Life course transitions and housework: Marriage, parenthood and time on housework', *Journal of Marriage and Family* 70: 259–272.

Bean, Clive 2005. 'Is there a crisis of trust in Australia?', in Shaun Wilson, Gabrielle Meagher, Rachel Gibson, David Denemark and Mark Western (eds), *Australian Social Attitudes: The First Report*, Sydney: University of New South

Wales Press, pp. 122–140.

Beck, Ulrich 2002. 'Zombie categories: Interview with Ulrich Beck', in Ulrich Beck and Elisabeth Beck-Gernsheim, *Individualization: Institutionalized Individualism and its Social and Political Consequences*, London: Sage, pp. 202–213.

Beck, Ulrich and Elisabeth Beck-Gernsheim 2002. *Individualization: Institutionalized Individualism and its Social and Political Consequences*, London: Sage.

Beck-Gernsheim, Elisabeth 2002. *Reinventing the Family: In Search of New Lifestyles*, London: Polity Press.

Bellafante, Ginia 1998. 'Feminism: It's all about me', *Time* 29 June, pp. 54–60.

Benn, Melissa 1998. *Madonna and Child: Towards a New Politics of Motherhood*, London: Jonathon Cape.

Bentley, Tom and Kate Oakley 1999. *The Real Deal: What Young People Really Think About Government, Politics and Social Exclusion*, London: Demos.

Bettie, Julie 2000. 'Women without class: *Chicas, cholas*, trash and the presence/absence of class identity', *Signs: Journal of Women in Culture and Society* 26 (1): 1–35.

Bittman, Michael and Jocelyn Pixley 1997. *The Double Life of the Family*, St Leonards: Allen and Unwin.

Bonnett, Alastair 2000. *White Identities: Historical and International Perspectives*, Harlow: Pearson Education.

Bourdieu, Pierre 1984. *Distinction*, London: Routledge and Kegan Paul.

Bourdieu, Pierre, Alian Accardo, Gabrielle Balazs, Stéphane Beaud, François Bonvin, Emmanuel Bourdieu, Philippe Bourgeois, Sylvain Broccolichi, Patrick Champagne, Rosine Christin, Jean-Pierre Faguer, Sandrine Garcia, Remi Lenoir, Françoise Œuvrard, Michel Pialoux, Louis Pinto, Denis Podalydès, Abdelmalek Sayad, Charles Soulié and Loïc J.D. Wacquant 1999. *The Weight of the World: Social Suffering in Contemporary Society*, Cambridge: Polity Press, translated by Priscilla Parkhurst Ferguson, Susan Emanuel, Joe Johnson and Shoggy T. Waryn.

Bourdieu, Pierre and Jean-Claude Passeron 1990. *Reproduction in Education, Society, and Culture*, London: Sage.

Bowman, Dina 2007. 'Men's business: Negotiating entrepreneurial business and family life', *Journal of Sociology* 43 (4): 385–400.

Bray, Abigail 2008. 'The question of intolerance: "Corporate paedophilia" and child sexual abuse moral panics', *Australian Feminist Studies* 23 (57): 323–341.

Brett, Judith and Anthony Moran 2006. *Ordinary People's Politics: Australians Talk About Life, Politics and the Future of Their Country*, North Melbourne: Pluto

Press.

Budgeon, Shelley 2003. *Choosing a Self: Young Women and the Individualization of Identity*, Westport and London: Praeger.

Budgeon, Shelley 2011a. *Third Wave Feminism and the Politics Of Gender in Late Modernity*, Basingstoke: Palgrave Macmillan.

Budgeon, Shelley 2011b. 'The Contradictions of Successful Femininity: Third Wave Feminism, Postfeminism and "New" Femininities', in Rosalind Gill and Christina Scharff (eds), *New Femininities: Postfeminism, Neoliberalism and Subjectivity*, Basingstoke: Palgrave, pp. 279–293.

Bulbeck, Chilla 1997. *Living Feminism: The Impact of the Women's Movement on Three Generations of Australian Women*, Cambridge: Cambridge University Press.

Bulbeck Chilla 2011. "You learn about feminists but they're all like years old": Young women's views of feminism and women's history', *Outskirts: Feminisms along the edge*, Volume 25, <http://www.outskirts.arts.uwa.edu.au/volumes/volume-25/chilla-bulbeck>, accessed 12 June 2012.

Bunting, Madeleine 2009. 'Again social evils haunt Britain. Do we still have the spirit to thwart them?', *The Guardian* 15 June 2009: 25.

Burchell, David 2005. 'The trouble with empathy', in Julianne Schultz (ed.), *People Like US: Griffith Review* 8: 115–132.

Burchell, David 2007. 'Trying to find the sunny side of life', in Julianne Schultz (ed.), *Divided Nation: Griffith Review* 15: 13–38.

Burns, April and Maria Elena Torre 2004. 'Shifting desires: Discourses of accountability in abstinence-only education in the United States', in Anita Harris (ed.), *All About the Girl: Culture, Power, and Identity*, New York: Routledge, pp. 127–137.

Bush, Melanie E.L. 2004. *Breaking the Code of Good Intentions: Everyday Forms of Whiteness*, Lanham: Rowman and Littlefield.

Butcher, Melissa and Mandy Thomas 2006. 'Ingenious: Emerging hybrid youth cultures in western Sydney', in Pam Nilan and Carles Feixa (eds), *Global Youth? — Hybrid Identities, Plural Worlds*, London: Routledge, pp. 53–71.

Butera, Karina J. 2008. '"Neo-mateship" in the 21st century: Changes in the performance of Australian masculinity', *Journal of Sociology* 44 (3): 265–281.

Calcutt, Lyn, Ian Woodward and Zlatko Skrbis 2009. 'Conceptualizing otherness: An exploration of the cosmopolitan', *Journal of Sociology* 45 (2): 169–186.

Campbell, Iain and Sarah Charlesworth 2004. 'Key work and family trends in Australia', Centre for Applied Social Research RMIT, Melbourne, <http://www.mams.rmit.edu.au/q0xq83s8849e.pdf>, accessed 10 May 2010.

Campo, Natasha 2005. '"Having it all" or "had enough"? Blaming feminism in the *Age* and the *Sydney Morning Herald*, 1980–2004', *Journal of Australian Studies* number 84: 63–72, 236–237.

Campo, Natasha 2009. *From Superwoman to Domestic Goddesses: The Rise and Fall of Feminism*, Bern: Peter Lang.

Cannold, Leslie 2005. *What, No Baby?: Why Women are Losing the Freedom to Mother, and How They Can Get it Back*, Fremantle: Fremantle Arts Centre Press.

Carpenter, Laura M. 1998. 'From girls into women: Scripts for sexuality and romance in *Seventeen* magazine, 1974–1994', *The Journal of Sex Research* 35 (2): 158–168.

Caterson, Simon 2005. 'A preposterous life', in Julianne Schultz (ed.), *People Like US: Griffith Review* 8: 57–63.

Chandler, Jo 2006. 'People who need help, any help', *The Age*, 16 October 2006, <http://www.theage.com.au/news/opinion/people-who-need-help-any-help/2006/10/15/1160850805425.html>, accessed 15 August 2009.

Chung, Donna 2005. 'Violence, control, romance and gender equality: Young women and heterosexual relationships', *Women's Studies International Forum* 28 (6): 445–455.

Chunn, Dorothy E., Susan B. Boyd, and Hester Lessard 2007. 'Feminism, law and social change: An overview', in Dorothy E. Chunn, Susan B. Boyd and Hester Lessard (eds), *Reaction and Resistance: Feminism, Law, and Social Change*, Vancouver: University of British Columbia Press, pp. 1–30.

Ciabattari, Teresa 2001. 'Changes in men's conservative gender ideologies: Cohort and period influences', *Gender & Society* 15 (4): 574–591.

Cimino, Richard and Don Lattin 1998. *Shopping for Faith: American Religion in the New Millenium*, San Francisco: Jossey-Bass.

Coates, Jennifer 1996. *Women Talk: Conversations Between Women Friends*, Oxford: Blackwell.

Coates, Jennifer 2003. *Men Talk: Stories in the Making of Masculinities*, Oxford: Blackwell.

Coles, Tony 2008. 'Finding space in the field of masculinity: Lived experiences of men's masculinities', *Journal of Sociology* 44 (3): 233–248.

Connell, Raewyn 1971. *The Child's Construction of Politics*, Melbourne: Melbourne University Press.

Connell, Raewyn 1990. 'A whole new world: Remaking masculinity in the context of the environmental movement', *Gender & Society* 4 (4): 452–478.

Connell, Raewyn 2000. *The Men and the Boys*, Sydney: Allen and Unwin.

Connell, Raewyn 2005. 'Change among the gatekeepers: Men, masculinities, and gender equality in the global arena', *Signs: Journal of Women in Culture and Society* 30 (3): 1801–1825.

Connell, Raewyn. 2008. 'A thousand miles from kind: Men, masculinities and modern institutions', *Journal of Men's Studies* 16 (3): 237–252.

Coombs, Anne 2009. 'How cyber-activism changed the world', in Julianne Schultz (ed.), *Griffith Review: Participation Society* 24: 105–111.

Coward, Ros 1999. *Sacred Cows: Is Feminism Relevant to the New Millennium?*, London: Harper Collins.

Coupland, Douglas 1991. *Generation X: Tales for an Accelerated Culture*, New York: St Martin's Books.

Cunningham, Sophie 2011. 'A long, long way to go: different tools for new wave of feminism', Crikey, 30 August 2011, <http://www.crikey.com.au/2011/08/30/a-long-long-way-to-go-different-tools-for-new-wave-of-feminism/>, accessed 21 November 2011.

Curthoys, Ann 1994. 'Australian feminism since 1970', in Norma Grieve and Ailsa Burns (eds), *Australian Women: Contemporary Feminist Thought*, Melbourne: Oxford University Press, pp. 14–28.

Dales, Laura 2005. 'Lifestyles of the rich and single: Reading agency in the "parasite single" issue', in Lyn Parker (ed.), *The Agency of Women in Asia*, Singapore: Marshall Cavendish, pp. 133–57.

Davies, Martin Brett 2007. *Doing a Successful Research Project Using Qualitative or Quantitative Methods*, New York: Palgrave Macmillan.

d'Ercole, Marco Mira 2005. *Extending Opportunities: How Active Social Policy Can Benefit Us All*, Paris: Organisation for Economic Co-operation and Development Publishing.

DeKeseredy, Walter S., Shahid Alvi, Martin D. Schwartz and E. Andreas Tomaszeweski 2003. *Under Siege: Poverty and Crime in a Public Housing Community*, Lanham: Lexington Books.

de Vaus, David 2004. *Diversity and Change in Australian Families*, Melbourne: Institute of Family Studies.

Dempsey, Ken 2001. 'Women's and men's consciousness of shortcomings in marital relations, and of the need for change', *Family Matters* 58: 58–66.

Denfeld, Rene 1995. *The New Victorians: A Young Woman's Challenge to the Old Feminist Order*, St Leonards: Allen and Unwin.

Denfeld, Rene 1997. *Kill the Body, the Head will Fall: A Closer Look at Women, Violence, and Aggression*, London: Vintage.

Department of Education, Training and Employment 2000. *Labour Force Experience of South Australian Government School Students*, Canberra: Department of

Education, Training and Employment.

Department of Housing, Community Services and Indigenous Affairs, 2012. 'Workplace Gender Equality Act 2012', <http://www.fahcsia.gov.au/sa/women/progserv/economic/Documents/EOWA_fact%20sheet.pdf>, accessed 10 June 2012.

Department of Immigration and Citizenship 2007. <http://www.citizenship.gov.au/should_become/guide/>, accessed 3 December 2011. The booklet is no longer available on line but the statement is reaffirmed in 'Quick guide to Australian Citizenship', <http://www.citizenship.gov.au/should_become/guide>, accessed 10 June 2012.

Dobson, Amy Sheilds 2008. 'Femininities as commodities: Cam girl culture' in Anita Harris (ed.), *Next Wave Cultures: Feminism, Subcultures, Activism*, New York and London: Routledge, pp. 123–148.

Dux, Monica and Zora Simic 2008. *The Great Feminist Denial*, Carlton: Melbourne University Press.

Dwyer, Peter and Johanna Wyn 2001. *Youth, Education and Risk: Facing the Future*, London: RoutledgeFalmer.

Easteal, Patricia and Keziah Judd 2008. '"She said, he said": Credibility and sexual harassment cases in Australia', *Women's Studies International Forum* 31 (5): 336–344.

Eckersley, Richard, Helen Cahill, Ani Wierenga and Johanna Wyn 2007. 'Generations in dialogue about the future: The hopes and fears of young Australians', Weston, Australian Capital Territory: Australian Youth Research Centre and Australia 21, <http://www.australia21.org.au>, accessed 15 December 2008.

Eisenstein, Hester 2009. *Feminism Seduced: How Global Elites Use Women's Labor and Ideas to Exploit the World*, Boulder, Colorado: Paradigm.

Elias, Norbert 1991. *The Society of Individuals*, Cambridge: Basil Blackwell, edited by Michael Schröter and translated by Edmund Jephcott, first published in 1987 as a collection of essays written between 1939 and 1987.

Elliott, Jane 2010. 'Imagining a gendered future: Children's essays from the National Child Development Study in 1969' *Sociology* 44 (6): 1073–1090.

Enloe, Cynthia 2004. 'Wielding masculinity inside Abu Ghraib: Making feminist sense of an academic military scandal', *Asian Journal of Women's Studies* 10 (3): 89–102.

Epstein, Barbara 2001. 'What happened to the women's movement?', *Monthly Review* May: 1–13.

Esping-Andersen, Gøsta 2009. *The Incomplete Revolution: Adapting to Women's New Roles*, Cambridge: Polity.

Evans, Ann and Edith Gray 2005. 'What makes an Australian family?', in Shaun Wilson, Gabrielle Meagher, Rachel Gibson, David Denemark and Mark Western (eds), *Australian Social Attitudes: The First Report*, Sydney: University of New South Wales Press, pp. 12–29.

Evans, M.D.R. and Jonathan Kelley 2002. *Australian Economy and Society 2001: Education, Work and Welfare*, Annandale: Federation Press.

Evans, M.D.R. and Jonathan Kelley 2004. *Australian Economy and Society 2002: Religion, Morality and Public Policy in International Perspective*, Annandale: Federation Press.

Everingham, Christine, Deborah Stevenson and Penny Warner-Smith 2007. '"Things are getting better all the time"?: Challenging the narrative of women's progress from a generational perspective' *Sociology* 41 (3): 419–437.

Ezzy, Douglas 2002. *Qualitative Analysis: Practice and Innovation*, Sydney: Allen and Unwin.

Flood, Michael 2005. 'Boys, young men and gender equality', presentation, United Nations Commission on the Status of Women, for the panel 'Future perspectives on the promotion of gender equality: Through the eyes of young women and men', New York, 9 March.

Flood, Michael 2007. 'Exposure to pornography among youth in Australia', *Journal of Sociology* 43 (1): 23–44.

Flood, Michael 2008. 'Men, sex, and homosociality: How bonds between men shape their sexual relations with women', *Men and Masculinities* 10 (3): 339–359.

Flood, Michael and Clive Hamilton 2008. 'Mapping homophobia in Australia', in Shirleene Robinson (ed.), *Homophobia: An Australian History*, Sydney: Federation Press, pp. 16–38.

Folbre, Nancy 2001. *The Invisible Heart: Economics and Family Values*, New York: New Press.

Frankenberg, Ruth 1997. 'Introduction: Local whitenesses, localizing whiteness', in Ruth Frankenberg (ed.), *Displacing Whiteness: Essays in Social and Cultural Criticism*, Durham and London: Duke University Press, pp. 1–34.

Franklin, Adrian 1999. *Animals and Modern Cultures*, London: Sage.

Franklin, Adrian 2006. *Animal Nation: The True Story of Animals and Australia*, Sydney: University of New South Wales Press.

Franzway, Suzanne, Rhonda Sharp, Julie E. Mills and Judith Gill 2009. 'Engineering ignorance: The problem of gender equity in engineering', *Frontiers: A Journal of Women Studies* 30 (1): 89–106.

Fraser, Nancy 1995. 'From redistribution to recognition? Dilemmas of justice in a "post-socialist" age', *New Left Review* 212 (July/August): 68–93.

Furlong, Andy, Dan Woodman and Johanna Wyn 2011. 'Changing times, changing perspectives: Reconciling "transition" and "cultural" perspectives on youth and young adulthood', *Journal of Sociology* 47 (4): 355–370.

Genovese, Ann 1996. 'Unravelling identities: Performance and criticism in Australian feminisms', *Feminist Review* 52: 135–153.

Gerson, Kathleen 2002. 'Moral dilemmas, moral strategies, and the transformation of gender: Lessons from two generations of work and family change', *Gender & Society* 16 (1): 8–28.

Gerson, Kathleen 2010. *The Unfinished Revolution: How a New Generation is Reshaping Family, Work, and Gender in America*, New York: Oxford University Press.

Giddens, Anthony 1991. *Modernity and Self-Identity: Self and Society in the Late Modern Age*, Cambridge: Polity Press.

Giddens, Anthony 1992. *The Transformation of Intimacy: Sexuality, Love and Eroticism in Modern Societies*, Cambridge: Polity.

Giddens, Anthony 1994. 'Replies and critiques', in Ulrich Beck, Anthony Giddens and Scott Lash, *Reflexive Modernization: Politics, Tradition and Aesthetics in the Modern Social Order*, Cambridge: Polity Press, pp. 184–197.

Gilbert, Pam 1994. '"And they lived happily ever after": Cultural Storylines and the construction of gender', in Anne Haas Dyson and Celia Genishi (eds), *The Need for Story: Cultural Diversity in Classroom and Community*, Urbana: National Council of Teachers of English, pp. 124–142.

Gill, Rosalind and Christina Scharff 2011. 'Introduction' in Rosalind Gill and Christina Scharff (eds), *New Femininities: Postfeminism, Neoliberalism and Subjectivity*, Basingstoke: Palgrave, pp. 1–17.

Gillespie, Marie 1995. *Television, Ethnicity and Cultural Change*, London and New York: Routledge.

Gilligan, Carol 1982. *In a Different Voice*, Cambridge and Massachusetts: Harvard University Press.

Gleeson, Kate and Hannah Frith 2004. 'Pretty in pink: Young women presenting mature sexual identities', in Anita Harris (ed.), *All About the Girl: Culture, Power, and Identity*, New York: Routledge, pp. 103–113.

Goffman, Erving 1974. *Frame Analysis: An Essay on the Organization of Experience*, London: Harper and Row.

Gold, Jodi and Susan Villari 2000. 'Peer education: Student activism of the nineties', in Jodi Gold and Susan Villari (eds), *Just Sex: Students Rewrite the Rules on Sex, Violence, Activism and Equality*, Lanham: Rowman and Littlefield Publishers, pp. 145–156.

Goot, Murray and Ian Watson 2005. 'Immigration, multiculturalism and national identity', in Shaun Wilson, Gabrielle Meagher, Rachel Gibson, David Denemark and Mark Western (eds), *Australian Social Attitudes: The First Report*, Sydney: University of New South Wales Press, pp. 182–203.

Gosden, Dianne 2006. '"What if no-one had spoken out against this policy? The rise of asylum seeker and refugeee advocacy in Australia', *Portal* 3 (1), <http://epress.lib.uts.edu.au/ojs/index.php/portal/article/view/121/87>, accessed 28 February 2006.

Gotell, Lisa 2007. 'The discursive disappearance of sexualized violence: Feminist law reform, judicial resistance, and neo-liberal citizenship', in Dorothy E. Chunn, Susan B. Boyd and Hester Lessard (eds), *Reaction and Resistance: Feminism, Law, and Social Change*, Vancouver: University of British Columbia Press, pp. 127–163.

Greer, Germaine 1999 *The Whole Woman*, London: Transworld Publishers.

Gross, Neil 2005. 'Detraditionalization of intimacy reconsidered', *Sociological Theory* 23 (3): 286–311.

Gunning, Isabelle R. 1992. 'Female genital surgeries', *Columbia Human Rights Law Review* 23 (2): 189–248.

Hage, Ghassan 1998. *White Nation: Fantasies of White Supremacy in a Multicultural Society*, Sydney: Pluto Press.

Hage, Ghassan 2003. *Against Paranoid Nationalism: Searching for Hope in a Shrinking Society*, Sydney: Pluto Press.

Hamilton, Clive 2008. *The Freedom Paradox: Towards a Post-secular Ethics*, Sydney: Allen and Unwin.

Hamilton, Clive and Elizabeth Mail 2003. *Downshifting in Australia: A Sea-change in the Pursuit of Happiness*, Canberra: The Australia Institute.

Hannan, Ewin 2008. 'Unions to recruit children', *The Weekend Australian* 2–3 August, pp. 1, 4.

Harris, Anita 2001. 'Revisiting bedroom culture: new spaces for young women's politics', *Hecate* 27 (1): 128–138.

Harris, Anita 2004. *Future Girl: Young Women in the Twenty-first Century*, New York and London: Routledge.

Harris, Anita, Johanna Wyn and Salem Younes 2007. 'Young people and citizenship: An everyday perspective', *Youth Studies Australia* 26 (3): 18–26.

Hawkes, Gail 2005. *Sex and Pleasure in Western Culture*, Cambridge: Polity.

Henderson, Margaret 2006. *Marking Feminist Times: Remembering the Longest Revolution in Australia*, Bern: Peter Lang.

Henderson, Margaret 2008. 'Feminism in the hearts and minds and words of men:

Revisiting men's cultural remembrance of Australian feminism in the new millennium', *Dialogue* 27 (3): 29–46, <http://www.assa.edu.au/Publications/Dialogue/dial32008.pdf>, accessed 2 February 2009.

Henderson, Sheila, Janet Holland, Sheena McGrellis, Sue Sharpe and Rachel Thomson 2007. *Inventing Adulthoods: A Biographical Approach to Youth Transitions*, London: Sage.

Henry, Astrid, 2004. *Not My Mother's Sister: Generational Conflict and Third-wave Feminism*, Bloomington, Indiana: Indiana University Press.

Hey, Valerie 1997. *The Company She Keeps: An Ethnography of Girls' Friendship*, Buckingham: Open University Press.

Heyes, Cressida J. 2007. 'Normalisation and the psychic life of cosmetic surgery', *Australian Feminist Studies* 22 (52): 55–71.

Heywood, Leslie 2008. 'Third-wave feminism, the global economy, and women's surfing: Sport as stealth feminism in girls' surf culture' in Anita Harris (ed.), *Next Wave Cultures: Feminism, Subcultures, Activism*, New York and London: Routledge, pp. 63–82.

High Resolves, 2011, 'High resolves initiative', <http://www.highresolves.org/SBHS_GenEq.html>, accessed 31 March 2011

Hillier, Lynne 2001. '"I'm wasting away on unrequited love": Gendering same sex attracted young women's love, sex and desire', *Hecate* 27 (1): 119–127.

Ho, Christina 2007. 'Muslim women's new defenders: Women's rights, nationalism and Islamophobia in contemporary Australia', *Women's Studies International Forum* 30 (4): 290–298.

Hochschild, Arlie Russell 1983. *The Managed Heart: Commercialization of Human Feeling*, Berkeley: University of California Press.

Hochschild, Arlie Russell 2003. *The Commercialization of Intimate Life: Notes from Home and Work*, Berkeley: University of California Press.

hooks, bell 1989. *Talking Back: Thinking Feminist, Thinking Black*, Boston: South End Press.

Hopkins, Susan 2002. *Girl Heroes: The New Face in Popular Culture*, Annandale: Pluto Press.

House of Representatives 2009. 'Making it fair: Inquiry into pay equity and associated issues related to increasing female participation in the workforce', Canberra: Parliament of Australia, <http://www.aph.gov.au/house/committee/ewr/payequity/report/chapter2.pdf>, accessed 15 November 2011.

Howard, Cosmo 2007. 'Three models of individualized biography' in Cosmo Howard (ed.), *Contested Individualization: Debates About Contemporary Personhood*, New York: Palgrave Macmillan, pp. 25–43.

Howarth, Caroline 2007. '"It's not their fault that they have that colour skin, is it?": Young British children and the possibilities for contesting racializing representations', in Gail Moloney and Iain Walker (eds), *Social Representations and Identity*, New York: Palgrave Macmillan, pp. 131–156.

Hughes, Kate 2005. 'The adult children of divorce: Pure relationships and family values?', *Journal of Sociology* 41 (1): 69–86.

Huntley, Rebecca 2006. *The World According to Y: Inside the New Adult Generation*, Sydney: Allen and Unwin.

Huppatz, Kate Elizabeth 2010. 'Class and career choice: Motivations, aspirations, identity and mobility for women in paid caring work', *Journal of Sociology* 46 (2): 115–132.

Imms, Wesley 2008. 'Boys engaging masculinities', *Journal of Interdisciplinary Gender Studies* 10 (2): 29–45.

Ingraham, Chrys 1994. 'The heterosexual imaginary: Feminist sociology and theories of gender', *Sociological Theory* 12 (2): 203–219.

Jamieson, Lynn 1998. *Intimacy: Personal Relationships in Modern Societies*, Cambridge: Polity.

Johansson, Thomas 2007. *The Transformation of Sexuality: Gender and Identity in Contemporary Youth Culture*, Aldershot: Ashgate.

Johnson, Carol 2005. 'Narratives of identity: Denying empathy in conservative discourses on race, class and sexuality', *Theory and Society* 34 (1): 37–61.

Jones, Adam 2006a. 'Governance and conflict', in Adam Jones (ed.), *Men of the Global South: A Reader*, New York: Zed Books, pp. 200–202.

Jones, Adam 2006b. 'The murdered men of Ciudad Juárez', in Adam Jones (ed.), *Men of the Global South: A Reader*, New York: Zed Books, pp. 235–237.

Kaminer, Wendy 1999. *Sleeping with Extra-Terrestrials: The Rise of Irrationalism and Perils of Piety*, New York: Pantheon.

Kelan, Elisabeth K. 2007. '"I don't know why" — accounting for the scarcity of women in ICT work', *Women's Studies International Forum* 30 (6): 499–511.

Kelly, Peter 2006. 'The entrepreneurial self and "youth at-risk": Exploring the horizons of identity in the twenty-first century', *Journal of Youth Studies* 9 (1): 17–32.

Kenway, Jane 1987. 'High status private schooling and the processes of an educational hegemony', thesis submitted for the degree of Doctor of Philosophy at Murdoch University.

Kenway, Jane, Anna Kraack and Anna Hickey-Moody 2006. *Masculinity Beyond the Metropolis*, Houndmills: Palgrave Macmillan.

Klein, Naomi 2000. *No Logo*, London: Flamingo.

Labaton, Vivien and Dawn Lundy Martin 2004. 'Afterword: Looking ahead and building a feminist future', in Vivien Labaton and Dawn Lundy Martin (eds), *The Fire this Time: Young Activists and the New Feminism*, New York: Anchor Books/Random House, pp. 279–290.

Lacroix, Carol 2006. 'Freedom, desire and power: Gender processes and presumptions of shared care and responsibility after parental separation', *Women's Studies International Forum* 29 (2): 184–196.

Lakoff, George 2004. *Don't Think of an Elephant: Know Your Values and Frame the Debate*, Melbourne: Scribe Publications.

Langer, Beryl and Estelle Farrar 2003. 'Becoming "Australian" in the global cultural economy: Children, consumption, citizenship', *Journal of Australian Studies* 79: 117–126, 236–238.

Lash, Scott 1994. 'Reflexivity and its doubles: Structure, aesthetics, community', in Ulrich Beck, Anthony Giddens and Scott Lash, *Reflexive Modernization: Politics, Tradition and Aesthetics in the Modern Social Order*, Cambridge: Polity Press, pp. 110–173.

Lemert, Charles and Anthony Elliott 2006. *Deadly Worlds: The Emotional Costs of Globalization*, Lanham: Rowman and Littlefield.

Levy, Ariel 2005. *Female Chauvinist Pigs: Women and the Rise of Raunch Culture*, Free Press: New York.

Lewis, Jane 2001. *The End of Marriage? Individualism and Intimate Relations*, Cheltenham: Edward Elgar.

Liamputtong, Pranee and Douglas Ezzy 2005. *Qualitative Research Methods, Second Edition*, Melbourne: Oxford University Press.

Lindsay, Jo and Deborah Dempsey 2009. *Families, Relationships and Intimate Life*, Melbourne: Oxford University Press.

Lobenstine, Lori, Yasmin Pereira, Jenny Whitley, Jessica Robles, Yaraliz Soto, Jeannette Sergeant, Daisy Jimenez, Emily Jimenez, Jessenia Ortiz and Sasha Cirino 2004. 'Possible selves and pastels: How a group of mothers and daughters took a London conference by storm', in Anita Harris (ed.), *All About the Girl: Culture, Power, and Identity*, New York: Routledge, pp. 255–264.

Lohm, Davina 2009. '"I just tell people that Australians are multicultural" — how young adults understand their national identity', *The Australian Sociological Conference Refereed Proceedings*, Canberra: Australian National University, 2–4 December.

Lupton, Deborah 1999. 'Crime control, citizenship and the state: Lay understandings of crime, its causes and solutions', *Journal of Sociology* 35 (1): 297–311.

Luttrell, Wendy 2003. *Pregnant Bodies, Fertile Minds: Gender, Race and the Schooling of Pregnant Teens*, New York: Routledge.

McCabe, Janice 2005. 'What's in a label? The relationship between feminist self-identification and "feminist" attitudes among U.S. women and men', *Gender & Society* 19 (4): 480–505.

McCalman, Janet 1993. *Journeyings: The Biography of a Middle-Class Generation 1920–1990*, Melbourne: Melbourne University Press.

McCann, Pól Dominic, Victor Minichiello and David Plummer 2009. 'Is homophobia inevitable? Evidence that explores the constructed nature of homophobia, and the techniques through which men unlearn it', *Journal of Sociology* 45 (2): 201–220.

McDermott, Elizabeth 2004. 'Telling lesbian stories: Interviewing and the class dynamics of talk', *Women's Studies International Forum* 27 (3): 177–187.

McDonald, Peter 2000. 'Gender equity, social institutions and the future of fertility', *Journal of Population Research* 17 (1): 1–16.

Mcintyre, David, 2011. 'BRW rich list puts Gina Rinehart Australia's richest person, the first woman at No.1', 25 May, <http://www.news.com.au/money/money-matters/brw-rich-list-puts-gina-rinehart-australias-richest-person-the-first-woman-at-no1/story-e6frfmd9-1226062751021#ixzz1Xn5TGv9V>, accessed 13 September 2011.

Mackay, Hugh 1997. *Generations: Baby Boomers, Their Parents and Their Children*, Sydney: Macmillan.

Mackay, Hugh 2007. *Advance Australia … Where? How We've Changed, Why We've Changed, and What Will Happen Next*, Sydney: Hatchette Australia.

Mackie, Vera 2005. 'In search of innocence: Feminist historians debate the legacy of wartime Japan', *Australian Feminist Studies* 20 (47): 207–217.

Mackinnon, Alison 2006. 'Girls, schools and society: A generation of change', *Australian Feminist Studies* 21 (50): 275–288.

Mackinnon, Alison and Elizabeth Bullen 2005. '"Out on the Borderlands": Time, generation and personal agency in women's lives', *Theory and Research in Education* 3 (1): 31–46.

Mackinnon, Alison, Simon Robb, Patrick O'Leary and Peter Bishop 2010. *Hope: The Everyday and Imaginary Life of Youth on the Margins*, Adelaide: Wakefield Press.

McLeod, Julie 2002. 'Working out intimacy: Young people and friendship in an age of reflexivity', *Discourse* 23 (2): 211–226.

McLeod, Julie and Lyn Yates 2006. *Making Modern Lives: Subjectivity, Schooling and Social Change*, Albany: State University of New York Press.

McMahon, Anthony 1999. *Taking Care of Men: Sexual Politics in the Public Mind*,

Cambridge: Cambridge University Press.

McNay, Lois 2000. *Gender and Agency: Reconfiguring the Subject in Feminist and Social Theory*, Cambridge: Polity Press.

McRobbie, Angela 2004. 'Notes on postfeminism and popular culture: Bridget Jones and the new gender regime', in Anita Harris (ed.), *All About the Girl: Culture, Power, and Identity*, New York and London: Routledge, pp. 3–14.

Maddison, Sarah, 2002. 'Bombing the patriarchy or just trying to get a cab: Challenges facing the next generation of feminist activists', *Outskirts*, volume 10, <http://www.chloe.uwa.edu.au/outskirts/archive/volume10/maddison>, accessed 19 March 2010.

Maddison, Sarah 2009. *Black Politics: Inside the Complexity of Aboriginal Political Culture*, Crows Nest: Allen and Unwin.

Maddison, Sarah and Emma Partridge 2007. 'How Well Does Australian Democracy Serve Australian Women?', Canberra: Democratic Audit of Australia, Australian National University, <http://democraticaudit.org.au/?page_id=21>, accessed 11 June 2012.

Magill, Pamela 2004. 'No sex please, we're modern', *West Australian* 3 July 2004: 3.

Maguire, Emily 2008. *Princesses and Porn Stars: Sex, Power, Identity*, Melbourne: Text.

Maguire, Emily 2010. *Your Skirt's Too Short: Sex, Power, Choice*, Melbourne: Text.

Maher, JaneMaree 2008. 'Forming Australian families: Gender ideologies and policy settings', *Social Policy Review* 20: 263–278.

Maher, JaneMaree and Jo Lindsay 2005. 'Conceptual orthodoxies and women's everyday labours: Rethinking the employment of mothers', Hawke Research Institute for Sustainable Societies, University of South Australia, <www.unisa.edu.au/hawkeinstitute/publications/downloads/wp31.pdf>, accessed 20 January 2009.

Maher, JaneMaree, Jo Lindsay and Anne Bardoel 2009. 'Modified maternalism: Nurses and their families managing work and care in Australia', *Journal of Comparative Family Studies* 40 (4): 661–675.

Maher, JaneMaree, Jo Lindsay and Suzanne Franzway 2008. 'Time, caring labour and social policy: Understanding the family time economy in contemporary families', *Work, Employment & Society* 22 (3): 547–588.

Mannheim, Karl 1959. *Essays on the Sociology of Knowledge*, London: Routledge.

Manning, Nathan 2006. 'Young people and politics: Apathetic and disengaged? A qualitative inquiry', thesis submitted for the degree of Doctor of Philosophy in the Department of Sociology, Flinders University, South Australia.

Marsh, David, Therese O'Toole and Su Jones 2007. *Young People and Politics in the*

UK: *Apathy or Alienation?*, Houndmills: Palgrave Macmillan.

Marsh, Ian 2000. 'Political integration and the outlook for the Australian party system: Party adaptation or system mutation?', in Paul Boreham, Geoffrey Stokes and Richard Hall (eds), *The Politics of Australian Society: Political Issues for a New Century*, Frenchs Forest: Pearson Education.

Marsh, Ian, Gabrielle Meagher and Shaun Wilson 2005. 'Are Australians open to globalisation?' in Shaun Wilson, Gabrielle Meagher, Rachel Gibson, David Denemark and Mark Western (eds), *Australian Social Attitudes: The First Report*, Sydney: University of New South Wales Press, pp. 240–257.

Martens, Lydia, Dale Southern and Sue Scott 2004. 'Bringing children (and parents) into the sociology of consumption: Towards a theoretical and empirical agenda', *Journal of Consumer Culture* 4 (2): 155–182.

Martino, Wayne 1999. '"Cool boys", "party animals", "squids" and "poofters": Interrogating the dynamics and politics of adolescent masculinities in school', *British Journal of Sociology of Education* 20 (2): 239–263.

Martino, Wayne and Maria Pallotta-Chiarolli 2005. *Being Normal is the Only Way to Be: Adolescent Perspectives on Gender and School*, Sydney: University of New South Wales Press.

Medd, Ruth 2008. 'Still no cracks in the glass ceiling', *The Drum*, ABC, 30 October 2008, <http://www.abc.net.au/unleashed/37524.html>, accessed 21 November 2011.

Messner, Michael A. 2007. 'The masculinity of the governator: Muscle and compassion in American politics', *Gender & Society* 21 (3): 461–481.

Mills, Martin, Wayne Martino and Bob Lingard 2007. 'Getting boys' education "right": The Australian Government's Parliamentary Inquiry Report as an exemplary instance of recuperative masculinity politics', *British Journal of Sociology of Education* 28 (1): 5–21.

Mills, Melinda 2007. 'Individualization and the life course: toward a theoretical model and empirical evidence', in Cosmo Howard (ed.), *Contested Individualization: Debates about Contemporary Personhood*, New York: Palgrave Macmillan, pp. 61–79.

Mills, Sara 2004. *Discourse*, London: Routledge, first edition published in 1997.

Morris, Meaghan 1998. *Too Soon, Too Late: History of Popular Culture*, Bloomington and Indianapolis: Indiana University Press.

Murachver, Tamar and Anna Janssen 2007. 'Gender and communication in context', in Ann Weatherall, Bernadette Watson and Cindy Gallois (eds), *Language, Discourse and Social Psychology*, Houndmills: Palgrave Macmillan, pp. 185–205.

Murphy, Kylie 2001. 'What does John Gray have to say to feminism?', *Continuum: Journal of Media and Cultural Studies* 15 (2): 159–167.

Natalier, Kristin 2003. '"I'm not his wife": Doing gender and doing housework in the absence of women', *Journal of Sociology* 39 (3): 253–269.

Nicolopoulou, Ageliki, Barbara Scales and Jeff Weintraub 1994. 'Gender differences and symbolic imagination in the stories of four-year-olds', in Anne Haas Dyson and Celia Genishi (eds), *The Need for Story: Cultural Diversity in Classroom and Community*, Urbana: National Council of Teachers of English, pp. 102–123.

Noble, Greg, Scott Poynting and Paul Tabar 1999. 'Lebanese Youth and Social Identity', in Rob White (ed.), *Australian Youth Cultures: On the Margins and in the Mainstream*, Hobart: National Clearing House for Youth Studies, pp. 130–137.

Nowra, Louis 2010. 'The Better Self?: Germaine Greer and "The Female Eunuch"' *The Monthly*, number 54, <http://www.themonthly.com.au/germaine-greer-and-female-eunuch-better-self-louis-nowra-2298>, accessed 15 August 2011.

Nollman, Greg and Hermann Strasser 2007. 'Individualization as an interpretive scheme of inequality: Why class and inequality persist', in Cosmo Howard (ed.), *Contested Individualization: Debates about Contemporary Personhood*, New York: Palgrave Macmillan, pp. 81–97.

O'Doherty, Kieran and Martha Augoustinos 2007. 'Australia and the Tampa: The use of nationalist rhetoric to legitimate military action and the marginalisation of asylum seekers', in Damien W. Riggs (ed.), *Taking up the Challenge: Critical Race and Whiteness Studies in a Postcolonising Nation*, Adelaide: Crawford House Publishing, pp. 225–247.

Office of the Status of Women 2004. *Women in Australia*, Canberra: Commonwealth of Australia.

Paechter, Carrie and Sheryl Clark 2007. 'Who are tomboys and how do we recognise them?', *Women's Studies International Forum* 30 (4): 342–354.

Pearson, Noel 2002. 'On the human right to misery, mass incarceration and early death', *Arena Magazine* 56: 22–31.

Peel, Mark 2003. *The Lowest Rung: Voices of Australian Poverty*, Cambridge: Cambridge University Press.

Peel, Mark 2005. 'Mothers who don't want to work and fathers who do', in Patricia Grimshaw, John Murphy and Belinda Probert (eds), *Double Shift: Working Mothers and Social Change in Australia*, Beaconsfield, Victoria: Circa, pp. 24–36.

Phillips, Lynn M 2000. *Flirting with Danger: Young Women's Reflections on Sexuality and Domination*, New York: New York University Press.

Pilcher, Jane 1998. *Women of Their Time: Generation, Gender Issues and Feminism*, Aldershot: Ashgate.

Pocock, Barbara 2001. *Having a Life: Work, Family Fairness and Community in 2000*, Adelaide: Centre for Labour Research, Adelaide University.

Pocock, Barbara 2003. *The Work/Life Collision*, Annandale: Federation Press.

Pocock, Barbara 2006. *The Labour Market Ate My Babies: Work, Children and a Sustainable Future*, Annandale: Federation Press.

Potter, Jonathan and Alexa Hepburn 2007. 'Discursive psychology: Mind and reality in practice', in Ann Weatherall, Bernadette Watson and Cindy Gallois (eds), *Language, Discourse and Social Psychology*, Houndmills: Palgrave Macmillan, pp. 160–182.

Powell, Anastasia 2008. '*Amor fati*? Gender habitus and young people's negotiation of (hetero)sexual consent', *Journal of Sociology* 44 (2): 167–184.

Probert, Belinda 2002. '"Grateful slaves" or "self-made women": A matter of choice or policy?', *Australian Feminist Studies* 17 (37): 7–17.

Probert, Belinda and Fiona Macdonald 1999. 'Young women: Poles of experience in work and parenting', in Dusseldorp Skills Forum (ed.), *Australia's Young Adults: The Deepening Divide*, Sydney: Dusseldorp Skills Forum, pp. 135–157.

Pusey, Michael 2003. *The Experience of Middle Australia: The Dark Side of Economic Reform*, Cambridge: Cambridge University Press.

Putnam, Robert D. 2000. *Bowling Alone: The Collapse and Revival of American Community*, New York: Simon and Schuster.

Quinn, Naomi 2005. 'Introduction', in Naomi Quinn (ed.), *Finding Culture in Talk: A Collection of Methods*, New York: Palgrave Macmillan, pp. 1–34.

Raddeker, Hélène Bowen 2006. 'Difference between the waves versus the "eternal return": Today's students of feminism' *Outskirts*, volume 14, <http://www.chloe.uwa.edu.au/outskirts/archive/volume14/raddeker>, accessed 24 March 2011.

Redfern, Catherine and Kristin Aune 2010. *Reclaiming the F Word: The New Feminist Movement*, London and New York: Zed.

Reekie, Gail 1998. *Measuring Immorality: Social Inquiry and the Problem of Illegitimacy*, Cambridge: Cambridge University Press.

Reid-Walsh, Jacqueline and Claudia Mitchell 2004. 'Girls' web sites: A virtual "room of one's own"?', in Anita Harris (ed.), *All About the Girl: Culture, Power, and Identity*, New York: Routledge, pp. 173–182.

Reynolds, Margaret 2004. *Australians Welcome Refugees: The Untold Story*, A Report to the 60th Session of the United Nations Commission on Human Rights, United Nations Association of Australia.

Rice, Esther and Michelle Swift 1995. 'Beyond "talking about my generation": What Anne Summers isn't hearing', in Anne Marée Payne and Lyn Shoemark (eds), *Women Culture and Universities: A Chilly Climate?*, Proceedings of national conference on the effect of organisational culture on women in universities, Sydney: Sydney Women's Forum, University of Technology, pp. 189–196.

Rich, Adrienne 1976. *Of Woman Born: Motherhood as Experience and Institution*, New York: Norton.

Rich, Emma, 2005. 'Young women, feminist identities and neo-liberalism', *Women's Studies International Forum*, 28 (6): 495–508.

Richardson, Laurel 1997. *Fields of Play: Constructing an Academic Life*, New Brunswick: Rutgers University Press.

Ricoeur, Paul 1980. 'Narrative and time', *Critical Inquiry* 7 (1): 169–90.

Robinson, Penelope A. 2008. 'A postfeminist generation: Young women, feminism and popular culture', thesis submitted for the degree of Doctor of Philosophy at the University of Western Sydney, <http://handle.uws.edu.au:8081/1959.7/37397>, accessed 24 March 2011.

Roseneil, Sasha 2007. 'Sutured selves, queer connections: Rethinking intimacy and individualization', in Cosmo Howard (ed.), *Contested Individualization: Debates about Contemporary Personhood*, New York: Palgrave Macmillan, pp. 117–134.

Roseneil, Sasha 2009. 'Transforming intimate citizenship: Movements for gender and sexual equality and change', 7th European Feminist Research Conference, Utrecht, June 4–7.

Rundle, Guy 2005. 'The rise of surplus culture', *Arena Magazine* 76: 45–46.

Rutherford, Jennifer 2000. *The Gauche Intruder: Freud, Lacan and the White Australia Fantasy*, Melbourne: Melbourne University Press.

Sade, Orly and Neuborne, Ellen 2011. *How Ella Grew an Electric Guitar: A Girl's First Adventure in Business*, Seattle: Createspace.

Saha, Lawrence J. 2000. 'Political activism and civic education among Australian secondary school students', *Australian Journal of Education* 44 (2): 155–174.

Saha, Larry, Murray Print and Kathy Edwards 2005. 'Youth Electoral Study: Research report 2: Youth, political engagement and voting', Canberra: Australian Electoral Commission, <http://www.aec.gov.au/About_AEC/Publications/youth_study/youth_study_2/index.htm>, accessed 24 March 2011.

Sawer, Marian 1999. 'EMILY's List and angry white men: Gender wars in the nineties', *Journal of Australian Studies* 62: 1–9, 236–237.

Sawer, Marian 2003. *The Ethical State? Social Liberalism in Australia*, Melbourne: Melbourne University Press.

Sawer, Marian and Barry Hindess (eds) 2004. *Us and Them: Anti-Elitism in Australia*, Perth: API Network, Curtin University of Technology.

Sawer, Marian 2004. 'Populism and public choice in Australia and Canada: Turning equality-seekers into "special interests"', in Marian Sawer and Barry Hindess (eds), *Us and Them: Anti-Elitism in Australia*, Perth: API Network, Curtin University of Technology, pp. 33–55.

Schultz, Julianne 2009. 'Introduction: Openness, collaboration and participation', in Julianne Schultz (ed.), *Griffith Review: Participation Society* 24: 7–10.

Scott, Jacqueline, Duane F. Alwin and Michael Bruan 1996. 'Generational changes in gender-role attitudes: Britain in a cross-national perspective', *Sociology* 30 (3): 471–493.

Scott, James 1987. *Weapons of the Weak: Everyday Forms of Peasant Resistance*, New Haven: Yale University Press.

Scourfield, Jonathan, Bella Dicks, Mark Drakeford and Andrew Davis 2006. *Children, Place and Identity: Nation and Locality in Middle Childhood*, London and New York: Routledge, Taylor and Francis.

Seabrook, Jeremy 2008. 'Why do people think inequality is worse than poverty?', Joseph Rowntree Foundation, <http://www.jrf.org.uk/publications/why-do-people-think-inequality-worse-poverty>, accessed 24 June 2009.

Sebastian, Savanth 2011. 'Gender wage gap biggest in 28 years', CommSec, 17 November, cited by UN Women National Committee Australia, <http://www.genderequalityonline.org.au/ForumRetrieve.aspx?ForumID=1873&TopicID=11060?>, accessed 10 June 2012.

Sedgwick, Eve Kosofsky 1990. *Epistemology of the Closet*, Berkeley and Los Angeles: University of California Press.

Segal, Lynne 1999. *Why Feminism? Gender, Psychology, Politics*, New York: Columbia University Press.

Simons, Margaret 2005. 'Ties that bind', in Julianne Schultz (ed.), *People Like US: Griffith Review* 8: 13–36.

Shoemaker, Nancy 1991. 'The rise and fall of Iroquois women', *Journal of Women's History* 2 (3): 39–57.

Skeggs, Beverley 1997. *Formations of Class and Gender: Becoming Respectable*, London: Sage.

Smart, Carol 2007. *Personal Life: New Directions in Sociological Thinking*, Cambridge: Polity.

Smart, Carol and Beccy Shipman 2004. 'Visions in monochrome: Families, marriage and the individualization thesis', *British Journal of Sociology* 55 (4): 491–509.

Smart, Diana and Anna Sanson 2003. 'Social competence in young adulthood, its nature and antecedents', *Family Matters* 64: 4–9.

Standing Committee on Education and Training 2002. 'Boys: Getting it Right', Australian Government, <http://www.aph.gov.au/house/committee/edt/eofb/report.htm>, accessed 7 November 2011.

Strauss, Claudia 2005. 'Analyzing discourse for cultural complexity', in Naomi Quinn (ed.), *Finding Culture in Talk: A Collection of Methods*, New York: Palgrave Macmillan, pp. 203–242.

Sullivan, Oriel 2004. 'Changing gender practices within the household: A theoretical perspective', *Gender & Society* 18 (2): 207–222.

Summers, Anne 1970. 'Women's Consciousness of Their Role-Structure', thesis presented in partial fulfilment of B.A. Honours degree in Politics, University of Adelaide.

Summers, Anne 1994. *Damned Whores and God's Police*, Ringwood: Penguin, first published 1975.

Summers, Anne 2003. *The End of Equality: Work, Babies and Women's Choices in 21st Century Australia*, Sydney: Random House Australia.

Taylor, Charles 1994. 'The politics of recognition', in Charles Taylor, K. Anthony Appiah, Jürgen Habermas, Steven C. Rockefeller, Michael Walzer and Susan Wolf, *Multiculturalism and the Politics of Recognition*, Princeton: Princeton University Press, pp. 25–73.

Taylor, Matthew 2009. 'Reflections on social evils and human nature', Joseph Rowntree Foundation, <http://www.jrf.org.uk/publications/reflections-social-evils-and-human-nature>, accessed 24 June 2009.

Thiel, Shayla Marie 2005. 'Identity construction and gender negotiation in the world of adolescent girls and instant messaging', in Sharon R. Mazzarella (ed.), *Girl Wide Web: Girls, the Internet, and the Negotiation of Identity*, New York: Peter Lang, pp. 179–202.

Thomas, Lyn 1995. 'In love with Inspector Morse: Feminist subculture and quality television', *Feminist Review* 51: 1–25.

Thomson, Rachel, Janet Holland, Sheena McGrellis, Robert Bell, Sheila Henderson and Sue Sharpe 2004. 'Inventing adulthoods: A biographical approach to understanding youth citizenship', *Sociological Review* 52 (2): 218–239.

Townsend, Helen 1994. *Real Men: What Australian Men Really Think, Feel and Believe*, Sydney: HarperCollins.

Threadgold, Steven and Pam Nilan, 2009. 'Reflexivity of contemporary youth, risk and cultural capital', *Current Sociology*, 57 (1): 47–68.

Tyler, Meagan 2008. 'Sex self-help books: Hot secrets for great sex or promoting the sex of prostitution', *Women's Studies International Forum* 31 (5): 363–372.

Uhlmann, Allon J. 2006. *Family, Gender and Kinship in Australia: The Social and Cultural Logic of Practice and Subjectivity*, Aldershott: Ashgate.

Vromen, Ariadne 2003. '"People try to put us down …": Participatory citizenship of generation X', *Australian Journal of Political Science* 38 (1): 79–99.

Vromen, Ariadne 2009. 'Youth participation from the top-down: Views and practices from policymakers and service providers', *The Australian Sociological Conference, refereed proceedings*, Canberra: Australian National University, 2–4 December.

Walker, Linley 1998. 'Under the bonnet: Car culture, technological dominance and young men of the working class', *Journal of Interdisciplinary Gender Studies* 3 (2): 23–43.

Walker, Rebecca 1995. 'Being real: An introduction', in Rebecca Walker (ed.), *To Be Real: Telling the Truth and Changing the Face of Feminism*, New York: Anchor.

Walker, Rebecca 2004. 'Foreword: We are using this power to resist', in Vivien Labaton and Dawn Lundy Martin (eds), *The Fire this Time: Young Activists and the New Feminism*, New York: Anchor Books/Random House, pp. xi–xx.

Walkerdine, Valerie 1984. 'Some day my prince will come', in Angela McRobbie and Mica Nava (eds), *Gender and Generation*, Houndmills, Basingstoke: Macmillan, pp. 162–184.

Walkerdine, Valerie 2005. 'Freedom, psychology and the neoliberal worker', *Soundings*, 29 (1): 47–61.

Walkerdine, Valerie 2008. 'A new gender order? Contemporary gendered subjectivities', seminar presented to Sociology Department, Birmingham University, 28 May.

Walkerdine, Valerie, Helen Lucey and June Melody 2001. *Growing Up Girl: Psychosocial Explorations of Gender and Class*, Houndmills: Palgrave.

Walsh, Mary and Mark Bahnisch 1999. 'Gangland and the political abjection of a generation', *Social Alternatives* 18 (2): 59–63.

Walter, James, with Tod Moore 2010. *What Were They Thinking? The Politics of Ideas in Australia*, Sydney: UNSW Press.

Walter, Natasha 1998. *The New Feminism*, London: Little, Brown and Company.

Walter, Natasha 2010. *Living Dolls: The Return of Sexism*, London: Virago.

Warner-Smith, Penny and Christina Lee 2001. 'Hopes & fears: The life choices, aspirations and well-being of young rural women', *Youth Studies* 20 (3): 32–38.

Watson, Juliet 2008. '"How can you put a title on something like that?" Marginalised young women's interpretations of their narratives', paper presented to Annual Conference of The Australian Sociological Association, Melbourne.

Weedon, Chris 1987. *Feminist Practice and Poststructuralist Theory*, London:

Blackwell Publishers.

West, Candace and Don Zimmerman 1987. 'Doing gender', *Gender & Society* 1: 124–151.

West, Candace and Sarah Fenstermaker 2002. 'Power, inequality and the accomplishment of gender: An ethnomethodological view', in Sarah Fenstermaker and Candace West (eds), *Doing Gender, Doing Difference: Inequality, Power, and Institutional Change*, New York: Routledge, pp. 41–54.

Western, Mark and Michael Emmison 1990. 'Social class and social identity: A comment on Marshall et al', *Sociology* 24 (2): 241–253.

Wetherell, Margaret and Jonathan Potter 1992. *Mapping the Language of Racism: Discourse and the Legitimation of Exploitation*, New York: Harvester Wheatsheaf.

White, Richard 1992. *Inventing Australia*, Sydney: George Allen and Unwin.

White, Rob and Johanna Wyn 2004. *Youth and Society: Exploring the Social Dynamics of Youth Experience*, South Melbourne: Oxford University Press.

Wicks, Deirdre and Gita Mishra 1998. 'Young Australian women and their aspirations for work, education and relationships', in Ed Carson, Adam Jamrozik and Tony Winefield (eds), *Unemployment: Economic Promise and Political Will*, Brisbane: Australian Academic Press, pp. 89–100.

Wierenga, Ani 2009. *Young People Making a Life*, Houndsmills: Palgrave Macmillan.

Wierenga, Ani 2011. 'Transitions, local culture and human dignity: Rural young men in a changing world', *Journal of Sociology* 47 (4): 371–387.

Wilkins, Amy C. 2004. '"So full of myself as a chick": Goth women, sexual independence, and gender egalitarianism', *Gender & Society* 18 (3): 328–349.

Wilkinson, Helen 1994. *No Turning Back: Generations and the Genderquake*, London: Demos.

Wilkinson, Helen and Geoff Mulgan 1995. *Freedom's Children: Work, Relationships and Politics for 18–34 Year Olds in Britain Today*, London: Demos.

Willis, Suzanne and Bruce Tranter 2006. 'Beyond the "digital divide": Internet diffusion and inequality in Australia', *Journal of Sociology* 42 (1): 43–59.

Wilson, Shaun, Gabrielle Meagher and Trevor Breusch 2005. 'Where to for the welfare state?' in Shaun Wilson, Gabrielle Meagher, Rachel Gibson, David Denemark and Mark Western (eds), *Australian Social Attitudes: The First Report*, Sydney: University of New South Wales Press, pp. 101–121.

Winchester, Hilary 1999. 'Lone fathers and the scales of justice: Renegotiation of masculinity after divorce', *Journal of Interdisciplinary Gender Studies*, 4 (2): 81–98.

Wise, Amanda 2005. 'Hope and belonging in a multicultural suburb', *Journal of Intercultural Studies* 26 (1–2): 171–186.

Wise, Amanda 2010. 'Sensuous multiculturalism: Emotional landscapes of interethnic living in Australian suburbia', *Journal of Ethnic and Migration Studies* 36 (6): 917–937.

Wiseman, Rosalind 2002. *Queen Bees and Wannabees: Helping Your Daughter Survive Cliques, Gossip, Boyfriends, and Other Realities of Adolescence*, New York: Three Rivers Press.

Wolf, Naomi 1993. *Fire with Fire: The New Female Power and How it Will Change the 21st Century*, New York: Random House.

Woodman, Dan 2009. 'The mysterious case of the pervasive choice biography: Ulrich Beck, structure/agency, and the middling state of theory in the sociology of youth', *Journal of Youth Studies* 12 (3): 243–256.

Woodman, Dan 2010. 'Class, individualisation and tracing processes of inequality in a changing world: A reply to Steven Roberts', *Journal of Youth Studies*, 13 (6): 737–746.

Wyn, Johanna 2009. *Youth, Health and Welfare: The Cultural Politics of Education and Wellbeing*, Melbourne: Oxford University Press.

Zevallos, Zuleyka 2005. '"It's like we're their culture": Second-generation migrant women discuss Australian culture', *People and Place* 13 (2): 41–49.

Index

This book is available as a fully-searchable pdf from
www.adelaide.edu.au/press

W